Multinational Enterprises, Innovative Strategies and Systems of Innovation

NEW HORIZONS IN INTERNATIONAL BUSINESS

Series Editor: Peter J. Buckley
Centre for International Business,
University of Leeds (CIBUL), UK

The New Horizons in International Business series has established itself as the world's leading forum for the presentation of new ideas in international business research. It offers pre-eminent contributions in the areas of multinational enterprise – including foreign direct investment, business strategy and corporate alliances, global competitive strategies, and entrepreneurship. In short, this series constitutes essential reading for academics, business strategists and policy makers alike.

Titles in the series include:

Globalizing Europe
Deepening Integration, Alliance Capitalism and Structural Statecraft
Edited by Thomas L Brewer, Paul A. Brenton and Gavin Boyd

China and its Regions
Economic Growth and Reform in Chinese Provinces
Edited by Mary Françoise Renard

Emerging Issues in International Business Research
Edited by Masaaki Kotabe and Preet S. Aulakh

Network Knowledge in International Business
Edited by Sarianna M. Lundan

Business Strategy and National Culture
US and Asia Pacific Microcomputer Multinationals in Europe
Denise Tsang

Learning in the Internationalisation Process of Firms
Edited by Anders Blomstermo and D. Deo Sharma

Alliance Capitalism and Corporate Management
Entrepreneurial Cooperation in Knowledge Based Economies
Edited by John H. Dunning and Gavin Boyd

The New Economic Analysis of Multinationals
An Agenda for Management, Policy and Research
Edited by Thomas L. Brewer, Stephen Young and Stephen E. Guisinger

Transnational Corporations, Technology and Economic Development
Backward Linkages and Knowledge Transfer in South East Asia
Axèle Giroud

Alliance Capitalism for the New American Economy
Edited by Alan M. Rugman and Gavin Boyd

The Structural Foundations of International Finance
Problems of Growth and Stability
Edited by Pier Carlo Padoan, Paul A. Brenton and Gavin Boyd

The New Competition for Inward Investment
Companies, Institutions and Territorial Development
Edited by Nicholas Phelps and Phil Raines

Multinational Enterprises, Innovative Strategies and Systems of Innovation
Edited by John Cantwell and José Molero

Multinational Enterprises, Innovative Strategies and Systems of Innovation

Edited by

John Cantwell

*Rutgers University, New Jersey, USA and
University of Reading, UK*

and

José Molero

*Professor of Applied and Industrial Economy,
Universidad Complutense de Madrid, Spain*

NEW HORIZONS IN INTERNATIONAL BUSINESS

Edward Elgar

Cheltenham, UK • Northampton, MA, USA

Published by
Edward Elgar Publishing Limited
Glensanda House
Montpellier Parade
Cheltenham
Glos GL50 1UA
UK

Edward Elgar Publishing, Inc.
136 West Street
Suite 202
Northampton
Massachusetts 01060
USA

A catalogue record for this book
is available from the British Library

ISBN 1 84376 479 2

Printed and bound in Great Britain by MPG Books Ltd, Bodmin, Cornwall

Contents

v

Figures

Tables

Contributors

Isabel Álvarez

Isabel Álvarez is Lecturer in Applied Economics at the Department of Economics Structure and Industrial Economics, Complutense University of Madrid, Spain, and a researcher associated to the Complutense Institute of International Studies, Research Group on Innovation Economy and Policy, where she acts as coordinator. Her main research topics focus on the internationalisation of technology and innovation policies. Among recent international projects, she has been involved in the MESIAS Network of the Strata Programme, as well as in the Assessment of Science and Technology Programme for Development in Iberoamerica, funded by the Secretary for the Iberoamerican Cooperation. Among recent publications, she has published a book about the regional system of innovation in the Canary Islands as well as several articles in Spanish and in international journals.

Daniele Archibugi

Daniele Archibugi is Technological Director at the Italian National Research Council in Rome, Italy. He graduated in Economics at the University of Rome and took his Ph.D. in Science and Technology Policy Studies at the University of Sussex, UK. He has worked and taught at the Universities of Roskilde, Sussex, Naples, Cambridge and Rome. He is an adviser to the European Union (EU), the Organisation for Economic Co-operation and Development (OECD), several United Nations (UN) agencies and various national governments. He has led many projects on science and technology policy studies for the European Commission and other international organisations. He is the author of several books and articles in refereed journals on the theory and measurement of technological change. Among his recent books, he has co-edited *The Globalising Learning Economy* (Oxford University Press, 2001), *Innovation Policy in a Global Economy* (Cambridge University Press, 1999), *Trade, Growth and Technical Change* (Cambridge University Press, 1998), *Technology, Globalisation and Economic Performance* (Cambridge University Press, 1997). He is also the co-author of a volume devoted to the measurement of the technological capabilities of OECD countries, *The Technological Specialization of Advanced Countries. A Report to the EEC on International Science and Technology Activities* (Kluwer, 1992).

John Cantwell

John Cantwell is Professor of International Business at Rutgers University in the US (from 2002), and Professor of International Economics at the University of Reading in the UK. He has also been a Visiting Professor of Economics at the University of Rome 'La Sapienza', Italy, the University of the Social Sciences, Toulouse, France, and the University of Economics and Business Administration, Vienna, Austria. He is the author of *Technological Innovation and Multinational Corporations* (Basil Blackwell, 1989), this book helped to launch a new literature on multinational companies and technology creation, beyond merely international technology transfer. He is a former President of the European International Business Academy (EIBA). In 2001 he was elected as one of four EIBA Founding Fellows.

François Chesnais

François Chesnais is Professor of International Economics at the University of Paris-Nord, France and senior researcher at the Centre for the Study of International Dynamics (CEDI), France. Previously he was Senior Economist in the Directorate for Science, Technology and Industry at the OECD. In that capacity he coordinated projects for the Committee on Science and Technological Policy (CSTP) and Industry Committee, *inter alia* on multinational enterprises (MNEs) and national scientific and technological capacity, trade in high technology products, technology and competitiveness and technological co-operation agreements. He was notably co-author and overall coordinator for the OECD report which concluded the Technology and Economy Programme (TEP) project, *Technology and the Economy, The Key Relationships* (OECD, Paris, 1992).

Alberto Coco

Alberto Coco graduated in Economics at the University of Rome 'La Sapienza' and took an M.Sc. in Economics at the University Luigi Bocconi in Milan, Italy. He has worked on data analysis and forecasting for Italian Telecom. He is currently a research associate at the Italian National Research Council and is attending a Ph.D. in Economic Sciences at the Catholic University of Louvain la Neuve in Belgium.

Vitor Corado Simões

Vitor Corado Simões is a Professor at the Instituto Superior de Economia e Gestao (Higher Institute for Economics and Business Administration) (Technical University of Lisbon, Portugal) and has worked on innovation, technology transfer and international investment issues. Dr. Simões has acted as a consultant to the European Commission, OECD and United Nations Industrial Development Organisation (UNIDO). He was a member of the Committee on Innovation and Technology Transfer (SPRINT programme-DGXIII) as representative of Portugal, as well as of the Community Innovation

Survey (CIS) Steering Committee. He is also actively involved with the EIBA, acting as President during 1993. His recent publications include three books: *Inovação e Gestão em PME, Inovação Tecnológica – Experiências das Empresas Portuguesas* and *Cooperação e Alianças Estratégicas nos Processos de Internacionalização.*

Jakob Edler

Jakob Edler is currently a senior researcher at the Fraunhofer Institute for Systems and Innovation Research, Karlsruhe, Germany. He received a Diploma in Business Administration as well as a degree as Master of Arts in Political Science and Economic History and has made his doctorate on European Research Policy. His main research areas are the dynamics of innovation systems and public and private innovation strategies – especially as regards the generation, transfer and protection of knowledge. One of his major interests is the internationalisation both of industrial research and development (R&D) activities and of public research and innovation policy. Furthermore, he has worked on the design and analysis of governance schemes for research and innovation in the European multi-level system. He has worked as an adviser to the European Commission and is a member of an OECD study group on Knowledge Management. As well as numerous articles on these subjects, his publications include a book on European R&D policy and he is co-editor of a book on the European Research Area.

Annamária Inzelt

Dr Annamária Inzelt is Founding Director of the Innovation Research Centre (IKU) (1991) and Founding Co-Director of the Centre for Innovation Policy Research and Education for Central and Eastern Europe, Budapest, Hungary (1999). She is a member of several international organisations and has organised some international conferences. She is the author and editor of several books, chapters and articles and regularly participates in international research projects. Her main research interests are: systems of innovation, the role of internationalisation in technology upgrading and research and development, knowledge flow through mobility and migration and brain circulation.

Elena Kosmopoulou

Elena Kosmopoulou is a Lecturer in the School of Business at Reading University in the UK. She completed her first degree on Business Administration and Management at Pireaus University in Greece and her Master of Science at Reading University in the UK. Her research work is in the area of international business and in particular: the internationalisation of corporate technology, technological innovation and its interactions with industrial structure and dynamics, innovation systems and the chemical and pharmaceutical industry.

José Molero

José Molero is Doctor in Economics at the Universidad Complutense de Madrid, Spain. He is also Professor of Applied Economics at this University. Today he is Vice-Rector of Postgraduate Studies and Continuing Education and Director of the Firms Incubator Programme for the Madrid Regional Government. Previously, he has been Director of the Complutense Institute for International Studies, Director of the Department of Applied Economics and Director of the Institute of Industrial and Financial Analysis at the same University. His research activity covers areas such as the economics of technical change, industrial economics and multinational corporations. In these fields he has conducted important national and international projects, mainly financed by the European Union. Among his recent publications, two books can be mentioned: *Technological Innovation, Multinational Corporations and New International Competitiveness: The Case of Intermediate Countries* (Harwood Academic Publishers, 1995) and *Innovación tecnológica y competitividad en Europa* (Sintesis, Madrid, 2001).

Rajneesh Narula

Rajneesh Narula is Professor in the Department of International Economics and Management (INT) at the Copenhagen Business School, Denmark, and at the Centre for Technology, Innovation and Culture (TIK), University of Oslo, Norway. He has worked variously as an engineer, analyst and academic in Nigeria, the US, Hong Kong, The Netherlands, Norway and Denmark. He has also been a consultant for the United Nations Conference on Trade and Development (UNCTAD), UNIDO, International Labour Organisation (ILO), The Inter-American Development Bank and the European Commission as well as several international companies.

Theodosios Palaskas

Theodosios Palaskas (thpal@panteion.gr) is Professor of Economic Analysis and Development Economics in the Department of Economics and Regional Development, Panteion University of Social and Political Sciences, Athens, Greece. He is also Research Director at the Greek Foundation of Economic and Industrial Research. He has been Teaching Fellow in Economics and Econometrics at the University of Oxford, UK. He has also acted as External Expert and Evaluator to the European Commission – DG Science, Research and Development and Consultant to the United Nations – UNCTAD. He co-authored a two-volume book on *Advanced Quantitative Methods of Economic Analysis – Theory and Applications*. He has also published several academic articles in international journals on modelling international economic development, trade trends and commodity pricing. He has coordinated international research projects financed, among others, by the World Bank, UNCTAD, the European Commission, the Economic and Social Research Council (ESRC), the Nuffield

Foundation, the Overseas Development Institute and the United States Agency for International Development (USAID). His recent research focuses on economic development, competitiveness, foreign direct investment, the competitive and innovative capacity of small to medium-sized enterprises (SMEs), and the related policy issues.

Guido Reger

Guido Reger is Professor of Business Administration and Innovation Management at the University of Applied Sciences in Brandenburg, Germany, and Director of the Institute of Innovation and Internationalization (I3) at the same university. His research focus is on innovation strategies and management, globalisation of research and technology, and evaluation of innovation policy. He is a senior adviser to Ministries, the Organisation for Economic Cooperation and Development, the Commission of the European Communities, and various high-technology firms.

Francesca Sanna-Randaccio

Francesca Sanna-Randaccio is Professor of Economics at the Department of Systems and Computer Sciences of the University of Rome 'La Sapienza', Italy. She studied at the University of Rome, Johns Hopkins University, USA (M.A. in International Relations) and Oxford University, UK (M.Litt. in Economics). She has been a visiting scholar at the University of California at Berkeley, USA, Duke University, USA, the London School of Economics, UK and a visiting professor at the University of Toulouse, France and the Free University of Bozen, Hungary. She has published a book and several articles in the fields of international economics, industrial organisation and the economics of innovation. In recent years her research has focused on the interaction between firms' multinational expansion and innovative strategy, R&D internationalisation, the impact of foreign direct investment (FDI) on host and home countries and the effect of national and multilateral FDI policies.

Maria Tsampra

Maria Tsampra (mtsam@geo.aegean.gr) is a Lecturer at the School of Geography, University of the Aegean, Greece. She is also Senior Research Officer at the Department of Economics and Regional Development, Panteion University of Social and Political Sciences, Athens, Greece. Her research and teaching interests centre on issues of regional diversity in the context of globalisation, and the relationship of economic viability and growth to territory-specific historical and socio-cultural characteristics and conditions. Her current research is on learning and innovation processes in regional agglomerations, the 'new economy' and competitive knowledge-based advantages, the role of regional socio-institutional structures in the development of technological capabilities, and the innovative and competitive capacity of firms.

Reinhilde Veugelers

Professor Dr Reinhilde Veugelers has been with the Catholic University of Leuven, Belgium, since 1985, where she obtained her Ph.D. in Economics in 1990 with a thesis on 'Scope decisions of Multinational Enterprises'. She is currently a full professor at the Department of Applied Economics, where she teaches managerial economics and international business economics. She was a visiting scholar at Northwestern University's Kellogg Graduate School of Management and at the Sloan School of Management, Massachusetts Institute of Technology (MIT), and visiting professor at University College, London (UCL), Belgium, Free University of Brussels, Paris I, France, University Pompeu Fabra (UPF) and University Autonoma of Barcelona (UAB), Barcelona, UMaastricht. With her research concentrated in the fields of industrial organisation, international economics and strategy and innovation, she has authored numerous publications on multinationals, R&D co-operation and alliances, trade policy, bargaining and market integration in leading international journals. She obtained research grants for projects on co-operation in R&D, the Europeanisation of Industry (EC), inter-firm networks and international competition (EC), and R&D strategies by Flemish Companies.

Acknowledgements

This book would not have been possible without the co-operation of the MESIAS network and all the institutions involved in it. As network coordinator, the Universidad Complutense de Madrid has helped with the administrative tasks that being in charge of such a broad project required. In particular, we acknowledge the Research Vice-rectorate and the Office for the Research Results Transfer (OTRI-UCM) in charge of the European Projects at the Complutense University level. Also, our acknowledgement should be extended to the Complutense Institute for International Studies (ICEI-UCM) where the project was located. On the institutional side, it should also be recalled that the institutions involved in the organisation of seminars have also been of great help in supporting the network activities.

We would also like to acknowledge the people and organisations not involved with the MESIAS network who actively participated in seminars as well as in the field research carried out during visits. In particular, we thank the representatives of companies and public administrations who have presented at the different seminars.

A very special acknowledgement goes to the European Commission and the STRATA Programme. The financial aid received (HPV1-CT-1999-003) was absolutely crucial for all the research collaboration. Moreover, we want to give our thanks to the officials who have been involved in the network. In particular, we acknowledge Hubert Couwenbergh with whom we have shared the contract preparation phase as well as the first period of the network. Also, to Christian Svanfeldt, an official in the last period, many thanks for his kindly co-operation, as well as to Mike Rogers from whom we have always received important ideas and help.

Lastly, our acknowledgement to Inés Granda for her careful help in editing this book.

Abbreviations

BERD	Business enterprise R&D
BG	Business group
CEDI	Centre for the Study of International Dynamics
CEE	Central and Eastern Europe
CEECs	Central and Eastern European post-socialist countries
CERN	Centre Européen Recherche Nucléaire
CIS	Community Innovation Survey
CMEA (or COMECON)	Council for Mutual Economic Aid
COCOM	Coordinating Committee on Multilateral Export Controls
COST	Co-operation in the field of Scientific and Technical Research
CSTP	Committee on Science and Technological Policy
CTO	Corporate Technology Officer
EBRD	European Bank for Reconstruction and Development
EC	European Commission
EEC	European Economic Community
EESD	Energy, Environment and Sustainable Development Programme of the 5th EU RTD Framework Programme
EFTA	European Free Trade Association
EIBA	European International Business Academy
EMBO	European Molecular Biology Organisation
EPAT	European Patent Office
EPO	European Patent Office
ERISA	Employment Retirement Income Security Act (US Congress)
ESA	European Space Agreement
ESEE	Encuesta de Estrategias Empresariales
ESF	European Science Foundation
ESRC	Economic and Social Research Council
EU	European Union
EU RTD FP	European Union Research and Technology Development Framework Programmes
EURATOM	European Atomic Energy Community

EUREKA	European Research Co-ordinating Agency
FAO	Food and Agriculture Organisation of the United Nations
FDI	Foreign direct investment
FEMIRC	Fellow Member in Innovation Relay Centres
FP	Framework Programme
GDP	Gross Domestic Product
GERD	Gross Domestic Expenditures on Research and Development
GM	General Motors
GPT	General purpose technology
GROWTH	Competitive and Sustainable Growth Programme of the 5th EU RTD Framework Programme
HCSO	Hungarian Central Statistical Office
ICT	Information and communication technology
IHP	Improving Human Research Potential and the Socio-economic Knowledge Base Programme of the 5th EU RTD Framework Programme
IKU	Innovation Research Centre
ILO	International Labour Organisation
IMF	International Monetary Fund
INCO	Confirming the International Role of Community Research Programme of the 5th EU RTD Framework Programme
IPO	Initial public offering
ISI	Institute for Systems Innovation and Research
ISO	International Organisation for Standardisation
IST	Information Society Technologies Programme of the 5th EU RTD Framework Programme
IT	Information technology
ITC	Information and telecommunication
KMÜFA	Central Technological Development Fund (Hungarian budgetary fund)
LIFE	Quality of Life and Management of Living Resources Programme of the 5th EU RTD Framework Programme
M&A	Mergers and acquisitions
MN	Multinational
MNCs	Multinational corporations/companies
MNEs	Multinational enterprises
NAFTA	North American Free Trade Agreement
NATO	North Atlantic Treaty Organisation
NCP	National Contact Points
NIS	National Innovation System

NSF	National Science Foundation
NUTS	Nomenclature of Territorial Units for Statistics
NYSE	New York Stock Exchange
OECD	Organisation for Economic Co-operation and Development
PCTPAT	World Patent Office
PD	Product division
PERA	Philips Research East Asia
PHARE	Polish-Hungarian Aid for Reconstruction
PIT Program	OECD Programme for Partners in Transition
PR	Philips Research
R&D	Research and development
RDC	Research Directors Conferences
RNUR	Régie Nationale des Usines Renault
RSA	Relative Scientific Advantage
RTA	Revealed technological advantage
RTD	Research and technological development
RWTH	Rheinisch-Westfälische Technische Hochschule
S&T	Science and technology
SCI	Science Citation Index
SDI	Strategic defence initiative
SEM	Single European Market
SME	Small to medium-sized enterprise
STK	5th Framework Programme
STP	Strategic technology partnering
TEP	Technology and Economy Programme
TNCs	Transnational corporations
TRIPs	Trade Related Intellectual Property Rights
TSER	Targeted Socio-Economic Research
UN	United Nations
UNCTAD	United Nations Conference on Trade and Development
UNIDO	United Nations Industrial Development Organisation
USAID	United States Agency for International Development
USPTO	US Patents Office
WIPO	World Intellectual Property Organisation
WTO	Word Trade Organisation

To Keith Pavitt from all MESIAS Network members
in gratitude for his brilliant teaching, loyal criticism and warm friendship.

Introduction

John Cantwell and José Molero

The national system of innovation is the network of institutions in the public and private sectors of each country that support the initiation, modification and diffusion of new technologies (Freeman, 1987; 1995). The nationally distinctive features of a system are reflected in the particular sectoral patterns of strength or technological capability that have been developed in private firms in each country (Nelson, 1993; Patel and Pavitt, 1994). The globalisation of technological innovation in multinational enterprises (MNEs), in the sense of an international corporate integration of geographically dispersed and locally specialised activities, tends to reinforce and not to dismantle nationally distinctive patterns of development or national systems of innovation (Cantwell, 1995). Contrary to what is sometimes alleged, globalisation and national specialisation are complementary parts of a common process, and not conflicting trends (as argued as well by Archibugi and Pianta (1992), and Archibugi and Michie (1997)). The incentive to organise affiliate specialisation is the desire to tap into the locally specific and differentiated stream of innovation in each centre but, by specialising in accordance with these local strengths, the latter are reinforced.

The creation of technological capability is in part tacit and context-specific, and hence becomes localised and embedded in social organisations (Nelson and Winter, 1982), and this organisational distinctiveness has a location-specific as well as a firm-specific dimension. The particular path of innovation followed in each country or region has historical origins (Rosenberg, 1976; 1982). In the period of globalisation since the late 1960s the general tendency has been for MNEs to become more technologically diversified as they establish newly integrated technological systems across borders, while countries or locations have become more specialised in their technological activity (Cantwell, 1993).

In developing their technological competence, firms evolve typically along paths in which their own past history plays a critical role, rather than through a series of discrete and unrelated steps. Yet either active technological cooperation or unintentional spillovers between firms that share some geographical or institutional proximity may facilitate some common systemic technological trajectories at the level of broader national of firms despite the remaining differences of more detailed focus between the individual companies concerned. Since the extent of interaction between the technological activities of firms tends to rise as geographical distance falls, national groups of firms tend to cluster around certain common areas of technological search and expertise. Hence, the degree of inter-firm variety in patterns of technological competence tends to increase over longer distances, which is what allows us to distinguish the specific features of geographically bounded national or regional systems of innovation. Such patterns are reinforced by the additional interaction of firms in developing new technology not only with other companies, but with other local institutions, including universities and scientific research facilities (especially in the science-based industries), other providers of specialised services, instruments and equipment, including innovative smaller firms and wider communities of engineering and allied expertise, as well as by the particular conditions of local markets. As a consequence, firms that have common origins in a national system of innovation are likely to cluster in certain industries and in the development of certain technological fields, in comparison with groups of firms that originated in other countries.

The degree of interchange between technological learning activities is typically greatest within the same firm, and becomes less intense in moving to inter-company connections within national groups of large firms. Yet since there are more likely to be technological complementarities between the learning efforts of large companies of common national origins in comparison with the different trajectories of firms from other countries, the closer inter-firm interchanges within national groups will reinforce the innovation of each company if they are in the same, or closely related, industries, through the ability of each firm to absorb as inputs into their own learning the knowledge generated by others of the same group. Hence, we can expect that the industrial patterns of technological development in each national group of the leading companies will be distinctive and will tend to persist over time (Cantwell, 2000).

Some MNEs have recently been able to establish closer cross-border connections between the most relevant geographical centres of innovation for their industry by exchanging knowledge between competence-creating subsidiaries and their parent companies. The largest MNEs have found ways of strategically combining alternative but complementary lines of innovation located in distant centres, through the emergence of internationally integrated corporate networks for dispersed technological development (Zander, 1997; 2002; Cantwell and Janne, 1999; Cantwell and Piscitello, 2000). The diversification of firms into new fields of competence creation is now achieved in part through these international strategies of geographically dispersed technology sourcing. The ability of the newer competence-creating subsidiaries to fulfil their role depends in turn on their embeddedness in local networks with other firms and other institutions (including universities) in their own vicinity.

However, not all kinds of corporate technological knowledge creation can be geographically dispersed in this fashion. In particular, the typical pattern of international specialisation in innovative activity within an MNE is for the development of technologies that are core to the firm's industry to be concentrated at home, while other fields of technological activity may be located abroad. In this sense, the internationalisation of research tends to be complementary to the home base (often termed home-base augmenting). Viewed from the perspective of the local area as opposed to the firm, most regions are quite highly specialised in their local capabilities and so attract foreign-owned activity in the same existing narrow range of fields, and thus witness intra-industry, inter-company technology spillovers (Cantwell and Iammarino, 2000; 2001). In contrast, in the major centres of excellence much of the locally sited innovation of foreign-owned multinationals does not match the specific fields of local specialisation, but is rather geared towards the development of general-purpose technologies of relevance in several industries (such as computing equipment or machinery). Here we also observe inter-industry technology spillovers (Cantwell, Iammarino and Noonan, 2001).

For competence-creating subsidiaries (unlike purely home-base competence-exploiting subsidiaries of the traditional kind), the presence of local skills, educational resources and research infrastructure is critical. A good science base is especially attractive to the location of internationally mobile corporate research facilities. Today, science–technology (university–industry) linkages matter much more to corporate research, owing to the deepening and widening character of much technological knowledge (Cantwell and Piscitello, 2002).

Through an intense scientific interchange, MESIAS Network members have dealt with new issues regarding the relationship between MNEs and local systems of innovation, as well as with the role played by academic research in the international activities of those companies and the upgrading of absorptive capacities as a means of accessing internationally available new knowledge. Efforts have been made with the objectives, first of conceptual clarification and formalisation and second to obtain new findings from more empirically oriented research. Regarding the scope of our work, although the core of the analysis is the European economy, comparisons with the US and Japan have been made and some particular analysis for the Eastern European accession countries has been included.

In relation to the complexity of the subject explored, there are different kinds of contributions, including formal essays (F. Sanna-Randaccio, R. Narula), and a variety of methods and sources of information have been used. In fact, the results come from a diversity of procedures. Some of them can be mentioned here such as: first, case studies (G. Reger, V. Corado-Simões); second, empirical analysis based on econometric estimations making use of important datasets, such as the Organisation for Economic Co-operation and Development (OECD) database through OLISNET (J. Molero), the one based on patents granted by the US Patent and Trademark Office, developed at the University of Reading (driven by J. Cantwell), as well as the SPRU database on the largest companies of the world, based on the Fortune 500 List (developed by K. Pavitt and P. Patel); third, a new exploitation of sources of information at the European level, such as the Community Innovation Survey (CIS) I and II (J. Molero); fourth, the generation of new sources such as surveys at the firm level in particular contexts (J. Edler, T. Palaskas, A. Inzelt).

A key question has to do with the explanatory mechanisms related to the firm's choices between centralised or decentralised key activities such as research and development (R&D) through its subsidiaries (Petit and Sanna-Randaccio, 2000; Sanna-Randaccio, 2002). It may be thought that when the latter prevails, it is plausible to wonder about the existence of international technological flows in both directions, from the parent to the subsidiary and vice versa and what the main determinants of these mutual exchanges are. This is a recent insight of a formal approach to the subject that tries to reflect the new organisational features and strategies of international companies, which are increasingly integrated into the systems of innovation of host countries.

Among the formal papers in this spirit, one recent one by Sanna-Randaccio and Veuglers (2002) should be noted, underlining the organisational implications for MNEs to benefit from a decentralisation choice. In particular, they explore the trade-off faced by an MNE when an active innovative role is assigned to a subsidiary, since the R&D subsidiaries can be used as a source of locally available know-how but, at the same time, they may provide a challenge to the effective appropriation of core technology. Based on a game theoretical model, this work shows the critical role of managing both internal and external spillovers and the recognition of absorptive capacities as a key to the use of the latter, from which important policy implications can be derived.

An interesting development based on the micro concept of absorptive capacities comes from considering the relationship between the ability of a country to absorb foreign knowledge and its stage of technological development (Criscuolo and Narula, 2001). This approach entails the macro perspective of the generation and absorption of knowledge capabilities, an issue which is closely related to the features of national systems of innovation. It is shown that the synergetic effects of inter-firm, inter-industry and systemic and institutional elements facilitate knowledge absorption. Through linking the absorption capacities with the technology-gap approach, the accumulation process seems to show a slower pace as a country approaches the frontier, which is of course especially relevant for catching up economies and for actions devoted to upgrading local capabilities.

Analysis of systems of innovation has been traditionally focused on institutions, networks and learning, but has paid relatively little attention to their financial aspects. This is a drawback given the rise of a finance-market-dominated accumulation regime. The new financial context generates important modifications in the availability and source of funding for long-term, innovation-related investment. The paper by Chesnais (2001) analyses precisely the US venture capital industry with the aim of assessing whether it might be a model to be easily borrowed, imported or adapted by other countries. This theme opens an interesting debate on the adequacy of the coordination of innovation and other policies at both a European and a national level. In this sense, institutional constraints are then stressed, which again highlights that the specificity of national systems of innovation still matters in the comprehension of the internationalisation of technology strategies.

Regarding the effects that internationalised R&D has for national systems of innovation, foreign-owned firms do not always show greater technology intensity than do domestically owned firms, and they account for a larger proportion of local industry production than they do of the local generation of technology.

Figure 0.1 illustrates the variety of profiles that the R&D activities of foreign affiliates may show, according to the R&D intensity of the countries. In particular, for a selection of countries, the relationship is presented between the national potential for knowledge generation, as proxied by R&D expenditure as a share of Gross Domestic Product (GDP), and the strength of MNEs, proxied by the R&D expenditure of affiliates as a share of total national business R&D. Leaving aside the special case of Ireland, there are a number of countries (Australia, Italy, Portugal, Turkey and even Spain) which show a positive relationship between the technological intensity of the country and the participation of MNEs in domestic R&D. On the upper left-hand side of the figure we find the most technologically developed countries, which are characterised by a share of foreign-owned MNEs that is low as compared with the national system, notwithstanding the fact that the majority of foreign-located R&D facilities of MNEs is concentrated in those countries. Interestingly enough, there is no example of a high technology intensive country whose local development is primarily due to the strong local participation of foreign-owned MNEs.

Some previous findings support the idea that national systems of innovation clearly condition the integration into the local environment of the innovative activities of MNEs. In fact, when innovative behaviour is analysed by comparing the activities of foreign-owned and domestically owned firms, there is little evidence of any great difference between the two groups. Indeed, the length of time for which a subsidiary has been operating in a country seems to be crucial in this respect. The similarity between subsidiaries and indigenous firms shows the adaptation of the former to local conditions over time (Molero, Buesa and Casado, 1995). Nonetheless, some structural variables seem to be the key to sustaining variety and limiting convergence in the behaviour and

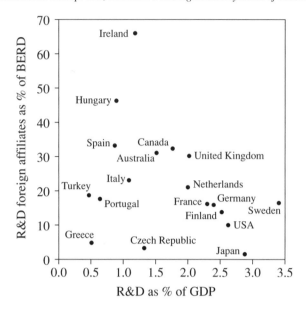

Note: BERD: Business Enterprise R&D.

Figure 0.1   R&D of foreign affiliates as a share of BERD and according to R&D intensity

influence of the different categories of firms in the national system of innovation. Recent analyses based on the CIS have confirmed that the higher the level of development of the system of innovation, the more likely foreign firms are to be integrated in the national economy (Molero, 2002).

When comparing foreign firms and indigenous firms that are also part of a larger company group (usually a domestically owned MNE), the results suggest that the differences associated with the nationality of ownership have more to do with the structural composition of activity than with innovation-related differences as such, and the influences of foreign-owned firms in the national system depend more on indirect mechanisms (Molero and Heys, 2002). In the case of intermediate countries like Spain (Molero, 2000) the larger average size of foreign-owned firms is crucial for international market competition and influences the approach taken to facing the risks linked to innovation too. Industry classification is another central factor since foreign-owned firms are mainly found in high technological opportunity sectors, characterised by a higher level of competition. The distinctive cross-industry distribution of investment of the foreign-owned group matters as well in terms of the maturity of industries and their technological content, as well as in the level of external openness, which would tend to be associated with a greater degree of international cooperation.

Another interesting aspect of foreign participation in the system of innovation is the distinction within the foreign-owned sector between subsidiaries with competence-creating mandates and those whose role is purely competence exploiting, each of which constitutes part of the international networks that some MNEs have now generated. While the traditional international business literature focused on hierarchical control from the parent company and assumed that the subsidiary had a competence-exploiting function (ie. exploiting established competence for the purpose of local-market servicing or local-resource extraction), more recent literature focuses on the possible establishment of some competence-creating subsidiaries whose functions are thus more widely defined. Considering both the degree of independence achieved by affiliates in R&D activities and their local competence in R&D and production, a typology of cases has been designed (Meyer-Krahmer and Reger, 1997). This typology has demonstrated its relevance and influence in the MESIAS debate. As shown in Figure 0.2, if both are low, the transfer of knowledge is just one way since the main function of the affiliate is to transfer knowledge about the local environment to the headquarters (to act as a local antenna). If there is low

	Low R&D Independence	High R&D Independence
Low Local Competence	Local antenna	R&D support activities
High Local Competence	R&D centralisation	Local centres of R&D competence

Source: Adapted from Meyer-Krahmer and Reger (1997)

Figure 0.2   Matrix for the evolution of possible impacts of R&D units

independence but high competence, R&D is mainly centralised and the external effects are moderate. On the other hand, when high independence prevails, although with little local competence, the generation of knowledge is mainly associated with adaptation to the local market. Finally, when both variables are at a high level, the unit contributes to the international generation of innovation and the impacts on the location are more profound.

In particular, once the external effects from decentralisation are allowed for, the qualitative nature of R&D seems to depend on whether or not the subsidiary is assigned a competence-creating mandate, as is shown by Cantwell and Mudambi (2001). Based on a strategic model of determination of the subsidiary's R&D intensity, the decision to grant a competence-creating mandate is endogenous and whether the subsidiary obtains the mandate depends on firm, industry and location factors. In this respect, the adequacy of local infrastructure, the educational system and the science base clearly influence the likelihood of foreign-owned R&D becoming competence creating. Also relevant is the previous position of the subsidiary, whether or not it has been designed as an independent unit for other strategic functions by the MNE's headquarters.

Regarding the scope of firms' choice of location and their determinants, recent research has begun to study the sub-national or regional level. More precisely, geographical proximity and agglomeration effects are considered since the existing knowledge base of a region plays an important role in the decision foreign-owned firms take for the sitting of technological activities. An analysis of the attractiveness of the German, Italian and UK regions is carried out in Cantwell and Piscitello (2002). The choice of location depends, on the one hand, on the strategy – home-base augmenting versus exploiting – and, on the other, on the characteristics of the location, it being possible to conceive of a hierarchy of regional centres in Europe according to cumulativeness in areas where MNEs have consolidated traditional specialisation against others characterised by high technological opportunities (Cantwell and Iammarino, 1998; 2000). In this sense, the degree of development and cohesion achieved by both technologies and the different elements of the local system of innovation appear as key aspects and, hence, impinge on the assessment of the impact that an MNE has in the system.

In spite of the great efforts made by foreign firms to develop new technologies, these are also supported by external sources of knowledge (Narula, 2001), and the science–technology relationship or university–industry proximity play an important role in this context. This is one manifestation of the increasing outsourcing trends followed by large firms, among which technological alliances have arisen as one of the main forms, fostering cooperation between different companies with the knowledge-generation objective. Policies which address the improvement of public infrastructure as well as scientific and technical capacities should still consider a perspective in which the attraction for the establishment of foreign firms plays its role. As Cantwell and Piscitello (2002) point out, foreign firms take care to be close to public research facilities, which is why the role of academic research may entail significant consequences for the analysis.

With regard to this, contrary to the pressure to make such support conditional on practical applications, a better understanding of the dynamics of the interaction between basic research and practice is needed. The linkages between disciplines, corporate functions and institutions are seen as an essential feature of the system and the discussion of the validity of US public support for basic research may be of great usefulness for the European context (Pavitt, 2001). Among Pavitt's findings, it can be underlined that a strong support for basic research seems to be a necessity for providing the skills and knowledge to compete in world markets on an innovation basis. This is why demand-driven strategies to support basic research may be considered a great danger. Nonetheless, the role of leading markets remains critical as has been underlined elsewhere (Meyer-Krahmer and Reger, 1999). Two aspects deserve more attention in Europe: the creation of new science-based firms linked to the universities, and the increasing internationalisation of the links between science and application. They too reflect some restrictions in basic research, inadequate local competences and local research resources available to foreign uses.

Based on a survey carried out among more than 200 firms, Reger (2002) shows again the existence of differences in the internationalisation of R&D and technology between European, Japanese and US corporations. Among his main findings, there is a growing tendency to acquire technology from foreign sources with similarities in patterns of foreign technology collaboration, although the motives for appropriation of the technological knowledge are still different. Moreover, the internationalisation of R&D is not global but takes place basically inside the Triad. Regarding differences in behaviour due to nationality, the lowest share of R&D abroad is obtained by companies from Japan while the largest corresponds to that of European-owned firms. On the other hand, US companies show a higher geographical diversification than the other two groups; the Japanese are mainly focused on North America, as are European companies outside Europe (although this depends on considering Europe as a combined entity).

Looking more closely at the European context, there are two groups of countries which have received special attention in our deliberations: the intermediate countries and the Eastern accession countries. Considering the former group, there are some remarkable findings. The centres of excellence literature suggests that the assignment to subsidiaries of this responsibility to assume the role of a specialised centre also reflects the existence of local capabilities. Based on case studies of firms in the metal processing and electrical industries, the processes of emergence and designation of centres of excellence in the context of acquisitions in the Portuguese economy have been analysed. It has been shown that domestic market inducements and subsidiary learning capabilities played a very important role in the emergence of centres of excellence (Simões and Nevado, 2000).

From a different perspective, it is interesting to analyse how a large internationalised company may generate strong effects on domestic firms from their intra-industry relationships. Based particularly on a case study of telecommunication firms, it is worth noticing the important role played by the largest Spanish information and telecommunication (ITC) multinational enterprises in the explanation of both innovation and internationalisation trends in small to medium-sized enterprises (SMEs), which enables us to differentiate firms' behaviour (Molero, López and Zlatanova, 2002). This phenomenon has important implications for countries where multinational companies are not numerous but where the links within an industry could permit actions to be defined that enhance the international and innovation capability of the SMEs connected to MNE networks.

A more particular case of an intermediate country is Greece, due to the clear dominance of SMEs in that national economy. Especial attention has been paid to the effect of industrial agglomerations within global networks as a way of accessing international knowledge sources for less-developed regions (Palaskas and Tsampra, 2002) and as a means to compete in international markets. Along these lines, similar to the Spanish case referred to earlier, the tendency among MNEs to build international networks can be seen as fundamental for national and regional policies that aim to enhance the attractiveness of a location and to facilitate development opportunities.

Finally, taking into account the Eastern European candidate countries, the first aspect to be considered is their background of limited internationalisation which enables us to understand foreign direct investment (FDI) inflows as an element in the transformation of the national economy itself. Nonetheless, the situation of different countries within this group clearly varies greatly in terms of the magnitude of inflows and the capacity to attract MNEs. Based on cross-border R&D, the results of the analysis for Hungary show that the access to national scientific and technological resources which enhances technology cooperation and learning processes depends on whether foreign-owned R&D activities respond either to market adaptation or to technology orientation (Inzelt, 2000). The scenario for the future and particularly for the enlargement of the EU in 2004, with ten more member countries, will bring further issues into the debate.

Despite the continuing significance of national systems of innovation (Nelson, 1993), there is no doubt that the role of the nation state is changing in the newly emerging global economy. The state is being undermined as a purely independent economic authority. It is not necessarily less important as a player in world economic affairs, but it cannot now act or formulate policy in isolation. However, while the state has less autonomy over macroeconomic policies such as the setting of interest rates, its role through many internal microeconomic policies has increased. This is most obviously the case for technology policy, in which it has become essential for governments to help facilitate innovation and encourage entrepreneurship in areas of local expertise and specialisation. The objective is increasingly to join more effectively an ever-expanding network of international knowledge flows in which each country searches for its niche position, rather than to view the process as one of techno-nationalist competition. To enhance the national contribution to cross-border technology creation the establishment of science–technology linkages have become more significant than ever at a local level, through the provision by the science base of skills, training and background supporting know how, much more than through the conduct of closer-to-market research in universities. Thus, we can conclude by briefly commenting upon the ways in which globalisation has changed the agenda for national policy.

The generation of local profitability and growth can be attributed either to the establishment of positions of market power (which has been the traditional focus of attention among economists and policymakers), or to innovation, of which the latter has become increasingly important (as reflected in a new-found interest among both economists and policymakers). With globalisation and the erosion of enclaves of market power within countries that were formerly associated with measures of national protection and separation, national policies must now instead be increasingly oriented towards the second type of strategy for growth rather than the first. From the perspective of the first line of argument, states can attract the investments of MNEs by lowering domestic wage costs and establishing protected markets or allowing the companies some degree of local market power. In doing so, states also thereby have the authority to bargain with MNEs to ensure that a 'fair' share of the returns on investments is retained locally. However, the scope for states to behave in this fashion is now diminished if the country wishes to participate in the international integration of activity being organised by MNEs elsewhere. Even if the strategy succeeds, it is likely to reduce local dynamism, as occurred in the import-substituting regimes of Latin America. It is also worth noting the failure of substantial parts of Central and Eastern Europe and a number of African countries to attract much investment on the basis of the supposed appeal of low wages, in economies in which the prospects for productivity growth have so far remained limited.

Following instead the second approach to economic growth through innovation, states are best advised to maintain a good local infrastructure and to encourage local institution building, and to facilitate local inter-company networks for cross-licensing and other schemes for the mutual enhancement of technological development. This type of strategy is increasingly likely to appeal to MNEs when they consider whether to extend capacity, and if so where. In this case, an industrial policy role very much remains for national governments, even (and perhaps especially so) in a global economy. There are certainly still problems for states in this view, but they are not the problems that are often traditionally perceived from the standpoint of the first perspective, such as a loss of bargaining power *vis-à-vis* MNEs. The problems are rather (among others) how to facilitate the most appropriate pattern of national specialisation, or in other words how best to build upon established local strengths in innovation, and how to encourage a greater international coordination of productive activity in such a way as to improve the ability to learn locally from what is being done elsewhere, in other parts of the neighbouring region or the world.

REFERENCES

Archibugi, D. and Michie, J. (1997), 'Technological globalisation and national systems of innovation: an introduction', in D. Archibugi and J. Michie (eds), *Technology, Globalisation and Economic Performance*, Cambridge and New York: Cambridge University Press.

Archibugi, D. and Pianta, M. (1992), *The Technological Specialization of Advanced Countries*, Dordrecht: Kluwer Academic Publishers.

Cantwell, J.A. (1993), 'Corporate technological specialisation in international industries', in M.C. Casson and J. Creedy (eds), *Industrial Concentration and Economic Inequality: Essays in Honour of Peter Hart*, Aldershot: Edward Elgar.

Cantwell, J.A. (1995), 'The globalisation of technology: what remains of the product cycle model?', *Cambridge Journal of Economics*, vol. 19, no. 1, February, pp. 155–74.

Cantwell, J.A. (2000), 'Technological lock-in of large firms since the interwar period', *European Review of Economic History*, vol. 4, no. 2, pp. 147–74.

Cantwell, J.A. and Iammarino, S. (1998), 'MNCs, technological innovation and regional systems in the EU: some evidence in the Italian case', *International Journal of the Economics of Business*, vol. 5, no. 3, pp. 383–408.

Cantwell, J.A. and Iammarino, S. (2000), 'Multinational corporations and the location of technological innovation in the UK regions', *Regional Studies*, vol. 34, pp. 317–32.

Cantwell, J.A. and Iammarino, S. (2001), 'EU regions and multinational corporations: change, stability and strengthening of technological comparative advantage', *Industrial and Corporate Change*, vol. 10, no. 4, pp. 1007–37.

Cantwell, J.A., Iammarino, S. and Noonan, C.A. (2001), 'Sticky places in slippery space – the location of innovation by MNCs in the European regions', in N. Pain (ed.), *Inward Investment, Technological Change and Growth*, London and New York: Macmillan.

Cantwell, J.A. and Janne, O.E.M. (1999), 'Technological globalisation and innovative centres: the role of corporate technological leadership and locational hierarchy', *Research Policy*, vol. 28, nos. 2–3, pp. 119–44.

Cantwell, J.A. and Mudambi, R. (2001), 'MNE competence-creating subsidiary mandates: an empirical investigation', University of Reading Discussion Paper in International Investment and Management, no. 285, July.

Cantwell, J.A. and Piscitello, L. (2000), 'Accumulating technological competence – its changing impact on corporate diversification and internationalisation', *Industrial and Corporate Change*, vol. 9, no. 1, pp. 21–51.

Cantwell, J.A. and Piscitello, L. (2002), 'The location of technological activities of MNCs in the European regions: the role of spillovers and local competencies', *Journal of International Management*, vol. 8, no. 1, pp. 69–96.

Chesnais, F. (2001), 'The impact of financial regimes on R&D decisions', Fourth Seminar of the MESIAS Network, Proceedings, Brandenburg.

Criscuolo, P. and Narula, R. (2001), 'A novel approach to national technological accumulation and absorptive capacity: aggregating Cohen and Levinthal', Third Seminar of the MESIAS Network, Proceedings, Budapest.

Freeman, C. (1987), *Technology Policy and Economic Performance: Lessons From Japan*, London: Frances Pinter.

Freeman, C. (1995), 'The "National System of Innovation" in historical perspective', *Cambridge Journal of Economics*, vol. 19, no. 1, pp. 5–24.

Inzelt, A. (2000), 'Foreign direct investment in R&D: skin-deep and soul-deep cooperation', *Science and Public Policy*, vol. 27, no. 4, pp. 241–51.

Meyer-Krahmer, F. and Reger, G. (1997), 'European technology policy and internationalisation. An analysis against the background of the international innovation strategies of multinational enterprises', paper written for the ETAN group on Technology Policy in the Context of Internationalisation. How to Strengthen Europe's Competitive Advantage in Technology, Karlsrule, July.

Meyer-Krahmer, F. and Reger, G. (1999), 'New perspectives on the innovation strategies of multinational enterprises: lessons for technology policy in Europe', *Research Policy*, vol. 28, pp. 751–76.

Molero, J. (2000), 'Las empresas multinacionales y el sistema español de innovación', in J. Molero (ed.), *Competencia global y cambio tecnológico*, Madrid: Pirámide.

Molero, J. (2002), 'The innovative behaviour of MNC subsidiaries in uneven European Systems of Innovation: a comparative analysis of the German and Irish cases', *The Journal of Interdisciplinary Economics*, vol. 13, nos. 1–3.

Molero, J., Buesa, M. and Casado, M. (1995), 'Technological strategies of MNE in intermediate countries: the case of Spain' in J. Molero (ed.), *Technological Innovation, Multinational Companies and New International Competitiveness. The Case of Intermediate Countries*, Chur: Harwood.

Molero, J. and Heys, J. (2002), 'Differences in innovative behaviour between national and foreign firms: measuring the impact of foreign firms on national innovation systems', *International Journal of Entrepreneurship and Innovation Management*, vol. 2, nos. 2–3.

Molero, J., López, S. and Zlatanova, G. (2002), 'Spanish TLC companies: a study of the innovative firms of network components', Sixth Seminar of the MESIAS Network, Proceedings, Lisbon.

Narula, R. (2001), 'Choosing between internal and non-internal R&D activities: some technological and economic factors', *Technology Analysis & Strategic Management*, vol. 13, pp. 365–88.

Nelson, R.R. (ed.) (1993), *National Innovation Systems: A Comparative Analysis*, Oxford and New York: Oxford University Press.

Nelson, R.R. and Winter, S.G. (1982), *An Evolutionary Theory of Economic Change*, Cambridge, Mass.: Harvard University Press.

Palaskas, T. and Tsampra, M. (2002), 'Technological capacity of labour intensive industries in vulnerable regions', Sixth Seminar of the MESIAS Network, Proceedings, Lisbon.

Patel, P. and Pavitt, K.L.R. (1994), 'National innovation systems: why they are important, and how they might be measured and compared', *Economics of Innovation and New Technology*, vol. 3, no. 1, pp. 77–95.

Pavitt, K.L.R. (2001), 'Public policies to support basic research: what can the rest of the world learn from US theory and practice? (and what they should not learn)', *Industrial and Corporate Change*, vol. 10, no. 3, pp. 761–79.

Petit, M. and Sanna-Randaccio, F. (2000), 'Endogenous R&D and foreign direct investment in international oligopolies', *International Journal of Industrial Organisation*, vol. 18, pp. 339–67.

Reger, G. (2002), 'Internationalisation of research and development in western European, Japanese and North American multinationals', *International Journal of Entrepreneurship and Innovation Management*, vol. 2, nos. 2–3, pp. 164–85.

Rosenberg, N. (1976), *Perspectives on Technology*, Cambridge and New York: Cambridge University Press.

Rosenberg, N. (1982), *Inside the Black Box: Technology and Economics*, Cambridge and New York: Cambridge University Press.

Sanna-Randaccio, F. (2002), 'The impact of foreign direct investment on home and host countries with endogenous R&D', *Review of International Economics*, vol. 10.

Sanna-Randaccio, F. and Veuglers, R. (2002), 'Multinational knowledge spillovers with centralised versus decentralised R&D: a game theory approach', CEPR Discussion Paper, no. 3151.

Simões, V. and Nevado, P. (2000), 'MNE Centres of Excellence and acquisitions: long evolutionary paths or capturing opportunities?', Second Seminar of the MESIAS Network, Proceedings, Madrid.

Zander, I. (1997), 'Technological diversification in the multinational corporation – historical evolution and future prospects', *Research Policy*, vol. 26, pp. 209–27.

Zander, I. (2002), 'The formation of international innovation networks in the multinational corporation: an evolutionary perspective', *Industrial and Corporate Change*, vol. 11, no. 2, pp. 327–53.

PART I

New Trends in MNE Technological Organisation:
Centralisation versus Decentralisation

1.   Global innovation strategies of MNEs: implications for host economies

Francesca Sanna-Randaccio and Reinhilde Veugelers

INTRODUCTION

With a global business environment where the pace and scope of changes in technological know-how and consumer taste are unprecedented, managing the innovative process has become more central in today's multinational corporations. Innovation strategies require increasingly more global sourcing: sensing new market and technology trends worldwide, while adequately responding to them through generating new ideas which are then implemented on a global scale. These tendencies imply a changing role of innovations in multinational companies, with important implications for the role of subsidiaries in recognising the potential for innovations and exploiting them. The subsidiary is increasingly being viewed as a vehicle to continually reassess and upgrade know-how on core products and technologies and to provide a basis for new generations of innovative products. A major challenge for the multinational enterprise (MNE) is to find an organisational system that is capable of transferring know-how across units and locations, allowing locally generated know-how to be used throughout the multinational organisation.

Changing innovative strategies will not only have implications for the internal know-how transfers within multinational firms: in addition, flows of know-how to and from external sources will be affected in the host markets. Technology sourcing will lead to more know-how being absorbed from local sources. At the same time, more innovation active subsidiaries may become more interesting vehicles for technology diffusion to the local economy. This leaves as an important question to examine what the overall impact of these changes is on the local host economy. Host economies have been actively vying for high-tech foreign direct investment (FDI), which is expected to increase the efficiency of local firms through transfers of technology. But a more active role for subsidiaries in sourcing locally available know-how for developing global innovations may have the worrying implication that valuable know-how leaves the country, while the subsidiary research and development (R&D) remains too dependent on the assimilation of know-how developed elsewhere in the company. When MNEs tie into the local innovation system and contribute to a further development of this system, strong host economies can become innovation centres in which MNEs participate directly, creating innovation, absorbing know-how from local parties, and generating know-how flows to local parties, thus creating further innovation in a 'virtuous cycle'. But at the same time the host economy can lose out from valuable know-how spilling out to multinational firms who may drive out weaker local competitors. Also Cantwell (1989) warns about 'vicious cycles', with MNEs keeping subsidiary know-how proprietary and/or restricting their affiliates to importing know-how intensive activities, developed elsewhere. By driving out weaker local competitors, they deprive the region of opportunities for technological advancement.

This chapter studies the motives of the MNE to internationalise their R&D and the impact of these decisions on the host economy. The discussion is based on an analytical model. The proposed model focuses on how the interplay of internal and external knowledge flows interacts with the nature of host market competition to influence the choice of MNEs in effectively dispersing their R&D internationally. At the same time, the model allows us to discuss the impact of these decisions on the local economy. Before presenting the model results, the chapter starts with an overview of recent literature and stylised evidence on the internationalisation of R&D and the impact on host economies, which is used to set up our model.

THEORETICAL AND EMPIRICAL LITERATURE ON THE INTERNATIONALISATION OF R&D AND THE IMPACT ON HOST ECONOMIES

Motives for MNEs to Internationalise R&D

In the traditional literature on multinationals, following the seminal work of Dunning (1988), multinational activities originate out of the R&D activities of the firm. R&D is a central headquarter function, which allows MNEs to capitalize on economies of scale from pooling R&D resources. The centrally developed know-how is transferred internally from the central R&D lab to geographically dispersed subsidiaries. This is home base exploiting FDI (Kuemmerle (1997)) or 'center-for-global' innovations in Bartlett and Ghoshal's (1997) terminology. In this view, the geographically dispersed subsidiaries can have a specific role in incremental innovations. Enjoying a direct geographic link between markets and production, they are best placed to adjust products and processes to (changing) local needs. Subsidiaries create location specific knowledge within the 'local-for-local' types of innovations, implying a decentralisation of development activities. These are the *demand oriented motives* for the decentralisation of R&D, where it is important to be close to 'lead users' and to adapt products and processes to local conditions, often related to host market regulations (see Granstrand et al. (1992)).

The emphasis in the literature has shifted more recently towards seeing the geographic dispersion of MNE activities as a source for knowledge creation, rather than as a result of knowledge creation. The pace and scope of technological and market change result in the increasing importance of sourcing technology externally on a global scale. All this implies a different role for subsidiaries in the innovative strategy of the MNE. The subsidiary, using location specific know-how, is now viewed in its capacity to contribute to the generation of central generic knowledge. Bartlett and Ghoshal (1997) distinguish two possible innovative processes in this new view. In 'locally leveraged' innovations, the know-how generated in one subsidiary is transferred across the company to benefit other subsidiaries. Units are engaged in a worldwide process of learning from each other and therefore location specific knowledge must flow from one location to another. In the 'globally linked' innovations the resources and capabilities of all units are pooled within the MNE to jointly create innovations, which can be used by all units. This strategy builds on exploiting synergies from combining complementary know-how from various locations. When the location holds a high level of technological capability for a particular innovative project, the subsidiary can be assigned a leading role as a 'centre of excellence', with a 'global product mandate', developing innovations which are implemented worldwide. This is 'home base augmenting FDI' in Kuemmerle's terminology; Pearce and Singh (1992) label these as 'internationally interdependent labs', whose role is in the long term basic research of the group, and who will have close collaboration with other similar labs.

Within an MNE's international technology sourcing strategy, the know-how flows are multiplex, with the subsidiary responsible for sourcing know-how in other units of the MNE (including headquarters), but also accessing externally available know-how. These external sources can be found in the local environment, if the technological capability of the subsidiary follows from being embedded in a performing 'national innovation system' (see, for example, Nelson (1993)). If only because of technological and scientific heritage, different locations have specific scientific expertise embedded in an interconnected system of local firms and research institutes. Local technological capabilities are country specific advantages, attracting foreign firms that are seeking R&D inputs and engage in FDI as a technology sourcing mechanism (Kogut and

Chang (1991)). These are the *supply related motives* for R&D decentralisation: acquiring access to a wider range of scientific and technological skills.

Empirical Evidence on the Internationalisation of R&D

Statistical evidence and survey results on R&D internationalisation suggest that most research still remains at corporate headquarters. On the basis of US patent data for 1969–1986 Patel and Pavitt (1992) found that for large US, German and Japanese firms less than 15% of their technological activities were located abroad. But nevertheless, the percentage of R&D carried out abroad is increasing rapidly (Granstrand et al. (1992), Caves (1996), Serapio and Dalton (1999), Meyer-Krahmer and Reger (1999)). For instance, Serapio and Dalton (1999) report that the R&D spending by US affiliates of foreign firms increased at a rate of 11.6% between 1987 and 1996. This is much faster than the R&D done by US firms, such that the share of foreign owned firms in US R&D spending had increased to 16.3% in 1996. This R&D internationalisation is mainly an intra-Triad phenomenon with the US and European Union (EU) the major locations for foreign R&D while US and EU firms have the largest shares of foreign R&D. Reger (2001) reports that in 1998 US and EU firms undertook respectively 30% and 28% of R&D abroad, and Japanese firms only 7%. Gerybadze and Reger (1999) found that firms from large countries, or from a country with a critical mass in R&D, and operating in science and technology based industries, are more likely to develop global innovative structures. The pharmaceutical industry typically has the most internationalised R&D.

Several studies indicate that MNEs mostly undertake development rather than research abroad. Von Zedtwitz and Gassman (2002) find that foreign R&D is twice as development oriented than domestic R&D. Also, labs undertaking development are generally operating within (or near) the production facilities of the same MNE. Pearce (1999) finds that only 16.7% of R&D labs created by foreign MNEs in the UK indicate that they operate independently of any producing subsidiary.

With respect to motives for R&D decentralisation, Hakanson (1992) found, on a sample of 150 subsidiaries of 20 Swedish MNEs, that local demand related factors were more important than local technology sourcing. Also, on an international sample, Pearce and Singh (1992) found limited evidence for supply-side factors such as the local scientific environment and the availability of researchers. But more recently Florida (1997) found, on a sample of 187 foreign R&D labs in the US, that although both technology and market driven motives are important, access to human capital and technological expertise is becoming a major force. Also Reger (2001) found, on an international sample, no single dominant motive since both product adaption and learning from lead markets go hand in hand with access to skilled researchers.

Empirical evidence on the role of subsidiaries in MNEs' innovative strategies relies on survey based analysis and has never been abundant. Although 44% of the 296 sample subsidiaries in Pearce and Singh (1992) report that they predominantly function as internationally interdependent labs, on average 60% regularly worked to adapt to local markets, 70% developed new products for local markets, while 45% developed new products also used in other markets. The authors conclude that on average adapting is still an important task, but development of products also used in other markets is gradually becoming more widespread (see also Pearce (1999)).

The internationalisation of R&D also has implications for the internal know-how flows between parents and subsidiaries. Empirical studies find no conclusive support for the transfer of know-how from subsidiaries to headquarters. Frost (1998), using US Patents Office (USPTO) data for 1980–1990, found evidence of the importance of headquarter patents for the innovations of subsidiaries, while patent data provided only limited evidence for the transfer of know-how from subsidiaries to headquarters.

The Impact of International R&D on the Host Economy

The impact of FDI on the host economies has received a lot of attention in the economic literature. In one of the early contributions, Caves (1974) distinguishes between three benefits of the presence of multinational firms in the host country. First, the increase in market competition due to the entry of a foreign subsidiary increases allocative efficiency and decreases the excess profits realised by the domestic firms. Second, domestic firms in monopolistic markets will increase their level of technical efficiency or X-efficiency. This benefit flows from either the competitive effect of the multinational's entry or from a demonstration effect.[1] Finally, the entry of the subsidiary of a multinational can speed up the transfer and diffusion of technology in the local market and hence increase the rate of innovation in the host country. Transfers of technology occur through interactions with local firms, such as technical support to local suppliers and customers or R&D contracting. However, internationally transferred know-how may also spill over to local competitors through many informal channels such as movement of personnel, conferences and meetings, and patent applications among other things.

Reviewing the empirical evidence on spillovers to the host economy from inward FDI at the firm level, Blomström and Kokko (1998) conclude that such spillover effects exist, but that both positive and negative effects on host economies can occur. Veugelers and Vanden Houte (1990) provide evidence for Belgium that the presence of foreign MNEs reduces innovative investment for local firms when foreign and domestic products are more homogeneous and the competitive pressure outweighs any positive impact from technology spillovers.

But even without competition effects, the potential benefits from FDI may not materialise, since a critical factor in exploiting spillovers is the technological capability of indigenous firms (Blomström and Kokko (1998)). Also Cantwell (1989) stresses the need for a high level of local competence to be able to absorb spillovers from multinational presence. Most of the empirical studies on developing countries have failed to find robust evidence of positive knowledge spillovers from multinational investment, accounted for by the lack of absorptive capacity in these host countries (see Aitken and Harrison (1999), Blomström and Sjöholm (1999), Blomström and Kokko (1998) for a review). Haskel et al. (2002) find a significant positive correlation, using firm level data from the UK, but this correlation is smaller for lagging domestic plants, again underscoring even for developed countries the need for absorptive capacity.

While most of the existing empirical literature derives the existence of technology spillovers through FDI indirectly from the effect this FDI has on local productivity growth, more recently the empirical literature on technology transfers has turned to more direct measures for technology transfers, using patent information to trace knowledge spillovers. The use of patent citation information for measuring knowledge spillovers has been pioneered by Jaffe et al. (1993). They use patent citation data to show that proximity matters and that being close to an external information source increases the impact of spillovers from that source on own know-how. Branstetter (2000) uses patent citations to foreign subsidiaries by local firms to measure international inter-firm knowledge spillovers through FDI. He finds on USPTO patent citation counts that Japanese FDI in the US is a significant channel of knowledge spillovers, i.e. increasing the likelihood of patent citations to the investing Japanese firm by the indigenous US firms. Similarly, Almeida (1996), using patent citations on a sample of foreign subsidiaries in the US semiconductor industry, finds that patents belonging to foreign firms located in the US are cited by local US firms more than expected, supporting positive technology transfers through FDI.

Patent information can also be used to trace technology transfers from local sources to foreign subsidiaries in search of a technology sourcing motivation. Almeida (1996), using US patent citations counts on a sample of foreign subsidiaries in the US semiconductor industry, finds foreign subsidiaries cite regionally located firms significantly more. Branstetter (2000) found Japanese firms investing in the US to have a significantly higher probability of citing other US firms' patents. Also Frost (1998) found subsidiaries to be citing local sources. Furthermore proximity mattered a lot, since patents from subsidiaries cited other entities located in the same state.

Linking Global Innovation Strategies of MNEs and the Impact on the Host Economy

A vast amount of information is transferred without being written down in patent applications, certainly in the case of internal transfers. Survey level evidence is another source of direct, albeit subjective, evidence of technology transfers arising through the affiliates of foreign firms. In a UK survey, Mansfield and Romeo (1980) found that two-thirds of the sampled firms indicated that their technological capabilities were raised by technology transfers from US firms to their overseas UK subsidiaries. But only 20% felt that this effect was important.

Survey data from a sample of Belgian innovation active manufacturing firms allow us to directly assess the occurrence of technology transfers between subsidiaries and other external local partners in both directions. Furthermore, it allows us to characterise the subsidiary's role in the parent's innovative strategy, as we are able to identify internal technology transfers between parents and subsidiaries.[2]

The Belgian sample contains 208 subsidiaries of foreign firms, which all have production activities in Belgian manufacturing. Of these foreign manufacturing subsidiaries 82% claimed to be innovation active in the considered period of 1990–92,[3] and 77% claimed to be engaged in R&D. This high number already indicates that R&D is an important subsidiary level function for foreign production plants in Belgium. Most of this R&D is development rather than basic research (Veugelers and Cassiman (2002)).

Overall, Table 1.1 indicates a two-way direction in external technology flows, with both acquiring know-how from and transferring know-how to the local economy reported by the subsidiaries. This reciprocity is further consummated in the large number of cooperative R&D agreements with local partners in which foreign subsidiaries are involved. But the data nevertheless suggest an asymmetry in knowledge flows, with foreign subsidiaries less frequently reporting transfers of know-how to the local economy than acquiring local know-how. Only 18% claimed to have transferred know-how to local partners.[4] About half of the firms reporting local transfers report the use of informal channels. It is interesting to note that in comparison to domestic firms, foreign subsidiaries report far fewer cases of know-how transfer through personnel mobility (27.5% for foreign subsidiaries versus 52% for local firms), suggesting that subsidiaries succeed better in keeping their personnel, thus protecting their know-how from spilling out.[5]

In terms of the extent to which foreign subsidiaries are sourcing local know-how (BUY), half of the subsidiaries reported having acquired know-how from local partners through various means, the most frequently reported means being recruiting R&D personnel (45), R&D contracting with local firms (43) and consulting contracts (29).

Table 1.1   External transfers between MNEs and the local economy

% R&D active (MAKE) subsidiaries (N=160) who		
Transfer technology to external national partners	SELL	18%
Receive know-how from external national partners	BUY	50%
Have cooperative agreements with external national partners	COOP	51%
Have cooperative agreements with local research institutes	$COOP_{RES}$	38%
Have cooperative agreements with local suppliers/customers	$COOP_{VERT}$	45%
Have cooperative agreements with local firms in the same industry	$COOP_{HOR}$	14%

Notes:
MAKE – innovative companies that have their own R&D activities and have a positive R&D budget.
BUY – innovative firms acquiring technology through licensing and/or R&D contracting and/or consultancy services and/or the purchase of another enterprise and/or hiring skilled employees and/or other informal forms.[6]
SELL – innovative firms transferring technology through licensing and/or R&D contracting and/or consultancy services and/or the purchase of another enterprise and/or hiring skilled employees and/or other informal forms.
COOP – innovative firms that have cooperation in R&D, where both parties have an active involvement.

Unfortunately we only have the reported transfers and acquisition of know-how from the subsidiary and cannot identify who is the local source or destination of these flows within the local economy. But for the cooperative R&D agreements with local partners, we can identify the type of local cooperative partner, i.e. whether these are research institutes, vertically linked firms (suppliers or customers) or firms in the same industry. The most frequently reported local external partners for cooperative R&D agreements are vertically related firms, with the local science base also being frequently reported as partner. Cooperative agreements with local firms which are directly competing in the same industry are rare, as Table 1.1 indicates.

The data further allow us to identify for foreign subsidiaries whether or not internal knowledge transfers occurred both to and from affiliated partners (parents or sisters) (Table 1.2).

Table 1.2 Internal transfers among affiliated partners

% R&D active (MAKE) subsidiaries (N=160) who		
Receive transfers from affiliated partners	BUY	59%
Generate transfers to affiliated partners	SELL	59%
Have cooperative agreements with affiliated partners	COOP	51%

Notes:
MAKE – innovative companies that have their own R&D activities and have a positive R&D budget.
BUY – innovative firms acquiring technology through licensing and/or R&D contracting and/or consultancy services and/or the purchase of another enterprise and/or hiring skilled employees and/or other informal forms.
SELL – innovative firms transferring technology through licensing and/or R&D contracting and/or consultancy services and/or the purchase of another enterprise and/or hiring skilled employees and/or other informal forms.
COOP – innovative firms that have cooperation in R&D, where both parties have an active involvement.

The data from Table 1.2 seem to suggest that in terms of internal know-how transfers among affiliated partners there is an important two-way flow between headquarters and subsidiaries. Note also the high occurrence of cooperative R&D agreements among affiliated partners.

On the basis of the pattern of internal transfers of know-how to and from the subsidiary, Veugelers and Cassiman (2002) construct a typology of foreign subsidiaries, characterising their role within the global innovative strategy of the parent firm. They found that the largest group of affiliates (39%) is the one that simultaneously receives and generates internal know-how transfers. The two-way internal flows in which these *integrated* foreign subsidiaries are engaged could indicate their leading role in 'locally leveraged' or even 'globally linked' innovations, but also a contributing role, with specific tasks in 'globally linked' innovations, could fit into this characterisation. The second largest group of foreign subsidiaries, about 31%, are those R&D active subsidiaries who receive no transfers and also generate no transfers to the group. These are *independent* or autonomous subsidiaries. They may be older, longer established subsidiaries that traditionally have built up an independent 'local for local' innovative strategy.[7]

We can now link the characterisation of internal know-how transfers to the external transfers of technology. The results are reported in Table 1.3. They strongly suggest a complementarity between technology transfers occurring within the MNE and transfers to the local economy. Foreign affiliates, when they are integrated in the multinational innovative process, are more likely to be interacting with the local economy at the same time, both acquiring local know-how and generating local transfers and cooperating with local partners. Those affiliates that are operating independently from their multinational structure are least likely to transfer know-how locally or to cooperate locally. This result suggests that a trend towards having subsidiaries playing a more integrative role in multinational innovations, although they are more actively engaged in local technology sourcing, is not necessarily detrimental for the host economy, since they are more likely to transfer know-how to the local economy.

Table 1.3   Linking internal and external transfers

	Independent subsidiaries	Integrated subsidiaries	All R&D active subsidiaries
% BUY	46%	56%	50%
% SELL	4%	25%	18%
% COOP	36%	60%	51%
% COOP$_{VERT}$	24%	45%	45%
% COOP$_{RES}$	18%	36%	38%

Notes:
The Chi-squared independence tests are significant for all row variables at the 1% level.
MAKE – innovative companies that have their own R&D activities and have a positive R&D budget.
BUY – innovative firms acquiring technology through licensing and/or R&D contracting and/or consultancy services and/or the purchase of another enterprise and/or hiring skilled employees and/or other informal forms.
SELL – innovative firms transferring technology through licensing and/or R&D contracting and/or consultancy services and/or the purchase of another enterprise and/or hiring skilled employees and/or other informal forms.
COOP – innovative firms that have cooperation in R&D, where both parties have an active involvement.

AN ANALYTICAL MODEL OF R&D DECENTRALISATION

The empirical evidence suggests that the internationalisation of R&D and subsidiaries as technology sources has become an important trend. A model can be useful to throw some light on the main issues involved with R&D internationalisation and its impact on the host economy. Although certain aspects of this phenomenon have been thoroughly studied, 'the overall processes are extremely complex and the outcomes/impacts are highly uncertain' (Meyer-Krahmer and Reger (1999, p. 752)). Thus we will describe here the structure and main implications of a game-theory model, developed in Sanna-Randaccio and

Veugelers (2002), which allows us to analyse more carefully the drivers of R&D internationalisation and the implications for host countries.

The theoretical model we will use discusses the trade-offs a MNE faces when assigning subsidiaries an active role in innovation and organising its R&D as decentralised or centralised. The model considers R&D decentralisation as a choice that allows the use of the specific know-how of the subsidiary and avoids having to adapt centrally developed innovations to local markets. In addition, R&D subsidiaries can be used to source locally available external know-how. But the MNE has to organise the transfer of local know-how internally so as to be able to benefit from this location specific know-how throughout the organisation. At the same time, decentralisation of R&D to the subsidiary level intensifies the challenge of effectively appropriating core technology know-how, since locating R&D resources in the foreign market will lead more easily to the spilling over of valuable know-how to local competitors.

A MNE investing in R&D in a foreign country interacts with local firms not only in the technological field (due to external flows of know-how) but also in the product market. Only by analysing what happens both at the technological level and at the level of product market competition may we understand the drivers and impact of R&D internationalisation. The proposed model focuses on how the interplay of internal and external knowledge flows interacts with the nature of host market competition, recognising that absorptive capacity is required in order to be able to use external spillovers.

The model has a number of features that are based on the main stylised facts which emerged from the empirical literature:

- R&D is undertaken abroad in association with production, and is typically of the development kind. The case of research outposts devoted to basic research, that are generally located separately from production, ignores product market interactions.
- Technological spillovers are localised: external technology spillovers, both dissipation and sourcing, can only occur when R&D is decentralised.
- The internal transfer of know-how between different units of an MNE are not costless.
- Both internal and external know-how flows may be two-way.
- There are economies of scale in R&D.

The model will be briefly and non-formally described here. A short analytical presentation can be found in the appendix, while Sanna-Randaccio and Veugelers (2002) present a more detailed discussion of the formal model. We consider two countries (countries I and II). Country I is the home base of an MNE (firm I) which is a monopolist in the home market and controls a production subsidiary in country II, where a local producer (firm II) also

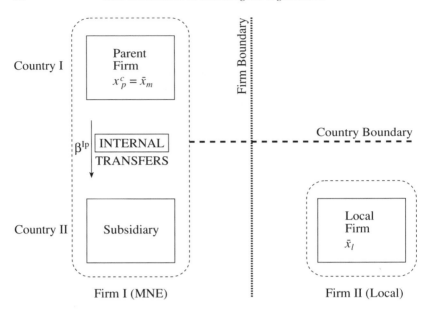

Figure 1.1a   Knowledge transfers with centralised R&D

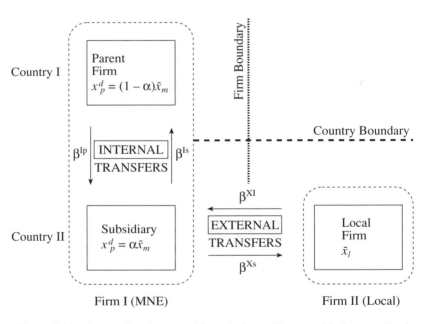

Figure 1.1b   Internal and external knowledge spillovers with decentralised R&D

operates (Figure 1.1). The MNE has to decide whether to concentrate all its R&D at the headquarters or to decentralise part of its R&D activities to the subsidiary. The decentralisation decision of multinational R&D is studied in a two stage game. In the first stage, firm I (the MNE) undertakes its R&D location choice. In the second stage, the subsidiary and the local producer, competing in production quantities with differentiated products, decide simultaneously how much to produce and sell in country II, while the parent chooses as a monopolist the output to be sold in country I.

Technological Innovation

Both the MNE and the foreign competitor are considered to be engaged in product innovation, which results in improved products.[8] Taking a short run perspective, we assume a fixed R&D budget at corporate level. This allows us to focus on the issue of how to allocate the fixed R&D budget between head-quarter and subsidiary. With $\bar{x}_m$ and $\bar{x}_l$ we indicate the given level of resources respectively invested in R&D by the MNE and the local producer (*own* R&D). Although the MNE's R&D resources are fixed at the corporate level, the R&D resources individually available to the parent and the subsidiary vary according to the MNE's R&D location decision. The MNE can locate all of its R&D resources in country I. This is the case of *centralisation* (Figure 1a). Alternatively, it can locate a share α of its total R&D resources in country II assigning an innovative task to the subsidiary, which is the case of R&D *decentralisation*[9] (Figure 1b).

The total knowledge which each plant can use for product innovation (defined as *effective* know-how) is not only composed of own R&D resources, but also includes the know-how the unit absorbs from other plants within the same firm or from other firms. As to internal knowledge transfer between subsidiary and parent, the know-how generated by the MNE in each market is transferred to the other unit. The parameter β^{lp} indicates the intensity of internal spillovers from parent to subsidiary, while β^{ls} indicates the share of know-how produced by the subsidiary which is transferred to the parent·

As to external knowledge transfer between the MNE and the local competitor we assume that there is knowledge dissemination only if there is R&D proximity, in this way capturing that external spillovers are geographically bounded. This implies that only when the MNE decides to decentralise its R&D, will there be external spillovers with the local competition. These spillovers are two-way (Figure 1b). On the one hand, decentralisation creates for the MNE the possibility to source local know-how, but on the other hand, locating R&D resources to the local market open up these resources for spillovers to the local competitors. The parameter β^{Xl} indicates the intensity of external spillovers from the local producer to the MNE's subsidiary, while β^{Xs} measures external spillovers from the MNE's subsidiary to the local firm. The assumption of localised spillovers furthermore implies that there is no dissipation to the local firm of know-how developed centrally and not transferred to the subsidiary.

In addition we account for the fact that the extent to which each unit benefits from external spillovers depends on the absorption capacity of the receiver. The own R&D resources serve to develop the absorptive capacity of the plant.

In total, the effective know-how base that a plant has at its disposition to generate innovations is composed of own R&D resources *plus* R&D resources from affiliated companies which are (at a cost) transferred internally *plus* R&D resources which are absorbed (imperfectly) from firms located in the same geographic market, at least if and to the extent that the plant has own R&D resources to absorb the external know-how.[10]

Market Competition

Firms also compete in the product market, which represents the second stage of the game. The effective know-how base will lead to product innovations which improve the product characteristics and hence lead to a greater willingness on the part of the customer to pay for the firm's product. While the parent firm is a monopolist in its home market, in the foreign market the subsidiary and the local competitor are engaged in (quantity) competition. In order to evaluate the effect of the intensity of product competition in country II we have allowed for the possibility of differentiation between the goods produced by the subsidiary and the local firm. The parameter ϕ captures the degree of product differentiation. The higher ϕ is, the greater the substitutability between the goods produced by the subsidiary and the local firm and thus the lower the product differentiation and the more intense the product market competition in country II. The equations for firms' profits are reported in the appendix.

THE COST AND BENEFITS OF R&D DECENTRALISATION FOR THE MNE

As MNE will decide to decentralise its R&D activities, i.e. to assign a role in its overall research effort to the subsidiary operating in a foreign country, if its overall profitability (i.e. the sum of parent and subsidiary profitability) increases as compared to the case of centralisation. Therefore we should assess the overall effect from R&D decentralisation on the MNE's profitability, giving due consideration not only to the impact on the subsidiary's profitability but also to the effects on parent's profitability and to the role of the additional costs due to foregone economies of scale in R&D).[11]

The Impact of R&D Decentralisation on the Subsidiary's Profitability

R&D decentralisation influences the subsidiary's profitability via three effects:

1. The benefits from avoiding the adaptation of central innovations by the subsidiary.
   The first positive effect is connected to the adaptation motive for R&D decentralisation. When the MNE allocates R&D resources to the host country instead of devoting them to the parent lab, the foreign lab's innovative effort can be tailored to satisfy local needs since it benefits from proximity to local production. Thus the subsidiary can avoid the adaptation costs that it would have to incur if the MNE had chosen to centralise all R&D in the home country. This positive effect can also be interpreted as reflecting the ability of the subsidiary to tailor its products better to local requirements (the same amount of R&D has a more powerful market enhancing effect if invested in the host market rather than at the parent level). The benefits of localising R&D where the market is will be greater the more the knowledge generated centrally by the parent needs to be adapted to local conditions (i.e. the higher $(1 - \beta^{lp})$).

2. The benefits from the incoming external spillovers to the subsidiary.
   The second positive effect reflects the supply related motives for R&D decentralisation, connected to the technology sourcing motive. It captures the effect of incoming external spillovers which arise because of the proximity between the subsidiary lab and the local producer lab. By decentralising R&D, the MNE becomes able to use its subsidiary to absorb know-how from the local firm, thus benefiting from incoming external spillovers. The results show that the positive effect of incoming external spillovers on the subsidiary's profitability is not affected by product market competition.

3. The costs for the subsidiary from outgoing external spillovers.
   There are also dangers associated with locating R&D resources close to local competitors, since there are also outgoing external spillovers. Due to lab proximity, at least part of the know-how created by the subsidiary will leak to the local competitors. The dissemination of the subsidiary's own R&D to the local firm has a negative impact on the subsidiary's profitability since it increases the local firm's competitiveness in the product market. Thus the outgoing external spillovers produce their effect via product market competition. The intensity of the negative impact of the outgoing external spillovers depends on the degree to which foreign and local products are differentiated (see Eq. (A13)). The more the products are similar (the higher ϕ), and thus the more intense the product market competition, the higher the costs of R&D proximity. The extent to which the local producer can

benefit from these spillovers depends on its absorptive capacity which in turn is determined by its own R&D resources. Thus the stronger the know-how base of the local competitor, the larger the negative impact on the subsidiary's profits of the outgoing external spillovers. A weaker local competitor with less absorptive capacity will be able to learn less, in which case the cost of the outgoing external spillovers will be smaller for the MNE.

The Impact of R&D Decentralisation on the Parent Plant's Profitability

R&D decentralisation influences the parent's profitability via two effects:

1. The costs due to lower R&D resources for the parent plant.
    Since we consider the total amount of resources devoted to R&D by the MNE as fixed, the choice of allocating R&D abroad implies lower R&D resources at home. This has a negative repercussion on the parent's equilibrium output and hence profitability. This effect is at least partly compensated for by the fact that the subsidiary transfers the know-how it creates back to the parent. This transfer is however imperfect ($\beta^{ls} \leq 1$). The negative effect is thus mitigated by internal transfers, and hence depends on the ability of the subsidiary to transfer know-how to the central level.
2. The benefits from the incoming external spillovers to the parent.
    R&D decentralisation has a positive effect on parent profitability because, by innovating in foreign countries, the MNE becomes able to gain access to the foreign pool of potential spillovers generated by local producers. The extent to which the parent benefits from the incoming external spillovers depends on how much the subsidiary will learn, which depends on the absorption capacity of the subsidiary which is a function of the latter's own R&D resources. However the benefit for the parent also depends on whether the subsidiary transfers back the acquired knowledge to the headquarters. The results clearly indicate that the ability of the subsidiary to channel back know-how is a crucial determinant of the effect of R&D decentralisation on parent's profitability, and thus internal knowledge management within the MNE has a pivotal role for the success of R&D investment abroad. Our findings hence highlight the importance of the interaction between internal and external knowledge transfer mechanisms.

The Impact of R&D Decentralisation on the MNE's Total Profits

Considering the overall impact on the MNE when R&D is located abroad in association with production, we have in total six effects that form the benefits and the costs of decentralisation:

- (**B.1**) benefits from avoiding the adaptation of central innovations by the subsidiary (first term in Eq. (A13))
- (**B.2**) benefits from the incoming external spillovers to the subsidiary (second term in Eq. (A13))
- (**B.3**) benefits from the incoming external spillovers to the parent (second term in Eq. (A12))
- (**C.1**) costs from foregone economies of scale in R&D (last term in Eq. (A9))
- (**C.2**) costs for the subsidiary from the outgoing external spillovers (third term in Eq. (A13))
- (**C.3**) costs from the loss of R&D resources for the parent plant which are decentralised to the subsidiary but not fully recoverable due to imperfect internal transfers (first term in Eq. (A12))

When the external spillover parameters are symmetric ($\beta^{Xl} = \beta^{Xs}$), for instance when the intensity of the external technological spillovers is sector or technology specific, the subsidiary's equilibrium profits will certainly increase when R&D is decentralised. This is the case since the positive effect of the incoming external spillovers is direct, with incoming external spillovers a pure externality, while the negative effect of the outgoing external spillovers is mediated via competition in the product market. On the other hand, if the intensity of the external spillovers is symmetric, the parent's profitability does not necessarily rise. This requires internal spillovers from the subsidiary to be sufficiently large.[12]

The case of research outposts, in which a foreign lab is created abroad not in association with production, presents several differences with the previous analysis. First there is no issue of adapting central innovations to the local market. Since there is no production in foreign countries, learning from local sources only matters for the parent firm, while generating spillovers to the local economy does not matter if the parent firm is not competing in the local market.[13] Hence, we can ignore B.1, B.2 and C.2 in the case of research outposts. This result helps to clarify why, as suggested by several studies, the drivers of decentralisation depend on the mission of the foreign lab. Given that the net impact on subsidiary profitability captured by (B.1+B.2+C.2) is likely to be positive,[14] it turns out that the prospect for immediate profitability is less likely for research outposts than for decentralised development labs, since research labs are trading off only B.3 on the benefits side to both C.1 and C.3. on the cost side. In this case however, the MNE might accept short term losses expecting a positive return only in a distant future.

The Drivers of R&D Decentralisation Decisions by MNEs

The local know-how base and the mechanisms for transfering know-how internally and externally have a critical role in influencing whether the decision to locate a lab abroad will have a positive or negative impact on subsidiary and parent profitability and hence on whether the MNE will decide to decentralise R&D.[15] Other factors, such as host market size, will contribute to determining the magnitude of these positive or negative effects, but not the sign. The model thus seems to suggest that there is a ranking in terms of importance of the different variables affecting the R&D decentralisation decision and thus a sequence in which the different variables should be considered: first the variables determining the sign (local know-how base, internal and external transfers of know-how) and then those determining the magnitude of the impact (host market size).

Local know-how base
A first important factor affecting the R&D decentralisation decision, is the local know-how base $\bar{x}_l$. From the above we know that a strong local know-how base is positive from a technology sourcing perspective since it increases the benefits from incoming external spillovers both for the subsidiary and the parent (B.2 and B.3). But at the same time it enlarges the cost of outgoing external spillovers (C.2) since the local rival will have a stronger absorptive capacity.

When evaluating the overall effect, it turns out that due to the cost of outgoing external spillovers, the local know-how base is not a univocally positive factor for R&D decentralisation. This would happen when the cost of outgoing external spillovers becomes very important. This cost would start to dominate when the learning is asymmetric (i.e. outgoing external spillovers β^{Xs} are high, while incoming external spillovers β^{Xl} are low) and competition is strong (i.e. ϕ is large). To understand this result it should be noted that while the positive effect of the incoming external spillovers is direct, the negative effect of the outgoing external spillovers is mediated via competition in the product market. Thus the latter effect is more intense the greater the substitutability between the goods produced by the MNE's subsidiary and by the local producer.

In the special case when the MNE subsidiary and the local firms are not direct competitors in production, the negative effect for the MNE of the involuntary dissemination of its subsidiary know-how to local producers vanishes. In this case the local know-how base is a univocal positive factor for decentralising R&D. Two cases come to mind where there are external spillovers with no interaction in the product market:

- The subsidiary and the local firms use related technologies but are unrelated in the product market. This may be due to vertical relationships between producers such as in the case of a producer of a complex good with its components suppliers or of the producer of a discrete product with a process equipment supplier (inter-industry spillovers).

- When the local party is a public research institution (universities or government labs), the local source of know-how has no production activities. Also in this case the subsidiary and the local partners only relate at the technological level. Note that in this case it is less likely that the know-how relates to development activities, but rather to fundamental research.

The model predicts that a large local know-how base is more likely to attract the location of R&D activity from foreign firms operating in different industries (i.e. ϕ is low) than from direct competitors (i.e. $\phi = 1$). This result is in line with the findings of Cantwell and Kosmopoulou (2002) who, studying the R&D activity undertaken abroad by the world's 792 largest industrial firms, find that 'inward penetration in location of technological excellence tends to be low in the same industry, but attract to a greater extent the investments of stronger firms from other industries....' (p. 26).

If the MNE wants to locate research abroad independently from production, the local know-how base will certainly have a positive effect in attracting this type of investment. In the case of research outposts, the local know how base will only have the positive technology sourcing effect on the parent's profitability while there will be no negative repercussions of outgoing spillovers since in principle there is no direct competition in the product market in the host country to worry about. In this case, the remaining negative effects linked with R&D decentralisation will be C.1 and C.3, which are not influenced by the size of the local know-how bases ($\bar{x}_l$).

Internal transfer of know-how

Another important factor determining the size of both the benefits and costs of decentralisation is the process of the internal transfer of know-how within the MNE.

We find that a more efficient internal know-how transfer process within the MNE from the subsidiary to the parent univocally acts to promote R&D decentralisation. A better internal transfer of know-how from subsidiary to parent results in lower costs of decentralisation (C.3) and in larger benefits from incoming external spillovers to the parent (B.3).

But on the other hand, a more efficient transfer of know-how from the parent to the subsidiary makes the motive for avoiding adaptation by the subsidiary less prevailing. Nevertheless it does not always discourage the MNE from investing abroad in R&D.

External transfer of know-how

Since both parent and subsidiary enjoy higher profits in the case of decentralisation when there are more spillovers from the local source (see

(B.3) and (B.2)), we can see that higher spillovers from the local source to the MNE univocally act as an incentive for R&D decentralisation. But of course, since subsidiary profits will decrease with higher spillovers to the local source (see C.2), a rise in β^{Xs} will be a disincentive decentralisation. Hence, being able to prevent spillovers to the local source univocally improves the case for R&D decentralisation, as well as being able to learn more efficiently from external sources.

Host market size

A large host market does not enhance the likelihood that decentralisation will be profitable *per se*. In fact both positive (B.1 and B2) and negative (C.2) factors determining the subsidiary's profitability are influenced by host market size. However, if decentralisation increases the subsidiary's profitability, then the host market size becomes a crucial location determinant since it determines the size of the profit gain.

In the technology outpost case, on the contrary, host market size has no direct role as a location determinant since B.1, B.2 and C.2 vanish. However, it might have an indirect influence, in so far as the local know-how base is linked to the size of the economy.

THE IMPACT OF R&D DECENTRALISATION BY THE MNE ON THE LOCAL ECONOMY

The Impact on the Local Know-how Base

In order to evaluate the effect on the host economy of decentralising R&D resources to the subsidiary, a central question is the impact of such investments on the local know-how base, which forms the backbone of the local innovation system. Our model can contribute to the understanding of some of the main issues involved since it allows us to assess the impact of inward R&D investments on the technological competitiveness of the local producer, as measured by its effective know-how base. In its current state, with R&D resources being fixed, the model only allows us to examine the short run effect on local technological competitiveness and profitability.

It emerges that the short term effect on the technological capability of the local producer is certainly positive, in line with the results of Serapio and Dalton (1999, p. 314). The technological level of the local producer is increased by having more R&D resources located at the subsidiary since, given the physical proximity of the R&D resources, the local firm benefits from technological spillovers generated by the subsidiary of the foreign MNE.

The long run impact, however, is less clear cut. It also depends on how inward R&D investments affect the local producer's incentive to invest in its own R&D.[16] It is due to this indirect effect that concerns may arise as to the erosion of the local economy technological competitiveness. Serapio and Dalton (1999) for instance raise such fears for the US.

The Impact on the Local Firm's Profitability

The model allows us to discuss the short run effects of R&D decentralisation on the local firm's profitability. Since R&D investments are largely financed out of current profits, and since future profits create the incentives for R&D investments, by examining the effect of the creation of a foreign owned lab on the local firm's overall profitability, we can get some indication of whether the resources that will be allocated to innovation by this firm will rise or decline in the future.

The profitability of the local producer is affected by inward R&D investment via three channels:

1. The benefits from the incoming external spillovers to the local firm.[17]
   Inward R&D investment by the foreign firm creates spillovers from the decentralised R&D resources to the local producer. This effect depends on the one hand on the amount of R&D resources allocated to the local economy by the foreign producer. But it also depends on the local firm's ability to profit from this potential pool of know-how generated locally, which is critically determined by the local firm's absorption capacity. This absorption capacity in turn is determined by the level of own R&D resources available to the local firm.
2. The costs for the local firm from outgoing external spillovers.[18]
   The know-how that the MNE's subsidiary, by investing in foreign countries in R&D, is able to absorb from the local economy increases its competitiveness. This has negative repercussions on the local firm's profitability if the two firms are competing in the product market. The intensity of the negative effect of these outgoing spillovers thus depends on how close competitors the two firms are in the product market, which depends on the similarity of foreign and local products (i.e. on the value of ϕ).
3. The costs for the local firm from the subsidiary's enhanced competitiveness due to lower adaptation costs.[19]
   When the MNE allocates part of its overall R&D resources in foreign countries, the subsidiary is able to avoid the cost of adapting know-how centrally generated by the parent. This enhances the subsidiary's competitiveness which has a negative impact on the local firm. This positive effect reflects the ability of the subsidiary to tailor its products better to local

requirements. The same amount of R&D has a more powerful market enhancing effect if invested in the host market rather than at the parent level. Again this effect unfolds via product market competition, and thus its intensity depends on how close the competition is.

In order to assess the overall impact of inward R&D investment on the local firm's profitability, it is useful to distinguish two scenarios:

1. External learning is asymmetric and heavily biased against the local producer.[20]
   In this case the net effect of external know-how transfer is negative and inward R&D investment will certainly decrease the profits of the local producer. The negative effect due to external spillovers in fact adds up with the negative impact due to the increased competitiveness of the MNE's subsidiary from being able to avoid adaptation costs.
2. External learning is symmetric or not heavily biased against the local producer.[21]
   In this scenario, external know-how transfers will have a net positive effect on the local firm's profitability. The overall impact of inward R&D investment will thus depend on whether the net positive effect of external spillovers more than compensates for the costs due to the enhanced competitiveness of the subsidiary from being able to tailor its products to local requirements better.[22]

These results have the following implications: first, the probability that inward R&D investment will raise the profitability of local firms is lower for industries characterised by a high unit cost of adapting to local conditions the know-how developed in the home country of the MNE (i.e. high $1 - \beta^{lp}$)). These costs may be high for instance when products are nationally differentiated. In other words, R&D proximity to production matters more when subsidiaries should be nationally responsive and thus the effect on the subsidiary's competitiveness is particularly pronounced in these cases. When tastes are nationally differentiated or if products are custom specific, decentralising R&D near the final users will increase the subsidiary's competitiveness, and thus increase competition for local firms, more than in sectors in which products are more standardised internationally. This is one reason why we expect that the effect of inward R&D investment should vary across industries.

Secondly, when external learning is symmetric or not heavily biased against the local producer, the probability that inward R&D investment is beneficial for local producers is higher the more technologically advanced the local firms are, i.e. the local firm's profit gains are increasing in its own R&D resources. The local firm's own R&D resources affect both the incoming spillovers, since they contribute to the absorption capacity of the local firm, and the outgoing spillovers, since they determine the pool of know-how from which the subsidiary can learn. It turns out that in this case the first effect dominates. Hence, own R&D resources are thus important for determining the ability of local firms to gain from inward R&D investment.

It follows that, if there are large gains in competitiveness for the subsidiary from tailoring its products better to local conditions when R&D is decentralised,[23] only the technologically more powerful local firms will benefit from inward R&D investment. If these gains are low however[24] local producers with lower R&D resources will also benefit from the creation in foreign countries of a foreign owned R&D centre. In other words, the level of local R&D resources required for local profits to increase depends on adaptation costs.

The results show that, only if the external know-how transfer is asymmetric and heavily biased against local firms, with foreign firms learning more from the local know-how than local firms will absorb from foreign resources, the probability that inward R&D investment will have a negative impact on the local innovative capacity is higher for a leading country. Thus, only within such a scenario could fears such as those emerging in the US be justified.

Thirdly, the impact of inward R&D investment on the profitability of local firms will be more beneficial when the MNE is not a direct competitor in the product market. In this case the negative effects due to the outgoing external spillovers and the enhanced competitiveness of the subsidiary due to tailoring its products better to local requirements no longer need to be considered. This suggests that inter-industry spillovers could be more beneficial than intra-industry spillovers. It also suggests that vertical relationships between foreign and local firms (forward and backward linkages) are more beneficial for host economy gains than horizontal relationships.

Similarly, the establishment of research outposts without production by foreign producers, *ceteris paribus*, could be expected to have a more positive effect on the profits of local firms, since it does not imply an increase in product market competition. However, it is unlikely that other things will be equal when comparing R&D abroad in association to production with research outposts. Furthermore, there are possible negative effects not captured by the model if the MNE and the local firms compete in product markets in other geographical areas.

Lastly, the size of the R&D resources allocated in foreign countries by the foreign MNE does not affect *per se* whether the impact on local producers is positive or negative. However, although it does not affect the sign, it increases the magnitude of the impact.

The Overall Welfare Impact on the Host Economy

In order to evaluate the overall impact on the host economy other considerations, beyond local firm profitability, should be added. To start with, the repercussions on local consumers should be considered. It can be shown that decentralising R&D in a foreign country results in lower prices in the host economy and thus in higher consumer surplus. This is due to an increase in the overall amount of R&D undertaken within the national border and of the enhanced know-how bases of the national producers and of the foreign firm operating in foreign countries. The increase in consumer surplus will take place irrespective of whether the MNE subsidiary and local producers are direct competitors in the product market. Consumers are not only able to buy at lower prices, they will also be able to buy products which are better adapted to their local preferences.

We have also additional effects via the impact on the product market. The rise in total production will have a positive impact via its effect on employment. In a regime of under-employment these effects can become very important for local policy makers, irrespective of whether the employment is in local firms or in foreign affiliates.

A SUMMARY OF THE MAIN FINDINGS

This chapter provides a theoretical framework for discussing the trade-offs which an MNE faces when it assigns a foreign subsidiary an active role in innovation, thus making its R&D decentralised instead of centralised. The proposed model analyses how the interplay of internal and external knowledge flows interacts with the nature of the host market competition to influence an MNE in choosing whether to disperse its R&D internationally and the impact of such a decision on the local economy. The chapter focuses on cases in which R&D activities are undertaken abroad in association with production. However some attention is also devoted to research outposts, i.e. to foreign labs created abroad which are separate from production.

We find that while R&D decentralisation is more likely to increase the equilibrium profits of the foreign subsidiary, the parent plant's profitability is less likely to increase, at least with symmetric external spillovers. The positive impact on the subsidiary's profitability increases with the relative size of the host country. The results thus help to explain why MNEs from small economies have been major R&D investors abroad, in larger markets.

A strong local know-how base is a positive factor for R&D decentralisation from a technology sourcing perspective since it increases the benefits from incoming external spillovers both for the subsidiary and the parent. But at the same time, a strong local know-how base enlarges the costs of outgoing external spillovers since the local rival will have a stronger absorptive capacity. These costs increase the more intense the competition is in the product market between the subsidiary and local firms. Hence, when R&D is undertaken abroad in association with production, the local knowledge base is not univocally a factor in attracting R&D investments by foreign MNEs, depending on the level of competition. The model thus predicts that a strong local knowledge base is more likely to attract inward R&D FDI from foreign firms operating in different industries than from direct competitors. In the case of research outposts, the local know-how base will only have the positive technology sourcing effect on the parent's profitability while there will not be the negative repercussions of outgoing spillovers since there is no competition in the product market in the host country to consider.

As to the impact on the local economy, the model shows that the short term effect on the technological level of the local producer is likely to be positive, as suggested also by Serapio and Dalton (1999). The long run impact, however, is less clear cut. In fact it also depends on how the new lab affects local producers' current profitability, and thus their incentive to innovate.

We find that inward R&D investment is less likely to increase the profitability of local firms in industries with products which are nationally differentiated. When tastes are nationally differentiated or if products are custom specific, decentralising R&D near the final users will increase the subsidiary's competitiveness, and thus increase competition for local firms, more than in sectors in which products are more standardised internationally. This is one reason why we expect that the effect of inward R&D investment should vary across industries.

The model also shows that inward R&D investment is more likely to be beneficial for local producers if local firms are technologically advanced. The local firm's own R&D investment affects both the incoming spillovers, via the absorption capacity, and the outgoing spillovers. But the impact is greater in the first case. Own R&D is thus crucial for determining the ability of local firms to gain from inward R&D investment. It follows that if there are large gains in competitiveness for the subsidiary from tailoring its products better to local conditions when R&D is decentralised, only the technologically more powerful local firms will benefit from inward R&D investment. If these gains are low, however, producers with lower R&D resources will also gain from the creation in foreign countries of a foreign owned lab.

Finally, the effects on the local firms are more beneficial if the MNE is not a direct competitor in the product market. In this case, the negative impact associated with the outgoing external spillovers and the enhanced competitiveness of the subsidiary due to tailoring its products better to local requirements diminishes. Thus, the positive effect of incoming external spillovers is likely to prevail. This seems to suggest that vertical relationships between foreign and local firms (forward and backward linkages) are more beneficial for the host economy than horizontal relationships.

APPENDIX

1. Firms Profits

$$II^c_m = \pi^c_p + \pi^c_s \tag{A1}$$

$$\pi^c_p = (p^c_l - c_p)q^c_p = [A_l + \bar{x}_m - b_l q^c_p - c_p]q^c_p \tag{A2}$$

$$\pi^c_s = (p^c_{II,s} - c_s)q^c_s = [A_{II} + \beta^{lp}\bar{x}_m - b_{II}(q^c_s + \phi\, q^c_l) - c_s]q^c_s \tag{A3}$$

$$II^c_l = (p^c_{II,l} - c_l)q^c_l = [A_{II} + \bar{x}_l - b_{II}(q^c_l + \phi\, q^c_s) - c_l]q^c_l \tag{A4}$$

$$II^d_m = \pi^d_p + \pi^d_s - \frac{\gamma}{2}\left(a\bar{x}_m\right)^2 \tag{A5}$$

$$\pi^d_p = (p^d_l - c_p)q^d_p = [A_l + (1 - \alpha)\bar{x}_m + \beta^{ls}\alpha\bar{x}_m \\ + \beta^{ls}(\beta^{Xl}\alpha\bar{x}_m)\bar{x}_l - b_l q^d_p - c_p]q^d_p \tag{A6}$$

$$\pi^d_s = (p^d_{II,s} - c_s)q^d_s = [A_{II} + \alpha\bar{x}_m + \beta^{lp}(1 - \alpha)\bar{x}_m \\ + (\beta^{Xl}\alpha\bar{x}_m)\bar{x}_l - b_{II}(q^d_s + \phi q^d_l) - c_s]q^d_s \tag{A7}$$

$$II^d_l = (p^d_{II,l} - c_l)q^d_l = [A_{II} + \bar{x}_l + (\beta^{Xs}\bar{x}_l)\alpha\bar{x}_m \\ - b_{II}(q^d_l + \phi q^d_s) - c_l]q^d_l \tag{A8}$$

where c stands for centralisation and d for decentralisation, p for the parent unit, s for the MNE subsidiary and l for the local producer in country II.

2. Solution of the First Stage Game

The MNE will choose decentralisation if:

$$\hat{II}^d_m - \hat{II}^c_m = \left(\hat{\pi}^d_p - \hat{\pi}^c_p\right) + \left(\hat{\pi}^d_s - \hat{\pi}^c_s\right) - \frac{\gamma}{2}\left(a\bar{x}_m\right)^2 > 0 \tag{A9}$$

It can be shown that:

$$Sign\ (\hat{\pi}^d_p - \hat{\pi}^c_p) = Sign\ (\hat{q}^d_p - \hat{q}^c_p) \tag{A10}$$

$$Sign\ (\hat{\pi}^d_s - \hat{\pi}^c_s) = Sign\ (\hat{q}^d_s - \hat{q}^c_s) \tag{A11}$$

where:

$$\hat{q}_p^d - \hat{q}_p^c = -\frac{\left(1 - \beta^{ls}\right)\alpha\bar{x}_m}{2b_l} + \frac{\beta^{ls}\beta^{Xl}\alpha\bar{x}_m\bar{x}_l}{2b_l} \tag{A12}$$

$$\hat{q}_s^d - \hat{q}_s^c = \frac{2\left(1 - \beta^{lp}\right)\alpha\bar{x}_m}{\left(4 - \varphi^2\right)b_{II}} + \frac{2\left(\beta^{Xl}\alpha\bar{x}_m\right)\bar{x}_l}{\left(4 - \varphi^2\right)b_{II}} - \varphi\frac{\left(\beta^{Xs}\bar{x}_l\right)\alpha\bar{x}_m}{\left(4 - \varphi^2\right)b_{II}} \tag{A13}$$

and $\hat{q}_j^k$ with $k = c, d$ and $j = s, l$ are the second-stage game solutions.

Thus the necessary and sufficient conditions for $(\hat{q}_p^d - \hat{q}_p^c) > 0$ and $(\hat{q}_s^d - \hat{q}_s^c) > 0$ represent sufficient conditions for the MNE's variable profits to increase when R&D is decentralised.

We also have:

$$Sign\ (\hat{\Pi}_l^d - \hat{\Pi}_l^c) = Sign\ (\hat{q}_l^d - \hat{q}_l^c) \tag{A14}$$

where:

$$\hat{q}_l^d - \hat{q}_l^c = \frac{2\left(\beta^{Xs}\bar{x}_l\right)\alpha\bar{x}_m}{\left(4 - \varphi^2\right)b_{II}} - \varphi\frac{2\left(\beta^{Xl}\alpha\bar{x}_m\right)\bar{x}_l}{\left(4 - \varphi^2\right)b_{II}} - \varphi\frac{\left(1 - \beta^{lp}\right)\alpha\bar{x}_m}{\left(4 - \varphi^2\right)b_{II}} \tag{A15}$$

We thus have that the necessary and sufficient condition:

for $(\hat{\pi}_p^d - \hat{\pi}_p^c) > 0$ is $\beta^{ls}(\beta^{Xl}\bar{x}_l + 1) > 1$ \hfill (A16)

for $(\hat{\pi}_s^d - \hat{\pi}_s^c) > 0$ is $2(1 - \beta^{lp}) + 2\beta^{Xl}\bar{x}_l > \varphi\beta^{Xs}\bar{x}_l$ \hfill (A17)

for $(\hat{\Pi}_l^d - \hat{\Pi}_l^c) > 0$ is $2\beta^{Xs}\bar{x}_l - \varphi\beta^{Xl}\bar{x}_l > \varphi(1 - \beta^{lp})$ \hfill (A18)

For a detailed analysis of the model and the way in which it is solved see Sanna-Randaccio and Veugelers (2002).

NOTES

1. Markusen and Venables (1999) show that FDI can be a catalyst for host economy growth, since FDI increases the demand in the intermediary sector. The linkage effect from the intermediary sector, with greater entry of domestic suppliers, more than compensates the higher competitive effect in the final market.
2. EUROSTAT's Community Innovation Survey for 1993, of which we use the Belgian subsample, was intended to develop insights into the problems of technological innovation

in the manufacturing industry and was the first of its kind organised in many of the partici-
pating countries. A representative sample of 1335 Belgian manufacturing firms was selected.
The response rate was higher than 50% (748). For more information on the sample see
Veugelers and Cassiman (2002).

3. Innovating firms are identified as having introduced new or improved products or processes
   and reported a positive budget for innovation.

4. But we are only recording here voluntary transfers of know-how as perceived by the sender,
   leaving uncovered a vast array of involuntary spillovers. Also for the total sample the
   percentage of innovative firms who report having transferred know-how to Belgian partners
   is low: 18.2%.

5. See also Veugelers and Cassiman (2003) for an econometric analysis of the firm characteristics determining the likelihood of transfers to the local economy.

6. We disregarded the 'embodied' purchase of equipment, mainly because too many firms
   responded positively on this item. The reported results are not affected by the inclusion or
   otherwise of the purchase of equipment in the BUY option. Probably not all of them interpreted the question as buying equipment with the explicit purpose of obtaining new
   technologies and as an alternative to developing the technology internally.

7. To complete the typology of foreign subsidiaries, only 9% of them receive internal transfers,
   but do not generate any internal transfers. These are the typical *adapting* subsidiaries, implementing 'central for global' innovations while adjusting them to the local market. This low
   number does not suggest that adaptation is not important, but that it is less important as the
   main innovative activity of affiliates. Subsidiaries that have a role as sensors, scanning technological developments to direct global innovations, receive no internal transfers, but generate
   transfers to affiliated companies. These *sourcing* subsidiaries account for the remaining 20%
   in the sample (see Veugelers and Cassiman (2002)).

8. Thus the position of the respective demand curve for each producer depends on its total
   knowledge (defined as effective know-how). The model can be easily adjusted to include the
   case of process innovations, improving the efficiency of production.

9. In the case of decentralisation, the R&D resources available to the parent are $\hat{x}_p^d = (1 - \alpha)\bar{x}_m$,
   while the subsidiary R&D resources amount to $\hat{x}_s^d = \alpha\bar{x}_m$.

10. For instance the effective R&D of the MNE's subsidiary in the case of decentralisation
    amounts to $X_s^d = \alpha\bar{x}_m + \beta^{lp}(1 - \alpha)\bar{x}_m + (\beta^{Xl}\alpha\bar{x}_m)\bar{x}_l$. Since the demand intercept depends on the
    effective know-how of each plant, the inverse demand function for the subsidiary is $p_{II,s}^k =$
    $A_{II} + X_s^k - b_{II}(q_s^k + \phi q_l^k)$ where X_s^k is the subsidiary effective R&D in the k state, with which
    $k = c, d$.

11. If R&D is decentralised, R&D economies of scale are not fully exploited, implying an increase
    in R&D expenditure for the same amount of resources devoted to R&D. This is captured by
    the negative $-\gamma/2(\alpha\bar{x}_m)^2$ term appearing in the MNE profitability in the case of R&D
    decentralisation (Eq. (A5)).

12. If $\beta^{Xl} = \beta^{Xs}$, $\beta^{ls} > 0.5$ is a necessary (although not sufficient) condition for the parent's prof-
    itability to rise with decentralisation.

13. Note that if there are firms present in the local market that may learn from the research outpost
    and may compete with the parent firm in other than the local market, this outgoing spillover
    effect may matter. This happens for example if other rival MNEs also have affiliates in the
    local market.

14. This is the case since the condition for the subsidiary's profitability to rise with decentrali-
    sation is not overly restrictive.

15. That is whether conditions (A16) and (A17) will be satisfied.

16. This depends on whether foreign and domestic R&D are substitutes or complements.
    Veugelers and Vanden Houte (1990) show that local R&D investments may decrease if the
    competition effect dominates the technology spillover effect. This issue is also analysed by
    Petit and Sanna-Randaccio (2000).

17. This effect is captured by the first term in Eq. (A15).

18. This negative effect is captured by the second term in Eq. (A15).

19. This negative effect is captured by the third term in Eq. (A15).

20. More specifically $\beta^{Xs} \leq (\varphi/2)\beta^{Xl}$.

21. More specifically $\beta^{Xs} > (\varphi/2)\beta^{Xl}$.
22. The local firms profits will rise iff condition (A18) is satisfied.
23. That is $(1 - \beta^{lp})$ is high.
24. That is $(1 - \beta^{lp})$ is low.

REFERENCES

Aitken, B. and A. Harrison (1999), 'Do domestic firms benefit from foreign direct investment? Evidence from Venezuela', *American Economic Review*, 89 (3), 605–18.

Almeida, P. (1996), 'Knowledge sourcing by foreign MNEs: patent citation analysis in the US semiconductor industry', *Strategic Management Journal*, 17, 155–65.

Bartlett, Christopher A. and Sumantra Ghoshal (1997), 'Managing innovation in the transnational corporation', in Michael Tushman and Philip Anderson (eds), *Managing Strategic Innovation and Change*, Oxford: Oxford University Press, 452–76.

Blomström, M. and A. Kokko (1998), 'Multinational corporations and spillovers', *Journal of Economic Surveys*, 12 (2), 247–77.

Blomström, M. and F. Sjöholm (1999), 'Technology transfer and spillovers: does local participation with multinationals matter?', *European Economic Review*, 43, 915–23.

Branstetter, L. (2000), 'Is FDI a channel of knowledge spillovers: evidence from Japanese FDI in US', National Bureau of Economic Research (NBER) Working Paper no. 8015.

Cantwell, John A. (1989), *Technological Innovation and the Multinational Corporation*, Oxford: Basil Blackwell.

Cantwell, J.A. and E. Kosmopoulou (2002), 'What determines the internationalisation of corporate technology?', in Mats Forsgren, Lars Hakanson and Virpi Havila (eds), *Critical Perspectives on Internationalisation*, New York: Pergamon.

Caves, R. (1974), 'Multinational firms, competition, and productivity in host-country markets', *Economica*, 41, 176–93.

Caves, R. (1996), *Multinational Enterprise and Economic Analysis*, Cambridge: Cambridge University Press.

Dunning, J. (1988), 'The eclectic paradigm of international production: a restatement and some possible extensions', *Journal of International Business Studies*, 19, 1–31.

Florida, R. (1997), 'The globalization of R&D: results of a survey of foreign affiliated R&D laboratories in the USA', *Research Policy*, 26, 85–103.

Frost, A. (1998), 'The geographic sources of innovation in the multinational enterprise: US subsidiaries and host country spillovers, 1980–1990', PhD, Sloan School of Management, MIT.

Gerybadze, A. and G. Reger (1999), 'Globalization of R&D: recent changes in the management of innovation in transnational corporations', *Research Policy*, 28, 251–74.

Granstrand, Ove, Lars Hakanson, Soren Sjolander (eds) (1992), *Technology Management and International Business*, Chichester: John Wiley and Sons.

Hakanson, L. (1992), 'Locational determinants of foreign R&D in Swedish multinationals', in Ove Granstrand, Lars Hakanson, Soren Sjolander (eds), *Technology Management and International Business*, Chichester: John Wiley and Sons, 97–116.

Haskel, J., S. Pereira and M. Slaughter (2002), 'Does inward FDI boost the productivity of domestic firms', Centre for Economic Policy Research (CEPR) Discussion Paper no. 3384, London.

Jaffe, A., M. Trajtenberg and R. Henderson (1993), 'Geographic localization of knowledge spillovers as evidenced by patent citations', *Quarterly Journal of Economics*, 58, 577–98.

Kogut, B. and S. Chang (1991), 'Technological capabilities and Japanese foreign direct investment in the US', *Review of Economics and Statistics*, 73, 401–13.

Kuemmerle, W. (1997), 'Building effective R&D capabilities abroad', *Harvard Business Review*, (March/April), 61–70.

Mansfield, E. and A. Romeo (1980), 'Technology transfer to overseas subsidiaries by US based firms', *Quarterly Journal of Economics*, 95 (4), 737–50.

Markusen, J. and A. Venables (1999), 'FDI as a catalyst for industrial development', *European Economic Review*, 43, 335–56.

Meyer-Krahmer, F. and G. Reger (1999), 'New perspectives on the innovation strategies of multinational enterprises: lessons for technology policy in Europe', *Research Policy*, 28, 751–76.

Nelson, R. (ed.) (1993), *National Innovation Systems, A Comparative Analysis*, Oxford: Oxford University Press.

Patel, P. and K. Pavitt (1992), 'Large firms in the production of the world's technology: an important case of non-globalization', in Ove Granstrand, Lars Hakanson, Soren Sjolander (eds), *Technology Management and International Business*, Chichester: John Wiley and Sons, 53–74.

Pearce, R. (1999), 'Decentralized R&D and strategic competitiveness: globalized approaches to generation and use of technology in MNEs', *Research Policy*, 28, 157–78.

Pearce, R. and S. Singh (1992), 'Internationalization of R&D among the world's leading enterprises: survey analysis of organization and motivation', in Ove Granstrand, Lars Hakanson, Soren Sjolander (eds), *Technology Management and International Business*, Chichester: John Wiley and Sons, 137–62.

Petit, M.L. and F. Sanna-Randaccio (2000), 'Endogenous R&D and foreign direct investment in international oligopolies', *International Journal of Industrial Organization*, 18, 339–67.

Reger, G. (2001), 'Differences in the internationalization of research and technology between Western European, Japanese and North American Companies', mimeo, University of Brandenburg.

Sanna-Randaccio, F. and R. Veugelers (2002), 'Multinational knowledge spillovers with centralised vs decentralised R&D: a game-theoretic approach', CEPR Discussion Paper no. 3151.

Serapio, M. and D. Dalton (1999), 'Globalization of industrial R&D: an examination of FDI in R&D in the US', *Research Policy*, 28, 303–16.

Veugelers, R. and B. Cassiman (2002), 'Innovative strategies and know-how flows in international companies: some evidence from Belgian Manufacturing', in Robert E. Lipsey and Jan Louis Muchielli (eds), *Multinational Firms and the Impact on Employment, Trade and Technology*, London: Routledge.

Veugelers, R. and B. Cassiman (2003), 'Foreign subsidiaries as a channel of international technology diffusion: some direct firm level evidence from Belgium', *European Economic Review*, forthcoming.

Veugelers, R. and P. Vanden Houte (1990), 'Domestic R&D in the presence of multinational firms', *International Journal of Industrial Organisation*, 8, 1–17.

Zedtwitz, M. von and O. Gassman (2002), 'Market versus technology drive in R&D internationalization: four different patterns of managing research and development', *Research Policy*, 31, 569–88.

2. Path-dependency and coherence in international networks of technological innovation

John Cantwell and Elena Kosmopoulou

INTRODUCTION

Firms and large multinationals in particular need a large number of technologies to support the production of their usually extensive product diversification (Granstrand, Patel and Pavitt, 1997). This phenomenon is enhanced by recent developments in communication, the fall of economic and other boundaries and the development of ever more technologically complex products. Although most research has been focused on firms' primary technological field (eg. chemical technologies for chemical firms) an extended portfolio of corporate technological competencies is necessary to enable firms to compete successfully. While different industries need an amalgamation of different technologies to support their activities there are a number of technologies of a very 'pervasive nature' for many sectors of the economy. These technologies that abide by the characteristics explored in the work of Breshahan and Trajtenberg (1995), are termed general purpose technologies (GPTs) and it is their composition and evolution that defines technological paradigms and signals their transition from one to another.

Different considerations may be relevant when international specialisation is concerned. Firms may pursue different strategies in their research abroad, through a division of labour with their technological efforts at home. There is a literature that explains the internationalisation of corporate technology on the basis of the explanatory framework Vernon's product cycle. In this context first, small countries internationalise more than larger countries; second, firms in less research-intensive industries internationalise proportionally more than firms in high research-intensive industries; and third, technologies developed abroad should primarily support the adaptation of products for local markets, rather than developing new competences for the international corporate group as a whole (to enhance the subsidiaries' productivity). However, there seems to be only limited empirical support for such a framework of internationalisation from the patenting activity of firms during the years 1969–95. Firms no longer diversify their corporate technology internationally just to support their servicing of international markets but also to tap into new sources of technological competence, which may include mutually beneficial technology spillovers between the subsidiary and a host industry or industries (ie. which may facilitate local spillovers of an inter-industry kind).

It is common practice for academics to measure the strength of an innovative economy with aggregate figures of research and development (R&D) or scores of patents and thus in many ongoing analyses there is an inherent, implicit assumption that scale is the only important factor when the innovative capacity of a country is examined. This overemphasis on scale as a univariate measure of technological prowess may mean that insufficient attention is paid to the cross-sectoral composition of innovation as part of a network of technological capabilities developed by firms and national industrial groups. It is widely accepted that a firm's overall capabilities are more than the sum of the constituent parts, and the concept of economies of scope in corporate technology can be employed at the micro, firm-level analysis to explain the insurgence and success of large, diversified firms. It is suggested that one important reason for firms' diversification, both at home and abroad, is in order to take advantage of economies of scope. In this process patenting data show that during the period 1969–95 some national groups of firms were more successful than others in successfully combining their limited innovative resources into coherent networks of technological innovation. Such excellence in the construction of coordinated networks of corporate technologies could have a major impact in national economies and potentially provide an explanation for the differential growth among national economies and for the failings of some national economies to achieve continuous successful growth.

Moreover, even once successful, coherent networks of innovation may eventually become less functional (or altogether obsolete) and can impede national growth. In particular, countries with once successful national systems of innovation can, if policy makers are not alert, be trapped into previously prevailing paradigms and fail to recognize evolution in terms of the most appropriate combination of activities.

DATA AND METHODOLOGY

In this chapter the data used are patents granted in the US to the world's largest firms during the period 1969–95. US patents are an established indirect measure of innovation, closer to production than other indirect measures and consistent historically. The study focuses on the patenting activity of the three most technologically important groups of firms from a selection of European countries (Germany, the UK, France, Netherlands, Switzerland, Sweden), the US and Japan.

The revealed technological advantage (RTA) index is a proxy measure of technological specialisation across different fields of technological activity. In this chapter the profile of technological specialisation across fields of innovative activity of a national group of firms in a specific industry (such as chemicals and pharmaceuticals) is measured by the RTA index. RTA is defined as the share of US patents granted to the group of firms in question in some given technological field, relative to that group's share of US patents in all technological fields granted to firms in the industry.

$$\text{RTA}_{ij} = (P_{ij} / \Sigma_j P_{ij}) / (\Sigma_i P_{ij} / \Sigma_i\Sigma_j P_{ij}),$$

where P is the number of US patents granted to large firms in a given industry, i is the technological sector of inventive activity, and j is the national group of firms.

The index varies around unity. The greater the value, the more a group of firms has a comparative technological advantage in the field of activity in question. The index controls for inter-sectoral and inter-country variations in the propensity to patent (Cantwell, 1993, 2000). An equivalent index is also used to portray the pattern of technological specialisation of national groups of firms as a whole (not restricted to a particular industry) relative to all other large firms in the world, either across industries (in which case i above would denote the principal industry of the firm to which a patent is granted) or across technological fields. We use this form of the index to establish the profile of national technological strengths and weaknesses – that is, the industries in which the largest firms originating from a given country are technological leaders.

The analysis of this chapter is concerned with corporate technological diversification and internationalisation within a specific industry of output, unlike in a previous study (Cantwell and Kosmopoulou, 2002) in which we referred to the technological diversification of firms from all industries organised by national group. Although it was not then our focus of attention, the existence of intra-industry technological diversification implicitly played a small but sometimes significant part in the analysis of the data organised by technological activity where the activity of all firms from all industries is considered collectively. This is because it need not be true that most of the technological activity of a field originates from the associated primary industry (eg. that the bulk of chemical patents come from the chemical industry), even though it may be true that a high share of patenting by chemical firms is in chemical technology. In other words, in the example just given of the chemical industry and its primary chemical technologies, the aggregate number of patents in chemical technologies performed by non-chemical firms in a country may exceed the number of chemical patents from that country's chemical industry.

In this study firms of different national origins are compared within selected industrial groups, rather than considering the firms of all industries collectively. Firms are treated together here where they belong to one of a narrowly selected combination of industries that are closely related historically in their technological activity. The significance of this grouping is that it allows us to compare like with like, as between different national groups, and it enables us to control any industry-specific shift in the underlying technological composition of patenting in one direction or another. For instance, firms in the chemical and pharmaceutical industries have the bulk of their patenting activity in chemical technologies. However, in recent years there has been a large increase in the development of pharmaceutical technologies in both industries; in the pharmaceutical industry in particular in what are for them the primary pharmaceutical technologies.[1]

It should be noted as well that we use the RTA index as explained to depict patterns of technological specialisation within industries across countries, and not absolute shares of patenting (ie. we control for the fact that all parts of, for example, the chemical industry have high shares of chemical patenting) which may account for some divergence in our focus of attention from that of some other studies. Thus, all chemical firms, for example, develop mainly chemical technologies whether at home or abroad if we work in terms of their patent shares across fields of activity (Patel and Vega, 1999). What we examine here, however, is whether they concentrate to a greater extent on chemical development at home compared to abroad, and how different national groups within the chemical industry compare with one another in their domestic vs. their international profiles of innovation.

Development of an Analytical Framework

In this context, we begin from, but then explore how to go beyond, two background propositions on the determinants of the internationalisation of corporate technological activity which can be found in the literature (see in particular Patel and Pavitt (2000)). While these propositions may be useful starting points for explaining cross-country and cross-industry variations in the degree of internationalisation they are insufficient. In showing that there are two further factors which also determine differences in the extent of technological internationalisation between countries and industries, we present a more general and comprehensive framework for the analysis of the international location of innovative activity in large firms. The two background propositions with which we start are as follows. First is the supposition that large firms from small countries tend to be more highly internationalised in their technological development strategies, while large country multinational corporations (MNCs) tend to be less internationalised. The reason is that the constraints of small country size compel large firms originating from such economies to become internationalised more rapidly. Taken alone this proposition is an overgeneralisation and may be misleading, since for example British firms have been highly internationalised for a long time while Swedish firms have been little internationalised until relatively recently. More importantly for our argument, the cross-national group pattern in the degree of internationalisation within each industry varies from one industry to another.

To explain the foundation for the second proposition, while firms develop a wide range of technologies to support a narrower range of products (Pavitt, Robson and Townsend, 1989; Granstrand, Patel and Pavitt, 1997), the geographical dispersion of production in multinational firms exceeds that of technological activity (Cantwell and Hodson, 1991). We might infer from this that technology is internationalised more in support of the geographical spread of production and markets than the other way round, and indeed until recently this has been largely true (Cantwell, 1995; Cantwell and Piscitello, 2000). Until around 1980 international direct investments tended to be market-seeking or natural-resource-seeking, and not technological-asset-seeking. So historically when the internationalisation of technology followed the internationalisation of production, which in turn was motivated by a search for markets or resources, the share of foreign-located research tended to be greatest where it was needed to adapt products to locally differentiated markets (like in food products) or to adapt resource extraction to local conditions (like in mining). It was lower in research-intensive industries, in which a higher proportion of research is directed towards the development of entirely new products and processes rather than simpler adaptation.

Thus, the second background proposition is that less research-intensive industries tend to be relatively more internationalised in their technological activity (in terms of foreign research shares) than are highly research-intensive industries. However, taken alone this is (also) an overgeneralisation that may be misleading. Chemicals, pharmaceuticals, petrochemicals and office equipment (computing) are all research-intensive industries that have on average a substantial internationalisation of technological endeavour among large firms. More importantly again for our purposes, the ranking from highly internationalised industries down to the least internationalised is not uniform if we compare the cross-industry distribution for the firms of different nationalities of origin. So rather than explaining why on average food and pharmaceuticals are highly internationalised industries while aircraft are not, we need to be able to explain why the food firms of some home countries of origin are highly internationalised in their technological efforts, but the food companies of other countries are not.

To clarify the nature of the supplementary arguments that are necessary to build upon but which qualify and go beyond the received wisdoms that technological development tends to be more internationalised on average in firms from smaller countries and in less research-intensive industries, we develop a new framework that embraces elements of these existing contentions. Yet at the same time our approach provides a more comprehensive explanation of the complex variations across countries and industries in the degree of internationalisation of technological activity that is observed in practice among large firms. Our framework introduces two new components in order to establish more precisely the determinants of the internationalisation of corporate innovative effort.

First, national groups of large industrial firms have unique and distinctive international technological profiles that reflect the path-dependent and historically bounded competencies that were originally developed in their home country (Cantwell, 2000). In industries in which national groups of firms are strongest as technological leaders the extent of internationalisation of technology development will be relatively high (Cantwell, 1989). However, such multinational firms utilise their international networks for innovation in large part to promote their own comparative technological diversification (Cantwell and Piscitello, 2000). The investment that they conduct abroad tends to be more oriented towards general technological systems, relevant to most industries, which are either core to the current technological paradigm (such as information and communication technology or new materials) or carried forward from past paradigms (such as mechanical devices and instruments), while they tend to retain at home a higher proportion of technological development in the primary fields for their own respective industries. Conversely, from the perspective of inward investment, if the industries in the host country are technologically strongest, the vibrant local presence of strong indigenous companies tends to deter foreign-owned firms of the same industry from conducting substantial levels of local development in the primary technologies of the industry in question. At the same time, the strongest firms of other industries might be attracted to locate development of the relevant technologies in such a centre of excellence, which lines of development for them would represent diversification from the primary technologies of their own industries. Since they are in another industry, they are not direct competitors of the local leaders.

In other words, the intensity of technological competition influences cross-sectoral patterns of international expansion. Competitive strengths in an industry on the part of a national group of firms encourage outward investment in foreign-located technological development but discourage the inward investment of foreign-owned companies in the same industry. However, the foreign-owned firms of other industries (which are not major competitors in output markets) may be attracted to source technology from a centre of excellence in the primary field of development in which local firms lead. Likewise, while the leading local companies tend to retain much of their development of their own primary technologies at home (given local expertise), what they locate abroad will be geared towards the foreign development of related or complementary fields.

Thus, in general, in the case of an area in which local firms are strong we expect to observe roughly the pattern illustrated in Figure 2.1 in terms of the degree of internationalisation of technological activity at the level of the industry, and at the level of the equivalent technological field. First, we expect outward investment in innovation to exceed inward investment, given the balance of corporate strengths. However, second, while in the case of outward investment the internationalisation of the industry will tend to exceed that in the corresponding technological field (since strong domestically owned firms

Home/Host Country Perspective

	Outward	Inward
Industry	High Degree of Internationalisation (H)	Local Deterrence in the Primary Industry (L)
Technology	Exploitation for Diversification (M)	Local Attraction for Diversification (M)

(Level of Analysis)

Notes:
H: High internationalisation of technological activity in the industry or technological field in question.
M: Medium-intensity internationalisation of technological activity in the industry or technological field in question.
L: Low internationalisation of technological activity in the industry or technological field in question.

Figure 2.1   The effect of leading locally-owned national groups on the degree and structure of internationalisation of innovation

diversify abroad), within inward investment the pattern tends to be the other way round (since foreign-owned firms in the same industry are those most deterred by the presence of dominant local companies).

However, to bring in now the second new component of our framework, a counterbalancing consideration may be observed in industries and countries in which the basis of strong local technological competitiveness is a tight inter-relatedness among companies in the industry with downstream local user firms or upstream supplier firms as the sources of innovation and providing crucial feedback to in-house innovation. This type of relationship places great importance on mutual trust and locally specific knowledge creation because it demands a commitment of substantial resources (Lee, 1998, pp. 47–8) that induces national industrial groups to remain local in their innovative strategies and 'has a cumulative and continuous property with a time dimension' (Lundvall, 1985, 1988). Hence, the more that the production of a national industrial group is aimed at local intermediate good markets, or depends upon locally specific suppliers of innovative equipment or other inputs, the less inter-nationalised they will tend to be in their research strategy.

We might expect this argument to apply in an industry such as metals, or machine tools, yet the same inward-looking approach to innovation may also be relevant to other industries with a strong indigenous advantage linked to inter-company and inter-industry interrelatedness. This is particularly likely to apply in the case of Japan, where a closely knit network of firms (such as in the form of *Keiretsu*) supports a broad dispersion of development across comple-mentary technological fields (Scher, 1997). For example, we have a variety of industries in Japan, such as the chemical, the computer, and the electrical equipment industries, whose technological development relies for support upon, and in turn helps to support, competence development in a focus industry, most notably motor vehicles. In this case the chemical, computer and electrical equipment industries can be regarded as to a greater extent than usual inter-mediate-good-oriented and much of their technological effort is directed to the innovative support of the car industry. Of course, this does not mean that these industries provide only for the local market or that in some later stage of their development they will not become more international in their innovative activity. Instead, the Japanese chemical industry is, for example, among the leading national groups in paints.

However, in general in a case in which the technological strength of local firms depends upon a tight localised inter-industry coupling of user–producer interaction in innovation, we expect to observe roughly the pattern illustrated in Figure 2.2, distinguishing again between the level of the focus industry and the level of the equivalent technological field. First, we expect outward investment in innovation to be low, quite likely to the extent that it is even weaker than inward investment. Yet in this case both outward and inward internationalisation in the industry will tend to be lower than in the corresponding technological field (since the firms of related industries may be better able to diversify into this field abroad or to tap into local excellence, while within the industry local firms would find it difficult to establish similar linkages or to operate more independently elsewhere, and foreign-owned firms find the inter-knit structure of the local industry a barrier to entry).

Home/Host Country Perspective

	Outward	Outward
Industry	Dependence on Local Users or Suppliers (L)	Deterrence due to Established Local Inter-Firm Linkages (L)
Technology	Exploitation of User or Supplier Capabilities (M)	Local Attraction for Diversification (M)

Level of Analysis

Notes:
M: Medium-intensity internationalisation of technological activity in the industry or technological field in question.
L: Low internationalisation of technological activity in the industry or technological field in question.

Figure 2.2   The effect of tight localised coupling of capable downstream user (or upstream supplier) firms as the source of innovation on the degree of internationalisation of technological activity

Patterns of International Technological Specialisation in Selected Industries

Table 2.1 traces the comparative advantage in innovation of national industrial groups over the 1969–95 period as a whole, in order to be able to apply the framework suggested by Figure 2.1 and to identify the national origins of the technological leaders in each industry. To start with, smaller countries have a

Table 2.1 The RTA of selected nationally-owned groups of firms, across industries, during the period 1969–95

Industries	United States	Germany	United Kingdom	France	Netherlands	Switzerland	Sweden	Japan
Food, Drink and Tobacco	1.16	0.00	4.74	0.48	0.19	1.18	0.03	0.41
Chemicals	0.75	2.58	1.10	0.96	0.89	2.78	0.31	0.76
Pharmaceuticals	1.24	1.05	0.87	0.94	0.00	3.98	0.84	0.22
Metals	0.69	2.19	1.03	1.34	0.45	0.94	2.37	1.00
Mechanical Engineering	1.19	1.01	1.01	0.24	0.00	1.69	6.74	0.32
Electrical Equipment	0.84	0.67	0.51	1.12	3.29	0.36	0.87	1.54
Office Equipment	1.46	0.02	0.11	0.49	0.00	0.00	0.00	0.80
Motor Vehicles	0.64	1.58	1.24	1.07	0.00	0.00	0.87	1.82
Aircraft and Aerospace	1.65	0.22	0.84	1.35	0.00	0.00	0.00	0.00
Coal and Petroleum	1.43	0.02	2.79	1.64	0.00	0.00	0.00	0.08
Instruments	0.82	0.28	0.02	0.00	0.00	0.00	0.62	2.46
Other Manufacturing	1.13	0.16	0.94	1.31	0.00	0.46	1.58	1.01
Standard deviation of sample	0.33	0.89	1.29	0.50	0.95	1.29	1.89	0.75
CV (= sd/mean)	0.31	1.09	1.02	0.55	2.37	1.36	1.60	0.87

Table 2.2 The RTA of selected nationally-owned groups of firms, across fields of technological activity, during the period 1969–95

Technological Sectors	United States	Germany	United Kingdom	France	Netherlands	Switzerland	Sweden	Japan
Food, Drink and Tobacco	1.33	0.36	2.41	0.27	0.23	1.11	0.79	0.29
Chemicals	1.00	1.58	1.18	0.99	0.52	2.23	0.33	0.65
Pharmaceuticals	0.93	1.80	1.56	1.22	0.40	3.59	0.86	0.45
Metals	1.11	0.67	1.11	1.05	0.67	0.64	1.80	0.83
Mechanical Engineering	1.08	0.89	1.36	0.97	0.59	0.66	2.22	0.72
Electrical Equipment	0.99	0.61	0.59	1.13	2.23	0.27	0.91	1.26
Office Equipment	0.87	0.42	0.26	0.83	1.50	0.07	0.27	1.89
Motor Vehicles	0.51	1.72	0.65	0.78	0.12	0.11	0.82	2.24
Aircraft and Aerospace	1.32	0.75	2.03	3.07	0.26	0.12	1.00	0.06
Coal and Petroleum	1.48	0.33	1.56	1.00	0.10	0.08	0.06	0.20
Instruments	0.90	0.83	0.67	0.74	1.16	0.46	0.86	1.52
Other Manufacturing	1.04	0.94	1.19	1.14	0.59	0.55	1.28	0.93
Standard deviation of sample	0.25	0.52	0.62	0.67	0.64	1.06	0.61	0.68
CV (= sd/mean)	0.24	0.57	0.51	0.61	0.91	1.29	0.66	0.74

narrower range of industries in which their firms compete successfully as worldwide technological leaders.

Table 2.2 shows the profile of national competencies in a variety of technological fields. In this table we can observe the relative technological advantage of national groups of firms from all industries at home and abroad. In general, firms sustain a wider research in a variety of technological fields to support a narrower range of products. As a result of this, the gap between large and small countries in the cross-sectoral dispersion of research is less pronounced than in Table 2.1. Moreover, a technologically competitive industry in most cases presumes a competitive primary technology and vice versa. However, this does not hold for computers in which two different national groups of firms share leadership. US-owned firms lead in the computing industry, while Japanese-owned firms have the strongest technological advantage in the development of the corresponding primary technologies, showing how Japanese firms are strongest in downstream industrial applications of computerised methods. In aircraft and aerospace UK-owned firms have an advantage solely in the technology (unlike US-owned and French-owned firms, that are leaders in the industry and in the technology), which is due to the British motor vehicle component firms whose expertise lies in engines in general.

In Tables 2.3, 2.4 and 2.5 we examine (i) the profile of technological specialisation of national groups of firms in each selected industry (distinguishing in particular between a special focus upon technologies that are primary for the industry in question, as opposed to those that are not), (ii) their spatial distribution of innovative effort between the relevant home country and the rest of the world, and (iii) the pattern of technological activity that host countries attract from foreign-owned firms in the industry in question.

Beginning with the chemical and pharmaceutical industry, Table 2.3 shows that according to our RTA calculations, German and Swiss domestically owned chemical and pharmaceutical industrial firms are focused at home on their primary technological activities, German-owned firms on chemical technologies (1.22) and Swiss-owned firms on both chemical (1.34) and pharmaceutical technologies (1.16). However, UK-owned firms, apart from their efforts in (primary) pharmaceutical (1.56) and petrochemical technologies (1.72), also develop mechanical engineering technologies (1.16), an important GPT for the support of production activity (Pavitt, Robson and Townsend, 1989). On the other hand, they develop extensive non-core technologies, in fact even more than primary ones. Dutch-owned firms innovate in chemical (1.11), mechanical (1.45) and petrochemical (1.44) technologies, and French-owned firms in pharmaceutical (1.11), metal (1.51) and mechanical engineering (1.55) technologies. Swedish firms innovate considerably in pharmaceutical technologies (1.81), but even more in a variety of other technologies such as instruments (2.56), metals (1.82), electrical equipment (1.54) and mechanical engineering (1.41).

Table 2.3   Chemicals and pharmaceuticals

Table 2.3a   The RTA from domestically-owned activity in selected host countries, across fields of technological activity, during the period 1969–95

Technological Sectors	United States	Germany	United Kingdom	France	Netherlands	Switzerland	Sweden	Japan
Food, Drink and Tobacco	1.60	0.36	0.61	0.52	0.61	0.29	1.37	0.58
Chemicals	0.92	1.22	0.89	0.99	1.11	1.34	0.53	0.98
Pharmaceuticals	0.96	0.89	1.56	1.11	0.68	1.16	1.81	0.62
Metals	1.40	0.52	0.64	1.51	0.40	0.08	1.82	0.61
Mechanical Engineering	1.13	0.73	1.16	1.55	1.45	0.26	1.41	0.91
Electrical Equipment	1.17	0.38	0.79	0.92	0.20	0.12	1.54	1.75
Office Equipment	0.87	0.47	0.19	0.09	0.00	0.21	0.61	3.21
Motor Vehicles	1.20	0.41	3.70	0.84	10.70	0.00	0.00	0.45
Aircraft and Aerospace	1.90	0.56	0.00	0.00	0.00	0.00	0.00	0.00
Coal and Petroleum	1.21	0.95	1.72	0.61	1.44	0.09	0.00	1.22
Instruments	1.08	0.66	0.40	0.41	0.37	0.45	2.56	1.71
Other Manufacturing	1.23	0.66	1.19	0.74	1.40	0.15	0.85	1.19
Standard deviation of sample	0.29	0.26	0.98	0.49	2.94	0.44	0.84	0.84
CV (= sd/mean)	0.24	0.40	0.91	0.63	1.92	1.28	0.81	0.76

59

Table 2.3b The RTA from foreign-located activity by firms of selected home countries, across fields of technological activity, during the period 1969–95

Technological Sectors	United States	Germany	United Kingdom	France	Netherlands	Switzerland	Sweden	Japan
Food, Drink and Tobacco	0.70	0.76	1.23	2.09	0.38	0.32	0.56	0.51
Chemicals	0.85	1.04	0.79	0.73	0.69	1.16	0.53	0.86
Pharmaceuticals	1.59	1.32	1.17	1.36	0.50	1.47	2.00	0.50
Metals	1.16	0.96	1.51	2.99	0.74	0.25	1.34	1.63
Mechanical Engineering	1.12	0.76	1.60	1.06	3.86	0.42	1.42	1.39
Electrical Equipment	1.24	0.55	1.54	1.11	1.82	0.10	1.08	2.64
Office Equipment	0.27	0.81	0.24	2.21	0.00	0.30	0.81	16.19
Motor Vehicles	*1.42*	*0.46*	*1.34*	*0.00*	*0.00*	*0.00*	*11.15*	*0.00*
Aircraft and Aerospace	*0.00*	*0.00*	*2.15*	*0.00*	*4.93*	*0.00*	*0.00*	*0.00*
Coal and Petroleum	0.48	0.36	0.72	0.48	0.87	0.26	0.00	1.92
Instruments	0.84	0.81	0.86	1.89	0.47	0.98	2.32	0.62
Other Manufacturing	0.85	0.74	1.37	0.60	1.54	0.26	0.96	0.62
Standard deviation of sample	0.47	0.34	0.50	0.93	1.55	0.48	3.01	4.46
CV (= sd/mean)	0.53	0.48	0.41	0.77	1.18	1.04	1.63	1.99

Note:
The sectors represented in italics have less than 1,200 patents.

Table 2.3c The RTA from foreign-owned activity in selected host countries, across fields of technological activity, during the period 1969–95

Technological Sectors	United States	Germany	United Kingdom	France	Netherlands	Switzerland	Sweden	Japan
Food, Drink and Tobacco	0.84	0.42	0.44	0.44	4.47	1.17	0.00	0.85
Chemicals	0.98	0.97	0.93	0.80	0.90	0.98	0.79	1.00
Pharmaceuticals	1.35	0.88	2.08	1.98	0.61	0.62	0.95	1.18
Metals	1.05	0.78	0.82	0.66	0.36	1.41	2.84	0.77
Mechanical Engineering	0.85	1.95	0.57	1.82	1.35	1.70	1.50	0.42
Electrical Equipment	0.83	0.98	0.40	0.38	0.58	0.85	0.00	1.96
Office Equipment	1.26	0.20	0.07	0.14	2.60	1.27	0.00	0.46
Motor Vehicles	*0.29*	*0.70*	*0.49*	*5.93*	*0.00*	*0.00*	*0.00*	*0.00*
Aircraft and Aerospace	*0.00*	*2.26*	*0.00*	*0.00*	*0.00*	*0.00*	*0.00*	*3.41*
Coal and Petroleum	0.53	0.40	0.18	0.19	3.39	0.74	0.00	0.47
Instruments	1.01	0.74	0.65	0.53	1.17	1.17	2.66	0.55
Other Manufacturing	0.64	0.91	0.47	0.38	1.61	0.97	1.01	1.44
Standard deviation of sample	0.39	0.60	0.54	1.64	1.40	0.52	1.05	0.91
CV (= sd/mean)	0.49	0.65	0.92	1.49	0.98	0.57	1.29	0.87

Note:
The sectors represented in italics have less than 1,200 patents.

Furthermore, US-owned firms do only average innovative research in the primary technologies (an RTA just below unity for both chemical and pharmaceutical technologies) while at the same time keeping a distributed research agenda in most of the non-core technologies for the industry.

The US national group of firms maintains in its foreign-located research a similar pattern to that pursued domestically, although foreign-located research is more geared towards the development of pharmaceutical technologies. German-and Swiss-owned firms are as focused abroad as they are in their domestic research, while all other national groups maintain the same diffused innovative portfolio. However, both US and German-owned firms are in this case very active in pharmaceutical technologies (1.59 and 1.32 in Table 2.3b) as opposed to the modest innovative performance in that area in their home country (0.96 and 0.89 in Table 2.3a).

In the UK for foreign-owned firms the balance is strongly in favour of research in pharmaceuticals (2.08), while in Germany foreign-owned chemical and pharmaceutical firms place their innovating activities neither in chemicals (0.97 in Table 2.3c) nor pharmaceuticals (0.88), but in mechanical engineering (1.95). This is consistent with the country's leading position in the world chemical and pharmaceutical industries, and the strong development by German indigenous firms of their core technological base in chemicals at home (Table 2.3a) makes it more costly for weaker firms from abroad to participate in the local development of the equivalent fields. In Switzerland, metals, mechanical engineering and instruments are among the most successfully researched technological areas of foreign-owned chemical and pharmaceutical firms. Mechanical engineering is for chemical and pharmaceutical companies a technological area of great importance. The relatively high competitiveness of France for pharmaceuticals (1.98) may be, to some extent, inflated by regulatory requirements rather than actually reflecting the local comparative advantage. In the Netherlands and Sweden, the foreign-owned research in the chemical and pharmaceutical industries reflects the comparative advantages of individual countries and concentrates in the countries' major fields of technological development. So in the Netherlands, foreign innovation is mainly in the areas of food (4.47), coal and petroleum (3.39), office equipment (2.60), mechanical engineering (1.35) and instruments (1.17), while in Sweden there is strong emphasis on metals (2.84), professional and scientific instruments (2.66) and mechanical engineering (1.50).

Table 2.4, which examines the profiles of large firms in the electrical equipment and electronics industry, shows that, as between their primary technological fields, firms tend to have a higher relative technological advantage in electrical equipment than they do in information and communication technologies (ICT). Among non-primary technologies instruments is the preferred choice of most national groups, in both their domestic and foreign-located

Table 2.4 Electrical and office equipment

Table 2.4a The RTA from domestically-owned activity in selected host countries, across fields of technological activity, during the period 1969–95

Technological Sectors	United States	Germany	United Kingdom	France	Netherlands	Switzerland	Sweden	Japan
Food, Drink and Tobacco	1.50	0.71	0.00	0.00	0.00	0.00	3.03	0.54
Chemicals	1.25	0.75	0.41	0.50	0.92	0.64	0.29	0.78
Pharmaceuticals	0.88	0.51	1.29	0.23	4.13	0.48	0.00	1.04
Metals	1.21	0.99	0.86	0.78	1.10	2.28	1.81	0.65
Mechanical Engineering	1.12	0.88	0.85	0.57	0.66	1.83	1.98	0.85
Electrical Equipment	0.97	1.07	1.11	1.23	1.19	0.97	1.06	0.97
Office Equipment	0.89	0.48	0.59	0.74	0.83	0.16	0.45	1.38
Motor Vehicles	0.40	0.78	0.44	0.34	0.07	1.56	3.98	2.30
Aircraft and Aerospace	1.57	0.14	4.23	4.23	0.63	0.00	0.00	0.13
Coal and Petroleum	1.09	2.76	1.09	0.77	0.62	0.00	0.00	0.73
Instruments	0.92	1.49	1.59	1.27	0.88	0.93	0.59	1.01
Other Manufacturing	1.09	1.42	1.04	0.90	0.81	2.06	1.45	0.83
Standard deviation of sample	0.31	0.67	1.07	1.09	1.05	0.84	1.29	0.53
CV (= sd/mean)	0.29	0.67	0.95	1.14	1.07	0.92	1.05	0.56

Note:
The sectors represented in italics have less than 1,200 patents.

Table 2.4b   The RTA from foreign-located activity by firms of selected home countries, across fields of technological activity, during the period 1969–95

Technological Sectors	United States	Germany	United Kingdom	France	Netherlands	Switzerland	Sweden	Japan
Food, Drink and Tobacco	0.00	0.00	0.00	0.00	0.59	0.00	0.00	0.00
Chemicals	1.19	0.36	0.88	0.23	0.70	0.68	0.30	0.51
Pharmaceuticals	1.42	1.56	0.40	0.00	1.62	0.00	0.77	0.00
Metals	1.09	0.56	0.80	0.32	0.78	1.50	2.24	0.63
Mechanical Engineering	1.33	0.35	1.16	0.30	0.58	0.94	3.05	0.54
Electrical Equipment	0.93	1.12	0.98	1.40	1.23	1.03	0.87	0.94
Office Equipment	0.89	1.28	0.44	1.54	0.63	0.09	0.13	1.97
Motor Vehicles	0.60	0.42	0.53	0.09	0.80	1.75	1.45	0.99
Aircraft and Aerospace	0.07	0.00	0.00	0.47	0.94	0.00	0.00	0.00
Coal and Petroleum	1.37	0.00	0.00	0.00	1.15	0.00	0.00	0.00
Instruments	1.03	1.49	1.72	0.48	1.30	0.71	0.58	0.95
Other Manufacturing	0.92	0.38	1.18	0.24	0.77	4.84	1.96	0.68
Standard deviation of sample	0.47	0.58	0.54	0.52	0.33	1.37	1.02	0.58
CV (= sd/mean)	0.52	0.93	0.81	1.22	0.35	1.42	1.07	0.97

Note:
The sectors represented in italics have less than 1,200 patents.

Table 2.4c The RTA from foreign-owned activity in selected host countries, across fields of technological activity, during the period 1969–95

Technological Sectors	United States	Germany	United Kingdom	France	Netherlands	Switzerland	Sweden	Japan
Food, Drink and Tobacco	0.00	0.73	0.00	0.00	0.00	0.00	0.00	0.00
Chemicals	0.67	0.58	0.62	0.46	2.10	0.48	0.21	1.94
Pharmaceuticals	0.64	0.42	4.45	1.43	0.00	0.54	3.83	0.22
Metals	0.78	1.27	1.24	0.56	0.93	0.64	1.11	0.53
Mechanical Engineering	0.67	1.52	1.05	0.54	1.82	1.17	1.06	0.74
Electrical Equipment	1.18	0.94	1.08	1.21	0.90	1.17	0.50	0.86
Office Equipment	1.06	0.69	0.75	1.14	0.35	0.54	0.52	0.88
Motor Vehicles	1.14	0.39	0.14	0.45	4.24	0.15	0.69	1.13
Aircraft and Aerospace	0.00	0.14	0.24	0.99	0.00	0.00	8.80	0.00
Coal and Petroleum	0.00	1.41	4.64	0.00	0.00	0.00	0.00	0.00
Instruments	0.96	1.20	1.20	1.03	0.75	1.27	3.64	1.59
Other Manufacturing	0.65	1.52	0.79	0.69	1.08	1.04	0.92	0.61
Standard deviation of sample	0.43	0.48	1.55	0.46	1.24	0.49	2.56	0.62
CV (= sd/mean)	0.67	0.53	1.15	0.65	1.22	0.83	1.44	0.88

Note:
The sectors represented in italics have less than 1,200 patents.

activities. Furthermore, the focus of technological activity generally coincides with whatever are the most prominent national industries. This applies in the case of motor vehicles in Sweden, metals and mechanical engineering in both Sweden and Switzerland, and chemicals in the US, and gives a hint of the direction of corporate diversification of the national groups of industries in question. Domestically owned firms in all European countries, apart from Switzerland, show a high degree of innovation in electrical equipment technologies. The RTA of both Switzerland and the US is about one (0.97 for both countries) and all national groups, apart from the UK and Sweden, innovate more abroad in their primary field of research than in their home country.

The US and, on the other side of the Atlantic, France display the highest degree of penetration from foreign-owned research in both electrical equipment and office equipment. In the UK and Switzerland the interest of foreign research is limited to electrical equipment. On the other hand, Germany and the Netherlands are much less affected by foreign-owned research in this area, while Sweden is not affected at all. The US innovates both at home and abroad, in non-core technological areas, while it attracts foreign innovation in some core ones and in motor vehicle technologies. France seems to draw relatively more from research situated abroad in both electrical equipment, and especially office equipment technologies, while the Dutch concentration of research at home in electrical equipment is not successfully challenged by foreign-owned firms. Foreign-owned electrical equipment firms however, are quite prevalent in developing motor vehicle and chemical technologies in the Netherlands.

In Table 2.5, which covers the metals and mechanicals industries, large firms show a higher research activity in the mechanical engineering technologies compared to metal technologies. Domestically owned firms, apart from Dutch-owned ones (in metal technologies) and Japanese-owned ones (in mechanical engineering technologies), all have a higher patenting activity at home in primary than in non-primary activities. However, especially conspicuous among the non-primary fields are the cases of French-, German- and Swiss-owned firms in chemical technologies (3.22, 1.68 and 1.39), and Swedish- and French-owned firms in electrical equipment technologies (1.65 and 1.37 respectively).

Foreign-located patenting activity is less diversified and more focused in the primary technologies. Exceptions to this are French-owned firms (in chemicals the RTA is 2.35), and German-owned firms (in motor vehicle and chemical technologies the RTA values are 1.47 and 1.30 respectively). Dutch and Swedish firms in mechanical engineering technologies and the Swiss in both primary technologies are more dynamic in their foreign-situated research, where their RTA figures for these technologies are significantly higher, in comparison to their domestic-situated research in the same technological fields. They are also less diversified in their research abroad although Sweden, with a strong

Table 2.5   *Metals and mechanical engineering*

Table 2.5a   *The RTA from domestically-owned activity in selected host countries, across fields of technological activity, during the period 1969–95*

Technological Sectors	United States	Germany	United Kingdom	France	Netherlands	Switzerland	Sweden	Japan
Food, Drink and Tobacco	*1.13*	*0.92*	*0.16*	*0.38*	*0.00*	*0.34*	*2.74*	*0.38*
Chemicals	0.84	1.68	0.91	3.22	1.14	1.39	0.44	0.95
Pharmaceuticals	*0.90*	*1.35*	*1.12*	*2.78*	*0.00*	*2.63*	*1.58*	*0.51*
Metals	0.97	0.57	1.27	1.06	0.77	1.00	0.94	1.42
Mechanical Engineering	1.06	0.95	0.90	0.42	1.51	1.14	1.03	0.68
Electrical Equipment	0.99	0.64	1.28	1.37	0.19	0.56	1.65	1.31
Office Equipment	*0.99*	*1.21*	*0.61*	*0.62*	*0.58*	*0.17*	*0.51*	*1.72*
Motor Vehicles	1.20	0.83	0.17	0.04	0.27	0.66	0.24	1.16
Aircraft and Aerospace	*0.89*	*1.96*	*1.60*	*0.38*	*0.00*	*0.00*	*4.04*	*0.21*
Coal and Petroleum	*1.11*	*1.37*	*0.29*	*0.92*	*0.00*	*0.41*	*0.47*	*1.06*
Instruments	1.06	0.83	1.31	0.44	0.85	0.49	0.96	1.27
Other Manufacturing	0.93	1.23	0.97	0.50	0.41	0.83	1.19	1.26
Standard deviation of sample	0.11	0.42	0.48	1.00	0.50	0.70	1.10	0.46
CV (= sd/mean)	0.11	0.37	0.54	0.99	1.06	0.87	0.84	0.46

Note:
The sectors represented in italics have less than 1,200 patents.

Table 2.5b   *The RTA from foreign-located activity by firms of selected home countries, across fields of technological activity, during the period 1969–95*

Technological Sectors	United States	Germany	United Kingdom	France	Netherlands	Switzerland	Sweden	Japan
Food, Drink and Tobacco	0.42	0.32	1.70	0.00	1.34	2.36	3.63	0.00
Chemicals	0.48	1.30	0.83	2.35	0.27	0.70	0.36	0.78
Pharmaceuticals	0.39	0.39	0.94	1.86	1.08	1.91	1.27	7.06
Metals	1.12	0.72	0.81	0.97	0.77	1.45	0.74	0.85
Mechanical Engineering	1.23	0.91	1.28	0.49	1.60	1.33	1.54	0.65
Electrical Equipment	1.03	1.11	1.02	0.62	0.54	0.45	1.02	0.85
Office Equipment	0.74	0.96	0.69	0.00	0.00	0.08	0.18	3.47
Motor Vehicles	0.90	1.47	0.51	0.00	0.16	0.08	0.43	2.46
Aircraft and Aerospace	0.00	1.90	1.52	0.00	0.00	0.00	0.00	0.00
Coal and Petroleum	0.57	0.00	0.84	1.39	0.00	0.20	0.15	2.10
Instruments	1.19	0.71	0.47	0.09	0.27	0.32	0.78	2.42
Other Manufacturing	0.64	1.36	0.81	2.43	1.14	0.83	0.42	1.05
Standard deviation of sample	0.38	0.54	0.38	0.94	0.57	0.78	0.99	1.97
CV (= sd/mean)	0.52	0.58	0.40	1.11	0.96	0.97	1.13	1.09

Note:
The sectors represented in italics have less than 1,200 patents.

Table 2.5c   The RTA from foreign-owned activity in selected host countries, across fields of technological activity, during the period 1969–95

Technological Sectors	United States	Germany	United Kingdom	France	Netherlands	Switzerland	Sweden	Japan
Food, Drink and Tobacco	*1.85*	*0.99*	*0.52*	*0.67*	*1.04*	2.95	*0.00*	*0.00*
Chemicals	0.75	0.49	0.72	0.53	0.55	0.82	0.75	1.22
Pharmaceuticals	*1.34*	*0.17*	*0.73*	*0.00*	*0.00*	2.77	*0.00*	*1.25*
Metals	1.06	1.03	1.18	0.70	1.94	0.74	0.81	0.94
Mechanical Engineering	1.05	1.42	1.29	1.40	1.14	1.38	1.34	1.00
Electrical Equipment	1.26	0.69	0.66	0.80	0.20	0.50	0.33	1.56
Office Equipment	*0.77*	*0.42*	*0.51*	*0.17*	*0.00*	*1.22*	*0.00*	*0.58*
Motor Vehicles	0.82	0.71	1.03	0.16	0.12	0.12	0.00	1.00
Aircraft and Aerospace	*0.57*	*0.00*	*0.00*	*0.00*	*0.00*	*0.00*	*0.00*	*0.00*
Coal and Petroleum	*0.18*	*0.59*	*0.00*	*0.81*	*0.62*	*0.00*	*0.00*	*1.39*
Instruments	0.61	0.90	0.64	1.61	0.76	1.24	0.50	0.57
Other Manufacturing	1.11	0.58	0.75	0.62	1.25	0.52	1.68	0.58
Standard deviation of sample	0.43	0.39	0.40	0.51	0.62	0.98	0.58	0.51
CV (= sd/mean)	0.46	0.58	0.59	0.82	0.97	0.96	1.30	0.60

Note:
The sectors represented in italics have less than 1,200 patents.

research base at home in electrical equipment technologies (for which the RTA is 1.65) maintains an average RTA figure (1.02) abroad.

In Europe, national groups in the metal and mechanical industry tend to situate their research abroad either in chemical technologies or electrical equipment technologies. This division is very distinct and strong. The industry's technological interest in chemicals is prevalent for French or German firms, in foreign as well as in domestically situated research. Swiss- and Dutch-owned firms on the other hand diversify considerably in chemicals but only in their domestic research activities. UK, German, Swedish and US firms, on the other hand, diversify into electrical equipment. Swedish and UK firms have a competitive advantage in electrical equipment development both at home and abroad, while German and US companies only do so in their foreign-located research. However, US domestically owned firms, and foreign-located German firms, diversify also in motor vehicle-related technologies. Foreign-owned firms do not seem to have any problem in getting into direct competition in the industry's core research activities, in the great majority of cases in mechanical engineering. However, foreign research activities are expanded into the areas of instruments (in France and Switzerland), electrical equipment (in the US), and motor vehicles (in the UK).

DISCUSSION

Corporate technological diversification at home, or abroad through internationalisation, can be seen as two complementary corporate strategies that have to balance the increasing necessity to tap into new technological areas while retaining the knowledge links with the established traditional connections in the home base. According to the model (Cantwell and Kosmopoulou, 2002) as illustrated in Figures 2.1 and 2.2 we identified the leaders in a selection of industries as the countries leading an industry and the industry's primary technology (Tables 2.1 and 2.2). Then under the assumption that the primary technology of an industry is also the industry's most important technology we examined the international diversification strategies of national groups of firms away from this primary technological area and towards other non-primary technological areas. The balance in Figure 2.1 is in favour of internationalisation of corporate technology as a diversification strategy by leading groups of firms, while in Figure 2.2 strong user–producer interaction puts a powerful constraint on the internationalisation of firms. On the other hand both Figures 2.1 and 2.2 show compelling pressure of leading national industries not to 'allow' direct invasion of their technological 'space' from other leading national industries that are direct competitors in the same product area, while other industries, not directly competitive with the firms of the leading centre in output markets, demonstrate a strong interest in spillovers from the leaders' area of comparative technological advantage.

In this part of the chapter we examine how far this model fits the empirical evidence presented here. The appropriateness of the model is to be explored in two separate cases: first, whether the leading national industries in their outbound investment in development abroad conform with Figures 2.1 or 2.2 and second, in terms of the composition of foreign-owned innovation conducted by the firms of a given industry in each location, whether the 'deterrence–attraction' relation between industries of different leading status is present. First, in Figure 2.1 it is maintained that firms tend to utilise their international networks of technological development mostly to promote their own comparative technological diversification (Cantwell and Piscitello, 2000), keeping their primary technologies at home and tapping into foreign centres of excellence for their innovative potential in related technologies or in GPTs. In accordance with this are the German-owned firms as leaders in the chemical industry and US-owned firms as leaders in the ICT industry. German-owned firms, the leaders in the chemical industry and technological area when considered among the chemical and pharmaceutical groups of firms, perform better in their domestic relative to their foreign-located research in the primary technology of chemicals, while they do more research abroad in the pharmaceutical technological area (see Tables 2.3a and 2.3b). US-owned firms, leaders in the ICT industry and technological area (Tables 2.1 and 2.2) perform about the same at home or abroad in ICT technologies, while the relative comparative advantage in electrical equipment technologies in domestic research is higher than the equivalent in foreign locations.

However, not all the empirical evidence on the leading groups in Tables 2.3, 2.4 and 2.5 sits happily with Figure 2.1 of our model. The leading national industries that do not are the Swiss-owned pharmaceutical group, the Dutch-owned electrical group, and the Swedish mechanical firms, all however originating from small countries. There seem to be significant constraints due to the size of the country, which can be brought into account here to explain this apparent inconsistency. First, the small size of the country confines not only the size of the market but also the supply of available resources, especially of high-quality skilled labour and second, the small size is often a sign that only a very few firms and sometimes only a single firm is present in the sample albeit with a very strong presence, for example Philips in the Netherlands. These two considerations might be of relevance to the Dutch-owned case in which firms have (the leading firm has!) a higher relative technological advantage in that industry's primary technology, electrical equipment, in foreign-located research than in home-based research (see Tables 2.4a and 2.4b) while in ICT technologies domestic research is relatively stronger than is the foreign-located.

The home country technology base may simply be too small when a leading world company originates from a small country.

Another factor that plays an important role is the nature of the technology, and in particular whether fields constitute GPTs, that is, technological areas relevant to most industries and characteristic of a technological paradigm. Broad electrical technologies (electrical communication and computing technologies) for instance, during the period 1969–95, account for 28% of the overall patenting activity and had significant growth during this period (from 25% in the period 1969–72 to 36% in the period 1991–95). However, the broad mechanical technological field (mechanical, metal and instrument technologies) is still the most important GPT accounting for 35% of the total patenting, although its role has steadily declined (from 38% during the period 1969–72 to 31% during the period 1991–95), and this decrease would be even larger if instrument technologies were not included. Swedish-owned firms, leaders in the industry and technological area of mechanical engineering, have a higher relative competitive advantage in foreign-located research in this field than they do in the home country, given that the primary field in which they specialise is that of a GPT that may be best developed in some all-round foreign centres of excellence, which pool together the potentially interactive efforts of firms of different industries.

Lastly, Swiss-owned firms are leaders in the pharmaceutical industry and technological area and have a higher comparative advantage in foreign-located research than in their home country (see Tables 2.3a and 2.3b). Although the size of the country has already been mentioned as being one of the reasons for this apparent departure from the expectations of Figure 2.1, in this case there are a number of additional reasons that may explain the higher RTA value in foreign-located research in comparison to the domestically located. According to recent research the most advanced research areas in pharmaceuticals rely increasingly on ICT. Surprisingly enough however Switzerland has neither a substantial IT industry nor technology (Tables 2.1 and 2.2) nor any significant indication of gaining any local IT spillovers, although the presence of ABB might suggest otherwise, for an internationally leading industry which would tend to require favourable local interaction with other industries in its home base (Tables 2.3 and 2.4). This void might have been one of the reasons why Swiss compatibility with the newly emergent paradigm was falling along with its position in chemicals and pharmaceuticals and led the industry into a merger wave (the creation of Novartis in 1996). Furthermore, following the same line of thought, the lack of expertise in an essential technological area and the pressure of expiring patents might have led to an increased internationalisation in research in the later stages of development, for example through new investments in the US, where the presence of strong pharmaceutical capabilities in ICT technologies and their successful interlinkage has helped to create the very recent emergence of a strong technological advantage in the area of pharmaceuticals and in particular in biotechnology (Nightingale, 2000).

The motivation to tap into new technological areas abroad can be contrasted with the need to maintain strong links with other parts of the industrial nexus of the technological base at home. For some industries the nature of production and for some countries historical contingencies make this necessity to maintain close supplier–buyer links essential. In Figure 2.2, the nature of the industry and its technological structure at a particular time are important determinants for the nature and direction of international activity. In our previous work (Cantwell and Kosmopoulou, 2002), the metal industry and Japan were identified as examples that best illustrate the argument, but it is obvious that the dividing line is very fine in a number of other cases. In the two examples discussed in our earlier work, both Japanese-owned firms and Swedish-owned firms as leaders in the electrical and metal industries comply with the model as described in Figure 2.2.

When examining the degree of foreign penetration from other industries in a leading host country, the results are very clearly supportive of the position proposed by the model. In no case has a leading industry received a higher penetration in the respective primary technology than occurs in the same technology in other countries in the same industry and in almost all cases (except mechanical engineering in Sweden and ICT in the US) the relative comparative advantage of foreign-owned firms from within the same industry in a leading centre's primary area of technological development is lower than unity. In addition, the relative technological advantage of foreign-owned firms investing locally in the primary technological areas is in all leading national groups lower than the equivalent value for the domestic comparative advantage of indigenous firms.

While until this point our focus of attention has been on the location of development efforts for the primary technologies of firms and the objectives of this locational choice, the remainder of this chapter is concerned with what else we can learn from the location of research efforts in the non-primary technologies. The generally quantified analysis of corporate patenting, in which the patents of a firm are allocated in their entirety to the primary industry or firm, or in which patents are assigned to the primary industry of use based on a patent class-Standard Industrial Classification (SIC) concordance, largely fails to appreciate the importance of corporate technological diversification from the perspective of the firm or the industry, while it ignores a valuable indicator for the interactive nature of the growth of firms, industries and countries.[2]

On the other hand, the location of efforts in developing those non-primary technologies in which industries invest is not randomly distributed, but often closely linked in the case of domestic research with other strong national industries, and abroad to other local industries in which the host economy may be a leading country or have been important at some time. In addition, in many cases the technological profiles of foreign-owned firms in a location are consistent with investment in what are the primary technologies of other industries that are locally strong in that host country, and hence suggestive of inter-industry technology linkages. In many of the cases that we can examine with the present data the potential link runs mainly from the oldest established and/or stronger industry as a source to the one that has more recently been established or has a lower competitive advantage as a recipient (Table 2.1).

By improving our understanding of the relationship between industries and technologies, and their evolution over time, we may come closer to explaining the underlying sources of firms' competence and national growth. Most importantly by linking the micro level (firm and industry level) and macro level (national level) of analysis we may be able to develop indicators for the use of policy makers and managers about the direction of industries and economies alike. In general, the domestic activity of firms is focused on at least some non-primary sectors in all three tables (2.3, 2.4 and 2.5). In all cases except for German- and Swiss-owned firms in chemicals and pharmaceuticals, and Dutch-owned firms in the metal and mechanical industrial groups, the specialisation in the primary technology has a lower RTA than do efforts in some other non-primary technologies developed by each national group.[3] Domestic activity seems to be very skillful in 'connecting' industries and in fusing together technologies. This is hardly surprising in the light of the recent development of the latest technological paradigm, with its growing emphasis on constructing combined packages of innovative effort that bring together the most – potentially – interrelated technologies.

Firms from smaller countries tend to have high RTA figures in only a handful of industries and technological fields (Tables 2.1 and 2.2), and so have less basis for technological diversification at home as a potential avenue for fruitful inter-industry knowledge exchanges. It is interesting to note that UK-owned firms have a singularly large number of both industries and technologies with high RTA values (above unity), although most national groups have a high relative comparative advantage in more technological sectors than industries, Germany and Switzerland being the main exceptions.

Links with national leaders and/or long established industries play an important role in the distribution of the development of non-primary technologies by US-owned firms. US-owned firms connect with food, motor vehicle, coal and petroleum and aircraft and aerospace technologies more in the home country (and sometimes abroad) than most other national groups of firm do. This is particularly obvious in the historically strong food industry (which remains in the US a strong industry and even stronger technological sector, 1.16 and 1.33 in Tables 2.1 and 2.2 respectively). Food technologies absorb a large amount of research sited in the US in all three main industrial groups' domestic activity (the RTA is 1.60, 1.50 and 1.13 in Tables 2.3a, 2.4a and 2.5a respectively) and attracts strong inward research from the broad metal and mechanical group of firms, with an RTA of 1.85 in Table 2.5c. The strong historical ties of US-owned firms in other industries with those of the motor vehicle industry, rather than its present day strength, and its technological links (mostly though with metal and mechanical technologies but not chemical and pharmaceutical) also seem to play an important role. There is relatively more technological activity directed towards motor vehicles than in developing primary technologies in both the chemical and pharmaceutical and metal and mechanical groups (see Tables 2.1, 2.2, 2.3a and 2.5a).

Although German-owned chemical and pharmaceutical firms are very focused in their domestic research agenda both the other broad groups invest in non-primary technologies such as petrochemicals (in both Tables 2.4 and 2.5), aircraft, metals and chemicals (the electrical and ICT group, Table 4) relatively more than in their primary fields of activity. These technological links may be associated with the historical strength of German industry in organic chemistry, which has hence connected with so many other lines of complementary research, and the presence of the Lufthansa airline (although there is not a significant independent presence in either Tables 2.1 or 2.2), and the leading position in the metal industry (Tables 2.1 and 2.2).

Dutch-owned firms dedicate more of their domestic research to the development of mechanical, petrochemical and motor vehicle technologies in the chemical and pharmaceutical group in which the country does not have any apparent strength – in either industry or technology – and so has a greater tendency to diversify away from the primary technologies of the group. In the electrical and ICT group as well relatively more research is done in pharmaceuticals than in the strong primary electrical field (few national firms research in this technology and small numbers may be a problem here). Moreover, internationally Dutch firms from the chemical and pharmaceutical group have a high RTA in aircraft, and a significant interest in food technologies among the metal and mechanical group of firms. Although it is not clear, the strength of these industries in the neighbouring UK and investment by foreign-owned car and component part companies (see Table 2.4c in which Dutch-owned firms are the only national group with high inward investment in the field, RTA = 4.24) may have a role to play in these odd deviations from the norm. Especially so since the figures of a small country such as the Netherlands may be highly influenced by a few multinationals (eg. the joint UK–Dutch Shell and Unilever).

The Swiss corporate technology profile resembles in many respects that of Germany. Both countries have a strong presence in chemicals and pharmaceuticals and are very concentrated in their domestic, as well as their foreign, specialisation in the primary technologies in this group, in which both are leaders. Moreover, Swiss-owned firms have a stronger technological advantage in the metal, mechanical and motor vehicle fields than in the primary electrical and ICT technologies (in Table 2.4) and more in pharmaceutical and chemical technologies in Table 2.5 than metal and mechanical technologies. These non-primary technologies correspond to the advantages of leading Swiss and German industries, another indication of the strong connection of Swiss industries to those of neighbouring Germany.

The UK seems to have one foot in Europe and the other in the US. The UK has a close connection with both continents, having had long historical inter-action with both the US and continental Europe. The wide range of industries and technologies in which UK-owned firms have a strong relative compara-tive advantage compares only to that of the US (six industries and eight technological fields in comparison to the seven US industries and an equal number of technological fields with RTA above unity, in Tables 2.1 and 2.2). However, the UK lacks the size the US has and trying to maintain this wide range of technological capabilities may well have been one of the reasons UK firms require such an internationalised effort and why the UK as a country has become a fertile ground for foreign-owned multinationals. UK-owned firms also diversify mostly at home but also in foreign locations into the primary technologies of other nationally strong industries. Both the electrical and ICT, and metal and mechanical groups of firms diversify in their domestic UK research into aircraft technologies to a relatively greater extent than they retain their interest in their primary fields (4.23 and 1.60 in Tables 2.4a and 2.5a respectively) while UK-owned firms in their operations abroad are also drawn into the aircraft field in the case of the chemical and pharmaceutical and metal and mechanical groups of companies (2.15 and 1.52 in Tables 2.3b and 2.5b respectively). In addition, the chemical and pharmaceutical group in the home country has a high RTA in motor vehicles and petrochemical technologies (3.70 and 1.72 in Table 2.3a). The UK coal and petroleum industry is by far the strongest (comparing RTA values in this industry across countries), as is the UK also in petrochemical technologies (Tables 2.1 and 2.2). However, the UK motor vehicle industry (RTA = 1.24) is far less competitive in comparison to the leaders in the industry and its strength lies in component parts firms. Lastly, the UK has the strongest food, drink and tobacco industry and both chemical and pharmaceutical, and metal and mechanical groups of firms tap into the resources of foreign locations in these fields (Tables 2.3b and 2.5b).

The French chemical and pharmaceutical group of firms invests domesti-cally in metals in which France is strong but not the leader (as well as in the mechanical field) and the electrical and ICT group develops aircraft technolo-gies (in which industry France is the leader). Furthermore, the mechanical group of firms has a high RTA abroad in petrochemical technologies (possibly to support activities related to mining and extraction in foreign locations) as the coal and petroleum industry is the most competitive in France during the period 1969–95 (far behind the UK national industrial group but ahead of the US).

Diversified technological activity closely related with the industries of domestic strength is also apparent among Swedish-owned firms. All groups have high comparative advantage in metal and mechanical technologies at home as well as in foreign locations (although less so the metal and mechanical group itself). Swedish-owned electrical and electronic firms devote effort to developing motor vehicle technologies as also do – quite intensively – the foreign-located chemical and pharmaceutical firms. Sweden also has a lot of research in instrument technologies from the chemical and pharmaceutical group of firms both at home and abroad (as well as a lot of inward investment, see Tables 2.3a–c). Finally, the development of food technologies interests all domestically owned firms equally, as well as the metal and mechanical companies abroad, although Sweden is not strong in the food industry or technological field.

The corporate technological diversification of Japanese-owned firms seems to be in close relation with the technologically stronger industries of the country, and the complementary technologies most needed by each industry. Japan seems to have the most coherent network of technologies among all the countries in the sample. Interestingly, although Japan is often rightly described as being little internationalised, some of the technologies developed by Japanese-owned firms in the particular industries examined here are quite highly internationalised. In particular, all three industrial groups have a strong diversification in ICT technologies both at home and abroad, while the electrical and ICT group also has at home and abroad a lot of research in motor vehicle technologies, as does the metal and mechanical group abroad.

SOME CONCLUSIONS

To recap on our discussion, we have reviewed the determinants of the internationalisation of corporate technological development in the largest firms. We have noted that where firms are part of a national innovation system that is characterised by a tight coupling of different industries (as applies especially in the Japanese system), the degree of internationalisation of corporate innovative effort is constrained. Otherwise, the technologically leading national groups in a given industry tend to be more internationalised, and typically their foreign-located development tends to promote their own corporate technological diversification. In relative terms their research abroad is more focused on the generation of complementary fields which support the greater continued concentration of efforts to develop the primary technologies of the relevant industry in the home base.

However, we have found three conditions under which leading groups do not use their foreign research efforts mainly to promote corporate technological diversification, but use foreign facilities at least as much to extend the geographical span of their innovation in the primary fields of their own industry (a strategy for deepening as much as widening their core technological base). This may apply first to the strong firms of small countries whose home base is inadequate for their core activities if they are to remain a major international player in their industry; second in an industry whose own primary technology is a general purpose technology (such as ICT or machinery), in which development is generally more internationalised to take advantage of inter-industry knowledge spillovers in the leading all-round centres of excellence for the technology in question (which attracts the firms of a wide range of industries to conduct their development work in this sphere of technology); third when the development of the primary technology of an industry itself requires some new inter-industry connections that may be lacking at home due to the absence of suitable capable firms in the new 'partner' industry. This last case calls our attention to the need to examine the strengths of firms in related industries when considering the determinants of the internationalisation of corporate research, and its capacity to facilitate inter-company knowledge spillovers. Strong industries tend to diversify and to connect in their home country with the primary technologies of other major national industries, often at the expense of a strong focus upon their own primary technologies. It seems that the amalgamation of technological competences at a national level has for some countries (like Japan) had a particularly strong influence upon the (lack of) diversification of research activity.

Historical path-dependency is also an important factor in an industry's technological structure that may give rise to national specificities. In other words, the connecting factor among industries within a country is often not the general relatedness of the primary technology of one industry to the core fields of another industry (which would apply everywhere), but rather the past and present development of some technology they happen to have held in common in a particular location. Another interesting finding is that the industry that tends to create the most links with technologies primary to other industries, in both the home and host country, is the longer established and stronger industry.

The data are obviously better suited to explain the pattern of internationalisation of development in the largest firms of the most highly industrialised countries with significant activity by multinationals, in which these large multinationals are responsible for a significant part of the country's economic activity. However, since only the very largest firms are included the results are bound to ignore significant technological ties that are the outcome of smaller-scale activities. Hence, the overall significance of the results depends on the degree to which multinational technological activity is representative of the overall technological activity in each country. More research should thus be conducted to determine the nature and importance of technological activity performed by small- and medium-sized firms, especially in their innovative interaction with the development efforts of larger companies.

NOTES

1. The data on the evolution of the technological structure of the pharmaceutical industry measured by the share of patenting show the very important increase of the primary pharmaceutical technologies that have become the most important technology of the industry, a position that until recently was held by chemical technologies.
2. '... nearly all the innovations in any one industry – not just electricity – had a significant impact on many other industries' (Chandler, 1990, p. 63). To the same end he also quotes Rosenberg (1979, p. 28), 'The growth in productivity of industrial economies is the complex outcome of large numbers of interlocking, mutually reinforcing technologies, the individual components of which are of a very limited economic consequence by themselves'. An example of this point is: 'In the refining of sugar and vegetable oil, where the process of production was similar to that of petroleum (in fact, several of the innovations in petroleum refining were borrowed from the sugar industry), modern production methods were adopted by a number of enterprises almost simultaneously' (Chandler, 1990, p. 149).
3. This does not mean, however, that the share of non-primary technologies – which is not examined here – is necessarily higher than that of the primary technologies.

REFERENCES

Breshahan, T.F. and M. Trajtenberg (1995), 'General Purpose Technologies: "Engines of Growth?"', *Journal of Economics*, 65, pp. 83–108.

Cantwell, J.A. (1989), *Technological Innovation and Multinational Corporations*, Oxford: Basil Blackwell.

Cantwell, J.A. (1993), 'Corporate Technological Specialisation in International Industries', in M.C. Casson and J. Creedy (eds), *Industrial Concentration and Economic Inequality*, Aldershot and Brookfield: Edward Elgar.

Cantwell, J.A. (1995), 'What Remains of the Product Cycle Model? The Globalisation of Corporate Technological Activity', *Cambridge Journal of Economics*, 19 (1), pp. 155–74.

Cantwell, J.A. (2000), 'Technological Lock-In of Large Firms Since the Interwar Period', *European Review of Economic History*, 4 (2), pp. 147–74.

Cantwell, J.A. and C. Hodson (1991), 'Global R&D and UK Competitiveness', in M.C. Casson (ed.), *Global Research Strategy and International Competitiveness*, Oxford: Basil Blackwell.

Cantwell, J.A. and E. Kosmopoulou (2002), 'What Determines the Internationalisation of Corporate Technology?', in V. Havila, M. Forsgren and H. Håkanson (eds), *Critical Perspectives on Internationalisation*, Oxford: Pergamon.

Cantwell, J.A. and L. Piscitello (2000), 'Accumulating Technological Competence – Its Changing Impact on Corporate Diversification and Internationalisation', *Industrial and Corporate Change*, 9 (1), pp. 21–51.

Chandler, A.D. (1990), *Scale and Scope: The Dynamics of Industrial Capitalism*, Cambridge, Mass.: Harvard University Press.

Granstrand, O., P. Patel and K.L.R. Pavitt (1997), 'Multi-Technology Corporations: Why They Have "Distributed" Rather Than "Distinctive Core" Competencies', *California Management Review*, 39, pp. 8–25.

Lee, Kong-Rae (1998), *The Sources of Capital Goods Innovation: The Role of User Firms in Japan and Korea*, Chur: Hardwood Academic Publishers.

Lundvall, B.-Å. (1985), *Product Innovation and User–Producer Interaction*, Aalborg: Aalborg University Press.

Lundvall, B.-Å. (1988), 'Innovation as an Interactive Process: From User–Producer Interaction to the National System of Innovation', in G. Dosi, C. Freeman, R. Nelson, G. Silverberg and L.L.G. Soete (eds), *Technical Change and Economic Theory*, London: Frances Pinter.

Nightingale, P. (2000), 'Economies of Scale in Experimentation: Knowledge and Technology in Pharmaceutical R&D', *Industrial and Corporate Change*, 9 (2), pp. 315–59.

Patel, P. and K.L.R. Pavitt (2000), 'National Systems of Innovation Under Strain: The Internationalisation of Corporate R&D', in R. Barrel, G. Mason and M. Mahoney (eds), *Productivity, Innovation and Economic Performance*, Cambridge and New York: Cambridge University Press.

Patel, P. and M. Vega (1999), 'Patterns of Internationalisation of Corporate Technology: Location vs. Home Country Advantages', *Research Policy*, 28 (2–3), pp. 145–55.

Pavitt, K., M. Robson and J. Townsend (1989), 'Technological Accumulation, Diversification and Organisation in UK Companies, 1945–1983', *Management Science*, 35 (1), pp. 81–99.

Rosenberg, N. (1979), 'Technological Interdependence in the American Economy', *Technology and Culture*, 20, pp. 25–50.

Scher, M.J. (1997), *Japanese Interfirm Networks and their Main Banks*, London: Macmillan.

3. Linking corporate-wide global R&D activities

Guido Reger

INTRODUCTION

Since the complexity of new technologies and products is increasing, the specialisation in the production of knowledge is growing as well. Thus, a central feature of the innovating firm is one of coordination. One of the most robust conclusions from empirical research on the factors affecting innovation success is the importance of coordinating learning and other change-related activities across organisational boundaries within firms (see Pavitt 1998, 443, and the cited literature there). This statement is especially true for large, multinational enterprises (MNEs) and their research and development (R&D) activities which build the centre for the internal technological knowledge production. R&D in multinational enterprises is highly differentiated and, broadly speaking, three main levels of R&D can be distinguished here: (1) research at the level of the corporation with a long- and medium-term orientation, conducted in corporate research laboratories, (2) short-term developments conducted in development laboratories, technology centres or development departments of divisions or subsidiaries and (3) foreign R&D units entrusted with various tasks.

This high division of labour puts the question of coordination and appropriate coordination mechanisms on the agenda: the main challenge for a large innovating firm is to improve coordination across organisational boundaries for a successful matching between the generation of technological knowledge and commercially successful applications or products. However, practical and theoretical knowledge of the organisational processes of coordination are still less well grounded than knowledge of the processes of technological advantages *per se* (see Pavitt 1998, 447).

Coordination plays a large part in most approaches to organisational theory as a complement to differentiation (see for instance Bleicher 1979 and 1991, Grochla 1982, Hill et al. 1989, Hoffmann 1980, Kieser and Kubicek 1992, Lawrence and Lorsch 1969, Pugh et al. 1968). Essentially, the two fundamental and contrasting aspects of the differentiation of work into various tasks, and the coordination of these tasks, can be regarded as the framework for mission fulfilment in any organised human activity. Accordingly, the structure of an organisation can be defined in simple terms as an integrated whole consisting of the totality of specialised tasks and their coordination.

Coordination of the R&D activities of internationally active enterprises is here understood to include, in a broad sense, not only relatively 'loose' (or informal) linkages but also integration and control activities. Further, in this chapter, the coordination across functions as well as across different countries is regarded as of central importance. Hereby, specific difficulties associated with culture-specific particularities or divergent socialisation can arise in the coordination of research and development. These problems may loom so large that an insufficient ability to coordinate leads to a limitation or re-centralisation of the internationalisation of R&D. However, the capability of coordinating international innovation processes may also hold a decisive competitive advantage: not only the parent company, but also the foreign subsidiary, is able to produce and exploit technological and market knowledge. In this respect, the coordination capability is the 'heart' of a global learning process.

This chapter aims to develop possible mechanisms for the coordination of corporate-wide, global R&D activities in internationally active enterprises and a conceptual framework for the use of suitable coordination mechanisms. A case study on the Dutch electronics company Philips illustrates the conceptual part. Conclusions are discussed in the final section.

From a methodological point of view this chapter is based on a broad literature analysis and interviews with Philips managers at different positions and locations between the middle and end of the 1990s.

COORDINATION MECHANISMS: THE 'GLUE' IN AN ORGANISATION

Coordination mechanisms are the (administrative) regulations used to coordinate work-related processes and orient individual activities towards the aims of the organisation. These '... can be regarded as the fundamental structural elements, as the glue that keeps the organisation together' (Mintzberg 1991, 113). Coordination mechanisms are used in the implementation of strategies that have already been formulated. In the literature (see, for instance, Kieser and Kubicek 1992, 95, Martinez and Jarillo 1989 and 1991) the term coordination instruments is used as a synonym for coordination mechanisms; this equivalence of terms is also adopted here.

The uncertain, unstructured and complex nature of research and development tasks, compounded by the increasing difficulties of coordination due to the internationalisation of R&D, would seem to imply the necessity for a particular set of instruments in the coordination of the R&D activities. Empirical studies dealing specifically with this aspect include, for instance, the studies by Bartlett and Ghoshal (1989, 1990), Casson and Singh (1993), Kenney and Florida (1994), Ghoshal and Nohria (1993), De Meyer and Mizushima (1989), De Meyer (1992), and Westney (1993, 1994). In these, however, the coordination mechanisms are not explicitly systematised and in most cases only a small selection of possible instruments are described or analysed. Bartlett, Ghoshal and Nohria, for instance, investigate only the three mechanisms centralisation, formalisation and socialisation in the coordination of global innovation processes.

By contrast, an analysis of the literature reveals a wide variety of coordination instruments that are also suitable for application in the coordination of globally distributed innovation activities (see Reger 1999, 16). Based on this literature, coordination mechanisms can be structured in four categories: (1) structural/formal, (2) informal, (3) hybrid and (4) internal markets/prices.

Structural/Formal and Informal Mechanisms

Following the studies by Barnard (1968), Martinez and Jarillo (1989) and Kieser and Kubicek (1992) the present study undertakes a systematisation into two categories: structural and formal mechanisms and informal mechanisms (Figure 3.1). Basically, this systematisation groups together structural and technocratic mechanisms, according to the definitions of Khandwalla (1972), Hoffmann (1984) and Macharzina (1993), under the rubric of structural and formal mechanisms. These include centralisation and decentralisation of the decision-making process, the structural coordination organs, programming and standardisation, planning and the control of results and behaviour. Person-oriented mechanisms, together with socialisation (in the sense of the formation of a cross-company culture transcending its component entities) forms the category of informal mechanisms. The separation into these two categories corresponds to the concept of a firm as consisting both of its formal organisation structure and of the organisation culture and informal strata underpinning this structure. This takes into account studies which attribute great significance to the formation of a company culture and to informal aspects in coordination, integration and control (see Martinez and Jarillo 1989 and 1991, Peters Waterman 1982, Perich 1993). The possibilities of the direct, plannable use of socialisation or culture as a control instrument are the subject of controversial discussion in the theory of organisation (see Perich 1993, 184, and the literature mentioned here). Socialisation and culture, unlike the structural and formal instruments of coordination, are not mechanisms with which coordination or its effects can be precisely planned or controlled (see Dierkes 1992, 20).

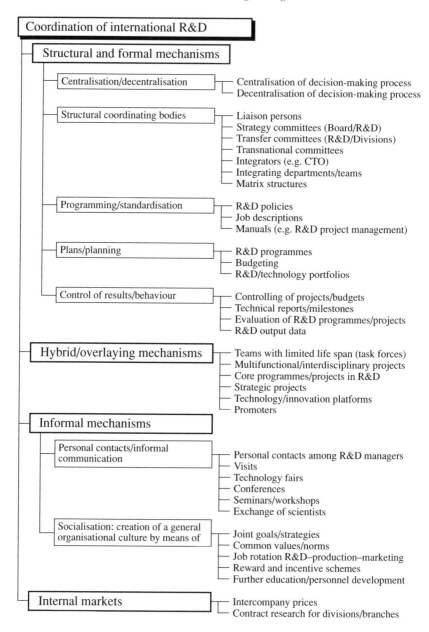

Source: Adapted from Reger (1999, 17).

Figure 3.1   Four categories of R&D coordination mechanisms

Hybrid Coordination Mechanisms

Hybrid coordination mechanisms constitute the third category. These include some elements of structured self-coordination and trans-departmental relations (Figure 3.1). These elements cannot be unequivocally classified as structural or informal mechanisms because many of the instruments are either not, or only to some extent, a part of the organisational structure. Hybrid mechanisms include task forces, interdisciplinary or multifunctional project groups, cross-company strategic projects, core programmes and core projects, technology platforms, and promoters. One characteristic of promoters, for example, is that they do not have formal executive powers but their influence is person-dependent or personality-dependent. The novel aspect of these coordination instruments is that they run crosswise to the formal organisational structure and overlay the hierarchy. The main hierarchical structure of the enterprise remains largely untouched. A study in 21 multinationals indicates that these hybrid mechanisms are becoming increasingly significant for the coordination of R&D (see Reger 1997 and 1999).

Internal Markets/Inter-Company Prices

Only a few of the studies address the issue of internal quasi-markets and internal prices (see Ouchi 1979, Kenter 1985, Welge 1989, Kieser and Kubicek 1992). Markets theoretically coordinate supply and demand, without the players necessarily having to pursue the same, or similar, goals (see Ouchi 1979, 834). Especially in multinational enterprises, with their independent divisions and subsidiaries, coordination of the exchange of services can take place via internal markets. Instead of planning and programming, more or less free negotiations can take place between potential supply and demand groups within the organisation, who coordinate their services via internal discounts or internally fixed prices. However, a prerequisite for the functioning of this internal market is the existence of profit centres – organisational units responsible for their own profits – since it is the profit-price relationship that determines the individual decisions. Consequently, this coordination instrument is based on the following three components (see Kieser and Kubicek 1992, 118): (1) the organisational units are responsible for their own profits, (2) they have autonomy of decision regarding clients and suppliers (3) there are internal inter-company prices. However, our study about the 21 multinationals showed that the R&D units are run as cost or performance centres and not as profit centres (see Reger 1997). Experimentation is going on with new forms of financing in R&D, aiming at the formation of internal quasi-markets. For this reason, a fourth category of internal markets and inter-company prices was formed (Figure 3.1).

A FRAMEWORK FOR THE USE OF COORDINATION MECHANISMS

The question arises whether there exists a framework to assess the use of suitable coordination mechanisms. Behind this lies the question of which factors influence the application of coordination mechanisms. Intensive empirical research in the 1970s and 1980s shows that coordination mechanisms are very much influenced by the technological and market context in which the firm is operating, the (corporate, business, internationalisation) strategies and the organisational structure of the company (see Pugh and Hinings 1976, Hoffmann 1980 and 1984 and the morphological box based on the literature overview in Reger 1997, 130). In this respect, the use of coordination mechanisms is at the end of management decisions on strategies and organisational issues. Other empirical research shows that the use of coordination mechanisms is influenced by various work- or task-related factors like the degree of uncertainty and novelty, the coordination task or the interdependencies between organisational units (see Thompson 1967, Egelhoff 1988, Galbraith 1970 and 1973, Nadler and Tushman 1988).

It may be concluded from both strands of literature that – in order to develop a framework for the use of coordination mechanisms – at least two different levels have to be distinguished: firstly, the normative/strategic level (which reflects the context of the company's environment) and, secondly, the operational level (which reflects the work- and task-related context). Regarding the normative/strategic level, the literature suggests the following core factors which influence the use of mechanisms to coordinate R&D in multinationals (see Baliga and Jaeger 1984, Bartlett and Ghoshal 1989 and 1990, Brockhoff 1998, Gerybadze and Reger 1999, Reger 1999, Westney 1993):

- the organisational element of process and structure (process orientation versus formal, structural orientation),
- the locus of decision-making (centralised versus decentralised),
- the location of competencies which is strongly related with the degree of the internationalisation of R&D (home-based versus foreign-based competencies),
- cultural differences between nations or regions (low versus high cultural differences).

Figure 3.2 presents the four mentioned influencing factors at the normative/strategic level and the four types of coordination mechanisms. First, formal mechanisms and internal markets are more related to the structural elements of the organisation and hybrid and informal mechanisms are more suitable to coordinate processes within the organisation.

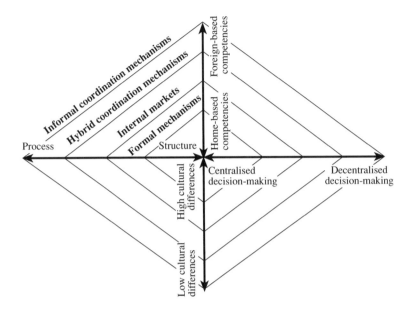

Source: Adapted from Reger (1999, 28).

Figure 3.2   Coordination mechanisms at the normative/strategic level

Second, the locus of decision-making describes whether decisions are made close to the corporate headquarters in the home country or close to the R&D laboratory abroad. In the first case (centralised decision-making), strong linkages need formal coordination mechanisms and in the second case (decentralised decision-making), more hybrid and informal mechanisms are appropriate.

Third, the location of competencies influences the use of coordination mechanisms. An R&D lab has strong competencies if it disposes of outstanding technological knowledge and researchers, the responsibility ('ownership') for a specific technology or product segment within the corporation, its own management and financial resources, and a strong influence on the overall organisation. The degree of the internationalisation of R&D is related to the extent to which competencies are based in the home country or globally dispersed. Empirical results show that companies with strong home-based competencies tie up their foreign R&D units with the help of formal mechanisms. However, strong and 'competent' R&D laboratories can not be linked together only through formal mechanisms – moreover, examples from Japanese companies point out that this will lead to inevitable conflicts (see Reger 1997). In contrast, hybrid and informal mechanisms are needed to link the different competencies at different locations if necessary.

Fourth, cultural differences between nations or regions require the use of different coordination mechanisms. Examples from Japanese companies indicate that the greater the distances between cultures, the less hybrid or informal coordination mechanisms are appropriate (see Reger 1997). This is due to the fact that informal mechanisms are based on joint norms, values and behaviour, and are not useful for coordination if these issues are lacking. In fact, this means that R&D units with different cultural 'distances' require the use of different coordination mechanisms.

Regarding the operational level, the application of mechanisms for coordinating R&D may be influenced through the following factors (see Brockhoff 1998, Galbraith 1970, Hedlund and Nonaka 1993, Nadler and Tushman 1988, Nonaka and Takeuchi 1995, Reger 1999, Thompson 1967):

- the possibilities of structuring tasks (highly unstructured versus highly structured),
- the degree of the uncertainty of the task and the novelty of the innovation (high novelty/uncertainty versus low novelty/uncertainty),
- the type of interaction between organisational units (reciprocal versus pooled),
- the codification of knowledge (codified/explicit versus uncodified/implicit).

The relationship between these four influencing factors and the use of coordination mechanisms at the operational level is portrayed in Figure 3.3. If the possibility of structuring a task is high, the degree of the uncertainty and the novelty of the innovation is low (incremental innovation), the resources are pooled, and the necessary knowledge is highly codified (explicit knowledge) the involved organisational units or persons can be linked together through formal mechanisms or internal markets. In contrast, if the possibility of structuring a task is low, the degree of the uncertainty and the novelty of the innovation is high (radical innovation), the resources are reciprocal, and the knowledge to be transferred is highly uncodified (implicit knowledge) the involved organisational units or persons can be coordinated through hybrid and informal mechanisms.

Summing up, the framework presented here is based on the assumption that different factors on the normative/strategic and the operational level have an effect on the use of suitable coordination mechanisms. This framework may serve as a starting-point to build bridges across organisational, disciplinary or cultural boundaries within large multinationals.

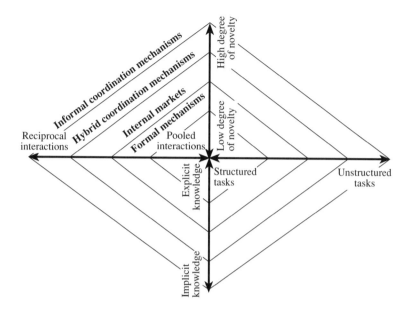

Source: Adapted from Reger (1999, 29).

Figure 3.3   Coordination mechanisms at the operational level

CASE STUDY ON PHILIPS ELECTRONICS

This case study is based on interviews with Philips R&D managers at different hierarchical levels and locations in the mid 1990s and follow-up interviews at the end of the 1990s. An interview guideline was developed and used for interviews in 21 multinationals in total, of which four detailed case studies were developed (see Reger 1997).

Philips Electronics of the Netherlands is one of the world's biggest electronics companies, with sales of EUR 32.3 billion in 2001. It is a global leader in colour television sets, lighting, electric shavers, medical diagnostic imaging and patient monitoring, and one-chip TV products. Its 184,000 employees in more than 60 countries are active in the six divisions of lighting, consumer electronics, domestic appliances, components, semiconductors, and medical systems. Philips is one of the 'global players', with less than half of its turnover made in Europe.

Since the beginning of the 1980s, Philips has undergone a fundamental structural change which has also had substantial impacts on research and development. Above all, the issue of innovative capability caused the corporation considerable problems, basically consisting of the following points:

- deficits in innovative strength compared to Japanese competitors,
- inadequate transfer of the research results of the autonomously acting central research labs into marketable products,
- duplication of activities and fragmentation of dispersed research laboratories,
- deficits in cooperation with the scientific community and the R&D of other firms,
- insufficient international orientation of the R&D management,
- excessively strong orientation towards technologies for their own sake ('choice of technologies') rather than applications ('choice of applications').

All in all, statements in our interviews predominated to the effect that Philips had paid dearly for learning from its negative experience of too much research autonomy and double work in globally dispersed research labs. For instance, Japanese competitors were quicker to the market with the video disc and video recorders – although Philips was in a technological lead position. These difficulties have led to a far-reaching re-orientation of R&D management, starting in the early 1990s.

Global Structure of R&D

In 2001, EUR 3.31 billion were spent on R&D, which is 10.2 per cent of sales (7.3 per cent in 2000). The increase in R&D intensity is due to the decrease of sales in 2001 and not to a high increase in R&D expenditure. Approximately 80 per cent of Philip's R&D budget is spent in Europe and around 50 per cent of R&D activities are performed in the Netherlands. Altogether, there are around 23,000 employees in R&D.

Founded in Eindhoven, the Netherlands in 1914, Philips now has one of the world's major private corporate research organisations (Philips Research – PR) with laboratories in the Netherlands, Belgium, England, France, Germany, the United States, East Asia and India. Two new Chinese labs (Shanghai and Xi'an) and an existing one in Taipei have formed one new Philips Research organisation, named Philips Research East Asia (PERA), effective from April 2000. The activities of PR became more global in recent years: whereas in the mid 1990s research labs existed in five countries (the Netherlands, England, France,

Germany and the US), the labs in East Asia and India established at the beginning of 2000 are a step forward to a stronger globalisation.

The number of employees in Philips Research shrank from 4,500 at the end of the 1980s to about 2,900 in 1994 and 2,500 in 2001. The annual research budget of Philips Research is slightly less than 1 per cent of Philips Electronics' annual sales. Roughly two-thirds of the corporate research work is geared to the activities of the Product Divisions of Philips Electronics, with contractual agreements about programmes and costs. The remainder is research of a more exploratory nature.

Research is performed worldwide by Philips in the laboratories of central research, as well as in the development laboratories, technology centres and product development departments of divisions and their subsidiaries (Figure 3.4). About 10 per cent of R&D activities take place in central research, and about 90 per cent in development in the divisions and their business groups (BGs). In the Philips corporation the central R&D is described, by definition, as research, although basic research constitutes the minor part of it and experimental development is also performed.

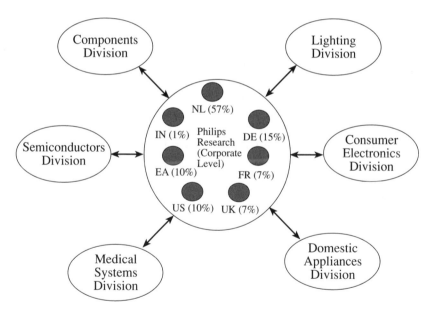

Figure 3.4   Structure of corporate-wide R&D in Philips

The broad business field of the corporation, oriented towards consumer goods, is based on a few core technologies. This situation favours the creation of technological synergies by central research, giving Philips Research great qualitative importance. The Philips laboratories see themselves as a strong, interdisciplinary, international industrial research organisation. They primarily conduct long-term preliminary research with a time horizon of 5–10 years. At present research and experimental development are being performed in the research labs in seven regions/countries (Figure 3.4). The technical and scientific competencies of the cross-corporate research are globally distributed between the research labs, which work mainly according to the principle of local-for-global, global-for-global and local-for-local in the sense of Ghoshal and Bartlett (1988). The range of topics depends on the size of the research laboratory concerned. Of the 2,500 employees, approximately two-thirds work as scientists, and are regionally distributed as follows (estimated):

- Netherlands (NL), Eindhoven: 57 per cent,
- Great Britain (GB), Redhill: 7 per cent,
- France (FR), Limeil-Brévannes: 7 per cent,
- Germany (DE), Aachen and Hamburg: 15 per cent,
- United States of America (US), Briarcliff and Palo Alto: 10 per cent,
- East Asia (EA), Shanghai, Xi'an, Taipei: 3 per cent,
- India (IN), Bangalore: 1 per cent.

Reasons for Internationalizing R&D

In Philips, internationalisation of R&D has been taking place since the 1950s; one important reason for this is necessarily that increasingly production and system developments have to be adapted to specific national or regional customer requirements and technical standards. However, this mainly affects the technology development of the divisions/business groups and not so much central research. Another important reason for the internationalisation of R&D is the limited availability of researchers and the limited size of the market in the Netherlands, making production abroad – and support by technology development – necessary early on.

One example of this internationalisation pattern due to domestic limitations is the setting up of the research laboratory in Aachen. At the beginning of the 1950s the electrical industry was booming and there were not sufficient researchers and engineers available in the Netherlands to cope with this upward swing. Philips looked for a suitable research location abroad. Since Aachen was only half an hour away from Eindhoven by car, and had an excellent technical university, the Rheinisch-Westfälische Technische Hochschule (RWTH), a laboratory of Philips Research was set up in Aachen in 1955. Three years later, a further German laboratory was established in Hamburg in order to support a subsidiary there.

The proximity to leading scientists and research establishments has played an important role in setting up the central research laboratories. Due to the frequent real coincidences of 'excellence in science' and 'lead markets' (as with microelectronics in Silicon Valley, California), market aspects were also indirect determinants of the choice of locations. Decisions on new locations are made by the board in agreement with the management of Philips Research.

Since the beginning of the 1990s, the distribution of topics among the research laboratories has been decided only on grounds of competence. Accordingly, international core competencies have crystallised out. The central criteria for assigning research topics to the globally distributed research laboratories are technical disciplines and responsibility for systems. How the distribution of competencies steers R&D projects can be illustrated through two examples. One case is the ultrasound group, for which the business responsibility lies in the USA. Since the research competence was in the French Philips laboratory, a contract research project was assigned there. The engineers of the American group participating in the project travelled several times a year to Limeil-Brévannes. An example of transferring the site for a research topic is shown by the case of fuzzy logic. According to the disciplinary responsibility for new basic software technologies, the Natuurkundig Laboratorium in Eindhoven was responsible, until finally the application and system relation to radio technology became the dominant factor and as a result the responsibility for fuzzy logic was shifted to the French laboratory with the competencies there.

Coordination of Philips Research with Divisions and Business Groups

The development of the R&D management of Philips Research with regard to the coordination of central research with the divisions and business groups can be described as taking place in three stages (Table 3.1). Until the end of the 1960s the R&D programmes were informally generated in negotiations with the corporation's top management. The central research was financed completely by corporate funds and the main instrument of R&D management was estimating the value of the research results obtained. At this time of growth, research aimed at diversification. In the 1970s and 1980s, R&D activities were formally – and no longer informally – negotiated. Central research continued to be financed by corporate funds. Project organisation and project management were also adopted as management instruments. Central research activities aimed at the in-depth exploration and renewal of technologies.

The R&D management of the 1990s is characterised by a split into contract research for the divisions (70 per cent) and basic research (30 per cent) (Table 3.1). The R&D programme in contract research is negotiated in a formalised procedure and the decision is made by the Management Committee. The product divisions (PDs) and business groups give contracts to the Philips Laboratories.

Table 3.1   Development of R&D management of Philips Research

	Generating R&D programmes	Financing central research	R&D management characteristics	Aims
To end of 1960s	Informal negotiation, advice	Financed from corporate funds	Appreciation, recognition	Diversification
1970s and 1980s	Formal negotiation, advice	Financed from corporate funds	Appreciation, recognition Projects	Intensification Renewal
Contract research From 1990s on Basic research	Formal decision of Management Committee Corporate research	Contracts financed by divisions/ groups (70%) Financed from corporate funds (30%)	Contract projects Portfolio Appreciation, recognition	Return on investment New business fields Synergies

Philips Research itself takes decisions on the basic research, which is financed from corporation funding. As well as recognition of research achievements and project organisation, this new generation of management is characterised by the generating of cross-corporation technology portfolios. Its aims are new fields of business, the creation of synergies and a measurable return on investment. The main change in the 1990s is definitely the installation of contract research. Critics of this system, however, see a danger that the strong emphasis on contract research might cause the orientation of cross-corporation research to become too short-term. The transition to a new generation of management is not yet complete. Philips' R&D management was characterised by several interviewees as still being very informal. They felt that although this was an advantage if there were good personal contacts, it could become a drawback if they were lacking.

The central element of motivation was, and is, the appreciation and recognition of researchers' achievements in finding particularly impressive techno-scientific solutions. According to one interviewee, this is also the case in many multinational enterprises in Western Europe, whereas in the USA it is mainly success in business terms that receives special recognition, and in Japan, particularly good planning and/or preparation. In the Philips corporation, the problems of orientation towards scientific success set the re-thinking process in motion.

Motivation in Philips Research is today provided by interesting topics and recognition from the contract clients. Competition for recognition and for the funding of the PD/BG is indirectly stimulating.

The core of Philips' strategic management of R&D is 'capability management', which has been used in Philips since the beginning of the 1990s, with the following aims:

- developing a long-term research strategy,
- building up and supporting qualifications and future competencies,
- employing new researchers,
- allocating funds according to strategic viewpoints and priority-setting in research topics,
- building up international centres of excellence,
- determining the future product policy, as a function of the research capabilities required.

'Capability management' is an important instrument for the identification of R&D strategies and the necessary capabilities, as well as for coordinating the R&D strategy of Philips Research with the product strategy of the PDs and BGs. It is active both at the strategic and operative levels. Using capability management, projects are strategically selected and steered. The various individual instruments ('tools') and their aims are shown in Table 3.2. Consistent use of the tools is intended to prevent the occurrence of isolated projects and projects that are personal favourites. Before the start of the project, the goals are established and the competencies necessary for carrying out the project are determined. This reinforces the close association of projects with divisions and business groups aimed at by the introduction of contract research. Coordination between Philips Research and the Board of Management is directly performed by the management of Philips Research without using a committee. All the activities in capability management are supported and controlled by the Corporate Research Bureau which is the planning office located as a staff function within Philips Research.

The position of a Chief Technology Officer (CTO) within a product division was created when Philips adopted the contract research model. The CTO is responsible for the technologies needed for product development and production of the product division and its business groups. His or her task is to support and give impulses for directions in technology that are not initiated by the business groups and to coordinate the necessary processes, for instance, with Philips Research (PR). He or she is the authorised signatory for assigning contract research projects that are given by the division to the central labs. The CTO's opposite number at PR is the Product Division Coordinator, who acts as the contact partner for one or two divisions. The Managing Director of the German Philips laboratories, for instance, is the PD Coordinator for the Lighting Division and the Communication Systems Division. Very large divisions have

Table 3.2   Aims and instruments of capability management

Tools	Aims	Responsible unit and level
Blue Books	Overview of existing capabilities of the research groups ('Capabilities Inventory')	Research group and its leader Operative level
Green Books	Listing R&D projects of the research groups ('Projects Capabilities')	Research group and its leader Operative level
Programme Matrix	Coordinating capabilities of PR with possible fields of application or products	Steering Committee Strategic level
Research Capability Profile	Coordinating capability profile of PR with capacity requirements of BGs	Steering Committee Strategic level
Research Project Portfolio	Comparing technological maturity and competitive position Coordinating R&D with strategies of PD/BG	Management Committee Strategic level
Road Maps	Overview over time of the basic technologies purely for products Coordinating R&D with long-term strategies of PD/ BG	Management Committee Strategic level
Microscopic Control (Daily)	Keeping to project milestones Professional R&D management	Project workers Project leader Operative level
Macroscopic Control (Annual)	Steering capabilities Setting-up, dissolving research groups Strategic planning, priority-setting and selection of topics	Management Committee Senior Managing Director Strategic level

several CTOs, each responsible for individual business groups such as Audio or Television.

Responsible for the technology throughout the whole corporation is one member of the Board of Management and the Group Management Committee. Contrary to the idea that predominates in the literature (see, for instance,

Rubenstein 1989, Adler and Ferdows 1990, Jonash 1995), the CTO at Philips is not installed at corporation level, but at the level of the product divisions. The purpose behind this arrangement is to ensure cross-group coordination of the technologies necessary for the business groups, while at the same time creating relatively close links between divisions, their business groups and Philips Research.

As well as coordination competence, the CTO also has autonomous decision competence. For this, more than 10 per cent of the division's R&D budget is generally at his or her disposal and can be used, for instance, to give contracts to PR on his or her own initiative. The CTO's main task is to act as an integrator between the division and Philips Research, and to represent the viewpoint of the division.

Another important coordination instrument is the transfer of researchers to the divisions and business groups. Researchers should work on average in Philips Research from the age of 25 to 35 approximately: then most of them should begin a career in development in the PD/BG. This technology transfer via personal knowledge is regarded as the main element in the transfer of knowledge from central research into the divisions and business groups. On average, researchers spend about five to seven years in Philips Research and then should move on to the PD and BG according to the personnel policy. It is particularly advantageous if a researcher moves together with his or her R&D project.

However, this essentially organic transfer of researchers in the context of contract research projects is not systematically supported by corresponding management instruments for personnel development. There is simply an informal agreement with the researcher to look for a job in the PD/BG after a maximum of ten years. This statement was reinforced by impressions gained in interviews with project and group leaders. It was regarded as a deficit that research careers were not explicitly planned or career perspectives described, but that only informal possibilities existed. Thus the most important element for the changeover to a PD/BG is direct personal contacts without them, transfer is virtually impossible. It is important to recognise that the inclusion of Philips Research in product strategies of the PD/ BG through programme matrices, portfolios and road maps, contract research and committees at different levels always has a global dimension in Philips.

Coordination of Global Centres of Excellence at Central Level

To combat the problems of fragmentation and duplication of activities in central research, Philips has adopted the strategies of forming centres of excellence and using several coordination mechanisms to link them together. The research laboratories in the five countries are integrated and coordinated via these mechanisms. Philips Research has come much closer to global coordination of the central laboratories. Nevertheless, the policy of forming centres of excellence, pursued since the beginning of the 1990s, has also been associated with a painful process of dwindling and fusion of locations (e.g. Hamburg with Aachen) and a decrease in the overall numbers of employees at Philips Research.

The distribution of projects between the globally scattered research laboratories now takes place according to the competencies of the laboratory concerned. The ideal concept being aimed for is concentration and focusing in one location, so that a clear assignment of R&D projects is possible. Since the project costs are reckoned as average values, real differences in costs between the research laboratories are not a criterion for distribution. Competition between the central labs is not encouraged and is regarded as impeding communication. The ideal is not always realised: for instance, materials technologies are broadly distributed between Aachen and Eindhoven.

In accordance with this concept of centres of excellence, R&D projects are conducted where the necessary capabilities are available and dispersed competencies are linked together. For example, the lab in Aachen, Germany, cooperates closely with the research lab in the USA, since Aachen possesses competencies in lighting technology and Briarcliff Manor has the relevant competencies in electronics. In the opinion of interviewees, the formation of centres of excellence has meant that, in tackling complex problems, coordination between the globally distributed Philips laboratories has become more important. In view of the growing complexity of products and technologies the concentration of specific capabilities in one laboratory and the avoidance of work duplication are leading to an increased need for coordination between the laboratories.

Within Philips Research, six Research Directors Conferences (RDCs) take place every year. The Managing Directors of the Philips laboratories and the Senior Managing Director attend. The purpose of the RDC is to coordinate the globally distributed central research labs at a strategic level. Here, decisions are made on strategic questions relating to project portfolios, success control, the initiation of new programmes and the further development of research capabilities. The Senior Managing Director has to give his final consent to decisions.

Other coordination instruments are big research conferences, which take place about twice a year, as well as personal and direct contacts among researchers.

Recently, technology platforms have come into existence at Philips, to cope with the tendency towards the fusion of various technologies and cross-corporation topics. At the time of our interviews in the mid 1990s the platforms 'storage' and 'multimedia' were already in existence. They cut across the departments of the research labs, which are mainly organised according to technical disciplines. Project proposals and applications can come from the research centres and the PD/BG worldwide. The participation is transnational and facilitates, besides the fusion of various technologies, the coordination among the central labs as well as of the central labs with the PD/BG. The platforms are headed by a Programme Director, whose position in the hierarchy is somewhere between that of department head and lab chief.

The example of the technology platform multimedia is taken here to illustrate the management. Since the beginning of the 1990s, enormous efforts have been put into orientating Philips Research towards the field of multimedia and digital TV. Although Philips' top management was aware that multimedia and the digitalisation of TV represented the decisive technologies of the future, there was no focal competence within the corporation in these technologies, and the question arose how Philips could position itself in this field.

Multimedia cuts across technical disciplines and cannot be clearly ascribed to any of them. Since the Philips Research sectors and groups are mainly organised according to technical disciplines, this transdisciplinary area could not find a focal location. Thus, the field of multimedia was established as a platform cutting across the technically oriented sectors and groups of the research laboratories, directly answerable to the Senior Managing Director and financed both by corporate funds and contract projects. The scientists continue to work in the sectors and participate in the multimedia programme in the form of projects. The new aspect of this coordination form is that, as a result of the multimedia programme, a corporate-wide research network has been formed, through which exchanges of information and communication take place successfully. This network definitely goes beyond the cooperation previously practised in Philips Research. Thus, for instance, a Multimedia Newsletter is brought out, with information on research activities throughout the corporation in this area.

Multimedia builds on existing technologies. It is therefore important to bring together already existing competencies in Philips throughout the world. There are very divergent country-specific views of multimedia: for instance, multimedia in the US centres on TV, and in Japan on the personal computer. Since the market in the US is very advanced, it is decisive for Philips to know more about the developments taking place there and possibly to transfer applications. In this context, the global R&D activities of Philips were named in the interviews as a definite advantage: 'If Philips only had a research laboratory in Eindhoven, it would now hypothetically speaking have to set up further laboratories worldwide, since market development in the interdisciplinary technologies like multimedia is very different from country to country.'

Discussion: Linking Dispersed R&D Activities in Philips

Until the 1980s, Philips' R&D management can be described as very informal. Thus the main starting points for change management were the installing of formal decision-making processes, customer orientation in research, steering a substantial proportion of research by inter-company prices and the integration of globally dispersed central laboratories. These changes are also clearly visible in a comparison of the various coordination mechanisms. The predominating informal mechanisms were, and still are, personal contacts and informal communication. To the well-developed informal coordination mechanisms of personal contacts and informal communication, the R&D management of the 1990s added structural and formal mechanisms. With regard to planning, these include the sophisticated instrument of capability management and the structural coordination organs comprising the various committees, integrating persons (CTO, PD/BG coordinators) and the Corporate Research Bureau. The last plays an important role in coordinating central research with the divisions and groups, and in coordinating central labs with corporate and business group strategies.

The main change in R&D management in the 1990s is the split into contract research for the divisions (70 per cent) and basic research (30 per cent). Critics of this system, however, see a danger that the emphasis on contract research may cause the orientation of cross-corporate research to become too short-term. Definite advantages are a stronger orientation of research towards customer requirements, towards targets, towards the needs of the divisions and the needs of markets. In addition, Philips Research enters into competition with external R&D institutions.

A new, hybrid coordination instrument is the setting up of platforms to manage transdisciplinary technologies. The participation is global and corporate-wide and facilitates the coordination of the central labs among themselves and across the corporation with the divisions and business groups. A further cross-cutting coordination mechanism is provided by R&D projects which are partly conducted in several countries.

The standardisation of decision-making procedures and success and behaviour control do not play a role as coordinating mechanisms. Seen as a whole, the decision-making process was characterised in the interviews by decentralisation and commitment.

CONCLUSIONS

The literature review shows that there is a rich number of coordination mechanisms available which can be used for linking globally dispersed R&D units of multi-divisional and multinational enterprises. However, not every coordination mechanism is suitable for every purpose. The framework developed here reveals that the use of coordination mechanisms differs according to the normative/strategic and the operational level and at least four further factors at each of these two levels.

From the case study conducted in Philips, it appears that, for the coordination of globally dispersed R&D, a set of various types of mechanisms is required. For linking central research with the divisions and business groups – both at various locations – the following mechanisms are used:

- capability management which includes planning and control (structural/formal mechanism),
- steering committees on different levels (structural/formal mechanism),
- Corporate Research Bureau (structural/formal mechanism),
- CTO at the divisional level and the PD coordinators at the central research level (structural/formal mechanism),
- joint transnational R&D projects (hybrid mechanism),
- technology platforms (hybrid mechanism),
- transfer of researchers from central research to divisions/business groups (informal mechanism),
- contract research (internal markets).

For the coordination of the global centres of excellence in seven regions/countries the following mechanisms are applied:

- forming centres of excellence (structural/formal mechanism),
- Research Directors Conferences (structural/formal mechanism),
- Corporate Research Bureau (structural/formal mechanism),
- joint transnational R&D projects (hybrid mechanism),
- technology platforms (hybrid mechanism),
- research conferences (informal mechanism),
- personal and direct contacts of researchers (informal mechanism).

The R&D management of Philips obviously does not rely on a single mechanism or a single type of coordination instrument, however, a great number and variety of mechanisms are applied to fulfil different coordination tasks. The case study presented here can have only illustrative character and no indicators were used to measure the efficiency of the applied mechanisms. However, my own research among 21 multinationals comes to the same conclusion (see Reger 1997 and 1999). It seems to be necessary to link the various instruments in order to reach a maximum coordination effect.

REFERENCES

Adler, P.S. and Ferdows, K. (1990), 'The Chief Technology Officer', *California Management Review*, Spring, 1990, 55–62.

Baliga, B.R. and Jaeger, A.M. (1984), 'Multinational Corporations: Control Systems and Delegation Issues', *Journal of International Business Studies*, 15, 2, 25–40.

Barnard, C.J. (1968), *The Functions of the Executive*, Cambridge, MA: Harvard University Press.

Bartlett, C.A. and Ghoshal, S. (1989), *Managing Across Borders: The Multinational Solution*, London: Harvard Business School Press.

Bartlett, C.A. and Ghoshal, S. (1990), 'Managing Innovation in the Transnational Corporation', in Bartlett, C.A., Doz, Y. and Hedlund, G. (eds), *Managing the Global Firm*, London, New York: Routledge.

Bleicher, K. (1979), *Unternehmensentwicklung und organisatorische Gestaltung*, Stuttgart, New York: Fischer.

Bleicher, K. (1991), *Organisation: Strategien – Strukturen – Kulturen*, 2nd edition, Wiesbaden: Gabler.

Brockhoff, K. (1998), *Internationalization of Research and Development*, Berlin: Springer.

Casson, M. and Singh, S. (1993), 'Corporate Research and Development Strategies: The Influence of Firm, Industry and Country Factors on the Decentralization of R&D', *R&D Management*, 23, 2, 91–107.

De Meyer, A. (1992), 'Management of International R&D Operations', in Granstrand, O., Håkanson, L. and Sjölander, S. (eds), *Technology Management and International Business. Internationalization of R&D and Technology,* Chichester, New York, Brisbane, Toronto, Singapore: John Wiley & Sons.

De Meyer, A. and Mizushima, A. (1989), 'Global R&D Management', *R&D Management*, 19, 2, 135–46.

Dierkes, M. (1992), 'Leitbild, Lernen und Unternehmensentwicklung: Wie können Unternehmen sich vorausschauend veränderten Umfeldbedingungen stellen?', in Krebsbach-Gnath, C. (ed.), *Den Wandel im Unternehmen steuern: Faktoren für ein erfolgreiches Change Management*, Frankfurt/Main: Frankfurter Allgemeine Zeitung: 19–36.

Egelhoff, W.G. (1988), *Organizing the Multinational Enterprise: An Information-Processing Approach*, Cambridge, MA: Ballinger.

Galbraith, J. (1970), 'Environmental and Technological Determinants of Organizational Design', in Lorsch, J.W. and Lawrence, P.R. (eds), *Studies in Organizational Design*, Homewood, IL: Michael D. Irwin.

Galbraith, J. (1973), *Designing Complex Organizations*, Reading, MA: Addison-Wesley.

Gerybadze, A. and Reger, G. (1999), 'Globalization of R&D: Recent Changes in the Management of Innovation in Transnational Corporations', *Research Policy*, 28, 251–74.

Ghoshal, S. and Bartlett, C.A. (1988), 'Innovation Processes in Multinational Corporations', in Tushman, M.L. and Moore, W.L. (eds), *Readings in the Management of Innovation*, New York: Oxford University Press.

Ghoshal, S. and Nohria, N. (1993), 'Horses for Courses – Organizational Forms for Multinational Corporations', *Sloan Management Review*, 34, 2, 23–5.

Grochla, E. (1982), *Grundlagen der organisatorischen Gestaltung*, Stuttgart: Schaeffer-Poeschel.

Hedlund, G. and Nonaka, J. (1993), 'Models of Knowledge Management in the West and Japan', in Lorange, P., Chakravarthy, B., Ros, J. and Van de Veen, A. (eds), *Implementing Strategic Processes: Change Learning and Cooperation,* Oxford: Blackwell Business.

Hill, W., Fehlbaum, R. and Ulrich, P. (1989), *Organisationslehre*, vol 1, 4th edition, Bern: Haupt.

Hoffmann, F. (1980), *Führungsorganisation. Band I: Stand der Forschung und Konzeption*, Tübingen: Mohr.

Hoffmann, F. (1984), *Führungsorganisation. Band II: Ergebnisse eines Forschungsprojekts*, Tübingen: Mohr.

Jonash, R.S. (1995), 'The Shift from R&D Management to Technology Management in the USA: The Challenges Facing a New Generation of CTOs', in Zahn, E. (ed.), *Handbuch Technologiemanagement*, Stuttgart: Schaeffer-Poeschel.

Kenney, M. and Florida, R. (1994), 'The Organization and Geography of Japanese R&D: Results from a Survey of Japanese Electronics and Biotechnological Firms', *Research Policy*, 23, 305–23.

Kenter, M.E. (1985), *Die Steuerung ausländischer Tochtergesellschaften. Instrumente und Effizienz*, Frankfurt, Bern, New York: Campus.

Khandwalla, P.N. (1972), *Uncertainty and the 'Optimal' Design of Organizations*, Working Paper of the Faculty of Management, McGill University, Montreal.

Kieser, A. and Kubicek, H. (1992), *Organisation*, 3rd edition, Berlin, New York: de Gruyter.

Lawrence, P.R. and Lorsch, J.W. (1969), *Organization and Environment. Managing Differentiation and Integration*, Boston, MA: School of Business Administration, Harvard University.

Macharzina, K. (1993), 'Steuerung von Auslandsgesellschaften bei Internationalisierungsstrategien', in Haller, M., Brauchlin, E., Wunderer, R., Bleicher, K., Pleitner, H.-J. and Zünd, A. (eds), *Globalisierung der Wirtschaft – Einwirkungen auf die Betriebs-wirtschaftslehre*, Bern, Stuttgart, Wien: Haupt.

Martinez, J.I. and Jarillo, J.C. (1989), 'The Evolution of Research on Coordination Mechanisms in Multinational Corporations', *Journal of International Business Studies*, 20, 489–514.

Martinez, J.I. and Jarillo, J.C. (1991), 'Coordination Demands of International Strategies', *Journal of International Business Studies*, 22, 429–44.

Mintzberg, H. (1991), *Mintzberg über Management. Führung und Organisation, Mythos und Realität*, Wiesbaden: Gabler.

Nadler, D.A. and Tushman, M.L. (1988), 'Strategic Linking: Designing Formal Coordination Mechanisms', in Tushman, M.L. and Moore, W.L. (eds), *Readings in the Management of Innovation*, Cambridge, MA: Ballinger.

Nonaka, I. and Takeuchi, H. (1995), *The Knowledge-Creating Company. How Japanese Companies Create the Dynamics of Innovation*, New York, Oxford: Oxford University Press.

Ouchi, W.G. (1979), 'A Conceptual Framework for the Design of Organizational Control Mechanisms', *Management Science*, 25, 833–48.

Pavitt, K. (1998), 'Technologies, Products and Organization in the Innovating Firm: What Adam Smith Tells Us and Joseph Schumpeter Doesn't', *Industrial and Corporate Change*, 7, 433–52.

Perich, R. (1993), *Unternehmensdynamik. Zur Entwicklungsfähigkeit von Organisationen aus zeitlich-dynamischer Sicht*, 2nd edition, Stuttgart, Wien: Haupt.

Peters, T.J. and Waterman, R.H. (1982), *In Search of Excellence. Lessons from America's Best-Run Companies*, New York: Harper & Row.

Pugh, D.S., Hickson, D.J., Hinings, C.R. and Turner, C. (1968), 'Dimensions of Organization Structures', *Administrative Science Quarterly*, 13, 65–105.

Pugh, D.S. and Hinings, C.R. (1976), *Organizational Structure: Extensions and Replications. The Aston Programme II*, Westmead, Farnborough, Hants: Saxon House.
Reger, G. (1997), *Koordination and strategisches Management internationaler Innovationsprozesse*, Heidelberg: Physica.
Reger, G. (1999), 'Internationalization and Coordination of Research and Development at Large Corporations', *International Management*, 3, 2, 13–32.
Rubenstein, A.H. (1989), *Managing Technology in the Decentralized Firm*, New York, Chichester, Brisbane, Toronto, Singapore: Wiley.
Thompson, J.D. (1967), *Organizations in Action*, New York: McGraw-Hill.
Welge, M.K. (1989), 'Koordinations- und Steuerungsinstrumente', in Macharzina, K. and Welge, M.K. (eds), *Handwörterbuch Export und Internationale Unternehmung*, Stuttgart: Poeschel, 1182–91.
Westney, D.E. (1993), 'Cross Pacific Internationalization of R&D by U.S. and Japanese Firms', *R&D Management*, 23, 2, 171–83.
Westney, D.E. (1994), 'The Evolution of Japan's Industrial Research and Development', in Aoki, M. and Dore, R. (eds), *The Japanese Firm. Sources of Competitive Strength*, New York, Oxford: Oxford University Press.

4. Germany and the internationalisation of industrial R&D: new trends and old patterns

Jakob Edler

INTRODUCTION

For more than a decade, the interest of both analysts and policy-makers in the internationalisation of research and development (R&D) activities of industrial companies has increased enormously. Empirical work has brought the scope and patterns of international activities in R&D to the fore. Although some arguments remain as to the relative importance of international R&D activities as compared to other international corporate activities like production, marketing or sales, the overall tendency seems to be clear: internationalisation of R&D has grown across the board, internationalisation of R&D has become a regular pattern in corporate strategies, and for many observers it is even the key to innovativeness and competitiveness in the globalised, knowledge-based and highly specialised economy.

However, it is obvious that the scope, pattern and motivations for international R&D activities differ, according to sectors, technologies and research phases (applied or basic). While this seems to be a rather trivial argument, it has nevertheless serious consequences. If we want to understand what drives companies to internationalise their knowledge-creating activities and what the consequences for sectors and technologies are, we need to look into technological, sectoral and country differences of international activities. In addition, the differences between basic and applied research need to be understood in order to estimate the impact of the activities, as well as to politically influence companies' behaviour and to optimise benefits for the host and home countries alike. Finally, we have to bear in mind that these patterns of international activities influence any given national innovation system in two ways: firstly through the activities of its domestic companies abroad (outward) and secondly through the activities of foreign companies in the country (inward).

This chapter looks at these patterns from the perspective of one single country – Germany – and analyses two company samples, one of German companies abroad and one of foreign companies in Germany.[1] The leading questions addressed are: What is the scale of international R&D activities and how has it developed over time? What sectoral and technological differences in the internationalisation of industrial R&D can be found and how have they changed over time? What emphasis do multinational enterprises (MNEs) have abroad as compared to their home-based activities and how can these differences be explained? What are the strategies behind the changes – does an increase in international activity mean that the companies do more of the same, or do companies increasingly focus their foreign activities? What differences are there as for the attractiveness of the German national innovation system between the various research activities (basic-applied) and between technological as well as scientific areas? What patterns of co-operations can be detected and what is the role of foreign parent companies as compared to their subsidiaries? Is the internationalisation of activities characterised by reciprocity within technological fields or is internationalisation a one-way track towards the strong markets?[2]

This chapter is organised as follows: it begins with a short introduction to the two company samples and the various methods used (indicator analysis, survey) in order to grasp the phenomenon from different angles and for the two company samples. In the main part of the chapter, the foreign activities of a sample of German MNEs and the German activities of a sample of international companies are discussed and compared. The analysis concentrates somewhat on indicator-based findings, since these are based upon a much larger number of companies. However, the survey results are selectively presented in order to supplement the analysis with qualitative data on motivations, knowledge absorption and exchange. The chapter finishes with some overarching conclusions on the empirical findings and the relative merit of the approach.

SAMPLES AND METHODOLOGY

The analysis focuses on the four most important manufacturing sectors (see Table 4.1). The companies were selected by relevance as to company size, scale of R&D activity as well as international activities.[3] Table 4.1 shows the composition of both company samples compiled and analysed.

For both samples, a multi-comparative analysis based on patent and (co-)publication analysis and a survey were conducted. In line with the research questions stated above, the methods and comparisons differ somewhat for the two samples (see Table 4.2).

Firstly, in order to detect application-oriented analysis,[4] a patent search was conducted for both samples, based on registered patents at the European Patent

Office (EPAT) and the World Patent Office (PCTPAT).[5] In order to detect all relevant patents, strings of consolidated companies were used in the database research that is – for the German MNEs all German and foreign subsidiaries, for the foreign MNEs in Germany all German subsidiaries were included in the research.[6] Each patent detected was assigned to the country in which the inventor was based.[7] Thus, for the German sample (the foreign sample) the patents registered at home (globally) and abroad (in Germany) in the year 1998 could be compared. For Germany, an additional search for 1990 was done in order to trace the development of R&D activities and profiles over time.

Table 4.1   Sectoral composition of the company samples

	Chemistry	Electronics	Vehicles	Mechanical Engineering	Others	Total
German companies	28	18	16	26	–	88
Foreign companies	16	12	11	4	4	47

Table 4.2   Methods and comparisons

Method	German MNEs abroad	Foreign MNEs in Germany
Patent analysis 1990	x	–
Patent analysis 1998	x	x
(Co-)publication analysis 1998/99	–	x
Survey	x	x
Micro data (business reports)	x	–
Comparison/analysis		
Home–abroad (resp. global–Germany)	x	x
Intersectoral	x	x
Intertechnological	x	x
Intertemporal	x	–
Applied–basic research	–	x

The patent analysis was executed along technological fields[8] to identify and compare technological emphases and profiles. To do this, for each field the share of foreign patents in all patents as well as the Revealed Technological Advantage (RTA) of each field were calculated. The RTA of a technological field x for a sample of companies y (or a country z) indicates how specialised this sample is in field x in relation to its overall activities. The RTA is calculated as the *relation* between:

- the share of patents of the sample y for field x in all patents of that sample (in a given time year) on the one hand and
- the share of all global patents in field x in all global patents.[9]

For this study, the RTA was mathematically transformed to values between the maximum +100 (extremely specialised) and minimum −100 (no activities), the technical annex at the end of this chapter displays for the formula of RTA.

To illustrate the relation between foreign (RTA_f) and domestic (RTA_d) activities in one variable, a foreign net-RTA (RTA_{fnet}) is calculated as follows: $RTA_{fnet} = RTA_f - RTA_d$. A positive RTA_{fnet} indicates relatively more intensive activities in a technology field abroad than at home. For the foreign companies the equivalent is the net German RTA: $RTA_{Gnet} = RTA_{Ger} - RTA_{glob}$, with RTA_{Ger} as the RTA for the patents registered in Germany and RTA_{glob} the RTA for the global patent registrations of the mother company. A positive RTA_{Gnet} indicates that in this specific technological field the foreign sample is – in comparison to its overall global activities – more intensively active in Germany.

Furthermore, the attractiveness of the German innovation system for foreign companies, not only for applied but also for basic research activities, was ascertained by a publication analysis, which lead (1) to publication profiles (Relative Scientific Advantage – RSA) – which are calculated analogously to the patent profiles – and (2) relative shares of German publications in global publications for the parent company.[10] Furthermore, the publication analysis enabled the determination of co-publications in order to assess the scale and pattern of co-operation between foreign industrial research and German researchers. In order to attain more stable results, the reference years for the publication analysis were 1998 and 1999.[11]

Indicators tell – to some extent at least – what, but they do not tell how and why. Therefore, the indicator-based findings were complemented by qualitative data. For both samples, a survey was conducted that asked for scale, forms, motivation and context conditions of their international R&D activities as well as for the knowledge-transfer activities, both within the host country and between foreign subsidiary and parent company.[12] Table 4.2 gives an overview of the various methods and the comparative analyses that could be conducted.

INTERNATIONAL R&D ACTIVITIES OF GERMAN MNES

General Tendencies and Technological Profiles

The German companies have almost doubled their overall patent registration from 1990 (5628) to 1998 (10 102). This period of intensified patent registration has seen an even stronger increase in international patents as the foreign share of patents has grown from 11.6 per cent (656) to 14.6 per cent (1500). To qualify this increase, it can be compared to the increase of international activities in general. For all companies for which data for 1990 was available (N = 69 out of 88), the share of foreign employees among all employees has grown from 33.3 per cent (1990) to 42 per cent (1998). For the same sample the increase in foreign patents was 12 per cent (1990) to 14.7 per cent (1998).[13] Thus, the relative importance of international R&D compared to overall international activity has somewhat decreased, as the share of foreign employees in 1998 was 3.34 times higher than the foreign patent share, while in 1990 the factor had been 2.76. The internationalisation of R&D is dynamic, however it is less so than the internationalisation of other company activities in general. This finding of Patel and Pavitt (1991) for the 1980s still seems to be true for the 1990s as well.

The regional distribution of the foreign activities has not changed much, although the number of foreign patents has more than doubled. The companies have registered about half of their foreign patents in the USA, followed by a group of medium-sized countries France, Japan and the United Kingdom.[14] The USA has about half the patents, having decreased only slightly from its share in 1990 (see Figure 4.1), while the United Kingdom especially has apparently had the highest gains.

While the German companies have not changed their regional pattern of foreign activity very much, they have somewhat changed their technological patterns and strategies abroad. The German companies of our sample have broadened their technological activities across the technological fields and the share of their international patents among all their patents has grown in all but two technological fields[15]. Still, the growth of the international activities has developed very unevenly across the technological fields. To illustrate this, Table 4.3 indicates the six technological fields with the highest and lowest foreign shares in 1998 and the difference to 1990. Three technological fields stand out: almost half of the patents in the biotechnology sector and more than a third in the fields of medical technology and pharmaceuticals have been registered abroad. Although starting from a relatively high level in the 1990s, the companies have even intensified their international activities in these fields in the 1990s. By far the highest dynamic, however, can be registered in the

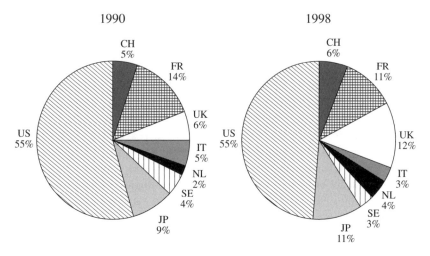

Figure 4.1   Host country distribution of foreign patents

semiconductor field, in which foreign R&D activities of the German MNEs of the sample in 1990 were almost non-existent.

How can we interpret the overall growth of international activities as well as the intensified internationalisation at the high end of international activities? A comparison of various technological profiles of the sample gives some indication. Firstly, if one compares the profile of the domestic RTA_d of the sample and the foreign RTA_f and looks at their development over time, it is obvious that in the course of the 1990s the activities of the companies abroad have come closer to the pattern at home. A simple correlation analysis of the RTA across 28 technological fields shows a relatively high correlation between the domestic and the foreign pattern in 1998 (0.7) while in 1990 the correlation was somewhat lower (0.6).[16]

This finding can be further specified by the comparison of the foreign technological profile of the sample RTA_f with the profile of the host countries of their research. The premise behind this comparison is that a high correlation of the foreign profile of the sample with the profile of a given host country indicates that the international R&D strategies of the companies are focused on the technological and market-related strengths of a host country. Due to the limitation of RTA calculation, which needs a critical mass of patents in order to result in sensible conclusions, this comparison is limited to the USA as by far the most important host country of German companies. The correlation between the technological profile of the US activities by the German companies of our sample and the technological profile of the USA in total is weak and statistically not significant in 1998, while it had been slightly stronger in 1990.

Table 4.3   Most and least internationalised technological fields of German MNEs in 1990 and 1998

Highest Foreign Share*	1998	1990	Diff.	Lowest Foreign Share*	1998	1990	Diff.
Biotechnology	43.58	30.67	12.91	Telecommunications	9.21	12.70	–3.49
Medical technology	38.41	33.83	4.58	Construction/Building	8.93	3.23	5.70
Pharmaceuticals	33.29	18.68	14.61	Transport/Aeronautics/			
				Weapons	8.13	3.61	4.52
Food processing	28.57	10.00	18.57	Environmental technology	8.09	3.17	4.91
Organic chemistry	24.18	13.18	11.00	Audiovisual technologies	6.67	16.13	–9.46
Semiconductors	24.04	4.35	19.69	Consumer goods	5.26	1.35	3.91

Note: * Share of international patents in all patents (%).

Therefore, across the board the growth of international, market-oriented R&D activities has not been driven by increased specialisation towards the specific scientific and technological strengths or market profiles of the host countries. Rather, it seems that the internationalisation of R&D has become a production-related, adaptation-oriented activity that accompanies local production and marketing activities.

However, this is only part of the story, as the data indicates a second pattern that somewhat runs across this finding: internationalisation has especially grown in a few fields that were already highly international in the early 1990s (Table 4.3). The discriminating variable seems to be the knowledge intensity of these technological fields, defined as the number of cited publications within a patent document (Grupp/Schmoch 1992; Schmoch 2001).[17] The argument is that the more knowledge intensive a technological field, the closer the related research is to the scientific forefront of knowledge. Indeed, there is a positive – and growing – relationship between the *knowledge intensity* of a technological field and its *net foreign specialisation* (RTA_{fnet}). Across all 28 fields the correlation in 1998 is 0.59 (1990 0.40).[18] Among the six most highly internationalised technological fields (see Table 4.3) are the four most knowledge-intensive ones (biotechnology, pharmaceuticals, organic chemistry and semiconductors). Apparently, although the companies have broadened their international R&D activities across the board, they have intensified their foreign activities even more in fields in which they need access to forefront knowledge, and therefore their presence in the global centres of excellence is important. This is in line with other findings on the knowledge-seeking motivation for international R&D (see for example Edler/Meyer-Krahmer/Reger 2001).

Sectoral Internationalisation: Different Stories

While the different sectors have intensified their overall international activities in a very similar fashion, the internationalisation of R&D is very diverse and has developed differently across sectors (see Table 4.5). The sectoral differences both for foreign shares in patents and for the relation between foreign R&D and foreign activities in general have increased over time. Most strikingly, while the foreign share has grown in three out of four sectors, the companies of the mechanical engineering sector show a stronger growth at home than abroad (Table 4.4), that is their international share has declined.

The German chemical companies show the highest foreign share in patents in 1998. However, this does not mean that these companies have increased their foreign activities most; on the contrary, the growth factor of their foreign patent registration is even lower. The simple explanation of course is that the growth in domestic patenting is negligible and that the chemical companies had already reached a high level of international R&D in 1990. Therefore, the German chemical companies are a good example of MNEs whose increase in R&D activities during the 1990s was to a high degree driven by foreign activities (Table 4.4). Due to this, the chemical sector is the only sector in which the relation of foreign share of employees and foreign share of patents has diminished, that is foreign R&D has gained importance relative to foreign activities in general. The analysis of the patterns of this increase shows that the chemical companies intensified their international activities in those fields in which they already had been highly internationalised, especially biotechnology (foreign share 42 per cent in 1998) and pharmaceuticals (32 per cent), which are – see above – most knowledge intensive. Moreover, the relative weight of these two most knowledge-intensive technological fields in all R&D activities is far bigger abroad than at home.

Table 4.4   Domestic and foreign patents in 1990 and 1998

	Total	Vehicles	Electronics	Chemistry	Mechanical engineering
	(N = 88)	(N = 16)	(N = 18)	(N = 28)	(N = 26)
1990					
Domestic	4972	487	1401	2617	467
Foreign	656	39	172	375	70
Foreign share (%)	**11.7**	**7.4**	**10.7**	**12.5**	**13.8**
1998					
Domestic	8602	1636	3167	2726	1073
Foreign	1500	149	510	694	147
Foreign share (%)	**14.7**	**8.4**	**13.6**	**20.3**	**12.6**
R&D expenses/turnover (%)	5.3	5.0	7.0	5.9	2.5
Differences 1990–1998					
Growth factor domestic					
patents	**1.73**	**3.36**	**2.26**	**1.04**	**2.30**
Growth factor foreign					
patents	**2.29**	**3.82**	**2.97**	**1.85**	**2.10**
Differences in growth factors	0.56	0.46	0.70	0.81	–0.20

The story is slightly different for the companies of the electronics sector, which have extremely intensified R&D activities – that is, patent registration – both abroad and at home and therefore show only an increase of their foreign share from 10.7 per cent to 13.6 per cent (Table 4.4). However, as the share of foreign employees has grown even stronger, the internationalisation of R&D was a bit less dynamic than the overall internationalisation (Table 4.5). Similar to the chemical companies, in the course of the 1990s the electronic companies have increased the foreign share most in those fields that have gained weight in the sector in general: semiconductors, information technologies, electrical energy and transport/space/weapon technologies. The only exception from that rule is, however, telecommunications, a field in which the German companies have almost quadrupled their patent registration from 1990 to 1998, but in which the increase abroad was slightly smaller than at home. The opposite is true for the field of semiconductors, in which a 400 per cent increase in overall patents has been to a large degree foreign driven, with a foreign share of 24 per cent in 1998 compared to 4 per cent in 1990. Semiconductors, a very knowledge-intensive field, is now by far the most internationalised of all relevant fields for the German electronics companies.[19] This is a good example of a catch-up strategy that heavily relies on the build up (or acquisition) of research potential abroad.

Table 4.5   Share of foreign patents and foreign employees in 1990 and 1998 (reduced sample)[1]

	Total	Vehicles	Electronics	Chemistry	Mechanical engineering
	(N = 69)	(N = 14)	(N = 9)	(N = 25)	(N = 21)
Share of foreign employees among all employees (%)					
1990	33.29	27.17	36.22	43.69	22.12
1998	49.03	47.03	49.93	58.11	36.36
Share of foreign patents among all patents (%)					
1990	12.07	7.22	10.41	12.85	13.15
1998	14.68	8.54	13.88	20.41	13.35
Relation share of foreign employees among all employees (%)/Share of foreign patents in all patents (%)					
1990	2.76	3.76	3.48	3.40	1.68
1998	3.34	5.51	3.60	2.85	2.72

Note:
[1] Due to limited availability of employee data for 1990 the sample had to be reduced for this comparison.

The German vehicles and vehicle supplier companies still show the lowest share of international patents (Table 4.4),[20] and the foreign share of employees has grown much stronger than the foreign share of patents (Table 4.5). However, the vehicles companies have nevertheless refocused their R&D activities and have started to take international R&D seriously. While in 1990 their foreign activities were both low and concentrated in peripheral technological fields, the analysis along technological fields shows that the international share of 10 per cent now represents the core technologies rather than peripheral fields as in 1990. In other words, the pattern abroad has very much converged to the pattern at home.

The mechanical engineering companies are the only ones that show stagnation (sample Table 4.5) or even a slight decrease (sample Table 4.4) in international R&D activities, while general international activities have increased. However, as the latter are – measured by employees – less important than in other sectors, the level of international R&D is remarkable. The ratio of general activities to patents is lowest of all sectors. At the same time, however, their international activity in general had been much lower than in other sectors. Nevertheless, the analysis along technological lines shows that the mechanical engineering companies have, like the other sectors, somewhat broadened the technological scope of their foreign R&D portfolios and converged the technological patterns to the patterns at home.

Motivation and Knowledge Absorption and Transfer

As we now have a picture of the scale and thematic patterns of foreign research, what are the main motivations to conduct research in Germany, and how do the companies integrate within the research system, absorb and exchange knowledge? A questionnaire that contained – among others – related questions was answered by 28 out of the 88 companies of the sample,[21] with the following sectoral distribution: vehicles 5, electronics 5, chemistry 9 and mechanical engineering 9. Breaking down the motivations to the well established dichotomy of market-adaptation vs. knowledge-seeking, it is fair to say that for the German MNEs the market-oriented motivations still somewhat dominate. Overall, adaptation of products to local market (4.0)[22] and close technological co-operation with clients (3.9) were the most important motives. Seeking the latest scientific and technological knowledge (3.6) received slightly lower values. Furthermore, the result of another recent survey (Edler/Meyer-Krahmer/Reger 2001) can be confirmed according to which regulatory framework conditions, costs or even subsidies were of minor importance for foreign R&D. Obviously, within the Triad region at least the decisive variables are market opportunities and scientific and technological excellence, not political framework conditions.

The sectoral differences are in line with the indicator analysis above. As especially chemical companies – and during the 1990s increasingly electronics companies – are very active in knowledge-intensive areas, they rate the knowledge-seeking motive, most of all the monitoring of current scientific knowledge (4.0 resp. 4.3), and the access to leading scientists in the relevant fields (3.8 resp. 4.3), higher than the whole sample (3.7 and 3.5). The opposite is true for mechanical engineering companies, whose home base is one of the strongest technological bases in their field and who rate market adaptation highest by far.

The German companies have adopted very similar strategies and practices to generate knowledge abroad,[23] with recruiting of scientific staff, (informal) contacts with scientists, training of personnel abroad and co-operation with public research being most important. This is in principle true for all sectors alike. The only significant difference between foreign and domestic activities is the lower intensity of co-operation with other companies and especially universities abroad for the companies of the mechanical engineering sector. Apparently, companies which are less dependent on scientific input satisfy their needs for the related input at home, while those companies for which scientific input is crucial for their R&D tend to tap into forefront knowledge globally.

Efficient international knowledge management includes furthermore the monitoring of knowledge abroad and the transfer of the knowledge acquired abroad back to headquarters. The means to absorb knowledge abroad are still rather traditional: publications, databases and international scientific conferences are rated most important, followed by own R&D units. The targeted acquisition of expertise or the build up of specific monitoring units, on the other hand, are still of minor importance. As for the forms of knowledge transfer back to headquarters, electronic means (intranet) are most important, followed by various forms of direct, intra-company, cross-border contacts and co-operation. Most surprisingly, the repatriation of scientists – in theory a cornerstone of knowledge transfer 'via heads' – has very little importance. Furthermore, and in line with intensive personal contacts and co-operation, the level of obstacles for intra-company knowledge transfer is rather low. Both for the forms and obstacles the sectoral variance is insignificant. The only – and telling – exception is the obstacle of 'differences in mentality and culture', which is rated highest for the sample but lower by the chemical companies. This confirms the findings of the patent analysis, according to which the more knowledge intensive the R&D activities of a sector are, the more 'natural' international activity, communication and integration becomes.

Finally, as domestic R&D still dominates the overall R&D of the companies, both scale and research directions, companies indicated a range of reasons why they leave so much of their R&D in the home country. The most important reasons are related to efficiency and based on synergy with other company activities (4.2), economies of scale in big, central R&D units (3.4) and the cost of the control of knowledge flows abroad (3.3). Of secondary importance are established co-operation structures with clients (3.4) and research institutes (3.3). Only after internal efficiency and external co-operation do the companies rate reasons related to better research conditions (high quality of staff and of public science, both 3.2; R&D programmes 2.8). The actual costs of absorbing the knowledge from foreign subsidiaries, on the other hand, are no obstacle, which is in line with the intranet being the most important means of internal communication and transfer.

GERMANY AS HOST OF FOREIGN INDUSTRIAL APPLIED AND BASIC RESEARCH

Overall Picture: A Pattern of the Attractiveness of Germany for Foreign Industrial Research

In order to analyse the attractiveness of Germany as a host for the R&D of foreign companies, the patents registered by the foreign subsidiaries in Germany were compared to the global patents of their parent companies as well as to the patent profile of Germany.[24] It is very clear that the traditional strength of Germany is still existent: for the foreign companies in our analysis Germany is by far most attractive in the seven technological fields that can be grouped in the mechanical engineering area, where on average the share of patents registered in Germany in all global patents of our foreign company sample is almost 20 per cent.[25] The only field in which the foreign companies show a German share above 20 per cent that is not within the mechanical engineering area is environmental technologies, where Germany has been a lead market in the 1980s and early 1990s, mainly due to challenging regulations. Furthermore, it is obvious that electronics is an area in which Germany plays no role whatsoever for applied research of global non-German companies, as the shares in semiconductors, information technologies or even telecommunications are below 2 per cent.

This very distinctive pattern is reflected through RTA analysis. Interestingly, the technological patterns of the foreign companies show quite different results as compared to the German MNEs (see above): firstly, while the technological pattern of the foreign activities of German MNEs shows no match with the technological profiles of their hosts – as was shown with the example of the USA – the technological pattern of the German activities of the foreign subsidiaries in Germany (RTA_{Gnet}) shows a significant correlation of 0.67 with the RTA of their host country, Germany. At the same time – and again in contrast to the activities of German companies abroad – the German activities (RTA_{Gnet}) of our foreign company sample show no match with the global (RTA_{Glob}) of their mother companies. This means the activities of the foreign companies somewhat mirror the German technological strengths. Secondly, emanating from the focus on mechanical engineering – which is characterized by low knowledge intensity – across the board of all activities the foreign companies show no correlation between knowledge intensity and activities in Germany. Interestingly, however, the foreign companies, just like the German ones, are very active in the four most knowledge-intensive areas (biotechnology, pharmaceuticals, semiconductors and organic chemistry), and here they show a positive German RTA_{Gnet} as well. Apparently the very knowledge-intensive areas are characterised by a reciprocal internationalisation emanating from globally distributed centres of excellence and a highly specialised division of labour. Although Germany has kept its traditional pattern of attractiveness in the mechanical engineering areas, the data show that the country has found its role within this division of labour in the knowledge-intensive areas.

To characterise the overall attractiveness of Germany for foreign industrial R&D, the picture can be expanded to more fundamental, basic industrial research by means of a publication analysis. Most importantly, the basic research activities of the companies are more dispersed and less concentrated than the ones in applied research. In the more basic oriented activities the companies show a high thematic match in their global and German scientific activity: the RSAs for the global (RSA_{gl}) and the German (RSA_{ger}) activities have a correlation of 0.6, in contrast to the relation between global and German activities as regards applied research which showed no correlation. This means that foreign MNEs are exploiting the possibilities to monitor and to tap into forefront knowledge abroad and to augment their homebase knowledge in a quite broad, extensive manner, while their more directed, application-oriented research is much more targeted.

As the spectrum of basic research for the sample of foreign companies in Germany is apparently broad, the variance as to the relative importance of single scientific areas is not extremely high. On average, the ratio of German to global publications is 8.8 per cent. Both measured as this ratio and as the net scientific advantage for the German activities (RSA_{Gnet}) the only scientific field in which Germany is extraordinarily attractive for basic research is medical technologies (with a ratio of German/global above 45 per cent): areas significantly above the average of 8.8 per cent are environmental technologies (18 per cent), medicine (13 per cent), chemical processing (12 per cent) and biotechnology (10 per cent). On the other hand, foreign companies are very hesitant to do fundamental research in organic chemistry.[26]

Table 4.6 summarises the overall attractiveness of Germany as a host for foreign industrial R&D. It contains the net German specialisation values of the patent profile (RTA_{Gnet}, 1998) and the publication activities ($RSA_{Gnet,}$ 1998/99).[27] Positive resp. negative values display an RTA_{Gnet}/RSA_{Gnet} that is at least ten points higher (lower) for the activities in a certain field within Germany as compared to the global activities, indicating a certain strength (or

Table 4.6 *Specialisation of foreign MNEs in Germany (whole sample): applied vs. basic research*

Applied research: RTA_{Gnet}[b]	Basic research: RSA_{Gnet}[a]		
	Positive[c]	Neutral[c]	Negative[c]
positive[c]	biotechnology; environmental tech.	polymers; materials; thermal processes	analysis/measurement/nuclear energy; organic chemistry; pharmaceuticals; mechanical engineering; civil engineering
neutral[c]	medical technology; chemical processing	basic materials; chemistry	
negative[c]		telecommunications; optics	information technologies; electrical engineering; food chemistry

Notes:

[a] RTA_{Gnet}: net Relative Technological Advantage for German activities: difference of the German patent profile (RTA_G) for the German patent activities of the German subsidiaries and the RTA_{glob} for the mother company globally.

[b] RSA_{Gnet}: net Relative Scientific Advantage for publication activities in Germany: difference of the German publication profile (RSA_G) of the company (subsidiary and foreign mother) and the RSA_G for the global publication activities of the company.

[c] Neutral: indices between + 10 and – 10; positive: indices above 10; negative: indices below 10.

weakness) of Germany as a host to foreign applied (patents) and basic (publications) research.

Firstly, the companies differentiate between foci in applied and in basic research. There is no strong link between applied and basic research in any given field: only five out of 18 fields have identical classifications. Secondly, they rate Germany as much more attractive in market-related research. While nine fields have positive RTA_{Gnet}, only five fields have positive RSA_{Gnet}. Thirdly, there are only two technological fields in which Germany has a distinct attractiveness both for applied and basic research. While for environmental technologies this was to be expected, given the high level of environmental regulation and the resulting take off for environmental technologies in Germany some years ago (lead market), it is somewhat surprising for biotechnology, since the general perception has been that in this area there was a drain of brain and R&D resources to other countries, especially the USA. Apparently, this learning abroad has not done harm to the German innovation and research system in biotechnology.

Further Different Sectoral Stories

In addition to the scientific differentiation for the whole sample, the picture can be further differentiated for three sectors (see Table 4.7).[28] For the foreign electronics companies in Germany, the market-related research in Germany plays a minor role, while their efforts in basic research in Germany are above average, especially the research related to medical technology and biotechnology which is extremely important. In fact, the electronics companies in the sample contribute a lot to the high basic research activities in biotechnology of the foreign companies in Germany. For the chemical and vehicles companies the picture is the other way round: for them the basic research plays no significant role in Germany (one exception being environmental technologies), while they put high emphasis on market-related R&D, the latter mainly in the areas of mechanical engineering.

Table 4.7   Foreign MNEs in Germany: applied vs. basic research differentiated for sectors

	Chemistry	Electronics	Vehicles	Whole sample
Ratio German/global patents (%)	11.6	3.3	8.7	4.83
Ratio German/global publications (%)	4.5	9.6	2.13	7.09

Co-operation, Motivation and Knowledge Exchange

To what extent do the foreign MNEs take advantage of their location abroad and try to integrate into the system of the host country, thereby exchanging knowledge with local actors in the national innovation system of the host country? What are the motivations for the companies to do research in Germany? With the methodology applied in this study, these questions can be tackled from two angles. Firstly, the publication analysis can be exploited as it delivers patterns of co-publication of all companies in the sample and thus determines and differentiates the co-operation in basic research. Secondly, this indicator-based analysis can be supplemented by some qualitative data of the survey which had a focus on knowledge transfer and co-operation schemes.

Patterns of Scientific Co-operation: Publication Analysis

The foreign MNEs doing research in Germany are very prone to co-operate with German partners. In 1998/99 their German subsidiaries had 257 publications without any German partner, but 298 with German partners (see Table 4.8). However, the most important – and surprising – 'discovery' of the publication analysis has been the scale of direct co-operation between the foreign headquarters and German partners despite a German subsidiary doing R&D in the country (439 joint publications with 510 partners). In some of these 439 cases the co-operation might have been done with the help of the subsidiary or even through a researcher of the subsidiary: however, as there is no intellectual property for scientific publications – in contrast to patents – there is no obvious and compelling incentive for the headquarters to claim the publication without actually having co-operated itself. This finding indicates that decentralisation of R&D – at least for basic research not linked to the local market – does not mean that the foreign subsidiaries are the foremost link to the national innovation systems of the host countries. Knowledge augmenting through international co-operation still happens to a large extent on the direct track. The central and strategic research departments of the MNEs still tap directly into knowledge systems abroad to a large degree. Whether this means that the linkage between national research systems and foreign industrial research is not in any case dependent on geographical proximity is still somewhat open, but indications are strong. The numbers also indicate, however, a slight difference in the intensity of contacts in projects leading to joint publication. While the average number of German partners is 1.34, the joint publications of the subsidiaries include – on average – 1.53 German partners, and those of the headquarters only 1.2. Geographical proximity certainly is a prerequisite to managing bigger project teams.

Table 4.8   (Co-)publications and contacts of foreign MNEs in Germany

	Publ. without German partner		Co-publ. with German partners			Number of contacts			Share of ind. contacts (%)[e]		Contacts per publication			Ratio M/S[a]	
	S alone[b]	S + M[c]	S[c]	M	all	S[d]	M	all	S	M	S	M	all	co-publ.	contacts
Chemistry	98	35	145	205	350	209	232	441	13.40	12.93	1.44	1.13	1.26	1.41	1.11
Electronics	143	45	129	177	306	170	211	381	16.47	18.48	1.32	1.19	1.25	1.37	1.24
Vehicles	3	22	11	17	28	15	18	33	26.67	27.7	1.36	1.06	1.18	1.55	1.20
Others	13	33	13	40	53	14	49	63	35.71	22.45	1.08	1.23	1.19	3.08	3.50
Total	**257**	**85**	**298**	**439**	**737**	**408**	**510**	**918**	**15.93**	**16.67**	**1.37**	**1.16**	**1.25**	**1.47**	**1.25**

Notes:
a   s = subsidiary, M = foreign mother.
b   Including co-publications with foreign, but not German, partner(s).
c   Co-publication mother and German subsidiary.
d   Contacts in common publications of mother and subsidiaries have been allocated to the subsidiary.
e   Share of industry contacts out of all contacts with German actors.

Another interesting – and somewhat surprising – finding is the high level of co-operation with German industry. While the average share of industrial publications in all publications for Germany is only around 6 per cent,[29] the share of industry partners in the co-publications across all companies in the sample is around 16 per cent. The co-operation with German companies is especially high in the scientific fields of the electronics/electrical engineering area,[30] in which one fourth to one third of the partners stem from industry. For the foreign MNEs geographical proximity does not influence the likelihood for co-operation with German industry, since the share of German industrial partners for the foreign headquarters and the German subsidiary are very similar.

Survey Data

Analogous to the section on the German companies abroad (see above), the discussion of the survey focuses on central aspects: motivation, knowledge-related co-operation, knowledge acquisition and intra-company knowledge transfer. The 16 companies that answered[31] show a mix of motivations related to the strong German market and its industrial players on the one hand, and related to the scientific capacities and human resources on the other. For the whole sample, the recruiting of scientific and technical personnel (as one form of *knowledge seeking*) is most important, however, followed by four variables related to the *market adaptation* or industrial potential of the country. Just as in the German company sample, the regulatory and political framework conditions do not play a significant role.

The activities to generate and acquire knowledge are somewhat different from what the German companies do abroad. The foreign companies also most importantly rely on the recruiting of scientific personnel, but co-operation – not only with universities but also with German companies – is more important than in the German sample.[32] In order to monitor the scientific developments in Germany, the companies rely very much on publications, databases and scientific conferences. However, and again in contrast to the German sample abroad, they also rate recruiting of scientific personnel as an important means for monitoring. Just like the German companies, the foreign companies in Germany have not built up specific monitoring units and do not seek to participate in subsidised programmes in order to tap into the knowledge pool of companies and universities.

Furthermore, it is obvious that the foreign companies doing R&D in Germany are highly integrated networks of knowledge. The companies indicate almost no obstacles for intra-company, cross-border knowledge transfer, and the vast majority has formal and informal processes at work that guarantee comprehensive transfer. The means utilised are very similar to those used by German companies, that is the intranet is the most important, followed by various forms of personnel co-operations. Again, the repatriation of personnel is not of any significant importance. However, the knowledge integration in the foreign MNEs is lopsided, as the knowledge flow towards the headquarters is more intensive and important than the flow from the headquarters to the German subsidiary.

Differentiating these overall results as for sectors, the results of the indicator-based analysis are confirmed and strengthened. The survey results of the electronic companies make it very clear that these companies follow a knowledge-seeking strategy in Germany. For example, recruiting scientific personnel is the most important motive, as well as the most important knowledge-seeking activity, and being up-to-date with scientific knowledge in Germany is much more important than for the rest of the sample. This is fully in line with the indicator analysis, which showed little relevance of patent (market-related) activities of the electronics companies, but high relevance of publication (science-related) activities. The opposite is true for the vehicles companies: market-related motives and activities are much more important for them, and at the same time their R&D activities are almost exclusively market-related. For the foreign chemical companies both the indicator-based analysis and the qualitative data indicate middle ground, as they combine aspects of market and science orientation more evenly.

SUMMARY

In a path-breaking analysis Patel and Pavitt (1991) have shown for the 1980s that (1) the MNEs did the bulk of their R&D activities at home, (2) that different sectors show different patterns of internationalisation and (3) that the National Innovation Systems (NISs) of the home country and the host country make a difference. The results of Patel and Pavitt for the 1980s can be partly confirmed for the 1990s and must also be further qualified: across the board of all German companies, the share of international R&D has further grown (confirming for example Cantwell/Harding 1998), but indeed, except for the chemical companies, this increase has been less dynamic than the build up of international activities in general. The leading German manufacturing companies have also shown quite different technological patterns of increase in the internationalisation of their R&D activities along sectoral lines – leading to even greater intersectoral differences in foreign shares in 1998 than in the 1990s. However, in each sector there was a tendency to broaden the scope of international activities and to let the activities converge towards what the parent company had been doing at home (confirming findings by Patel/Vega 1999 and Le Bas/Sierra 2002),[33] while at the same time the correlation with the pattern of the host countries – shown by way of the example of the USA – was reduced.

The picture must be further differentiated as diversity in the pattern of internationalisation has grown. First of all, there are some specific technological fields, mainly in knowledge-intensive areas like pharmaceuticals and biotechnology and semiconductors, in which the foreign activities seem to have actually been key drivers for activities at home. In these areas, the requirement to absorb excellent basic science knowledge in science-intensive areas quickly is a key driver of the internationalisation of R&D (for example Kuemmerle 1999).[34] This was confirmed by the survey data, as chemical and electronic companies rate knowledge–seeking motivations much higher than the rest of both samples. The majority of these companies also report a high degree of knowledge integration, confirming the new mode of international learning company (see also Meyer-Krahmer/Reger 1997). However, both the qualitative and the quantitative data confirmed that market adaptation and lead markets in many areas are still the most important drivers. Furthermore, this chapter has confirmed the importance of the origin of the foreign company, as foreign companies in Germany, which are mainly US companies, seem much more focused on the market as driving force, while European companies tend to put higher emphasis on the knowledge-seeking motive, which confirms other recent studies (Grandstrand 1999 for Swedish and US companies, and Edler/Meyer-Krahmer/Reger 2001 for the three Triad regions).

Finally, a further dimension of knowledge integration has come to the fore that seems to be somewhat underrated by analysts so far. The non-German MNEs analysed serve their need to tap into knowledge and to monitor scientific activities abroad to a high degree through international co-operation between headquarters and partners in Germany, although they have subsidiaries in the country. This might be an increasingly important strategy of the companies to adapt to the rapid developments of ever new pockets of excellence globally and to cope with the growing diversification of knowledge inputs into the research process, with the consequence of ever more complex international knowledge networks.

What could all this mean for policy making? While the causes and especially the effects of international R&D still need further analysis, one conclusion seems obvious: governments should not be afraid of their MNEs going abroad to do research. This is very obvious in the market-related dimension. However, foreign activities in knowledge-intensive technological areas such as biotechnology or pharmaceuticals are also an imperative for successful MNEs: a transnational knowledge integration is evolving, and MNEs that want to take advantage of this need to play the game, and governments that want their NIS to profit need to secure access to their knowledge systems and support the lead market. Funding programmers or tax subsidies are of secondary importance, and regulatory obstacles for foreign MNEs or special incentives for domestic MNEs to stay at home are certainly counter-productive.

TECHNICAL ANNEX: SPECIALISATION INDEX REVEALED TECHNOLOGICAL ADVANTAGE

We have defined the Revealed Technological Advantage as follows:

$$RTA_{ij} = 100 \tanh \ln [(Pat_{ij}/\Sigma i\ Pat_{ij}) / (\Sigma j\ Pat_{ij} / \Sigma_{ij}\ Pat_{ij})]$$

with:

Pat_{ij} = number of patents of a country (or a group of companies etc.) i in the technological field j. Logarithm: symmetrical values around zero.

Tangent Hyperbolicus: value limitation between ±1. Factor 100: simply for visibility. Base (denominator): all (global) EPAT + PCTPAT patents in the respective year possible values from −100 to + 100.

NOTES

1. The empirical work was conducted in a study financed by the German Federal Ministry for Education and Research in 2001 and 2002. This study was done in co-operation between the Fraunhofer Institute for Systems and Innovation Research (ISI) and the Rheinisch West-fälisches Institut für Wirtschaftsforschung, Essen (Roland Döhrn; Michael Rothgang). The latter provided company data and conducted the survey of the German companies abroad. The whole study is published as Edler, Döhrn and Rothgang (2003).
2. The regional distribution of foreign R&D activities in Germany will not be dealt with. For detailed work on this dimension see Cantwell/Noonan (2001).
3. For the sample of foreign companies four highly relevant 'other' companies were included in order to enlarge the sample size.
4. We are aware that patents only reflect part of the picture for applied research. However, they indicate the output of corporate research activities with a demonstrated market potential ('applied'). In view of the lack of sufficient and comparable data on input, it is still the best quantitative indicator for research we have. The drawbacks of patents as indicators for research are obvious: most importantly patent intensity is not stable overtime or across sectors. However, for our analysis the empirical fact that the relation between research activities (input) and number of patents has changed in recent years – due to a tendency towards more strategic patenting – does not have a great effect, as a higher patent intensity is true both for national and international application. Similarly, different patent intensities across sectors do not affect the conclusion to be drawn from inter-temporal and inter-technological analysis.
5. Double counting was systematically avoided.
6. In both cases minimum share is 50 per cent.
7. For methodological reasons, the foreign host countries included in this search were the USA, the United Kingdom, France, Japan, Sweden, Switzerland, the Netherlands and Italy. However, a test search found that these countries covered more than 90 per cent of the foreign patents.
8. Following the established classification jointly designed by Fraunhofer Institute for Systems and Innovation Research (ISI) and the Observatoire des Sciences et des Techniques (OST).
9. See the technical annex for the RTA formula used.
10. The database used was the Science Citation Index (SCI).
11. As with the relation between patents and applied research, it is true that publications are only one possible (output) indicator for 'basic' research, but more appropriate and comprehensive input indicators are not available at the level of a distinct set of companies. Moreover, the term 'basic' does not mean that the findings published need necessarily reflect cutting-edge

research. However, it indicates findings that are based on research work at a pre-competitive, pre-application stage, as this is the corporate prerequisite for publication in the first place.

12. For the German sample, the survey data could be complemented by company indicators from an existing company database based on business reports.

13. There is of course a time-lag between the increase in foreign employees and increase of R&D activities on the one hand and the resulting patent registration on the other. However, the existing inaccurateness is true both for 1990 and 1998 and might, for the sake of illustration, be neglected here.

14. The high share of the UK in 1998 is mainly due to the acquisition of Rover by BMW – that is history already as BMW has sold most of the acquisition meanwhile – and that was, moreover, not motivated by the R&D potential of the British car company.

15. In the two technological fields telecommunications and audiovisual technologies, both from the electronics area, internationalisation has decreased.

16. Both correlations are significant at the level 0.01.

17. Grupp/Schmoch have determined the knowledge intensity by analysing patent documents for the 28 technological areas and calculating knowledge indexes for each technological area. While the average index across all technological fields is 0.88 citations per patent, at the high end it is 2.65 for biotechnology, 1.87 for pharmaceuticals and at the low end 0.18 for construction/building and 0.22 for consumer goods.

18. Level of significance 0.01.

19. 'Relevant' meaning that more than 5 per cent of all patents are registered in a given field.

20. The fusion of Daimler Benz with Chrysler was not yet reflected in the patent statistics of 1998.

21. Due to limitations in space, the discussion based on the survey confines itself to a selection of questions most relevant to motivations, integration and knowledge exchange. The response rate was 32 per cent.

22. The answering scale was 1 for 'not important at all' to 5 for 'extremely important'.

23. However, it must be noted that the persons answering the questionnaire were representatives from the domestic parent company and not from the subsidiaries abroad.

24. For all companies and technological areas, the number of German patents equals 4.77 per cent of the global patents of the sample. However, this number alone does not tell us much, since it cannot be compared to the German MNE foreign patent share, given that the foreign companies in Germany only have one country as a 'foreign' R&D location.

25. Thermal processes (31 per cent) and engines and turbines (28 per cent) show the highest values. This attractiveness is confirmed by the RTA profiles: the RTA_{Gnet} of the sample of foreign companies is extremely high while at the same time the RTA_{gl} of the parent company is negative.

26. This does not mean, however, that for chemistry in general the attractiveness is low, since the average of all chemical science fields is 7.0.

27. In order to achieve this, some fields of the patent classification had to be somewhat aggregated, mainly in the area of mechanical engineering. Therefore, Table 4.6 is only based on 18 fields, instead of the 27 of the original patent classification.

28. The sample of mechanical engineering (four companies) is too small for a sound sectoral analysis.

29. If the areas without direct links to technology, medicine, biology, physics, agriculture, mathematics and geosciences are excluded, the share is 9 per cent.

30. As the companies of the electronics sector have not confined their activities to the scientific areas of electronics and electrical engineering, the numbers for the sector are lower.

31. The response rate was 34 per cent, among five chemical, four electronic, four vehicle, two others, and one mechanical engineering company.

32. In fact, when asked for the conditions for doing research in Germany, these three dimensions are the most highly rated by the companies.

33. Thus, the finding of Cantwell/Kosmopoulou (2001), which find that big companies tend to invest in R&D activities in complementary and peripheral areas, cannot be confirmed for the mid 1990s.

34. This finding confirms Cantwell (1995), Florida (1997), Edler/Meyer-Krahmer/Reger (2001) and Kumar (2001).

REFERENCES

Cantwell, J. (1995), 'The globalisation of technology: what remains of the product life cycle model', *Cambridge Journal of Economics*, 19 (1), pp. 155–74.

Cantwell, J. and Harding, R. (1998), 'The internationalisation of German companies' R&D', *National Institute Economic Review*, 163, pp. 99–124.

Cantwell, J. and Kosmopoulou, E. (2001), 'What determines the internationalisation of corporate technology', in Forsgren, M. et al. (eds), *Critical Perspectives on Internationalisation*, mimeo.

Cantwell, J. and Noonan, C. (2001), 'The regional distribution of technological development', in Feldmann, Maryann and Massard, Nadine (eds), *Institutions and Geography in the Geography of Innovations*, Boston: Kluwer, pp. 199–230.

Edler, J. Döhrn, R. and Rothgang, M. (2003), *Internationalisierung industrieller Forschung und grenzüber-schrietendes Wissensmangrment*, Heidelburg: Springer.

Edler, J., Meyer-Krahmer, F. and Reger, G. (2001), 'Managing technology in the top R&D spending companies worldwide – results of a global survey', Special Issue of the *Engineering Management Journal*, 'Managing high technology research organizations', 13 (1), pp. 5–11.

Florida, R. (1997), 'The globalization of R&D: results of a survey of foreign-affiliated R&D laboratories in the USA', *Research Policy*, 26, pp. 85–103.

Grandstrand, O. (1999), 'Internationalisation of corporate R&D: a study of Japanese and Swedish corporations', *Research Policy*, 28, pp. 275–302.

Grupp, H. and Schmoch, U. (1992), *Wissensbindung von Technik: Panorama der internationalen Entwicklung und sektorales Tableau für Deutschland*, Heidelberg: Physica.

Kuemmerle, W. (1999), 'Foreign direct investment in industrial research in the pharmaceutical and electronics industry – results from a survey of multinational firms', *Research Policy*, 28, pp. 179–93.

Kumar, N. (2001), 'Determinants of location of overseas R&D activity of multinational enterprises: the case of US and Japanese corporations', *Research Policy*, 31, pp. 159–74.

Le Bas, Christian and Sierra, Christoph (2002), '"Location versus home country advantages" in R&D strategies: some further results on multinationals' locational strategies', *Research Policy*, 31, pp. 589–609.

Meyer-Krahmer, F. and Reger, G. (1997), 'Konsequenzen veränderter industrieller FuE-Strategien für die nationale Forschungs- und Technologiepolitik', in Gerybadze, A., Meyer-Krahmer, F. and Reger, G., *Globales Management von Forschung und Innovation*, Stuttgart: Schäffer-Poeschel, pp. 196–215.

Narula, R. (2000), 'Explaining inertia in R&D internationalisation: Norwegian firms and the role of home country effects', MERIT Research Memorandum, 2000–021.

Patel, P. and Pavitt, K. (1991), 'Large firms in the production of the world's technology: an important case of "non-globalisation"', *Journal of International Business Studies*, 22 (1), pp. 1–22.

Patel, P. and Vega, M. (1999), 'Patterns of internationalisation of corporate technology: location vs. home country advantages', *Research Policy*, 28, pp. 145–55.

Schmoch, U. (2001), *Interaktion von akademischer und industrieller Forschung*, Karlsruhe: manuscript.

5. Understanding the growth of international R&D alliances

Rajneesh Narula

INTRODUCTION

Firms are not restricted just to a dichotomy of choices – either staying at home or relocating to acquire immobile sources of knowledge. There are a variety of 'in-between' options available to access location-specific resources, and these include cooperative agreements. Such agreements are also a useful organisational mode when firms seek technologies that are specific to other firms.

It should be apparent even to the most casual observer of business news that cooperative agreements are being signed continuously, and in ever-greater numbers with every passing year. This is a phenomenon that has sparked the attention of managers, national and supra-national regulators, policy-makers and academics alike. It is argued by some that this phenomenon is the death knell of the traditional firm, that firms will become increasingly 'virtual'. One of the main points that the literature highlights is that there are limits to the extent to which firms can use cooperative agreements as a substitute for in-house activity. To paraphrase Samuel Clemens, I believe that the death of the firm is greatly exaggerated. I feel that there are a great many misconceptions about cooperative agreements, some of which I shall seek to address in this chapter.

The growth of collaborative agreements is undoubtedly greatly influenced by the process of globalisation, which is taken here to mean the growing interdependence of locations and economic units across countries and regions (Narula 2003). As with globalisation, the effect varies across industries, and is particularly acute in sectors where consumption patterns are increasingly homogenous across countries, and which are capital-intensive as well as knowledge-intensive, in terms of (1) investing in innovation and technology, (2) requiring large plant scales, and (3) depending on new and fast-evolving technologies. These are sectors where firms have expanded internationally fastest, as they are thus able not just to compete in the various markets simultaneously, but also to exploit and acquire assets and technology that may be specific to particular locations.

It is axiomatic that firms in some sectors need to innovate in order to survive, which, in this day and age, implies being present in all the major international markets where competitors are present. This is not just to meet demand, but also to overcome supply constraints – companies wish to exploit the particular characteristics of given countries that represent inputs to the innovative process, required to generate new competitive advantages. Unfortunately, given the capital-intensity of these activities and the inherent risk of innovation, firms cannot afford to be omnipresent. Internalising and undertaking all (or even most) aspects of value-adding activity through wholly owned subsidiaries in every location is no longer possible, and in many instances not even desirable. Over the past two decades, firms have increasingly sought to undertake activities through collaborative efforts. Although collaborative activity is not a new practice, it is undeniable that there has clearly been a process of evolution whereby there is an increasing use of alliances explicitly for strategic purposes. Its novelty is not as an organisational form – economic units have collaborated for millennia. Intricate linkages between economic entities that create informal and formal networks to undertake value-added activity dates back to before the 17th century, where production of goods was undertaken by 'putting out'. Rapid Japanese industrial growth over the last century has been partly attributed to the cooperation between interlinked firms with limited equity cross-holdings within industrial groups referred to in the post World War II era as *Keiretsu* (see for example, Gerlach (1992), Nakamura (1981)). Dunning (1995, 1997) and others suggest that this represents a new 'age of alliance capitalism' whereby flexible economic arrangements find increasing favour, shifting away from the older paradigm of hierarchical capitalism where hierarchies represented the primary mode through which economic activity was undertaken. What is particularly unique about the 'age of alliance capitalism' is its widespread use by firms of all sizes and nationalities, and its use in a growing variety of activities which have hitherto been centralised and internalised, such as research and development (R&D). Furthermore, cooperative activity has a growing international element, and is not just limited to related firms but is often undertaken with international competitors. In addition, even within international strategic technology partnering (STP), there has been a gradual shift away from equity-based partnering to non-equity forms of agreements.

The rest of this chapter focuses on evaluating some of these trends. First, I will clarify some definitional issues. There are a wide variety of cooperative agreements, all of which have fundamental differences in their structure and objectives, but are often referred to interchangeably as strategic alliances, collaborative agreements, or networks or outsourcing. I intend to clarify this issue. My primary objective is to focus on R&D alliances, but in the process I intend to deal also with more general aspects that apply to all kinds of cooperative agreements.

Second, cooperative agreements have different objectives, depending on what aspect of the value-added chain we are dealing with. This chapter focuses on the narrow area of collaborative R&D activity. I intend to explain what role cooperative agreements play in technological competence development, in light of the growth of what is best described as the multi-technology corporation. I propose that these trends can be explained by combining a resource-based view of the firm, in addition to traditional economic rationale, and by acknowledging the special nature of innovative activity, which has certain unique characteristics that separate it from production activities, as well as the strategic nature of firm-decision making. I will illustrate my arguments with particular reference to some data on European Union (EU) strategic technology partnering, explaining why alliances have become increasingly important to firms.

THE CHARACTERISTICS OF OWNERSHIP ADVANTAGES AND TECHNOLOGY

There are many motives for undertaking R&D alliances which Hagedoorn (1993) classifies into those relating to general characteristics of technological development; those relating to the innovation process; and those relating to market access and opportunities. One of the primary objectives of R&D collaborative ventures is to learn, for the basic reason that the ability of firms to compete effectively for market share is a function of their ability to maintain and renew their firm-specific assets. These assets are commonly referred to as ownership advantages. An important distinction needs to be made about the nature of ownership advantages of companies, which, in knowledge-intensive firms, comprise two different forms of knowledge. First there is technical knowledge which is made up of what might traditionally be defined as technology, both embodied in plant and equipment (and to a large extent codifiable), as well as the employee-specific knowledge that is only to a limited degree non-tacit. Second, there is organisational knowledge which comprises knowledge of transactions, both *intra-firm* and *inter-firm*. In general, throughout theis chapter, I focus on R&D alliances whose primary purpose is to acquire technical knowledge and to generate innovations. Although innovations can (and frequently do) occur through the acquisition of organisational improvements, and/or the ability to undertake inter-firm transactions more efficiently, I limit myself here to studying alliances to undertake *overt* R&D.[1]

There are different ways of classifying innovatory activities. In this chapter innovation is viewed along a continuum between basic research and development, with the determining factors being (1) the generic nature of the innovation and (2) the distance from market. By generic nature, I refer to a distinction

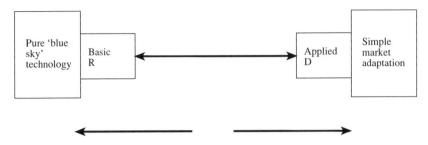

Technology is tacit, and property rights undeveloped – alliance possible, but depending on speed and uncertainty.
Object is to invent and share costs and risks of innovation – R&D alliance only likely if technology likely to have systemic influence of background or main technological competence; in-house R&D will be preferred.

Technology is more codifiable. Possible to subcontract objective is to 'sell' innovation, and share cost of making product saleable. R&D outsourcing more likely: if technology is part of core competences, then R&D alliance likely, but probably equity-type agreement.

Figure 5.1   'Distance-to-market' issues in the innovation process

introduced originally by Kuznets (1962) and used in a modified way by Arora and Gambardella (1994) and Trajtenberg et al. (1997). Figure 5.1 summarises the basic argument. Knowledge that is 'basic' or 'generic' represents knowledge that is not country- or demand-specific, and is less appropriable than 'applied' or 'specific' ('applied D' in Figure 5.1). It is important to highlight that we are speaking of *research outcomes*, since laboratories are often engaged in several similar (and often related) projects simultaneously, and since technological development is an uncertain process, it is not always possible to say *ex ante* whether a certain project is applied or basic research. Nonetheless, a distinction can be made between the extremes. On the one hand, firms can explicitly engage in projects that are more 'blue sky', or pursue scientific research that has no clear market value in the short run, aim to change the technological paradigm, or have a major impact in defining general laws rather than solving particular problems. On the other hand, demand-specific modifications or adaptations can be explicitly undertaken, which are more context-specific and are clearly 'applied D'. It is worth noting that regardless of the basic-ness or generic nature of the knowledge, there is always some extent of context specificity. Even codifiable technology is context-specific to at least some extent (Cantwell 1991). Because technology is the cumulative sum of innovations and proceeds incrementally based on 'localised search' patterns centred on the technology possessed by the firm in previous periods, the technology of any given firm is unique, such that no two firms can have exactly the same kind of technology.

EXPLAINING STRATEGIC TECHNOLOGY PARTNERING: SOME DEFINITIONS

It is germane to begin this discussion with some fundamental definitions of terms as used throughout this chapter. Before proceeding further, some distinction needs to be made of the difference between the following three terms which are often mistakenly used as synonyms: cooperative (or collaborative) agreements, networks and strategic alliances. Cooperative agreements include all inter-firm cooperative activity, while strategic alliances and networks represent two different (though related) subsets of inter-firm cooperation.

By strategic alliances I refer to inter-firm cooperative agreements which are intended to affect the long-term product–market positioning of at least one partner (Hagedoorn 1993). I am specifically interested in strategic technology alliances where innovative activity is at least part of the agreement. What differentiates a strategic alliance from a network is the underlying motive of the cooperation (Figure 5.2). This differentiation has its roots in an ongoing debate within the management literature of the relative merits of various underlying theories explaining the behaviour of firms to use markets and hierarchies (see Madhok (1997) for a more in-depth analysis of the various aspects of this debate). On the one hand, there is the transaction costs/internalisation perspective, which derives its roots in the work of Williamson (for example, (1975)) and Coase (1937) which explains the behaviour and organisational mode and the mode of entry of firms based on their need to *minimise net transaction costs* faced by the firm. This body of literature has been expanded by others including Buckley and Casson (for example, 1976), Hennart (for example (1993)) and Rugman (for example (1980)). On the other hand, there is also the organisational capability and technology based view of the firm developed in parallel by several schools, including behavioural theory (Cyert and March 1963) and the economics of technological change (for example Nelson and Winter (1982)). Other work includes Kogut and Zander (1993), Hill et al. (1990), and Cantwell (1991) who have highlighted the fact that firms undertake decisions based on the need to enhance their technological and organisational capabilities because they need to *enhance the value* of the firm. Underlying the difference between these two perspectives is a fundamentally different view of the way firms make decisions, since the transactions cost school assumes that firms are driven by opportunism while the technology/knowledge view assumes that firms are boundedly rational. I do not intend to debate the views here, but accept

Madhok's (1997) perspective that the two schools may be regarded as complementary to each other, although an organisational learning and technology based view underlies our understanding of strategic technology partnering.

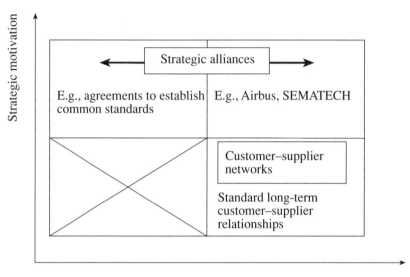

Cost-economising motivation

Source: Narula and Hagedoorn (1999).

Figure 5.2   Explaining the underlying differences between strategic alliances and customer–supplier networks

   The approach favoured here is that both transaction cost minimising and value-enhancing reasons underlie most of the behaviour of firms. Firms would prefer to increase short-term profits through cost-economising as well as long-term profit maximising through value enhancement, but this is not always possible. It is important to emphasise that very few agreements are distinctly driven by one motivation or the other. What I am trying to establish here is that agreements that are established with primarily short-term cost efficiencies in mind are generally customer–supplier networks, while agreements where a long-term value enhancement is the primary objective are strategic alliances. Figure 5.2 illustrates my basic argument with a few examples.

   Decisions to conduct a vertical alliance may tend to be primarily cost-economising, but also have a strategic element to them, in that by collaborating with the supplier firm you may have pre-empted a similar move by a competitor. The behaviour of firms within Japanese *Keiretsu*, to a greater extent, tend to have cost-based benefits. Collaborations such as these are primarily cost-economising and may be defined as *networks*. On the other hand, cooperative agreements such as the one between Sony and Philips to develop DVD technology, or the Sematech partnership, are clearly aimed at improving the future value of the various partnering firms and are thus more strategically motivated rather than cost-economising. As such they represent strategic alliances rather than networks. It should be noted that it is particularly difficult to clearly delineate strategic alliances from networks, given that firms have no incentive to reveal their true motives to the public and, more importantly, to their partner firm, especially where these might prove detrimental to the proposed relationship.

Collaborative agreements of all sorts have been undertaken for strategic, economic and diplomatic reasons since the beginning of history. However, what differentiates their current popularity is that until recently they represented a second-best option, utilised only where full internalisation was not possible. It was conventional wisdom that firms preferred, wherever possible, to establish wholly owned subsidiaries, and, where this was not possible for whatever reason, to maintain a controlling (which generally implied majority) stake in its affiliate. In general, firms preferred to maximise their equity stake in all their activities, particularly so when entering or expanding in foreign markets. Over the past two decades or so, alliances and networks have come to represent a *first-best* option. Indeed, there are four primary characteristics that differentiate collaborative activity in the era of alliance capitalism from those in earlier periods (Narula and Dunning 1998). First, agreements are not primarily made to overcome market failure. Second, alliances are increasingly made not just to achieve vertical integration, but also horizontal integration. Third, alliance activity is no longer a phenomenon peculiar to certain countries such as Japan (Gerlach 1992), but typical of most advanced industrialised economies (see Narula and Sadowski (2002) for a discussion on developing country alliances). Fourth, while agreements were primarily made to enhance or achieve market entry or presence (i.e., asset-exploitation), an increasing number of alliances are now made to protect or enhance the technological assets of firms (i.e., asset-creation or acquisition). It is worth noting that alliances involving marketing and sales are, more often than not, cost-economising in nature, while R&D alliances are more strategic in character. Two independent surveys of alliances (Culpan and Costelac 1993, Gugler and Pasquier 1996) found that sales and marketing accounted for 41% and 38% of all alliances surveyed, while R&D alliances accounted for only 10.8% and 13% respectively. One of these studies noted, however, that R&D alliances had tripled in relative importance since the 1980s.

Organisational Modes of Alliances

Figure 5.3 describes the range of inter-firm organisational modes generally utilised in collaborative agreement activity. There are a wide range of types of

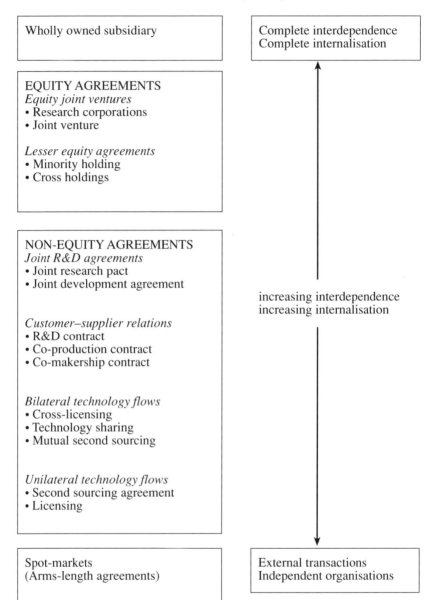

Source: Narula and Hagedoorn (1999).

*Figure 5.3   Organisational modes of inter-firm cooperation and extent of
            internalisation and interdependence*

agreements, reflecting various degrees of inter-organisational interdependency and levels of internalisation. These range from wholly owned subsidiaries, which represent complete interdependency between the firms and full internalisation, at the other extreme, to spot-market transactions, where totally independent firms engage in arms-length transactions in which both firms remain completely independent of the other. As Figure 5.3 illustrates, we include within the rubric of collaborative agreements two broad groupings of agreements that can be regarded as representing different extents of internalisation, or what may succinctly be described as quasi-internalisation. Although it is difficult to be specific and concrete regarding the ordinal ranking, it is safe to say that equity-based agreements represent a higher level of internalisation and interorganisational interdependence than non-equity agreements.

Not all equity cooperative arrangements are alliances. For instance, joint ventures have always been a popular means for undertaking business activity in developing countries, but this was often because of government restrictions on the ownership of domestic companies by foreign investors. In other words, these joint ventures were only undertaken because government restrictions prevented the establishment of majority or wholly owned subsidiaries. Very often, the partner would be a government corporation or ministry, which would act as a silent partner. As such, these so-called joint ventures actually represent a subsidiary of a multinational rather than a true joint venture, since the local partner is not sharing managerial control and providing a proportional input in a strategic sense. In addition, traditional joint ventures were generally undertaken across several activities, often including marketing and production. Newer joint ventures are increasingly single activity: joint ventures that are formed primarily to conduct R&D are often referred to as research corporations.

The Growth of Alliance Activity

There is little doubt that the growth of R&D alliances mirrors the globalisation process. Although there was some growth in R&D alliances in the 1960s and 1970s, inter-firm agreements began to grow exponentially since the 1980s (Hagedoorn 2002). Figure 5.4 illustrates this trend with data from 1980 onward.

The growth of partnerships is associated in part with economic imperatives. Nonetheless, simply by invoking globalisation one cannot explain the growth of this form of economic activity. I intend to shed some light on the determinants of this sustained interest in cooperative agreements in R&D.

One of the fundamental reasons for the growth in alliances lies in the reduction of transaction costs. These have occurred due to, *inter alia*, (1) the introduction of new space-shrinking technologies (particularly information and computer technologies) which have reduced cross-border communication, information and organisational costs; and (2) the harmonisation of regulations and

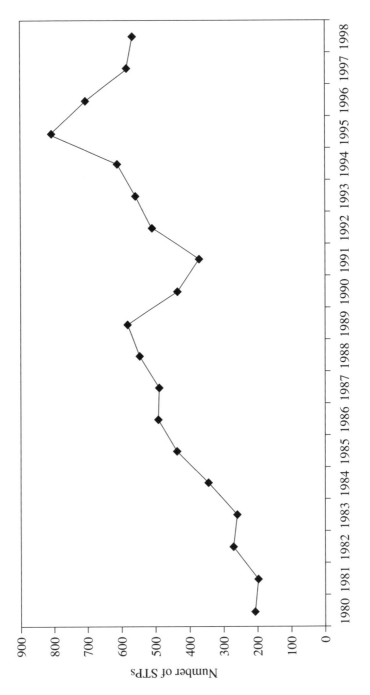

Source: MERIT-CATI database.

Figure 5.4 Growth of STP, 1980–1998

barriers as a result of growing economic liberalisation. These have been further enhanced by the establishment of supra-national regional and inter-regional agreements such as the North American Free Trade Agreement (NAFTA), and the EU, as well as multilateral protocols and agreements under the auspices of the World Trade Organisation (WTO), World Intellectual Property Organisation (WIPO), etc. These agreements have, *ceteris paribus*, reduced the risks of shirking as the costs of monitoring and enforcing cross-border alliances have fallen. The case of the EU is particularly useful in illustrating the growth of alliances because the EU is not only at a rather advanced stage of economic integration, achieved over the last 50 years, but EU firms are at the technological cutting edge, and some EU locations are important agglomerative locations (see for example, Cantwell and Iammarino (2003)). From a transactions costs perspective, the harmonisation of regulations within the Single European Market (SEM) initiative in such a view represents a more advanced version of this activity, and further lowers transaction costs for firms within the Union. As Narula and Hagedoorn (1999) have shown, there are no significant country-specific differences in the propensity to engage in alliances. As such, the benefits of integration have resulted in lower costs for all firms regardless of nationality. However, there continues to be a considerable bias of multinational enterprises (MNEs) towards the home country in terms of the concentration of value-adding activity: it can thus also be argued that, *ceteris paribus*, greater absolute cost-reductions might occur for EU firms since the extent of their European value-added activity is generally higher and the significance of their European operations much larger to their total worldwide activity. This reasoning might suggest that, *ceteris paribus*, EU firms should derive a larger benefit when engaging in collaboration with other EU firms as a result of European integration relative to *collaboration* involving non-European firms. As Figure 5.5 shows, intra-European cooperation did gain briefly in popularity relative to EU–Japanese and EU–US alliances, but this growth was not sustained for long, as predicted by Kay (1991).

It is important to remember that the decline in transaction costs due to the SEM has also reduced costs for other organisational modes (Kay 1991, 1997). The costs associated with full internalisation will have also proportionally fallen, and *ceteris paribus*, alliances would still be a second-best option. Certainly, reduced transaction costs might lead firms that otherwise might have considered full internalisation to undertake collaborative agreements. Firms that might not have had the resources to expand (whether domestically or internationally) on their own would now also be able to consider it, since a collaboration could require fewer resources than it might otherwise have done before European integration. In other words, this line of reasoning would suggest *ceteris paribus*, the number of firms undertaking alliances within the EU would have increased since the 1980s in response to integration.

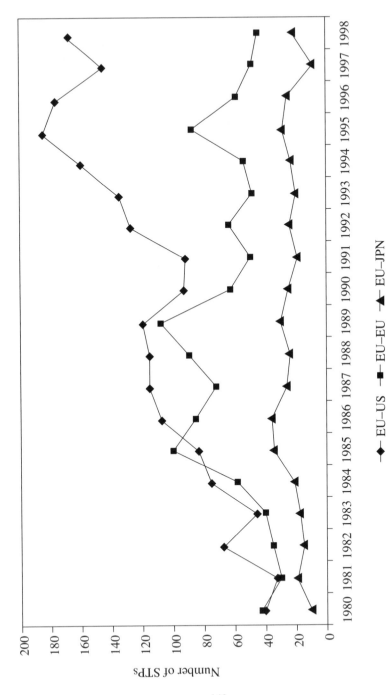

Figure 5.5   Number of new STPs by year for EU firms, by nationality of partner

However, transaction costs provide only a partial explanation for the growth in alliances, and only suggest why one group may derive greater benefits from collaboration than other groups. It does not completely explain why firms increasingly prefer quasi-hierarchical arrangements to fully internalised ones. If transaction cost theory were to provide a complete explanation, the decline in costs due to either globalisation or integration should lead to at least the similar extent of benefits for traditional hierarchical arrangements. To understand the non-transaction cost based reasons for alliances, it is useful to return to the motives for alliances as discussed in Figure 5.2, and reflect on the word 'strategic' in strategic alliances. What differentiates a strategic alliance from a customer–supplier network is the underlying motive of the cooperation. The primary motivation for a customer–supplier network is that it is primarily cost-economising in nature, while strategic alliances embody a second motivation, which is strategic in nature. By 'strategic' they suggest that such agreements are aimed at *long-term profit-optimising* objectives by attempting to enhance the value of the firm's assets.

Several reasons exist for the growth in popularity of cooperative agreements which embody a strategic element. One explanation is based on the increased competition due to liberalisation of markets and the globalised nature of the operations of firms. Such increased competition has led to a low-growth scenario over the past two decades or so, and firms need to seek cheaper sources of inputs or divert sales from slow or negative growth markets (Buckley and Casson 1998). Such changes often need to be undertaken with rapidity. Declining transaction costs associated with contractual or quasi-internalised relationships in addition to falling profits margins have led to a *dis-integration* of certain firms in particular industries, as they seek flexibility and lower risk, which have hitherto preferred vertical integration. Indeed, some notice has been made of the process of dis-investment, that, coincidentally or not, appears to have become quite commonplace during the last decade (Benito 1997).

In addition though, the emergence of new technological sectors (such as biotechnology) and the growing technological convergence between sectors (such as computers and automobiles, or new materials with transportation) have also played an important role. The cross-fertilisation of technological areas has meant that firms need to have an increasing range of competencies (Granstrand et al. 1997). This encourages the use of alliances to seek complementary assets. As has been emphasised by others (for example Kogut (1988)), the use of mergers and acquisitions (M&A) is not a viable option where the technology being sought is a small part of the total value of the firm. Greenfield investment does not represent a viable option either, in most instances, as the time and costs of building new competencies from scratch may be prohibitive. It should be noted that in some instances alliances are used as a precursor to M&A (Hagedoorn and Sadowski 1999). In connection with this, there has also been a growing cost of development, and of acquiring the resources and skills necessary to bring new products and services to market. Increasing the market size, and the sharing of costs and risks associated with staying on the cutting-edge of technology, creates strong motivation to undertake alliances, no matter how much firms may prefer to go it alone.

Last but not least, there are the game-theoretic considerations. As Kay (1997: 215) explains, 'it is necessary to engage in networks with certain firms not because they trust their partners, but in order to trust their partners'. In addition, there is the follow-my-leader strategy, as originally highlighted by Knicker-bocker (1973). Firms seek partnerships in response to similar moves made by other firms in the same industry, not always because there is sound economic rationale in doing so, but in imitation of their competitors.

If firms do go it alone, they forgo the opportunity to observe what the other firms in the same industry are up to. This goes for firms that have proven abilities in a given area of specialisation, as well as firms that do not. In addition, where new technologies are concerned, there is an increasing need to seek a broad range of competencies in unrelated fields. Firms generally have limited resources and cannot possibly engage in vertical and horizontal integration to internalise all their needs. As I have noted earlier, there is a growing tendency to focus on a few selected core technologies, rather than to vertically integrate. By engaging in alliance activity rather than internalisation, as Buckley and Casson (1998) have noted, firms are able to be more flexible, and can respond to low growth scenarios and, at the same time, optimise returns. In addition to the benefits of flexibility, the need for complementary assets, market power and economies of scale, there are other reasons which are peculiar to strategic technology partnering which I will discuss in the next section.

The Special Case of Strategic Alliances to Conduct R&D

R&D alliances are of a different and special nature: this is the one aspect of value-adding activity that continues to be highly centralised and internalised, even in a domestic scenario. In general, while production activities have gradually been increasingly internationalised, R&D tends to stay 'at home' (see for example Kumar (2001), Narula (2002)). Nonetheless, it is worth noting that there has been some growth in the technological development activities of MNEs relative to its level 20 years ago, and these changes indicate two trends worthy of note. First, in addition to overseas R&D activities associated with demand-side factors, there has been a growing extent of foreign R&D activities by firms in response to supply-side factors (Florida 1997, Kuemmerle 1996). Second, there has been a growing use of external or quasi-external techno-logical sources. Tidd and Trewhella (1997) suggest that the most important external sources of technology are: universities, consortia, licensing, customers and suppliers, acquisitions, joint ventures and alliances and commercial research organisations. Although there is little systematic and thorough analysis of this process, companies such as Philips and Akzo-Nobel are currently attempting to externally source 20% of their technology needs (van Hoesel and Narula 1999). Indeed, there is a direct relationship between how much R&D a firm does internally, and its external acquisition of technology – Veugelers (1997) demonstrates that there is a positive relationship between external technology sourcing and internal R&D. Indications are that collaborative arrangements to undertake R&D are becoming ever more popular, having tripled in significance since the early 1980s (Gugler and Pasquier 1996).

These special characteristics of alliances require certain important caveats to be noted. To begin with, there is a fundamental difference in the definition of R&D alliances and non-R&D alliances. Traditionally alliances have been defined as agreements which have a long-term and formal aspect which links aspects of their businesses (Porter and Fuller 1986). Strategic technology partnering, as used here, refers to agreements that are intended to undertake specific tasks and are generally terminated at the completion of these tasks, and are by definition short- (and often fixed-) term in nature.

There are other important considerations due to the special nature of R&D alliances. First, it is important to note that there is a strong causality between size and the propensity to engage in STP, given the need to have sufficient resources to undertake R&D (Hagedoorn and Schakenraad 1994). Second, trade barriers have not played a major role in inhibiting the relocation of R&D, except where such R&D is associated with production (i.e., adaptive R&D). Stand-alone R&D facilities, which are common in knowledge-intensive sectors, are often located due to supply-related considerations. Such activities have not necessarily been affected by the decline in transaction costs due to the SEM initiative – skilled human capital and knowledge (in either tacit or non-tacit form) have long enjoyed relatively restriction-free freedom of movement across borders. Although certain improvements, such as the common patenting system, and the harmonisation of regulations may have lowered costs in general, the benefits of lowered communication costs (due *inter alia* to information and communication technologies (ICTs) have occurred on a global level.

Although the reduction in trade barriers may affect both exporting and foreign direct investment through wholly owned subsidiaries, R&D alliances are largely unaffected by these. While it is true that firms engaged in asset-exploiting activities such as production or sales have a broader choice of options that include wholly owned subsidiaries and arms-length technology acquisition, some of these options are simply not available to firms that are seeking to undertake R&D. This is for several reasons associated with the particular value of technological innovation: for instance, because technology is tacit by nature, and as far as technology development is concerned, even more so.

Arms-length transactions are simply not as effective, particularly in technology-intensive sectors or new, 'emerging' sectors, even if markets for these technologies were to exist. The further away these technologies are from the market (i.e., more research-oriented than development-oriented) the less likely that technology can be obtained through market mechanisms. Besides, its partly-public good nature prevents prospective selling firms from making technologies available for evaluation, and without doing so, the prospective buyer is unable to determine their worth. Markets, therefore, are liable to fail, or, at least, will function inefficiently. It is no surprise, therefore, that technology partnering has grown fastest in high-technology sectors where market options are less well-developed, while partnering activity in low- and medium-technology sectors has steadily declined as a percentage of all agreements (Hagedoorn 2002).

The choice of partner in R&D alliances can be international or domestic. There has been considerable variation in the international aspect of R&D alliances over time, although broadly speaking this reflects the gradual internationalisation of firms and competition. Country size differences persist: small countries tend to engage in more alliances than large countries – the US has the smallest level of international partnerships with less than 50% being international, while Switzerland has an international share greater than 90%. There are also considerable differences by industry (Hagedoorn 2002). Why do firms prefer in certain instances to partner with a foreign firm rather than a domestic firm? This is related to the question of why firms do not undertake all the R&D at their home location in the first place. The literature suggests that this is due to both supply and demand issues. The demand issues are well-known, and are generally associated with adaptive R&D in response to specific market conditions. More recently attention has been drawn to the supply issues. Firms are seeking to utilise immobile assets, which may be either firm-specific or location-specific. In the case where they are firm-specific, they are often associated with clusters of firms, and country-specific characteristics. It is well acknowledged that location advantages are idiosyncratic and path-dependent, and the nature of innovatory activities in a given location is associated with the national systems of innovation (Edquist 1997, Lundvall 1992). The nature of the benefits arising from a non-cooperative arrangement require physical proximity to the firm or cluster, in order to seek indirect technology spillovers, which can be a highly costly, uncertain and random procedure that requires a long-term horizon. In the case of basic research, for instance, this might occur through the hiring of researchers that hitherto worked for a competitor. Where such immobile assets are country- but not firm-specific, they may be embodied in aspects of the national systems of innovation. Whether the advantage being sought is firm- or country-specific, the establishment of a greenfield laboratory is a feasible option, but involves high start-up costs, and considerable time. In fields where innovation is rapid, it may not provide a fast-enough response. The use of M&A is even less attractive when the area where the complementary resources are sought only cover a small area of the firm's interests. Even where a firm wishes to acquire an R&D facility, it is generally not possible to do so, except in rare circumstances.

It is true, nonetheless, that there are also strategic *limitations* to the use of alliances. First, there is a danger that an alliance may represent a precursor to M&A. Indeed, Hagedoorn and Sadowski (1999) show that 2.6% of strategic technology alliances lead to M&A, a figure that is quite significant given the high percentage (estimates vary between 50 and 70%) of alliances that are terminated before completing their stated objective (Inkpen and Beamish 1997).

Why would a potential partner wish to collaborate with another which has limited or as-yet-undemonstrated resources to offer? First, because of the nature of innovation, the only way to determine the nature of a potential partner's research efforts is to examine them. One way this can be done is by engaging in some form of mutual hostage exchange, which an alliance provides. Second, even where the partner's resources prove to be of a limited or inappropriate nature, and the alliance is terminated prematurely, information about its former partner's competencies are then available to either firm in future periods, should it require competencies similar to those on offer by its ex-partner. Third, as Hagedoorn and Duysters (2002) have argued, while selecting partners that are well-established players in existing technologies may represent a profit-maximising situation, it is optimal only in a static environment. In a dynamic environment, where there is a possibility of technological change (or even a change in technological trajectories), having ties to a wide group of companies, including companies that have yet to demonstrate their value, represents a higher learning potential.

Strategic technology alliances are not only undertaken by firms seeking complementarity of resources. As Narula and Dunning (1998) note, firms may also engage in alliances in order to co-opt the competition. Take the situation where two firms in the same industry are pursuing an important new breakthrough. Neither can be certain that they will win the race to innovate. As such, it may be in their best interest to collaborate, thus ensuring both that they are jointly 'first': half a pie may be considered better in conditions of uncertainty while there is a probability that there may be none at all.

The evidence on strategic technology partnering points to the fact that the need for complementary assets and the reduction of risk have become increasingly important as these are global phenomena, while open markets may have aggravated the use of need to co-opt and block competitors, since firms are obliged to restructure to strengthen or even maintain their competitive position, either through aggressive or defensive means. Indeed, such a restructuring of EU industry has occurred since the early 1980s in response to the impending single market agreement (Dunning 1997). Many of the EU-subsidised R&D programmes were aimed at achieving this renewed competitiveness, and indeed were undertaken in earnest by most firms with a view to being able to compete on equal terms with other EU firms as well as US and Japanese firms by 1993. As Peterson (1991) has pointed out, although technological collaboration has constantly remained high on the agenda of European policy-makers, pan-European R&D activities have only systematically been developed by policy-makers since the 1980s. Several initiatives by the European Commission have been implemented over the past two decades in an attempt to bolster the competitiveness of European firms, particularly in high-technology sectors. Indeed, Hagedoorn and Schakenraad (1993) show that there was a concurrent rise in non-subsidised and subsidised R&D during the latter half of the 1980s. Nonetheless, in a study of non-subsidised R&D collaboration by European firms, Narula (1999) shows that while intra-EU cooperation did in fact increase during the second half of the 1980s, this level was not sustained through the 1990s (as illustrated in Figure 5.5). The initial rise in intra-EU alliances reflected the fact that European industry began to undertake a much more serious view of alliances in the mid 1980s, with a doubling of activity over a short period. This can in part be attributed to three things. First, that the process of economic integration had by this time been seen to be a reality. Second, European firms had begun to realise by the mid-1980s that they were technologically lagging in new core high-technology sectors such as information technology, and leading European firms had begun to cooperate by this period (Mytelka and Delapierre 1987, Mytelka 1995). By the end of the 1980s this growth in intra-EU activity declined, but EU firms showed a continued propensity to undertake EU–US and EU–Japanese R&D collaboration, particularly in the information technology, biotechnology and new materials sectors. The subsequent decline of the number of new alliances in the 1990s is quite dramatic. Narula (1999) postulated that this reflected the result of re-structuring of European industry, in part through the series of M&A that occurred in the run-up to the single market (for example Nixdorf by Siemens, ICL by Fujitsu, Plessey by Siemens-GEC) as well as the re-positioning of firms' technological profiles (e.g., the exit of Philips from computers, and its entry into the telecommunications sector with AT&T) (Mytelka 1995).

The second reason for the decline in intra-EU alliances may have to do with the growth of extra-EU alliances. As Figure 5.5 shows, the propensity for EU firms to engage in alliances with Japanese and US firms also increased in the mid-1980s. This reflects in part the desire for Japanese and US firms to seek strategic positions within European industry prior to 1992 to avoid any question of being excluded from 'fortress Europe'. In addition, there had been some attempt to spur transatlantic R&D cooperation though the strategic defence initiative (SDI) programme of the US government in the mid-1980s (Carton

1987). Perhaps most significantly of all, however, EU firms were primarily spurred to partner with US and Japanese firms given the technological lead that US firms possessed in information technology and bio-technology and, to a lesser extent, new materials, while Japanese firms had a technological lead in information technology and new materials. In other words, EU firms would be interested in partnering with firms regardless of nationality, depending primarily on their relative competitive positions in the industry, or the presence of significant clusters at given locations.

It is important to note that the definition of strategic technology alliances includes both equity and non-equity agreements, as discussed in an earlier section. As such, while we have made general comments about the choice between markets, hierarchies and quasi-hierarchies, there is a significant difference between various organisational modes of STP. Broadly speaking though, it is possible to consider these as being of two major groups – equity-based agreements and contractual, non-equity based agreements. It is significant to note that the choice of alliance mode is determined by the technological characteristics of sectors of industry (Hagedoorn and Narula 1996). Equity agreements are preferred in relatively mature industries while contractual alliances are more common in so-called high-tech industries.

There is, however, another dimension that is worth noting. There has been a decline in the use of equity agreements on a global basis, whereby the percentage of equity STP has fallen steadily from 46.9% in 1980–1984 to 26.1% during the period 1980–1994 (Narula and Hagedoorn 1999). A similar tendency has been noted for all alliance groupings by region. This points to an important issue which relates to the process of learning. Given the novelty of R&D alliances, it can be hypothesised that firms prefer to undertake more hierarchical arrangements, but, as they have acquired experience with this form of technological innovation, they have gradually switched to more flexible, but inherently riskier agreements.

European R&D alliances have demonstrated a similar tendency, and, indeed, the fact that these patterns demonstrate industry-wide trends rather than national ones suggests that the same process of learning about the mechanics of alliance formation and management apply to all firms regardless of nationality. It also highlights the need for firms, again regardless of nationality, to partner with the most appropriate firms regardless of national origin.

CONCLUSIONS

This chapter has focused attention primarily on a rather 'macro' scale on the reasons why firms of a given nationality tend to engage in R&D alliances. Within this discussion I have dealt with some of the firm-level issues that determine why firms prefer alliances to full internalisation. Our admittedly simplistic analysis lends support to, and confirms, some of the trends and patterns observed by the technology-partnering literature. First, that strategic technology partnering as a phenomenon is best explained using an organisational-learning framework. Recent theoretical studies have suggested that firms' decisions regarding what extent to internalise value-adding activity is determined not just by a cost-minimisation strategy driven by short-term profit optimisation, but also by an interest in enhancing the value of the firm in a more long-term horizon. It does so by improving the nature and types of technological/knowledge-based assets it possesses. Given the firm's bounded rationality, however, this decision is more of a strategic one. This is what determines the primary difference between networks and alliances.

There has clearly been an explosion in the use of alliances to undertake innovative activity, and this trend is closely related to the process of globalisation. Globalisation has affected the need of firms to collaborate, in that firms now *seek* opportunities to cooperate, rather than identifying situations where they can achieve majority control. In addition, the increasing similarity of technologies across countries and cross-fertilisation of technology between sectors, coupled with the increasing costs and risks associated with innovation, have led to firms utilising STP as a *first-best* option. STP, as with most forms of innovative activity, is primarily concentrated in the Triad countries. However, the propensity of firms of a given nationality to engage in STP varies according to the characteristics of the country. This is because small and technologically less advanced countries tend to be focused in fewer sectors than large countries, due, *inter alia*, to the differences in economic structure and demand. We also see that strategic alliances are dominated by large firms, and there is indeed a positive relationship between firm size and STP levels by firm. We also observe a high percentage of STP utilised on a cross-border basis. That is, a considerable share of STP seems to be undertaken with partners of other nationalities. There seems to be some suggestion that, while some firms undertake STP as a means of complementing their existing R&D activity, others seek to use STP as a substitute.

There seems to be no clear relationship between the extent to which firms engage in international production and the extent to which they engage in technology partnering. This difference is not mediated, as might have been expected, by nationality of ownership or by R&D expenditures, but preliminary indications suggest that differences exist on a sectoral basis, suggesting that it is an industry-specific phenomenon.

There is also a clear shift of alliance activity towards non-equity forms of agreements, and this has occurred more or less uniformly across countries. We attribute this change partly to the improved enforceability of contracts and intellectual property protection, and partly to the increasing knowledge and familiarity firms now have in conducting international business activity. On a firm-level basis, the propensity to use equity agreements is associated with industry-specific differences, rather than country-specific differences.

It would seem that countries are increasingly engaged in promoting the competitiveness of their domestic firms, in what can loosely be described as 'techno-nationalism' (Ostry and Nelson 1995), with the intention of developing 'national champions'. Most of the major industrial economies practice some sort of government intervention to boost the ownership advantages of their firms. While some governments do so through indirect means that improve the quality of location-bound resources and capabilities to attract mobile ownership advantages of domestic and foreign-owned firms, others attempt more direct intervention by directly participating in ownership advantage-generating activities.

Much of this intervention was originally a response to globalisation, with the desire of protecting weak domestic firms from international competition. Ironically, this has led to a greater use of alliance- and network-forming activity. As such, techno-nationalism is doomed to failure, as the question of 'who is us' and 'who is them' makes such policies increasingly redundant (Reich 1990, Strange 1998). National champions are equally willing to act as free agents, and are in some instances receiving national treatment (and support) from several governments, both national and regional. The example of IBM being involved in several research consortia funded by both the EU and the US governments best illustrates this point.

As for the underlying motive of improving levels of R&D activity, this too would seem to be in doubt. It should be noted that R&D alliances are even more footloose than traditional majority-owned production or R&D activities, and, it must be stressed, R&D alliances do not provide significant levels of spillovers to the host economies where they might be located. Funds invested in joint research by governments are notoriously hard to track down, in terms of their application, both in a geographic and a technical (i.e., project-specific) sense. Furthermore, firms are more interested in establishing themselves near centres of agglomeration, regardless of where these might be located (Narula 2003). This indicates a very real danger of entering into an incentive war, with so many countries willing to subsidise R&D (Niosi 1995), and with so few obvious spillovers therefrom.

NOTE

1. For a discussion of organisational knowledge, see Inkpen (1996, 1998).

REFERENCES

Arora, A. and Gambardella, A. (1994), 'The Changing Technology of Technological Change: General and Abstract Knowledge and the Division of Labor', *Research Policy*, vol. 23, pp. 523–32.

Benito, G. (1997), 'Divestment of Foreign Production Operations', *Applied Economics*, vol. 29, no. 10, pp. 1365–77.

Buckley, P. and Casson, M. (1976), *The Future of the Multinational Enterprise*, New York: Holmes & Meier.

Buckley, P. and Casson, M. (1998), 'Models of the Multinational Enterprise', *Journal of International Business Studies*, vol. 29, no. 1, pp. 21–44.

Cantwell, J. (1991), 'The Theory of Technological Competence and its Application to International Production', in McFetridge, D. (ed.), *Foreign Investment, Technology and Economic Growth*, Calgary: University of Calgary Press.

Cantwell, J. and Iammarino, S. (2003), *Multinational Corporations and European Regional Systems of Innovation*, London: Routledge.

Carton, A. (1987), 'EUREKA: A Western European Response to the Technological Challenge Posed by the SDI Research Programme', in Brauch, H. (ed.), *Star Wars and European Defense*, New York: St. Martin's Press, pp. 311–28.

Coase, R. (1937), 'The Nature of the Firm', *Economica*, vol. 4, no. 4.

Culpan, R. and Costelac, E. (1993), 'Cross National Corporate Partnerships: Trends in Alliance Formation', in Culpan, R. (ed.), *Multinational Strategic Alliances*, New York: International Business Press, pp. 103–22.

Cyert, R. and March, J. (1963), *A Behavioral Theory of the Firm*, Englewood Cliffs: Prentice-Hall.

Dunning, J. (1995), 'Reappraising the Eclectic Paradigm in the Age of Alliance Capitalism', *Journal of International Business Studies*, vol. 26, pp. 461–91.

Dunning, J. (1997), *Alliance Capitalism and Global Business*, London: Routledge.

Edquist, C. (1997), *Systems of Innovation*, London: Pinter.

Florida, R. (1997), 'The Globalisation of R&D: Results of a Survey of Foreign-Affiliated R&D Laboratories in the USA', *Research Policy*, vol. 26, pp. 85–103.

Gerlach, M. (1992), *Alliance Capitalism*, Oxford: Oxford University Press.

Granstrand, O., Patel, P. and Pavitt, K. (1997), 'Multi-Technology Corporations: Why They Have "Distributed" Rather Than "Distinctive Core" Competencies', *California Management Review*, vol. 39, pp. 8–25.

Gugler, P. and Pasquier, M. (1996), 'Strategic Alliances of Swiss Firms: Theoretical Considerations and Empirical Findings', Institut für Marketing und Unternehmungsführung, Working Paper No. 27.

Hagedoorn, J. (1993), 'Understanding the Rationale of Strategic Technology Partnering: Inter-Organizational Modes of Cooperation and Sectoral Differences', *Strategic Management Journal*, vol. 14, pp. 371–85.

Hagedoorn, J. (2002), 'Inter-Firm R&D Partnerships: An Overview of Patterns and Trends since 1960', *Research Policy*, vol. 31, pp. 477–92.

Hagedoorn, J. and Duysters, G. (2002), 'Satisficing Strategies in Dynamic Inter-firm Networks – The Efficacy of Quasi-Redundant Contacts', *Organisation Studies*, vol. 23, pp. 525–666.

Hagedoorn, J. and Narula, R. (1996) 'Choosing Modes of Governance For Strategic Technology Partnering: International and Sectoral Differences', *Journal of International Business Studies*, vol. 27, pp. 265–84.

Hagedoorn, J. and Sadowski, B. (1999), 'Exploring the Potential Transition from Strategic Technology Partnering to Mergers and Acquisitions', *Journal of Management Studies*, vol. 36, pp. 87–107.

Hagedoorn, J. and Schakenraad, J. (1993), 'A Comparison of Private and Subsidised R&D Partnerships in the European Information Technology Industry', *Journal of Common Market Studies*, vol. 31, pp. 374–90.

Hagedoorn, J. and Schakenraad, J. (1994), 'The Effect of Strategic Technology Alliances on Company Performance', *Strategic Management Journal*, vol. 5, pp. 291–311.

Hennart, J. (1993), 'Explaining the Swollen Middle; Why Most Transactions are a Mix of Market and Hierarchy', *Organization Science*, vol 4, pp. 529–47.

Hill, C., Hwang, P. and Kim, W. (1990), 'An Eclectic Theory of the Choice of International Entry Mode', *Strategic Management Journal*, vol. 11, pp. 117–28.

Hoesel, R. van and Narula, R. (1999), 'Outward Investment from the Netherlands: Introduction and Overview', in Hoesel, R. van and Narula, R. (eds), *Multinationals from the Netherlands*, London: Routledge, pp. 1–31.

Inkpen, A. (1996), 'Creating Knowledge through Collaboration', *California Management Review*, vol. 39, pp. 123–40.

Inkpen, A. (1998), 'Learning and Knowledge Acquisition through International Strategic Alliances', *Academy of Management Executive*, vol. 12

Inkpen, A. and Beamish, P. (1997), 'Knowledge, Bargaining Power, and the Instability of International Joint Ventures', *Academy of Management Review*, vol. 22, pp. 177–202.

Kay, N. (1991), 'Industrial Collaborative Activity and the Completion of the Internal Market', *Journal of Common Market Studies*, vol. 29, pp. 347–62.

Kay, N. (1997), *Pattern in Corporate Evolution*, Oxford: Oxford University Press.

Knickerbocker, F. (1973), *Oligopolistic Reaction and the Multinational Enterprise*, Cambridge (Mass.): Harvard University Press.

Kogut, B. (1988), 'Joint Ventures: Theoretical and Empirical Perspectives', *Strategic Management Journal*, vol. 9, pp. 319–32.

Kogut, B. and Zander, U. (1993), 'Knowledge of the Firm and the Evolutionary Theory of the Multinational Enterprise', *Journal of International Business Studies*, vol. 24, pp. 625–46.

Kuemmerle, W. (1996), 'Home Base and Foreign Direct Investment in R&D', unpublished PhD dissertation, Boston: Harvard Business School.

Kumar, N. (2001), 'Determinants of Location of Overseas R&D Activity of Multinational Enterprises: The Case of US and Japanese Corporations', *Research Policy*, vol. 30, pp. 159–74.

Kuznets, S. (1962), 'Inventive Activity; Problems of Definition and Management', in Nelson, R. (ed.), *The Rate and Direction of Inventive Activity*, Princeton: Princeton University Press.

Lundvall, B.-Å. (ed.) (1992), *National Systems of Innovation: Towards a Theory of Innovation and Interactive Learning*, London: Pinter Publishers.

Madhok, A. (1997) ,'Cost, Value and Foreign Market Entry Mode: The Transaction and the Firm', *Strategic Management Journal*, vol. 18, pp. 39–61.

Mytelka, L. (1995), 'Dancing with Wolves: Global Oligopolies and Strategic Partnerships', in Hagedoorn, J. (ed.), *Technical Change and the World Economy*, Aldershot and Brookfield: Edward Elgar, pp. 182–204.

Mytelka, L. and Delapierre, M. (1987), 'The Alliance Strategies of European Firms in the Information Technology Industry and the Role of ESPRIT', *Journal of Common Market Studies*, vol. 26, pp. 231–53.

Nakamura, T. (1981), *The Post-War Japanese Economy*, Tokyo: University of Tokyo Press.

Narula, R. (1999), 'Explaining Strategic R&D Alliances by European Firms', *Journal of Common Market Studies*, vol. 37, no. 4, pp. 711–23.

Narula, R. (2002), 'Innovation Systems and "Inertia" in R&D Location: Norwegian Firms and the Role of Systemic Lock-in', *Research Policy*, vol. 31, pp. 795–816.

Narula, R. (2003), *Globalisation and Technology: Interdependence, Innovation Systems and Industrial Policy*, Cambridge: Polity Press

Narula, R. and Dunning, J. (1998), 'Explaining International R&D Alliances and the Role of Governments', *International Business Review*, vol. 7, pp. 377–97.

Narula, R. and Hagedoorn, J. (1999), 'Innovating through Strategic Alliances: Moving towards International Partnerships and Contractual Agreements', *Technovation*, vol. 19, pp. 283–94.

Narula, R. and Sadowski, B. (2002), 'Technological Catch-Up and Strategic Technology Partnering in Developing Countries', *International Journal of Technology Management*, vol. 23, pp. 599–617.

Nelson, R. and Winter, S. (1982), *An Evolutionary Theory of Economic Change*, Cambridge: Belknap Press.

Niosi, J. (1995), *Flexible Innovation: Technological Alliances in Canadian Industry*, Montreal: McGill-Queens University Press.

Ostry, S. and Nelson, R. (1995), *Techno-Nationalism and Techno-Globalism: Conflict and Cooperation*, Washington: The Brookings Institution.

Peterson, J. (1991), 'Technology Policy in Europe: Explaining the Framework Programme and EUREKA in Theory and Practice', *Journal of Common Market Studies*, vol. 29, pp. 269–90.

Porter, M. and Fuller, M. (1986), 'Coalitions and Global Strategy', in Porter, M. (ed.), *Competition in Global Industries*, Boston: Harvard Business School Press.

Reich, R. (1990), 'Who Is Us?', *Harvard Business Review*, January-February, pp. 53–64.

Rugman, A. (1980), 'Internalisation as a General Theory of Foreign Direct Investment, A Reappraisal of the Literature', *Weltwirtschaftliches Archiv*, vol. 116, pp. 365–79.

Strange, S. (1998), 'Who are EU? Ambiguities in the Concept of Competitiveness', *Journal of Common Market Studies*, vol. 36, pp. 101–14.

Tidd, J. and Trewhella, M. (1997), 'Organizational and Technological Antecedents for Knowledge Creation and Learning', *R&D Management*, vol. 27, pp. 359–75.

Trajtenberg, M., Henderson, R. and Jaffe, A. (1997), 'University versus Corporate Patents : A Window on the Basicness of Invention', *Economics of Innovation and New Technologies*, vol. 5, pp. 19–50.

Veugelers, R. (1997), 'Internal R&D Expenditures and External Technology Sourcing', *Research Policy*, vol. 26, pp. 303–15.

Williamson, O. (1975), *Markets and Hierarchies: Analysis and Anti-Trust Implications*, New York: Free Press.

PART II

The Interactions between MNEs
and Systems of Innovation

6. Partnerships for knowledge in business and academia: a comparison between Europe and the USA

Daniele Archibugi and Alberto Coco

COLLABORATING FOR KNOWLEDGE: A POSITIVE SUM GAME

International collaborations are a significant and increasingly important channel of diffusion of knowledge in both the public and the business sectors. Their importance has grown, as the number of partnerships among public research centres, universities and firms testify (OECD (2000) and National Science Foundation (NSF) (2002)). Collaboration for knowledge has received a widespread consensus from analysts. It has been stressed that collaboration allows increasing the number of agents able to benefit from knowledge, and that it provides expanding learning opportunities. It permits partners to acquire the expertise of each other, by enriching the overall know-how (Hagedoorn, Link and Vonortas, 2000). Collaborations can be seen as a positive sum game and the partners acquire more advantages than disadvantages, although the net gains are not always equally distributed among them (see Archibugi and Michie (1995) and Gambardella and Malerba (1999), part II especially).

Much collaboration has occurred without a deliberate promotion by public policies. Firms have found it convenient to split the costs and risks associated with innovative programmes, and this has often induced them to share strategic know-how with actual and potential competitors. Academic researchers – a social group that has traditionally been open to sharing their knowledge inside and outside the borders of their state – have substantially benefited from the new information and communication technologies to work in co-ordination with colleagues in geographically remote areas.

Policy-makers have been keen to further enhance the mood to share know-how. Governments have welcomed the idea of devoting public resources to collaborative ventures since it increases the number of players receiving the benefits of public support and it promises to multiply the benefits of investment in knowledge. It is therefore not surprising that schemes to promote collaboration within academia, within firms and across academia and firms have proliferated. These policies have not been confined at the national level. On the contrary, more attention has been dedicated to bi-lateral and multi-lateral international co-operation as an instrument for acquiring and disseminating expertise that is not available at the country level.

A straightforward example is the European science and technology policy, which aims to enhance European co-operation in the activities of research and technological development (RTD). European institutions have based their policy of sustenance to scientific and technological development on promoting collaboration as a rather 'natural' outcome of a multi-government policy. Europe as a whole has felt the need to bridge (or – at least – not to increase) the scientific and technological gap with the USA. The budgets and the competencies of each European country – including those of the largest ones such as Germany, France and the UK – would not allow them to compete in the majority of fields with the USA. This has led European institutions, and in particular the European Union (EU), to fund research on a co-operative basis as a way to reach a sufficient critical mass to obtain excellence and with a view to disseminating the results across all member countries. At the same time, this was also conceived as an instrument to increase cohesion within the Union.

The idea to increase collaboration in the EU through public policies has counterbalanced the fact that the main competitors of European firms are likely to be other firms based in Europe (and not in the USA). The closest neighbour is likely to be also the fiercest competitor. Policies to induce European firms to collaborate among themselves should also overcome the reluctance of competitors to share such a crucial strategic asset as technological expertise.

The main instrument used by the EU is a plan of financial aid to research projects known as the various Framework Programmes (FPs), promoted every four years by the European Commission, with the approval of the Council and Parliament (for more information, see <www.cordis.lu>. The bulk of the resources are attributed through competitive tenders which, among a range of requirements, also privilege co-participation from private and public organisations based in more than one EU member country.

In recent years, European institutions have concentrated more and more of their resources on 'priority' research areas, corresponding to the most innovative sectors (life-science and biotechnology; information society; energy and environment; sustainable growth). In their policy, they also have considered three main objectives, considered strategic for both economic and social reasons:

• to support small and medium enterprises (SMEs), critical for innovation and job creation;

- to involve the least developed areas around the EU (Eastern Europe, the Newly Independent States, the Mediterranean countries) through a plan of international co-operation;
- to upgrade human capital, by means of an intense process of training and mobility of researchers that allows a continuous acquisition and exchange of knowledge across academia, industry and other institutions.

Co-operation among firms and public research organisations across countries would help to achieve all these goals.

The EU had to face another dilemma, namely to make sure that the financial resources provided to one, or a group of, economic agents would not distort competition. European integration has started as a custom union in order to develop a 'common' but also 'competitive' market, and it would have been contradictory for the EU itself to carry out some policies that would distort competition. But in the field of science and technology it has traditionally been more acceptable than in other traditional fields – such as agriculture or steel – to provide funds to some organisations only, since it was expected that the benefits of RTD would have been propagated across the whole Union.

This has led to funds being made available for so-called 'pre-competitive' research. It has long been argued whether anything like 'pre-competitive' research exists. But, as a rule of thumb, the Commission is probably right in assuming that if a research grant is assigned to a consortium, composed of a variety of organisations in different countries, it is less likely that it is going to benefit a national industry only and to disadvantage potential competitors. And the Commission is certainly right in assuming that the production of knowledge would generate direct and indirect benefits not only for the players receiving EU funding.

How influential is the EU's science and technology policy? Concerning the financial budget, this has grown for every FP, having reached the sum of 16,270 million euros, for the current one (FP6, for the period 2002–2006) an 18 per cent increase compared to FP5 (1998–2002) and a 36 per cent increase compared to FP4 (1994–1998). But it remains limited, and it takes no more than 5 per cent of the total EU budget and just 5.5 per cent of the total spending of member state governments for civil RDT (see Sharp (2001), p. 243), European Commission (2002, p. 20). For a more comprehensive assessment of EU policy, see Peterson and Sharp (1998). The impact of these resources is probably larger than their simple quantitative weight since the EU finances additional projects, it privileges co-funded projects and it has a greater flexibility than the national budgets.

This chapter aims to analyse whether and how the European Union policy has influenced the dimension and the trend of European international collaborations. We will take into account two forms of international collaboration for sharing know-how: 1) strategic technology agreements among firms from different countries; and 2) academic collaborations among researchers from different countries.[1]

We assume that collaborations can be taken as an indicator of the vitality of a national knowledge system and that they are beneficial for the country as a whole. A country is often involved in collaboration if its institutions have an attractive knowledge-base that is of interest to institutions based in other countries. At the same time, collaborations allow institutions to plug into the knowledge systems of other countries, allowing national institutions to upgrade their competencies (Cantwell and Iammarino (2003)).

In the next two sections we will present some evidence on international collaborations for science and technology across the Triad (Europe–USA–Japan), by focusing in particular on the comparison between Europe and USA. Our data show that the USA has substantially augmented its participation in strategic technology partnering among firms, while Europe has lost significant positions. But in academic collaboration, Europe has taken a greater role, and the USA has relatively declined.

STRATEGIC TECHNOLOGY AGREEMENTS

A strategic industrial technology agreement is defined as a partnership that has the following three characteristics: 1) it involves a two-way relationship where knowledge is a crucial component; 2) it is contractual in nature with little or no equity involvement by the participants; 3) it is strategic in the sense that it is a long term planned activity (Mowery (1992) and Mytelka (2001)).

It is well known that this form of agreement has substantially increased in the last 20 years. Figure 6.1 reports the trend from 1980 to 2000 of the absolute number of yearly interregional technological alliances for the USA, Europe and Japan. Data are taken from the database developed by John Hagedoorn and his colleagues (see Hagedoorn (1996, 2002); and the National Science Foundation (2002). The USA and Europe split the same trend: a uniform growth except the two drops following the Gulf War in 1990–1991 and the Kosovo War in 1999. Foreign alliances of Japanese companies have kept steady in the last 20 years.

International technology agreements are a source of knowledge and signal where companies seek expertise (Narula and Hagedoorn (1999)). Some evidence on the distribution of inter-firm technological collaboration is reported in Table 6.1. We consider the strategic technology alliances between and within the three main economic blocs.[2] International alliances have more than doubled. Alliances among blocs represent 42.4 per cent of total alliances.

The geographical distribution of the alliances shows that the largest and most increasing portion of them takes place within the United States. 45.8 per cent

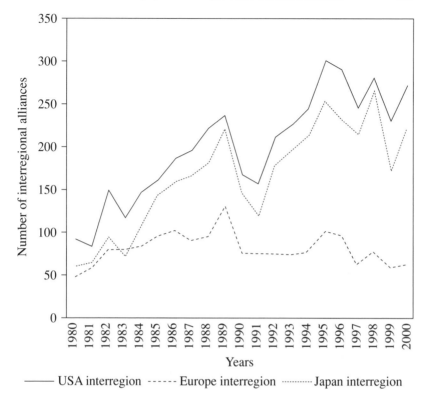

Source: National Science Foundation (2002); Hagedoorn (1996, 2002).

Figure 6.1 *Trend of interregional alliances in the Triad, 1980–2000*

of all the strategic technological alliances recorded in 1998–2000 occurred among American firms only, and the share has increased greatly with respect to the past (they were 34.7 per cent of the total at the beginning of the 1990s and 24.6 per cent in the 1980s). Of all US alliances, 45.6 per cent are Pan-American, and 54.6 per cent involve foreign firms. But the US firms have strong ties on both the Atlantic and the Pacific shores: in the recent period, US companies have participated in as much as 84.7 per cent of all recorded technology alliances (against 69.5 per cent in the first period). Inter-firm strategic technological alliances almost always imply the participation of at least one American company (an analysis of the US case is presented in Vonortas (1997)).

On the contrary, the share of intra-European strategic technological alliances has substantially declined: they accounted for 18.2 per cent in 1980–1982, and

Table 6.1 *Distribution of strategic technology alliances between and within economic blocs, 1980–2000*

Year	Total	Interregional alliances								Intraregional alliances						
		Eur-Jap		Eur-US		Jap-US		Subtotal		Europe		Japan		USA		Subtotal
		number	%	number	%	number	%			number	%	number	%	number	%	
1980–1982	203	16	7.9	48	23.6	43	21.2	107		37	18.2	9	4.4	50	24.6	96
1989–1991	404	25	6.2	101	25.0	57	14.1	183		74	18.3	7	1.7	140	34.7	221
1998–2000	542	19	3.5	173	31.9	38	7.0	230		53	9.8	11	2.0	248	45.8	312

Source: Our elaboration from National Science Foundation (2002).

less than 10 per cent in 1998–2000; they have even decreased in absolute terms in the last decade (from 74 in 1989–1991 to 53 in 1998–2000). Besides, European–US partnerships have gone up, both in relative (from 23.6 to 31.9 per cent) and absolute terms (more than three times with respect to two decades ago, from 48 a year in 1980–1982 to 173 a year in 1998–2000). While American companies do not need to plug into the innovation systems of other countries, and manage to exploit their know-how abroad even in the absence of international strategic partnerships, European firms (even more than Japanese firms) feel the need to share competencies with American counterparts (Narula and Hagedoorn (1999)).

But the most striking result is the decline of Pan-European strategic technology partnerships, especially in the light of the policies carried out at the EU level to foster them (see Narula (1998)). One possible explanation would be that the absolute amount of resources devoted to science and technology is higher in the USA, so that the greatest flow of alliances in this continent would simply be the outcome of the amount of investment in knowledge by US companies. In order to control for this factor, we have divided the number of European alliances by the total amount of, respectively, European, US and Japanese business enterprise R&D (BERD). This provides an indicator of the European companies' propensity towards collaboration in each of these regions. The results are reported in Table 6.2.

Although the attractiveness of the US economy is a bit smaller in relative terms, it is confirmed that European companies have a greater propensity for American rather than European partnerships. In the 1998–2000 period, there are 1.07 European–US partnerships for each billion US dollars of BERD, while the equivalent figure for Pan-European alliances is just 0.62. This result is even more striking if compared with the past trend. In fact, the European business community has considerably reduced its propensity for partnership: in 1980–1982 and 1989–1991, European companies had a larger propensity for European rather than American partners. The figures were, respectively, 0.80 and 0.61 agreements for each billion US dollars of BERD in 1980–1982, and 1.03 and 0.86 in 1989–1991. Another confirmation of the American attractiveness for European firms is found by looking at the agreements signed with Japanese companies: the European propensity has in fact constantly decreased.

To have a homogeneous picture, we also report (in the lower part of Table 6.2) the propensity of American companies to undertake alliances across regions. US companies are now keener to undertake joint ventures with European partners and this is a result of the overall increase of their engagement in collaborations. They have become less attracted to partnerships with Japanese companies: the propensity has reduced to one-third between the first and last periods.[3] Besides it is supported by the great propensity for internal partnerships, which has grown about three times in the last 20 years.

Table 6.2   Propensities for strategic technical partnerships, 1980–2000

Propensity of European firms for European, US and Japanese technological partners

Number of agreements involving European firms by BERD of the region (in billion US $ at constant dollars PPP)

Period	Europe	USA	Japan
1980–1982	0.80	0.61	0.71
1989–1991	1.03	0.86	0.50
1998–2000	0.62	1.07	0.32

Propensity of US firms for European, US and Japanese technological partners

Number of agreements involving US firms by BERD of the region (in billion US $ at constant dollars PPP)

Period	Europe	USA	Japan
1980–1982	1.03	0.64	1.90
1989–1991	1.41	1.20	1.15
1998–2000	2.03	1.54	0.65

Notes: Methodology – the number of strategic technological agreements recorded by the MERIT database has been divided by the business expenditure on R&D of the region expressed in constant 1992 purchasing power parity US billion $. It reads for example that in 1980–1982 there have been 0.8 strategic technology agreements involving European firms for each US dollar billion of European BERD.

Source: Our elaboration from National Science Foundation (2002) (data from MERIT database) and from Organisation Economic Co-operation and Development Statistics, *Main Science and Technology Indicators 2001–2002*.

Therefore, also keeping out the differences in investment in knowledge, it is confirmed that intra-European, inter-firm strategic technology alliances are low. These trends have occurred in spite of EU policies: the FPs aimed to increase European technology partnering but it has decreased. Some observations can help to account for this.

First, the FP budget is very low, as compared to the request of the business community: remember that the current one amounts to 16,270 million euros for four years, so approximately 4,000 million euros a year, when the annual BERD in Europe has a magnitude of about 100,000 million euros (OECD (2002)).

Second, the EU funds have different destinations: in the main research areas, they are mainly devoted to financing pre-competitive research projects, which, as mentioned before, do not always coincide with the aims of industrial research, which is more inspired by criteria of competitiveness. Furthermore, a significant share of resources is destined to non-industrial purposes (the involvement of the weakest areas, the upgrading of the human base).

In the end, what remains for European collaborative industrial projects is not much, so that the choice European firms effectuate about partners is fundamentally dictated by managerial criteria. On the one hand, partners in the USA seem to be more reliable generators of knowledge than European ones. On the other hand, they are less likely to compete directly in the European market. The deepening of economic integration in Europe has increased competition, and this has made companies less keen to share technology (Narula, 1998; Molero and Heys, 2001). Much greater policy instruments would have been needed to reverse these trends. Still, it should be explained how Pan-American technological joint-ventures – in the absence of specific policies and in a market which is certainly more integrated and competitive than the European one – continue to grow.

It is well known that the bulk of these technology alliances have taken place in emerging fields, and in particular in information technology (IT) and biotechnology. Table 6.3 shows that these two sectors only represent two-thirds of the total agreements that have occurred in recent years. Bearing in mind that these fields involve the highest costs and risks, the result is not a surprise. Biotechnology shows the highest growth rate in the last decade, by climbing from 12 to 29 per cent of the total alliances. From a geographical viewpoint, Europe is involved in alliances in biotechnology as much as in IT, while Japan and the USA show a great prevalence in IT. This suggests that Europe is relatively stronger in biotechnology and weaker in IT with respect to the USA and Japan. The amount of FP funds in the key areas of research in some sense confirms this evidence.

ACADEMIC COLLABORATIONS

Partnerships and collaborations promoted by public research institutions and universities play an equally crucial role in the international dissemination of knowledge. The scope, complexity and cost of some of today's scientific problems suggest and often compel international collaborations among institutions of different countries. They can take a variety of forms: joint research centres, exchange of students and of academic staff, sharing of scientific information. One of the ways to measure these collaborations is by looking at internationally co-authored scientific papers. A dramatic increase in internationally co-authored papers – also facilitated by the diffusion of Internet and email – is evident in all countries. Table 6.4 reports the internationally co-authored scientific papers in absolute terms for the years 1986 and 1999. The

Table 6.3   International strategic technology alliances, by technology and selected region/country, 1980–2000

Total	1980–1982	%	1989–1991	%	1998–2000	%
Total	229	100	465	100	607	100
Information technology	68	30	206	44	228	38
Biotechnology	41	18	54	12	179	29
New materials	20	9	34	7	30	5
Aerospace and defense	14	6	47	10	21	3
Automotive	12	5	24	5	42	7
Chemicals (nonbiotechnology)	32	14	57	12	49	8
Other	42	18	43	9	58	10
United States						
Total	155	100	321	100	499	100
Information technology	49	31	159	49	192	39
Biotechnology	32	21	39	12	154	31
New materials	12	8	23	7	22	4
Aerospace and defense	9	6	29	9	16	3
Automotive	5	3	15	5	29	6
Chemicals (nonbiotechnology)	20	13	34	11	37	7
Other	28	18	22	7	49	10
Europe						
Total	108	100	231	100	265	100
Information technology	32	29	83	36	80	30
Biotechnology	13	12	29	12	79	30
New materials	12	11	18	8	14	5
Aerospace and defense	8	7	29	13	12	4
Automotive	8	7	9	4	24	9
Chemicals (nonbiotechnology)	15	14	34	15	32	12
Other	20	19	29	12	24	9
Japan						
Total	72	100	98	100	75	100
Information technology	23	32	44	45	37	50
Biotechnology	12	17	8	8	11	15
New materials	5	7	9	9	8	11
Aerospace and defense	3	4	4	4	2	2
Automotive	4	5	11	11	7	9
Chemicals (nonbiotechnology)	11	16	15	15	3	4
Other	14	20	7	7	7	9

Notes: Total alliances are less than the sum of the alliances of the USA, Europe and Japan because the transnational alliances are counted once for each region involved.

Source: Our elaboration from National Science Foundation (2002).

number of internationally co-authored papers has at least doubled, and in some countries it has tripled. It is interesting to examine the geographical evolution. The USA is still the country with the highest participation in internationally co-authored papers, and this is not surprising taking into account the size of its scientific community. But if we look at the dynamics, the situation changes abruptly: in the last 15 years the USA and Canada are the countries with the lowest growth rates. This has lead to a decrease in the USA in the world's share of internationally co-authored scientific papers. We can check for this in Figure 6.2, where we observe that from 1986 to 1999 EU and Japanese shares increased and the USA decreased.[4]

Table 6.4   Internationally co-authored papers, 1986 and 1999

	Internationally co-authored articles in 1986	Internationally co-authored articles in 1999	Annual growth rate from 1986 to 1999 (%)
USA	17.187	39.669	6.6
Japan	2.509	9.275	10.6
Austria	687	2.369	10.0
Belgium	1.313	3.733	8.4
Denmark	1.025	2.813	8.1
Finland	589	2.214	10.7
France	4.932	13.905	8.3
Germany	5.805	18.340	9.3
Greece	362	1.250	10.0
Ireland	243	753	9.1
Italy	2.620	8.551	9.5
Netherlands	1.830	5.654	9.1
Portugal	160	1.129	16.2
Spain	911	5.569	14.9
Sweden	1.935	4.887	7.4
UK	6.554	16.806	7.5
Canada	4.375	8.665	5.4
Norway	568	1.589	8.2
Switzerland	2.174	5.385	7.2

Notes: Article counts are on a whole-count basis where each country author receives a whole count on internationally co-authored papers. Internationally co-authored papers consist of papers that have at least one international co-author. We could not calculate the EU total because the sum of EU countries would contain multiple countings (a paper co-authored by a French and a Belgian would be counted twice and so on).

Source: Institute for Scientific Information, Science Citation and Social Citation Indexes; CHI Research, Inc., Science Indicators database; and National Science Foundation, Division of Science resources Statistics, 2002.

Internationally co-authored articles 1986

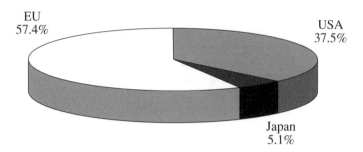

Internationally co-authored articles 1999

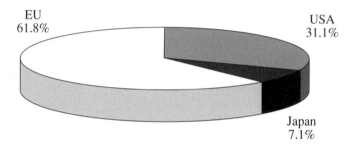

Notes: Articles are assigned to every country on a fractional basis (one half if it is co-authored between two countries and so on).

Source: Our elaboration from National Science Foundation (2002).

Figure 6.2   Distribution of internationally co-authored articles across the Triad, 1986 and 1999

Table 6.5 presents the same data as Table 6.4 from another visual angle: internationally co-authored articles are divided by the total scientific articles for 1986 and 1999. In this way, we can compare the evolution of total scientific articles and of internationally co-authored ones. The percentage nearly doubles in the considered period, and this represents a clear signal of globalisation in the generation of knowledge.

It also emerges that European countries have a higher ratio of articles in international collaboration than the USA and Japan. This fact is not surprising given the smaller size of the scientific community in each individual European country (Pianta and Archibugi, 1991; Archibugi and Pianta, 1992), but it also indicates that the academic community in Europe is perceived as a valuable asset for the acquisition of knowledge and expertise.

Table 6.5 Percentage of internationally co-authored scientific papers in selected countries in all scientific papers, 1986 and 1999

	Internationally co-authored in 1986 (%)	Internationally co-authored in 1999 (%)	Annual growth rate from 1986 to 1999 (%)
USA	9.2	21.6	6.8
Japan	7.5	17.6	6.7
Austria	25.2	47.6	5.0
Belgium	29.9	52.5	4.4
Denmark	24.4	48.5	5.4
Finland	18.7	42.0	6.4
France	21.0	39.6	5.0
Germany	20.1	38.4	5.1
Greece	26.6	42.1	3.6
Ireland	26.7	44.7	4.0
Italy	22.9	39.4	4.3
Netherlands	19.8	41.2	5.8
Portugal	34.8	52.8	3.3
Spain	17.0	36.2	6.0
Sweden	22.2	44.1	5.4
UK	15.7	34.1	6.1
Canada	18.9	35.4	5.0
Norway	21.9	44.9	5.7
Switzerland	32.2	52.4	3.8

Notes: National rates are based on total counts: each collaborating country is assigned one paper (a paper with three international co-authors may contribute to the international co-authorship of three countries and so on). We could not calculate the EU total, as it would contain multiple countings.

Source: Our elaboration from National Science Foundation (2002) (data from ISI – Institute for Scientific Information).

From a dynamic viewpoint, however, the rate of increase has been higher in the USA and Japan than in European countries. This finding deserves attention: from 1986 to 1999 the USA has grown more than Europe and Japan in the percentage of internationally co-authored articles on total articles (Table 6.5); but its absolute number has grown less (Table 6.4). This means that the USA has not only decreased its world share as regards internationally co-authored articles – as Figure 6.2 shows – but also as regards total scientific articles.

Not only this, but the loss of shares in total scientific output has been greater than the loss of shares in the portion constituted by internationally co-authored scientific articles.[5]

A way to see graphically the relation between the absolute and relative size of the academic collaborative phenomenon is to put the countries in a two-dimensional space, where on the horizontal axis we measure the absolute number of internationally co-authored articles[6] and on the vertical one their percentage over the total articles. In Figure 6.3, the regression line shows an inverse relationship since, as expected, the propensity to collaborate is inversely related to the size of a country. But it is interesting to check how individual countries have different propensities to collaborate. Those below the line are relatively less internationally open, or more self-sufficient, while those above the line show a greater propensity to international collaboration. From the inspection of the graph we note that Japan is a long way below the line, with a negligible share of internationally co-authored articles. The USA is on the extreme right of the line, with its large share, and below it, although less so than Japan. Spain, Finland, Ireland and Greece are a little below the line but the distances are negligible. The scenario for 1986 is not so different. Globally, the graphs confirm what Table 6.5 has shown: European countries are more open internationally than the other two components of the Triad, and this is not only due to the smaller size, but also to a greater propensity towards collaboration.

To complete the analysis, we look at the distribution of internationally co-authored articles across collaborating countries in the Triad. This allows a comparison with the analysis on the industrial side. Does the European academic community also share the same preference of European firms for American rather than for European partners? From Table 6.6, we note that Europe is by far the greatest collaborator for the American academic community. In 1995–1997 as much as 60.3 per cent of the US internationally co-authored papers involved a European partner. Also Europeans have a strong propensity to collaborate with each other. This fact could be misleading if we think that a paper co-authored by a Dutch and a Belgian scientist is classified as 'international', while a paper co-authored by a Californian and a New Yorker is classified as national. Still, the USA remains the single nation most collaborated with by every European country.

But what is significant about these data is the dynamic analysis (not affected by the different size of the countries). By comparing the period 1986–1988 to the more recent 1995–1997, it emerges that the share of inside-EU collaborations has greatly increased (from 56.6 to 69.4 per cent of all EU internationally co-authored papers), while the share of US collaborations has decreased for the EU as a whole (from 31.9 to 29.0 per cent) as well as for each EU member country. If we look at Japan, we note that it has increased its percentage of collaborations with the EU (from 33.3 to 39.4) and decreased that with the

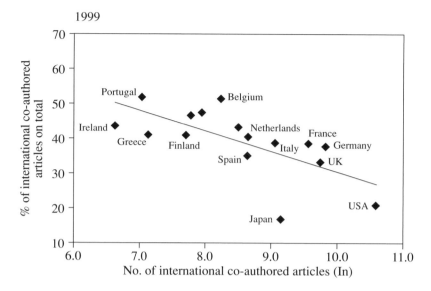

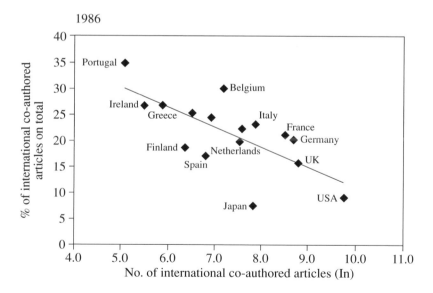

Source: Our elaboration from National Science Foundation (2002).

Figure 6.3   *Relation between the absolute dimension of international co-authored articles and their ratio to total articles, 1986 and 1999*

Table 6.6 Distribution of internationally co-authored papers across collaborating countries, 1986–1988 and 1995–1997

Country	Year	USA	Jap	EU	UK	Ger	Fra	Ita	Neth	Swe	Den	Finl	Belg	Aus	Irel	Spa	Gre	Por
USA	1986–1988		8.2	54.9	12.7	11.8	8.3	5.7	3.4	4.1	1.7	1.2	1.9	1.0	0.3	1.7	0.9	0.2
USA	1995–1997		9.6	60.3	12.4	12.8	8.9	6.7	4.2	3.5	2.0	1.6	2.0	1.4	0.4	3.1	0.9	0.4
Japan	1986–1988	54.0		33.3	7.0	10.2	5.1	2.1	2.0	2.0	0.8	0.6	1.5	0.8	0.2	0.8	0.2	0.0
Japan	1995–1997	45.6		39.4	9.1	9.9	5.7	3.5	2.7	2.6	1.1	1.1	1.2	0.7	0.2	1.1	0.3	0.2
EU	1986–1988	31.9	3.1	56.6	10.3	10.4	9.0	5.8	4.7	4.0	2.4	1.5	3.4	1.7	0.6	2.7	0.8	0.5
EU	1995–1997	29.0	4.5	69.4	12.1	12.1	10.9	7.6	5.8	4.1	2.9	2.1	3.7	2.0	0.8	5.0	1.1	1.6
UK	1986–1988	33.9	2.9	46.3		10.2	8.2	6.1	4.8	3.7	2.4	1.1	2.4	0.9	1.6	2.8	1.3	0.8
UK	1995–1997	30.6	4.7	60.2		12.6	10.7	7.8	6.5	3.8	3.0	1.5	3.1	1.4	1.8	5.0	1.7	1.3
Germany	1986–1988	31.1	4.1	47.9	10.2		9.5	5.5	5.1	3.7	2.3	1.4	2.8	4.1	0.3	1.9	0.8	0.3
Germany	1995–1997	30.0	4.9	58.6	11.9		11.5	7.1	5.9	3.8	2.7	1.7	3.0	4.5	0.5	3.7	1.6	0.7
France	1986–1988	28.9	2.7	54.7	10.7	12.5		8.6	4.0	2.9	1.5	0.7	6.0	1.0	0.4	4.6	1.1	0.7
France	1995–1997	26.1	3.5	66.7	12.7	14.4		10.1	5.0	3.1	1.9	1.4	6.2	1.4	0.5	6.9	1.8	1.3
Italy	1986–1988	35.7	2	64.3	14.5	13.1	15.5		4.3	3.9	2.0	0.9	3.6	1.7	0.4	3.6	0.6	0.2
Italy	1995–1997	32.6	3.5	76.3	15.4	14.8	16.7		5.7	3.6	2.7	1.7	3.5	2.1	0.6	6.5	1.9	1.1
Netherlands	1986–1988	31.1	2.7	73.7	16.4	17.5	10.4	6.2		3.9	2.3	2.0	9.4	1.9	0.7	2.2	0.4	0.4
Netherlands	1995–1997	29.2	3.9	85.4	18.4	17.6	11.8	8.1		4.6	3.5	2.3	9.5	1.8	1.0	4.6	1.0	1.2
Sweden	1986–1988	36.1	2.7	61.2	12.0	12.1	7.4	5.4	3.7		8.8	5.8	2.5	1.2	0.2	1.2	0.7	0.2
Sweden	1995–1997	28.8	4.5	73.2	12.6	13.5	8.8	6.0	5.4		9.1	7.3	3.7	1.4	0.5	3.1	0.9	0.9
Denmark	1986–1988	29.6	2	73.2	15.4	14.8	7.3	5.5	4.4	17.2		3.4	1.6	1.0	0.2	1.6	0.4	0.4
Denmark	1995–1997	29.0	3.4	94.1	17.9	16.4	9.6	8.1	7.3	15.9		4.5	3.0	2.1	0.7	5.5	2.3	0.8
Finland	1986–1988	33.1	2.4	71.3	11.2	14.7	5.6	4.1	6.1	18.0	5.4		2.6	1.8	0.4	0.9	2.4	0.2
Finland	1995–1997	32.1	4.8	89.0	12.4	14.9	9.3	7.1	6.7	17.7	6.3		3.8	2.1	0.8	3.7	1.1	1.8
Belgium	1986–1988	25.9	3	83.7	11.8	13.8	22.8	7.5	13.7	3.8	1.3	1.3		2.0	0.6	3.3	1.1	0.7
Belgium	1995–1997	22.9	2.9	97.6	14.1	14.8	23.8	8.2	15.5	5.0	2.4	2.2		1.4	1.0	5.3	2.1	1.8
Austria	1986–1988	25.8	3	78.5	8.4	38.6	7.0	6.5	5.1	3.4	1.4	1.6	3.7		0.3	2.3	0.2	0.0
Austria	1995–1997	25.1	2.8	82.1	10.1	34.5	8.5	7.6	4.8	3.0	2.6	1.9	2.2		0.5	4.3	1.7	0.4
Ireland	1986–1988	22.3	1.8	78.2	42.6	7.9	8.8	4.1	5.2	1.5	0.9	1.0	2.9	0.9		1.4	0.4	0.6
Ireland	1995–1997	21.8	2.5	101.3	40.6	12.3	10.2	7.4	8.1	3.2	2.9	2.3	5.0	1.5		4.8	1.6	1.4
Spain	1986–1988	28.9	1.9	79.6	18.2	12.6	22.5	9.9	4.2	2.4	1.6	0.5	4.3	1.6	0.3		0.3	1.2
Spain	1995–1997	25.4	1.9	84.5	16.9	13.1	19.5	11.1	5.5	3.1	3.2	1.6	3.9	2.0	0.7		1.7	2.2
Greece	1986–1988	42.0	1.1	69.2	22.5	14.5	14.9	4.4	2.3	3.6	1.0	0.5	3.7	0.4	0.3	0.9		0.2
Greece	1995–1997	31.2	2.5	122.1	23.5	23.3	21.0	13.8	5.1	3.9	5.6	4.1	6.6	3.3	1.0	7.0		3.9
Portugal	1986–1988	24.2	0.4	88.4	29.3	11.6	20.8	3.4	4.8	1.8	2.5	0.7	5.4	0.2	0.9	6.6	0.4	
Portugal	1995–1997	21.0	2.1	126.5	25.9	15.8	22.2	11.5	8.9	5.6	2.9	4.4	7.9	1.1	1.3	13.4	5.6	

Notes: Row percentages may add up to more than 100 because articles are counted in each contributing country and some may have authors in three or more countries.
With regard to the European Union, internationally co-authored articles also include those among member countries.
Rows report the percentage of the total number of international co-authorships of the country. Columns indicate the relative prominence of a country in the portfolio of internationally co-authored articles of every country.

Source: National Science Foundation (2000).

USA (from 54.0 to 45.6). Finally, the USA has increased its share of international collaborations both with Japan (from 8.2 to 9.6 per cent) and the EU (from 54.9 to 60.3 per cent). The data for American academia support the above trend: the share of nationally co-authored articles on the total number of co-authored articles (nationally and internationally) involving a US-based scholar has declined from 78.2 per cent in 1986–1988 to 64.2 per cent in 1999 (National Science Foundation, 2002, Table 5.45). On the other hand, American co-authorship with scholars based in the EU has grown from 11.6 per cent in 1986 to 19.1 per cent in 1997 (National Science Foundation, 2000, Tables 6.60 and 6.61).

Thus, the attractiveness of the American national system, so clear for industrial collaborations, seems to encounter a drastic reduction regarding academic production. These data confirm the decrease of the US share in international article co-authorship already assessed in Table 6.4. Indeed, they reveal that European academia has increased its weight in international collaborations.

Concerning the composition by field of academic collaborations, the sector in which most scientific articles are internationally co-authored is earth and space sciences, followed by physics and mathematics (Table 6.7). There are also important academic partnerships in biomedical research and biology. If from international co-authorship we turn to total co-authorship, which includes co-authoring internal to a country (these data reflect substantially the position of the USA which is the country with the most internal articles), we find that the sector most co-authored becomes clinical medicine, followed by biomedical research and earth and space sciences. As regards the growth in the period examined, the greatest progress is shown by physics and psychology.

We stress the existence of an opposite trend in collaborations in industry and academia. Regarding the American slowdown, the data also reflects the lower level of attention that public research institutions have received from the Federal Government, which has devoted its resources to business priorities. We are aware that these data also reflect the fact that the academic journals composing the Science Citation Index (on which these data are based) are more and more open to non-English speaking countries, and this has somewhat reduced the dominion of the Anglo-Saxon academic community. But overall it is possible to conclude that European academia has become more attractive and has increased its significance.

Can these positive trends also be associated with EU policies? All FPs have dedicated a whole expenditure chapter to improving human capital (1280 million euros in FP5, increasing to 1580 in FP6). An intense process of training of researchers and acquisition of knowledge has begun through various measures: by sustaining the mobility of researchers to and from abroad (by means of fellowships), by fixing awards for the achieving of excellent results in research, by enhancing the access to infrastructures (for an assessment of the European impact on university research, see Geuna (1999)). The aim of the FPs has been to build a European 'knowledge society' that can link academia, industry and institutions. At least the FPs' goal to increase co-operation in academia has been reached.

Table 6.7   Fields of co-authorship and international co-authorship, 1986–1988 and 1995–1997

World	Co-authored (%)		Internat. co-authored (%)	
	1986–1988	1995–1997	1986–1988	1995–1997
Total science & engineering	*38.6*	*50.1*	*7.8*	*14.8*
Physics	32.2	49.0	11.1	22.4
Chemistry	26.7	38.5	6.7	12.8
Earth & space sciences	39.7	54.3	13.3	24.1
Mathematics	28.6	38.2	14.4	20.6
Biology	31.4	44.5	7.4	13.9
Biomedical research	41.5	54.9	9.1	16.2
Clinical medicine	52.4	61.3	6.3	11.5
Engineering	29.9	39.8	7.1	12.7
Psychology	30.6	38.6	4.1	8.5
Social sciences	23.4	29.2	5.4	8.6
Health & professional fields	29.6	36.7	3.3	6.4

Source: National Science Foundation (2000).

A complementary piece of evidence is represented by collaboration between academia and firms. Preliminary information from Pavitt and Patel (2002) has indicated that European firms are keener to collaborate with American rather than with European universities (as measured by jointly co-authored scientific papers). The willingness, and ability, of American universities to work for firms may have diverted some energies from typical academic collaborations. At the same time, the evidence also suggests that in the old continent there is a potential, and dangerous, divergence between the research trajectories followed by 'public academia' and 'business technology'.

CONCLUSIONS

This chapter has commented on a significant divergent trend in international collaborations for knowledge. On the one hand, American companies have considerably increased their recourse to strategic technology agreements as a source of innovation and this has also affected European firms, which have become more willing to collaborate with American partners, and less interested in sharing know-how with other European companies. European firms have looked for partnerships in those countries where they can split more easily the costs and risks of research and absorb a greater flow of know-how, minimising the danger of 'sleeping with the enemy', i.e. with the most relevant market competitors. On the other hand, European academia has increased its attractiveness as measured by international co-authorship, and European scholars have augmented their collaborations not only within the old continent, but also with American scholars.

We have assumed that partners are more often sought when they have a substantial knowledge dowry: the institutions of a country are often sought as partners if the overall national knowledge system is vital. Certainly, the attractiveness for potential collaborators is only one of the many ways to assess the strengths of a national scientific and technological system. However, it is logical to assume that it is good news when a science and technology (S&T) system increases its links with other parts of the world. It is more difficult to explain how in the last decade Europe has become more attractive in 'public science' and less attractive in 'business technology', while precisely the opposite trend has occurred in the USA.

Can these trends also be associated with deliberate public policies carried out in Europe and in the USA? We have referred to the impact of the EU R&D policy, which has increased its importance in the last decade as a tool for creating and diffusing innovation. By means of the Framework Programmes, European institutions have financed co-operation across industry and academia. Four main reasons induce us to consider collaborations so important, especially for a union of different states: they permit sharing of the high costs and risks of research; they allow absorption of expertise and know-how from other countries; they facilitate expansion of the size of the market; they can accelerate the process of integration in a wider sense.

But EU budget and instruments, although growing, continue to be very limited and subject to many constraints (Pavitt, 1998, p. 567). The share effectively gone to industrial research of a collaborative nature has always been very low compared with the requirements (EU funds cover just 5.5 per cent of the total European public civilian expenditure on R&D). Thus the EU policy seems not to come out uniform. It still has not been able to make Europe become a junction of technological exchange. European firms should probably call for more help via national sources and policies. Also in the case of sharing know-how in the business sector, it emerges that the EU should use a wider battery of instruments than the (limited) financial ones (Barry, 2001; Pavitt, 1998). Regulation, standards, procurement, competition, real services and large-scale co-operative civilian projects seem to be more important instruments to create a European Research Area than the (limited) financial instruments (Lundvall, 2001).

However, it is significant what happened in the academic sector. It testifies that Europe owes a human capital able to allow future growth. But it has also pointed out that European academia is becoming more and more isolated from business, up to the point that European companies prefer to contract research and to collaborate with American, rather than European, universities (Pavitt and Patel, 2002). A greater integration between business and academia also seems essential if Europe wants to become – as policy-makers have reiterated since the Lisbon Summit of 2000 – the greatest society of knowledge of the 21st century.

NOTES

1. We will not take into account collaborations between firms and academia since data are not easily available (Pavitt and Patel, 2002).
2. We do not include alliances involving countries outside the Triad, which constitute less than 10 per cent of the total.
3. This also depends on the decreasing propensity of Japanese firms towards international collaborations.
4. To build this graph, we had to sum the internationally co-authored scientific articles of each country by avoiding multiple counting. We first considered the number of total scientific articles for each country in which every internationally co-authored one is counted on a fractional assignment basis (it is counted as one half if it is co-authored between two countries and so on); these data are furnished by National Science Foundation (2002, Table 5.41). We subtracted from them the number of national scientific articles for each country (obtained from Table 5.48 as the difference between the number of total articles and the number of internationally co-authored articles, in which each internationally co-authored article is counted on a whole-count basis, that is counted as one independently from the number of foreign partners). By so doing, we got the number of internationally co-authored articles for each country on a fractional assignment basis: each article is assigned to a country only for the fraction that involves it, so that no article can be counted more than once when we aggregate the countries we want to analyse.
5. Let us call *GintUS* the growth rate of US internationally co-authored articles and *GtotUS* the growth rate of total US scientific articles; let the corresponding rate for Europe be *GintEU* and *GtotEU*. We know from Table 6.4 that in the period 1986–1999:

$$GintUS < GintEU \qquad (1)$$

Table 6.5 says that in the same period $G(intUS/totUS) > G(intEU/totEU)$, which can be written:

$$GintUS - GtotUS > GintEU - GtotEU \qquad (2)$$

From (1) and (2), we derive: *GtotUS < GtotEU*. The disequation (2) above can also be written: *GtotEU – GtotUS > GintEU – GintUS*, which means $G(totEU/totUS) > G(intEU/intUS)$.
6. We considered the logarithm of the number of articles.

REFERENCES

Archibugi, D. and Lundvall B.-Å. (eds) (2001), *The Globalising Learning Economy*, Oxford: Oxford University Press.

Archibugi, D. and Michie, J. (1995), 'The Globalisation of Technology: A New Taxonomy', *Cambridge Journal of Economics*, 19, 121–40.

Archibugi, D. and Pianta, M. (1992), *The Technological Specialisation of Advanced Countries. A Report to the EC on International Science and Technology Activities*, Dordrecht: Kluwer.

Barry, A. (2001), *Political Machines. Governing a Technological Society*, London: Athlone Press.

Cantwell, J. and Iammarino, S. (2003), *Multinational Enterprises and Regional Systems of Innovation in Europe*, London: Routledge.

Dodgson, M. (1993), *Technological Collaboration in Industry*, London: Routledge.

European Commission (1997), 'Second European Report on S&T Indicators', EUR 17639, Brussels.

European Commission (2002), 'Science, Technology and Innovation. Key Figures 2002', Luxembourg.

Gambardella, A. and Malerba, F. (eds) (1999), *The Organization of Economic Innovation in Europe*, Cambridge: Cambridge University Press.

Geuna, A. (1999), 'Patterns of University Research in Europe', in Gambardella and Malerba (1999).

Hagedoorn, J. (1996), 'Trends and Patterns in Strategic Technology Partnering since the Early Seventies', *Review of Industrial Organisation*, 11, 601–16.

Hagedoorn, J. (2002), 'Inter-Firm R&D Partnership: An Overview of Major Trends and Patterns since 1960', *Research Policy*, 31, 477–92.

Hagedoorn, J., Link, A., Vonortas, N. (2000), 'Research Partnerships', *Research Policy*, 29, 567–86.

Lundvall, B.-Å. (2001), 'Innovation Policy in the Globalising Learning Economy', in Archibugi and Lundvall (2001).

Molero, J. and Alvarez, I. (2002), 'Multinational Enterprises and Systems of Innovation Assessment. Consequences for National and European S&T Policies', paper presented at the final MESIAS meeting, Brussels, July 1–2.

Molero, J. and Heys, J. (2001), 'The Differentiated Impact of Innovative Strategies of MNCs and National Firms on European Systems of Innovation', paper presented at the MESIAS meeting, Budapest, March 8–10.

Mowery, D. (1992), 'International Collaborative Ventures and the Commercialization of New Technologies', in Rosenberg, Landau and Mowery (1992).

Mytelka, L.K. (1991), *Strategic Partnership. States, Firms and International Competition*, London: Pinter Publishers.

Mytelka, L.K. (2001), 'Mergers, Acquisitions, and Inter-Firm Technology Agreements in the Global Learning Economy', in Archibugi and Lundvall (2001).

Narula, R. (1998), *Strategic Technology Alliances by European Firms since the 1980s: Questioning Integration?*, Oslo, Step Group, April.

Narula, R. and Hagedoorn, J. (1999), 'Innovating through Strategic Alliances. Moving towards International Partnerships and Contractual Agreements', *Technovation*, 19, 283–94.

National Science Foundation (2000), *Science and Engineering Indicators 2000*, Washington, DC, US Government Printing Office.

National Science Foundation (2002), *Science and Engineering Indicators 2002*, Washington, DC, US Government Printing Office.

Organisation for Economic Co-operation and Development (2000), 'International Strategic Alliances in Industrial Globalization', STI Working Papers Series, available from <www1.oecd.org/dsti/sti>.

Organisation for Economic Co-operation and Development (2002), *Main Science and Technology Indicators 2001–2002*, Paris: OECD.

Pavitt, K. (1998), 'The Inevitable Limits of EU R&D Funding', *Research Policy*, 27, 559–68.

Pavitt, K. and Patel, P. (2002), 'Unpublished Statistics on Business and Academic Joint Publications', paper presented at the final MESIAS meeting, Brussels, July 1–2.

Peterson, J. and Sharp, M. (1998), *Technology Policy in the European Union*, Houndmills, Macmillan.

Pianta, M. and Archibugi, D. (1991), 'Specialization and Size of Scientific Activities: A Bibliometric Analysis of Advanced Countries', *Scientometrics*, 22, 341–58.

Rosenberg, N., Landau, R. and Mowery, D. (1992), *Technology and the Wealth of Nations*, Stanford, Stanford University Press.

Sharp, M. (2001), 'The Need for New Perspectives in European Commission Innovation Policy', in Archibugi and Lundvall (2001).

Vonortas, N. (1997), 'Research Joint Ventures in the US', *Research Policy*, 26, 577–95.

7. The technological strategies of multinational enterprises: their implications for national systems of innovation

José Molero and Isabel Álvarez

INTRODUCTION

Multinational enterprises (MNEs) have a crucial role in globalisation trends via their contribution to the internationalisation of both economic and technological activities. In fact, they are the main protagonist of direct investments flows and intra-firm international trade and one of the most important sources for the international transfer of technology experiences and know-how. On the particular debate of the effects that foreign direct investment (FDI) generates in recipient economies, the internationalisation of knowledge generation and exploitation is gaining increasing importance, despite the still controversial aspect of the role of governments in dealing with FDI. In this vein, the attraction and absorption capacities as well as the features of national systems of innovation may be seen as fundamental issues when understanding and assessing the impact of multinational affiliates on their locations. There is enough evidence on national disparities to affirm that country specificity matters and should be explicitly considered for both analytical and policy implication aims.

In the present phase of the European Research Area, some interesting questions may be raised in relation to technological internationalisation and the activity of transnational corporations, on the one hand, with regard to the strategies of large European firms and, on the other, due to the attraction and absorptive capabilities that European economies show. These two angles enable us to analyse whether the internationalisation of technology is being favoured by the regional integration process or whether it is threatened inside the European Union (EU) framework, allowing for some explanations of those trends. The underlying question, with clear implications for policies, is whether the behaviour of MNEs in Europe permits us to think in terms of a European system of innovation (as Archibugi and Coco (2001) discuss) or, on the contrary, whether national differences still persist. This is an interesting point with consequences which need to be specially considered regarding the enlargement of the EU.

In this chapter, the European situation is explored, focusing on the presence of MNEs and supported by previous empirical evidence on the issue. After a revision of the main theoretical background, in section two, an initial description of the FDI movements and the largest European MNEs is given in section three, with particular attention to the technological activities. Section four is devoted to observing the existence of differences and similarities in the innovative behaviour of foreign and domestic firms and their relation with the national system of innovation, paying special attention to Spain as a case of an intermediate economy. Finally, the aim of section five is to derive some concluding remarks and reflections for policy implications based on the arguments presented in the previous sections.

INTERNATIONALISATION AND TECHNOLOGY: BACKGROUND AND NEW INSIGHTS

The spread of the internationalisation of technical change and innovation due to the effect of MNEs' technological strategies is an issue which has been explored in numerous theoretical and empirical essays in recent decades. A part of this body of literature has been focused on the impact of MNEs' subsidiaries in the host countries, obtaining interesting results and still raising new research questions for analysis.

An initial aspect has to do with the role of MNEs as a channel of technology transfer, which may be made either directly, to the affiliates, or indirectly, to the domestic firms of the host economy.[1] This aspect can be explored in terms of the extension of the phenomena: the picture seems to be changing thanks to the increasing incorporation of other countries as sources of investment flows. A second aspect is related to another key changing aspect – the decentralisation of strategic functions of MNEs, and particularly research and development (R&D) activities, which allows affiliates a more independent way of functioning. This almost seems to become a necessary condition for technology transfer, also determined by the features of the national systems of innovation. With regard to these, there was considerable consensus on the need for clarifying the meaning of internationalisation of technology. Basically, the typology proposed by Archibugi and Michie (1995) has been accepted as a good tool for the study: first, through the exploitation of technology at a world level; second, taking into account the increasing international scientific and technological collaboration; and third, through the creation of new technology on a truly international basis.

In fact, opposing those who appreciate that the process is considerably extended, at least among developed or industrialised countries, there are others who do not agree with this argument. In favour of this statement, a number of indicators come to demonstrate the relatively reduced dimension of that internationalisation due to the fact that MNEs considered as a whole only internationalise a minor fraction of their technological activities and when they do, it simply involves a reduced number of economies – which has been called 'Triadisation'. Likewise, there is a great heterogeneity of situations. While Japanese and US companies are those with the lowest levels of technological activities outside their borders, European MNEs, on average, carry out more of those tasks in foreign countries; this behaviour mainly corresponds to firms from the smallest, highly-advanced European economies.

To throw some light on how global the international generation of knowledge is (Pavitt and Patel, 2000), the analysis of the top 500 largest companies in the world shows that nearly 13 per cent of the patents in the US were granted to foreign subsidiaries abroad (Patel, 1995; Patel and Vega, 1998). Similarly, for a large sample of MNEs from the US and EU, 15 per cent of the patents in the US were granted by foreign subsidiaries (Cantwell, 1995). On the other hand, regarding R&D expenditures, two main features can be underlined: there is an increasing trend in the volume of R&D done by subsidiaries abroad, and important differences between countries have been observed. Particularly, Beise and Belitz (1997) found a considerable acceleration of the expenditures of foreign subsidiaries located in the UK during the second half of the eighties. Nonetheless, it should be noted that Japanese and US firms internationalised R&D less than European companies, for which the level of R&D abroad is very high (Reger, 2001; Molero, 2001).

While recent case studies have shown that firms in the UK have declared that they learn from the presence of MNEs from the US established in their country, (Pearce, 1999), there is, however, still some room for further explanations. A necessary condition for technology transfer seems to have to do with the international generation of knowledge suggested type (Archibugi and Michie, 1995), a plausible assumption being that the activities subsidiaries carry out are either only production-oriented or also carry out R&D activities in their location. Related to this aspect, a very interesting distinction was established between *home base exploiting* strategies, which sought to exploit the technological advantage a firm has from its domestic activity, and *home base augmenting*, in which the bulk of the activity is oriented to increasing the technological basis with the incorporation of other created assets available in advanced foreign countries (Kuemmerle, 1999). Moreover, differences arise when the time dimension is taken into consideration. In fact, the evolution of firms' strategies in foreign countries changes over time, generally towards being more integrated with local firms and institutions (Pearce, 1999). In fact, the expression of technological change in their locations is manifested in different ways: the increase of competition due to the presence of foreign owned firms, their demonstration effects, as well as the mobility of a highly skilled labour force. Nonetheless, there is not strong support for the positive external effects that MNEs' subsidiaries generate – on the contrary, the evidence is not clear and differences among countries are found (see the survey by Blomström and Kokko (1998)).

The overall rationale is then that multinational companies may play a fundamental role in the relationship between the international generation and diffusion of knowledge and welfare improvements. Therefore, among new works, a key question has to do with the explanatory mechanisms related to a firm's choice between centralised or decentralised key activities such as R&D through its subsidiaries (Petit and Sanna-Randaccio, 2000; Sanna-Randaccio, 2002). It may be thought that when the latter prevails, it is plausible to wonder about the existence of international technological flows in both directions, from the parent to the subsidiary and vice versa, and what are the main determinants of them.[2] Some formal essays (Sanna-Randaccio and Veugelers 2002; Chapter 1 in this book) underline the organisational implications for MNEs to benefit in the case of a decentralisation choice. In particular, they explore the trade-off faced by an MNE when an active innovative role is assigned to a subsidiary, since the R&D subsidiaries can be used as a source of locally available know-how and, simultaneously, it provides a challenge for the effective appropriation of core technology. Based on a theoretical game model, this work shows the critical role of managing both internal and external spillovers and the recognition of the absorptive capacities as a key to the use of the latter. These findings have important policy implications.

Regarding the complexity of the subject explored, a variety of methods and sources of information are being used. In fact, the empirical results come from a variety of procedures such as: case studies; empirical analysis based on econometric estimations making use of relevant datasets, such as the US patent office or the Organisation for Economic Co-operation and Development (OECD) database; the exploitation of sources of information at the European level, such as the Community Innovation Survey (CIS I and II); and the generation of new sources, such as surveys at firm level in particular cases. It is interesting to notice that there have been increasing efforts in the development of instruments for measuring the phenomenon. Certainly, there were two central trends and empirical works have been focused on two basic indicators. On the one hand, there is the gathering of aggregated data concerning flows of technological activities such as R&D expenditures of foreign affiliates, and the number of patent applications carried out abroad by national firms or domestically by MNEs. The spread of strategic technological alliances and the international transaction of technologies reflected in the Technology Balance of Payments are also measurements of the phenomena. On the other hand, monographic studies try to provide a better understanding of the particular strategies pursued by single firms or groups; in this case the method combines surveys with interviews with managers of the firms. Taking into account these two trends, the basic result to be highlighted is that heterogeneity dominates the behaviour of MNEs in the international scenario.

The particular position of European companies is therefore remarkable. Thus, after considering different aspects of the tendency towards the decentralisation of technological activities by European MNEs, three basic issues came up for discussion; first, the evidence that they constitute the most active group, with some country cases in which outside activity accounts for 50 per cent of the technological activity of the company; second, a relatively less dynamic capacity to host the R&D tasks of non-European firms; and third, the growing number of technological alliances with US enterprises. Significant enough is the fact that, in spite of the promotion of European policies fostering Euro-alliances (Narula, 1999; Chapter 5 in this book), intra-European alliances have achieved a much lower rate of growth (Hagerdoorn and Narula, 1996). There is also a trend to increase the concentration of a very relevant number of new techno-logical activities in particular regions or sites. The so-called *Hollywood Effect* (Solvell and Zander, 1995) means that, just as in the cinema industry, there are other centres which are compulsory references for all international actors wanting to compete in growing globalising markets and with access to similar facilities to those of their competitors. Thus, the tendency to agglomerate in selected places constitutes a main factor in discussing new policies.

The debate about policies in that new context may be also mentioned here. A central issue has to do with the role of national systems of innovation. In fact, insofar as they continue to be a determining factor for deciding innovatory activities, national policies can still maintain some effective tasks, notwith-standing the fact that interaction between firms and national systems has changed in the *globalising learning economy* (Archibugi and Lundvall, 2001). Nevertheless, that intense debate gives rise to important topics for research which have been addressed with insufficient intensity, thus underestimating their economic and political importance. One substantial aspect is the role played by basic research and academic institutions in the new division of tech-nological work. Again, there is not much knowledge about this but partial evidence suggests that there have been very significant changes, with public institutions playing a very important role as attractive factors for high technology investment and as a mechanism for increasing the domestic absorptive capabilities (Pavitt, 2001). Then, a new role is assigned to academic research and the upgrading of absorptive capacities within the relationship between the multinational companies and the systems of innovation.

An interesting development based on the micro concept of absorptive capacities (Cohen and Levinthal, 1990) has been made by considering the relationship between the ability of a country to absorb foreign knowledge and its stage of technological development (Criscuolo and Narula, 2001). It is shown that the synergetic effects of inter-firm, inter-industry and systemic and institutional elements facilitate absorption. By linking the absorption capacities with the technology gap approach, the accumulation process seems to show a slower pace as the country approaches the frontier, an aspect notably relevant for catching up economies and for actions devoted to upgrading local capabilities.

Summarising, a vast majority of the theoretical and empirical research has been carried out on the basis of statistical evidence provided by the most developed countries, including the US, Japan and the core of highly industrialised European countries. However, the experience of countries outside that cluster does not always fit easily within the same parameters – worst for the laggard countries. On the one hand, this is because, with a few exceptions, they are not headquarters for big MNEs from that cluster and, therefore, they do not experience the consequences of those firms spreading their innovative activities into other economies. On the other hand, it is because their technological level does not usually match that required by MNEs in technological asset seeking, which means they mostly host subsidiaries of the *home base exploiting* kind. Similarly, the case of East European countries has been scarcely considered until recently. The arguments expressed above are relevant because of the lower level of technological development of these economies. Moreover, we can add another two significant facts: one related to the lack of comparable statistics to measure the process and another derived from the fact that those countries have been relatively divorced from the internationalisation process until very recently. Nevertheless, in recent years they have advanced considerably in their internationalisation, with some cases receiving important flows of FDI (see Chapter 9 in this book). Insofar as some of them will join the EU in the near future, there is a clear necessity for having better knowledge of the extent to which they are part of the internationalisation process and the particularities they show with respect to western countries.

INTERNATIONALISATION AND TECHNOLOGY: THE RECENT TRENDS

In the economy and technology globalisation trends, FDI has been achieving a crucial role, the behaviour of MNEs being a key aspect in that evolution. In fact, FDI has become at the end of the century more notable than other economic operations, such as gross capital formation, royalties and licence fees as well as exports. A special indicator of global trends is manifested by the importance acquired by the movements of mergers and acquisitions (the growth rate of which doubled during the nineties) since these operations are increasing their share to a greater extent than green-field types. However, recent convulsions in the international economic scenario have affected both.

Regarding the direction and evolution of FDI since the beginning of the eighties, the existence of geographical differences persists and its behaviour is not similar in the different world regions. Although there has been a greater diversification, and the relative importance of the Triad has diminished from the middle eighties to the present day, geographical distribution of FDI still shows a notable concentration in the US, Japan and the EU: 71 per cent of world FDI inflows. According to the United Nations Conference in Trade and Development (UNCTAD, 2002) the share of outward and inward stock by country shows the relevance of the Triad in 2001, being higher in outward than in inward. The former represents nearly 78 per cent of the outward and the latter 59 per cent of the inward stock in the world. However, it should be noted that over half of the outward world stock corresponds to the EU, double the US share. However, the difference between outward and inward shares is more notable in the European region than in the US. Japan, on the other hand, accounts for nearly 5 per cent of the outward share and only for less than 1 per cent of world inward. The EU has a high concentration of the stock in the largest economies: it is notable in the UK, Germany and France, who represent more than one half of the European share.

There has been, nonetheless, a remarkable shift in the trend in recent decades. Today, it can be observed that among the largest recipients of FDI, more countries than before are involved in the internationalisation process. For this reason, the volume of FDI and the factors explaining the intensity and direction of the flows have been gaining a notable relevance for the design and application of economic policies (UNCTAD, 2001). Beyond the differences existing among countries, important enough is the fact that seven economies maintain their position of being simultaneously the largest recipient and source of FDI, mainly the European and North American countries, Japan not being among them. Nonetheless, countries like Spain lost their position of being a large recipient in favour of Mexico in 2001, while Hong-Kong–China ceases to be one of the largest sources, Italy taking its place.

Figure 7.1 shows the position of those countries according to the Balassa Index applied to FDI[3] and used by Chesnais, Ietto-Gillies and Simonetti (2000). A similar profile is shared by Japan and Switzerland as *predominantly home countries*, while the UK and France are featured as such only in the year 2000. On the other hand, Germany seems in 2001 to have lost its position of being *a predominantly host country*, which is clearly occupied by countries such as Mexico, China and Hong Kong–China. Finally, most of the EU economies are represented, as well as the North American countries, as mixed type, being both *host and home* without predominance of either of the extreme positions. It confirms the high level of internationalisation of these latter countries.

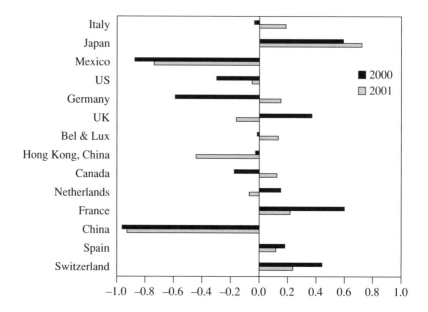

Source: UNCTAD (several years), own elaboration.

Figure 7.1   Internationalisation index, 2000–2001: the largest recipients and sources

Considering the economic relevance of FDI for the national economy, through the inward and outward stock position in relation to their Gross Domestic Product (GDP), it can be observed in Table 7.1 that the evolution of this ratio in the last decade has been more notable in Japan and also important in the European Union, more than in the US economy. Nonetheless, the greatest change in the ratio in the nineties does not correspond to the Triad but to the Central and Eastern European countries. Although in these countries the backwardness explanation[4] should be taken into account, since they evolved from a very low position regarding internationalisation, the importance of foreign capital measured by the FDI inward stock as a percentage of GDP at the end of the nineties has multiplied to more than eight times the value of the same ratio at the beginning of that decade. Some Nordic countries, such as Sweden and Finland, have also experienced an important fourfold increase in that period. Regarding their internationalisation potential, proxied by their FDI outward position in relation to their economy, again as a share of GDP, it is well noted that the evolution of this indicator is notable for the intermediate countries, such as Portugal and Spain, as well as for the Central and Eastern European countries. This latest similar behaviour may give some key points for the analysis of the candidate countries, based on the Iberian experiences. From the macro perspective on the investment development path hypothesis (Dunning and Narula, 1994, 1996; Lall, 1996), by which FDI may enable us to observe how countries evolve through different stages, defining patterns of FDI behaviour in their development path, these intermediate countries have followed a similar evolution. It can be said that they are located at the stage in which they improve the behaviour of their outward position in relation to their inward position – stage three moving on to stage four in the hypothesis referred to. The candidate countries, on the other hand, would still respond to stage two with a notable increase in their inward position and where outflows of FDI are still low.

Another fact which deserves attention is the modifications in the distribution of the 100 largest MNEs. Although 90 per cent of the 100 largest MNEs are from the Triad, three of them originate from developing countries, an aspect new in the geography of the largest companies in the world. By industries, electrical and electronic, automobiles and petroleum are the most representative among the world MNEs. Regarding the EU position, it is noticeable that over 50 per cent of the largest MNEs originate from the EU countries but host only 7.6 per cent of the affiliates. The territory of the European Union does not seem, therefore, to be one of the most preferable locations. On the other hand, empirical estimation of the degree of internationalisation of European companies has been provided according to the two indexes, attempting to measure the degree of international projection and the degree of spread of the networks among countries (Ietto-Gillies, 2002). Results confirm that EU companies show a higher level of internationalisation in comparison to MNEs originating from the US and Japan, regardless of the index used. Within Europe, MNEs from Finland, France, The Netherlands and the UK are the most internationalised according to both their degree of projection and the spread of their foreign linkages. With regard to industries, the lowest values of the internationalisation index correspond to industries such as telecommunications, aerospace and military, among others, for which the home country still persists as the main location.

When considering the location of industrial activities, there are three main factors: the role of liberalisation policies with a clearly increasing trend, which favour the climate for the entry of FDI; the importance of technical change; and the evolution of entrepreneurial strategies (UNCTAD, 2002). In fact, it is agreed that technology is behind the existing differences between countries and sectors and technological evolution is one of the critical variables

Table 7.1   Inward and outward FDI stocks as share of GDP

	Inward (%)				Outward (%)			
	1980	1990	1998	2000	1980	1990	1998	2000
European Union	6.1	10.6	17.3	30.3	6.1	11.6	22.9	40.1
Austria	4.0	6.1	11.3	16.1	0.7	2.6	8.2	13.2
Belgium & Luxembourg	5.8	27.8	61.7	174.0[1]	4.8	19.4	50.2	154.1[1]
Denmark	6.1	6.9	17.4	39.6	3.0	5.5	19.4	39.4
Finland	1.0	3.8	13.1	20.0	1.4	8.2	23.4	43.0
France	8.2	8.2	11.7	19.9	3.6	9.9	15.9	33.4
Germany	3.9	7.1	9.3	24.1	4.6	8.8	17.3	25.2
Greece	9.3	9.4	18.3	11.1	6.0	3.5	0.7	5.1
Ireland	7.9	7.2	32.7	68.2	n.a.	5.8	12.4	19.4
Italy	2.0	5.3	8.8	10.5	1.6	5.2	14.1	16.8
Netherlands	10.8	23.3	48.0	65.9	23.7	36.3	68.9	83.8
Portugal	12.3	14.8	20.8	26.5	1.7	1.3	8.6	16.7
Spain	2.3	12.8	21.5	25.8	0.9	3.0	12.5	29.6
Sweden	2.2	5.3	22.5	36.1	2.8	21.3	41.3	53.8
United Kingdom	11.8	20.6	23.3	30.5	15.0	23.2	35.9	63.2
Japan	0.3	0.3	0.7	1.1	1.8	6.6	7.1	5.8
North America	4.5	8.0	10.5	13.5	7.9	8.1	12.5	14.5
Canada	20.4	19.6	23.9	28.8	8.9	14.7	26.9	32.4
United States	3.0	6.9	9.5	12.4	7.8	7.5	11.5	13.2
Latin America & the Caribbean	6.5	10.4	19.5	30.9	1.2	1.8	3.3	6.2
Asia	13.0	14.8	20.2	31.6	0.9	2.7	0.5	15.2
Central & Eastern Europe	n.a.	1.7	12.1	18.9	n.a.	0.4	1.7	2.7
Developing Countries	10.2	13.0	20.0	30.9	1.7	2.8	6.7	11.9

Note: [1] The data were revised to reflect the value of transactions related to cross-border mergers and acquisitions (M&A) deal, as the transaction and the related value were determined and reflected in the balance-of-payments statistics only retroactively.

Source: UNCTAD (2002).

explaining them. Subsidiaries of technology intensive industries tend to concentrate in particular locations of developed economies while the choice of less technologically intensive industries is more oriented to developing countries. Consequently, adequate policy actions are addressed either to the attraction of FDI, or to the creation of the conditions to attract FDI, not necessarily in labour intensive industries but in high technological content industries. Nonetheless, with regard to the choice of location, it depends, on the one hand, on the changing strategies of MNEs – home base augmenting versus home base exploiting – as well as whether subsidiaries are assigned on a competence creating mandate. On the other, are the location characteristics such as adequate infrastructure, public research facilities, and the educational system and science base of the location (Cantwell and Piscitello, 2001; Cantwell and Mudambi, 2001).

With regard to the manner of the internationalising technology, its generation and exploitation, a common feature is its traditional concentration in developed economies. This aspect has allowed us to confirm that technological internationalisation, whatever its expression, has not been contributing to the globalisation trend but has been mainly focused in the Triad.[5] In this respect, a first aspect to be considered is whether MNEs perform knowledge generation activities mainly at home or abroad through their subsidiaries. The decision of the MNEs to decentralise or not R&D expenditure to be performed by foreign affiliates in their locations may serve as a proxy to measure this fact.

Figure 7.2 shows, for a selection of countries, the relationship between the national potential for knowledge generation, proxied by R&D expenditure as a share of GDP, and the strength of MNEs, proxied by the R&D expenditure of affiliates in relation to national business R&D. The latest indicator reveals that the importance of these activities performed by MNEs abroad differs by country and according to the importance of R&D activities in those economies. The special case of Ireland can be observed as a country where, although R&D intensity is below 1.5 per cent of GDP, the R&D expenditures of foreign companies represent more than 50 per cent of the R&D of the national business sector. This aspect deals with the role achieved by FDI in the business sector of that economy in recent decades, and has clear implications for its importance within the Irish system of innovation. The closest performance is Hungary, with a lower R&D intensity but where economic changes have favoured the attraction of FDI and foreign companies are performing R&D activities (Inzelt, 2000), which represent between one third and one half of the R&D expenditure of enterprises.

To a lesser extent, Spain shares this performance – also in the first quadrant – with an intensity of R&D lower than 1 per cent of GDP and where affiliates' R&D represents 34 per cent of business enterprise R&D (BERD). Italy, Portugal and Turkey also show a moderate R&D share but with an importance of affiliates' R&D less than 35 per cent, Australia being in the frontier between the first and the third quadrants. With modest levels of R&D in their economies combined with a low R&D share of the affiliates are the Czech Republic and Greece. The other countries, the most advanced economies, are mainly placed in the fourth quadrant of the figure, where R&D performed by affiliates only represents less than 30 per cent of total enterprises but these economies are highly R&D intensive. It should be noted that in Japan and the US, although R&D as a share of GDP is high, the relative magnitude of R&D by affiliates is very modest.

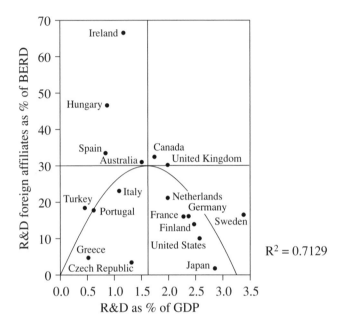

Source: Own elaboration with information from AFA/FATS database, OECD.

Figure 7.2   R&D of foreign affiliates as a share of BERD and according to national R&D intensity in the nineties, average values

The second quadrant, on the other hand, is virtually empty – with the exception of Canada – an aspect which means that the R&D of MNE subsidiaries has more relative importance in less technologically active countries and there are no situations of both high national and foreign R&D efforts. Once a regression line is adjusted to the dispersion graph, a non-linear relationship is found. In fact, a binomial form seems to fit the best, adopting an inverted U form which may be interpreted in terms of the importance that the features of national systems of innovation have for the R&D strategies of MNEs. The positive slope and concave shape of the curve is due to the fact that a minimum threshold is expected by MNEs to carry out knowledge generation activities, such as R&D activities, in their foreign locations. Nonetheless, once achieved, the relative magnitude of the foreign R&D carried out by subsidiaries versus national is decreasing and losing relevance. So the more consolidated are the national R&D systems, notwithstanding the fact that, in absolute terms, the bulk of foreign R&D activity of MNEs is mainly carried out in that last group of countries.

Meanwhile regarding any thought about the possibility of a European system of innovation, with both common objectives for R&D and policies related to a knowledge-based society, Figure 7.2 shows that differences among less developed countries inside the Union call for special attention once the role of multinationals is taken into account. In particular, some different groups of countries may be defined: one formed by Ireland and Spain and another by Portugal, Greece and Italy, while the more advanced economies behave very differently. Moreover, in the near future this raises important policy issues for actions considering foreign capital and the candidate countries, since among the latter, the performance is also very different.

Data in Table 7.2 show that differences in the behaviour of affiliates of multinational (MN) companies arise according to the host countries. In particular, data on R&D expenditure levels show the predominance of the US, followed by the UK and Germany, which is positively associated with the magnitude of the activity of foreign affiliates, turnover and number of employees. However, when the relative R&D indicator is taken, on the one hand, the value of R&D expenditure per enterprise or establishment is notably higher in the US (1.46) than for the other countries, followed by Japan (0.86). On the contrary, for Central and Eastern European countries, the value of this indicator is negligible. On the other hand, relative to the number of researchers of foreign affiliates, although no data are available for many countries, the Czech Republic shows the highest value and it is also significant for Japan and higher than in the US, the UK and Germany.

Some additional data about patents in the US provide a picture of the technological activity of foreign affiliates, which allows us to observe the decentralisation versus centralisation trend (Patel and Vega, 1999; Patel and Pavitt, 2000). From the SPRU database, built with data from the world's 359 largest companies[6] which were technologically active in the nineties, the propensity to perform technological activities abroad has been observed. Innovative activities, proxied by the patents in the US, are still predominantly carried out at home by large multinational companies. Regarding the Triad, European firms are again the most internationalised, with a propensity to patent from abroad higher than in Japan and the US, and below average value for the latter. Nonetheless, it is important to underline the different behaviour of firms according to their nationality and how structural features matter in the EU. In particular, in three small open advanced countries, the proportional share of US patents from abroad is over 50 per cent, also in the UK. On the contrary,

Table 7.2   Activities of foreign affiliates in the nineties by recipient country, average values

	No. of entrep./ establishment	Number of Employees (1)	Turnover (2)	R&D Expenditures (2)	Number of Researchers (1)	R&D Exp./ establishment	R&D Exp./ researchers
Czech Republic	11.893	304.333	66.337	37.34	75	0.00	0.50
Finland	1.386	90.609	21.510	306.45	4.156	0.19	0.07
Germany	8.178	820.200	255.300	3.303.53	33.527	0.41	0.10
Hungary	20.622	496.789	84.401	100.35	n.a.	0.00	n.a.
Japan	1.020	139.921	61.428	888.11	4.862	0.86	0.18
Netherlands	3.087	347.831	134.837	843.83	n.a.	0.26	n.a.
Poland	5.870	503.589	83.321	n.a.	n.a.	n.a.	n.a.
Sweden	2.465	n.a.	45.978	649.46	n.a.	0.28	n.a.
United Kingdom	9.551	1.368.355	482.710	4.576.65	38.600	0.50	0.12
United States	11.468	4.974.667	1.464.215	16.309.78	111.557	1.46	0.15

Notes:
(1) Units or full-time equivalent.
(2) Million US dollars PPP, current prices.

Source: Own elaboration with information from AFA/FATS database, OECD.

Germany and Italy are more notably home oriented in the innovative performance of large companies. Taking a time perspective, although the trend to patent from abroad has been increasing, especially in the data for France, particular behaviour is shown by Swedish companies from the eighties which denotes a predominance of home activities at present more than before.

National specificity is then an aspect which seems to matter. In fact, different innovative behaviour can be observed due either to the nationality of the MNE or due to the host country where its subsidiaries are localised. It has been shown that the variables determining their technology strategies are different when considering firms from the US and Japan (Meyer-Krahmer and Reger, 1999; Reger, 2001). These results have clear implications for the effects the foreign firm generates in the host systems of innovation. Some findings indeed support the idea that national systems of innovation clearly condition the integration of the innovative activities carried out by MNEs. In fact, recent analysis based on the CIS has confirmed that innovatory foreign firms are likely to be more integrated in the national economy, the higher the level of development of the system of innovation (Molero, 2002). When comparing foreign firms and domestic ones belonging to a company group, the results clearly show that the differences are more related to structural than innovative factors. Then, the influences of foreign firms on the national system are more dependent on the structural features of the firms, such as size and industry, as well as on indirect mechanisms (Molero and Heijs, 2002). The reasons behind these facts can be found in the characteristics of the national systems of innovation and the importance of their specific analysis, as is seen in the next section.

SOME NEW INSIGHTS ON THE INNOVATIVE BEHAVIOUR OF MNES' SUBSIDIARIES AND DOMESTIC FIRMS IN SPAIN

Focusing the analysis on the intermediate economies, Spain may serve as a good example to study the innovative behaviour of multinational firms in comparison to domestic firms and in relation to the national systems of innovation. As an intermediate country, Spain has been highly attractive for FDI inflows since the sixties, with an extraordinary growth in the eighties, accelerated by the accession to the EC – an aspect which has conditioned the stage achieved by this country in investment development path patterns (Campa and Guillén, 1996). In fact, the size of the internal market as well as the macroeconomic stability conditions were the main explanations for the remarkable growth of inward FDI as a share of the GDP in Spain, which was even above the European average after entry (Bajo and Sosvilla, 1992; Martín and Velázquez, 1996).

However, that difference has been diminishing in more recent years, the rate of growth being more moderate in the late nineties and under the EU average. In fact, in the early nineties Spain was one of the top OECD countries ranked according to the volume of received inflows in both absolute and relative terms as a share of GDP (Bajo and López Pueyo, 1996). Empirical essays show that, while cost variables were scarcely significant, the technological advantages of the FDI inflows and GDP levels and growth seemed to have a notable importance in the explanation (Bajo, 1991; Bajo and Sosvilla, 1992). The more recent trends underline the importance achieved by disinvestment movements, as well as the increasing role played by the holding companies of international shares but the Spanish economy is not the final destination of the investment (Fernandez-Otheo, 2002).

Regarding the degree of internationalisation of the sectors, services has the main role of FDI in Spain, including outflows and inflows, an aspect which is also confirmed for stock data. For manufacturing, the internationalisation position permits it to be classified as a clear flows recipient. Nonetheless, there are some important differences by industry, varying from industries with an important foreign presence, such as vehicles and other transport, petroleum, chemicals, rubber and plastics, to others in which the relative volume of inflows and outflows is not so unbalanced, such as machinery, computers, TV and communications. According to their technological content, previous empirical tests made at the industry level have revealed that the manufacturing sector recipients of FDI in Spain are, in absolute terms, characterised by being of both high and medium technology intensity (measured by R&D expenditure over total sales) as well as having high export and import propensity.

When FDI is weighted by the contribution of the industry to the added value, those industries with a foreign presence over that contribution are those representatives of industrial development in the country but not always the highest technological content, such as the automotive and chemical industries (Buesa and Molero, 1998). At the micro level, among other noted differences, foreign owned firms in Spain show a higher dependence on technological resources from abroad, employ a more skilled labour force and mostly show a higher R&D intensity than domestic ones (Alonso and Donoso, 1994). According to data from the Spanish Innovation Survey, MNEs in Spain are mainly located in industries with high technological opportunities and act differently from domestic ones in the national system of innovation, conceding a higher importance to learning sources external to the firm (Molero, 2000).

Table 7.3 summarises the main existing evidence in this particular for the Spanish case. In relation to the external effects that MN companies may generate in their location, the analysis of the differences in the strategies and results between foreign and domestic firms in Spain confirms the quantitative and qualitative superiority of foreign owned firms over domestic ones in physical and human resources and, particularly, in technology variables (Molero, 1996). However, although foreign owned firms show higher R&D intensity, higher technology imports and higher productivity, there is no confirmation of a positive influence of foreign firms on the market strategies and the results of the domestic ones (Merino and Salas, 1995). Furthermore, when controlling by structural variables such as size, differences between foreign owned and domestic firms tend to clearly diminish (Molero, 2000). In particular, the analysis of the innovative behaviour of the largest firms reveals that although MNEs' subsidiaries perform a higher R&D effort, they seem to be more active only in product innovation, and concede less importance to public programmes (Círculo de Empresarios, 1995).

In a recent theoretical development, which has been applied to the Spanish case, the consequences of foreign presence for the innovation decisions of domestic firms as an external effect or spillover have been explored (Merino and Salas, 2001). The hypothesis was that foreign presence increases the competition in the market and it can be observed as a factor of improvement for the technical capacities of domestic firms. The empirical works distinguish between product and process innovations, confirming that the openness and the stimuli generated by the presence of foreign firms is important for the improvement of innovations in large firms, the external effects being practically nil for smaller firms. Based on the Central Bank dataset, a recent test at the micro level does not confirm either that the presence of foreign companies introduces higher levels of competition or positive induced effects in the domestic market. In fact, long run effects on the profits of domestic firms were only found limited to R&D intensive industries (Sembenelli and Siotis, 2002).

Moreover, once the technological transfer and technological spillover from foreign to domestic firms has been tested for the Spanish manufacturing sector, using firm panel data for the nineties, some interesting results arise (Álvarez et al., 2002). On the one hand, technology transfer from the headquarter to the subsidiaries established in Spain has a significant effect from FDI while no intra-industry spillovers to domestic firms are found. On the other hand, R&D performance does not seem to improve the results used as a proxy for domestic absorptive capacities. Nonetheless, trade is still an important channel to acquire technology since knowledge in capital goods and equipment imports still seems to be significant for the efficiency gains of domestic firms.

The new evidence here deals with the behaviour of foreign and domestic companies in Spain in relation to their technological effort, their innovative performance and the importance of public programmes to enhance R&D, using micro data from a national survey for manufacturing firms, the Encuesta de Estrategias Empresariales (ESEE).[7] As a first structural feature, it can be noted

Table 7.3 Some available evidence of comparisons between foreign and domestic firms

Reference	Analysis	Sample and Data Source	Results
Molero (2002)	Domestic vs MN (belonging to a group and total), Ireland and Germany, Multivariate analysis	Irish and German firms, Community Innovation Survey CIS I	– The more integrated the MN companies, the more developed the national system of innovation
Molero & Heijs (2002)	Domestic vs MN, Multivariate analysis	Italian, Norwegian, Irish, Dutch and German firms, Community Innovation Survey CIS I	– Differentiating elements are more structural than innovation related – Similarities in the innovative behaviour of foreign firms and domestic firms belonging to a group were found – Influence of foreign firms in the national system of innovation depends more on indirect mechanism
Sembernelli & Siotis (2002)	Competitive and efficiency effects of foreign presence on Spanish firms, Panel data	Firm level data Central de Balances	– Long run effects on profitability of domestic firms found, but limited to firms belonging to R&D intensive industries
Molero (2000)	Foreign vs domestic, Multivariate analysis	Innovative companies in Spain, CDTI database	– Largest differences among the large firms – More similar by industry – MNEs collaborate more with firms of the group and are more active in technology transfer
Álvarez, Damijan, Knell (2002)	Test of spillover, Panel data	Manufacturing firms, Encuesta de Estrategias Empresariales	– Technology transfer to the subsidiaries significantly found – No intra-industry spillovers occur – R&D expenditures do not seem to improve the capacities of domestic firms for the absorption of productivity spillovers

Author (Year)	Topic / Method	Sample / Source	Findings
Merino & Salas (2001)	Internationalisation effects in domestic firms, Multivariate analysis	Manufacturing firms, Encuesta de Estrategias Empresariales	– The presence of foreign firms in Spanish manufacturing discourages product innovation in domestic firms while the opposite occurs through imports – A positive effect in process innovation is found only in large domestic firms, being insignificant in small to medium-sized enterprises
Molero, Buesa, Casado (1995)	Estrategies of German and Dutch subsidiaries in Spain	151 innovator firms in Madrid, Generated survey	– No differences between foreign and domestic firms were found
Merino & Salas (1995)	Foreign vs domestic Multivariate analysis	Manufacturing firms, Encuesta de Estrategias Empresariales	– No differences in R&D activities between foreign and domestic firms when controlling by size and sector – Foreign firms utilise technologies more intensive in capital and more qualified human resources – Foreign presence does not influence the R&D performance of domestic firms
Círculo de Empresarios (1995)	Large firms in Spain, Description from specifically generated survey	305 large firms; Encuesta del Círculo de Empresarios	– MN more active in product innovation – MN shows higher R&D intensity, higher importance to users – MN gives scarce importance to Public Programmes

from Table 7.4 that, considering the distribution of firms between foreign and domestic, the presence of foreign firms differs according to industry and technological content. Foreign presence is over 50 per cent in high and medium technology content industries, such as chemicals and motor vehicles respectively, and can be seen to a lesser extent even in low tech sectors. It is also observed that foreign firms are predominantly large firms, with more than 200 employees. This aspect should be taken into account and leads one to wonder about the importance of this feature when assessing whether their technological features and innovative behaviour truly differ from domestic firms due to the ownership of capital assets.

To have a rough idea of the technological performance, a relative index has been built with data on patents granted in Spain and abroad by both domestic and foreign owned firms (Table 7.5). It can be observed that foreign owned firms do not show higher patent propensity for the whole group of industries but it is related to the technological content. In particular foreign owned ones are relatively more specialised in higher technology sectors while domestic firms show a higher patent propensity in some medium technology sectors and mainly in low-tech industries. Taking these results into consideration, a set of relative variables, expressive of technology and innovation activities, has been selected for the two kinds of firms. The aim is to test whether differences exist and to what extent these are explained by the national system of innovation's characteristics.

A first test at the firm level is presented in Table 7.6, which permits us to confirm that indeed foreign and domestic firms do not show a similar technological profile, according to the first test where all the firms are considered. Differences are statistically significant for all the variables with the exception of the patents granted abroad and the ability to obtain funds for R&D from public funds. However, these differences diminish when controlled by size. In particular, foreign and domestic firms with more than 200 employees are technologically similar and only differ in technology transfer activities such as licence fee payments. Moreover, among the firms equal to or smaller than that size, there are statistically significant differences again in licence fees, and this time also in revenues and to a lesser extent in R&D expenditures and patents granted in Spain. Regarding innovative performance, on the other hand, no differences have been found.

Finally, to address the question of which main variables permit us to differentiate the behaviour of foreign and domestic firms in the Spanish system of innovation, a single discriminate analysis has been made, again in three steps, considering that size may permit differences to be erased (Table 7.7). The analysis for all firms (D1) manifests that the importance of technology transfer mechanisms, the resources devoted to the generation of knowledge and the performance in process innovation are the main elements which differentiate

Table 7.4 Distribution of Spanish manufacturing firms, foreign and domestic, by industry and technological content

Industry by technological content	% of Firms	% of Foreign	% of Domestic	% of Foreign	
				Fewer than 200 employees	More than 200 employees
Low Technology					
Basic metals	2.64	46.43	53.57	1.29	56.01
Non metallic minerals	8.0	25.88	74.12	3.36	56.64
Manufactured metals	9.42	14.0	86.0	6.56	14.42
Meat and meat preparations	3.3	20.0	80.0	2.16	4.80
Food and tobacco	10.64	22.12	77.88	1.01	74.11
Beverages	2.45	23.08	76.92	0.00	32.85
Textiles	9.89	15.24	84.76	2.32	21.32
Leather products	2.45	3.85	96.15	1.76	0.00
Pulp and paper products	7.53	17.5	82.5	3.03	26.42
Medium Technology					
Machinery and equipment	6.03	34.38	65.63	7.76	68.58
Motor vehicles	5.18	54.55	45.45	0.35	94.62
Other transport equipment	2.54	18.52	81.48	0.17	11.68
Wood products	4.52	6.25	93.75	2.66	8.13
Rubber and plastics products	5.37	35.09	64.91	5.36	60.76
High Technology					
Chemical and chemical products	7.44	53.16	46.84	4.60	73.02
Office machinery and computers	1.04	27.27	72.73	0.69	67.45
Electrical machinery	9.42	39.0	61.0	1.65	68.27
Other manufacturing	2.17	17.39	82.61	0.00	32.47
Total	100	26.93	73.07	1.85	66.20

Source: Own elaboration with data from ESEE (several years).

Table 7.5 *Technology relative index*

	Patents Abroad		Domestic Patents		
	Relative Index Domestic	Relative Index Foreign	Relative Index Domestic	Relative Index Foreign	
Basic metals	0	3.83	0	2.40	F
Non metallic minerals	0.90	1.27	0.85	1.20	F
Chemical and chemical products	1.18	0.48	0.76	1.32	f
Manufactured metals	0.23	3.16	0.97	1.04	F
Machinery and equipment	0.50	2.41	0.61	1.54	F
Office machinery and computers	0.16	3.36	0.21	2.10	F
Electrical machinery	0.07	3.61	0.78	1.30	F
Motor vehicles	1.21	0.40	1.37	0.47	D
Other transport equipment	1.35	0	1.71	0	D
Meat and meat preparations	0	0	0	0	–
Food and tobacco	1.31	0.10	1.46	0.34	D
Beverages	1.35	0	1.65	0.07	D
Textiles	0.31	2.95	1.21	0.69	f
Leather products	1.35	0	0	0	d
Wood products	1.35	0	1.71	0	D
Pulp and paper products	1.35	0	1.38	0.45	D
Rubber and plastic products	1.29	0.16	1.70	0.01	D
Other manufacturing	1.08	0.76	0.12	2.22	f
Total	1	1	1	1	

Notes:
(F) Higher propensity of foreign owned firms over domestic ones.
(f) Higher propensity only in one kind of patent.
(D) Higher propensity of domestic firms over foreign ones.
(d) Higher propensity of domestic only in one kind of patent.

Source: Own elaboration with data from ESEE (several years).

Table 7.6 T-test of differences in means: foreign versus domestic firms in Spanish manufacturing

Variables	All firms		Firms larger than 200 employees		Firms Equal to or smaller than 200 employees	
	t-value	Significance	t-value	Significance	t-value	Significance
R&D expenditure per employee	6.3	**	1.5	n.s.	1.8	*
Patents granted in Spain per employee	-1.8	*	-0.4	n.s.	-2.4	*
Patents granted abroad per employee	-0.7	n.s.	-1.5	n.s.	0.11	n.s.
Product innovations as share of total innovations	1.7	*	-0.14	n.s.	0.79	n.s.
Process innovations as share of total innovations	2.9	**	-1.0	n.s.	1.1	n.s.
Public funds for R&D as share of total R&D expenditure	1.5	n.s.	0.5	n.s.	0.3	n.s.
Licence fee revenues as share of total sales	2.2	*	-0.18	n.s.	3.2	**
Licence fee payments as share of sales	12.0	**	5.7	**	6.5	**

Notes:

(**) At the 99% confidence level.
(*)   At the 95% confidence level.
(n.s.) Not significant.

foreign and domestic firms in Spain. These results are not the same when the analysis is done for large firms only (D2), the resources to acquire technology being the only dissimilar aspect between the two groups. Finally, when considering only smaller firms (D3), the variables in the explanation of the differences are not related to innovation but to technology transfer and the absorptive capacities, proxied by R&D activities.

Table 7.7 Discriminatory analysis

	D1	D2	D3
R&D expenditures per employee	0.47**	n.s.	0.22*
Patents granted in Spain per employee	n.s.	n.s.	n.s.
Patents granted abroad per employee	n.s.	n.s.	n.s.
Product innovations as share of total innovations	n.s.	n.s.	n.s.
Process innovations as share of total innovations	0.22**	n.s.	n.s.
Public funds for R&D as share of total R&D expenditure	n.s.	n.s.	n.s.
Licence fee revenues as share of total sales	n.s.	n.s.	0.44**
Licence fee payments as share of sales	0.89**	0.99**	0.89**
Chi-Square	165.7	31.6	52.1
Cases rightly classified (%)	77	61	89
Number of observations	1.061	393	668
Lambda Wilks	0.85	0.92	0.92

Notes:
D1   All firms.
D2   Firms larger than 200 employees.
D3   Firms equal to or smaller than 200 employees.
(**)   At the 99% confidence level.
(*)   At the 95% confidence level.
(n.s.) Not significant.

The results presented here may allow us to affirm that, firstly, although foreign firms present some specific characteristics when compared to domestic firms in Spain, the differences are scarcely related to technology results, measured by patents both national and abroad, or to innovation in products. In fact, the differences are related more to the exploitation of foreign technology than to the generation of new technology in Spain as a foreign location. This, nonetheless, can also be interpreted as an ownership advantage,[8] since foreign firms may be more dependent on technological knowledge coming from abroad due to the relatively scarce autonomy conceded by the headquarters to the affiliates. Secondly, although there has been a kind of exclusion of foreign firms from public technology programmes, as previous evidence shows (Heijs, 2002), the more recent evidence as shown here manifests that there is no differentiated behaviour once their participation in public programmes is considered, proxied by their accession to public R&D funds. This aspect may be considered as an expression of the fact that MNE subsidiaries seem to be more integrated in the national system and the Spanish policy to foster R&D activities does not discriminate along the lines of nationality of firms.

CONCLUDING REMARKS

Internationalisation of technology is still a scarcely known and uneven phenomenon. Probably, the consequences for national systems of innovation and domestic policies are just partially known, in spite of the recent research carried out. In fact, it is possible to notice the importance of the diversification of FDI, considering both inward and outward flows.

Regarding the effects that multinational enterprises have on the host national system of innovation, an important aspect to be underlined has to do with the MNEs' strategies and, particularly, with the decision about R&D decentralisation; it is likely that, once the latter prevails, increased positive external effects and technology dissemination can be expected. Moreover, this is not a 'territory-less' phenomenon but, on the contrary, it is also thought that national differences matter.

In fact, it has been shown that here there is not a sole defined pattern of foreign R&D activities made by MNEs' affiliates. The number of factors intervening in that process is quite large and very heterogeneous and it corresponds both to the features of the MNEs' country of origin, to the characteristics of the host system of innovation, and to some structural variables such as the sector of activity. Therefore, the necessity for establishing different categories and patterns is one of the most promising analytical works to perform.

This also has important implications for Europe since heterogeneity prevails as a crucial character of the Union. Since it is confirmed that the features of the technological capabilities for the generation and absorption of foreign knowledge become crucial, enlargement of the Union brings a new and uncertain scenario to which European policies have to respond. Nonetheless, it might be noticed that the peculiar set of intermediate countries still calls for special attention, mainly due to the notable role that foreign capital tends to play in their development path and the still large distance from the more advanced European countries. Being focused on *catching up* countries such as Spain, foreign and domestic firms seem to show a similar innovatory behaviour.

However, some interesting findings may be taken into account: first, cross border technological transfer is still a more likely path for foreign companies than for local ones; second, structural variables show that the closer in size firms are the fewer the technological differences; third, differences dealing with public technology policies seem to be declining between foreign and national players. Moreover, it can be pointed out that a determining aspect thus seems to be the level of integration achieved inside the national system of innovation, and how the actors behave in relation to the rest of the elements of the economy.

NOTES

1. Some of the pioneering contributions in this particular field are from Dunning and Cantwell, when analysing the effects of US companies in Europe (Dunning, 1958; Cantwell, 1989).
2. The model developed by Siotis (1999) is a good attempt at this.
3. The Balassa Index of FDI is calculated as follows:

$$BI = \frac{FDIxw - FDIwx}{FDIxw + FDIwx}$$

   where *FDIxw* is the FDI of country *x* in the world and *FDIwx* is the FDI of the world in country *x*. Values of BI between −1 and −0.33 denote predominantly a host country; between −0.33 and 0.33 a host and home country; between 0.33 and 1 predominantly a home country.
4. The Gerschenkron explanation on the benefit from backwardness (Gerschenkron, 1962).
5. Confirmation of this can be found in, among others, Patel (1995) and Pavitt & Patel (2000).
6. From the Fortune 500 list.
7. The authors acknowledge the help of the Fundación Empresa Pública, under the auspices of the Spanish Ministry of Industry – now the Ministry of Science and Technology – for access to this dataset.
8. In Dunning's *eclectic theory* sense (Dunning, 1973; 1980).

REFERENCES

Alonso, J.A. and Donoso, V. (1994), *Competitividad de la empresa exportadora española*, Madrid: ICEX.
Álvarez, I., Damijan, J. and Knell, M. (2002), 'Do Spanish firms get technology through FDI and Trade?', paper prepared for the Macrotec Final Conference, Brussels.
Archibugi, D. and Coco, A. (2001), 'The globalisation of technology and the European innovation system', Instituto Complutense de Estudios Internacionales (Complutense Institute for International Studies) (ICEI) Working Paper, DT09/2001.
Archibugi, D. and Lundvall, B.-Å. (2001), *The Globalizing Learning Economy*, Oxford: Oxford University Press.
Archibugi, D. and Michie, J. (1995), 'The globalisation of technology: a new taxonomy', *Cambridge Journal of Economics*, 19, pp. 121–40.
Bajo, O. (1991), 'Determinantes macroeconómicos y sectoriales de la inversión extranjera directa en España', *Información Comercial Española*, August–September, 696/697, pp. 53–74.

Bajo, O. and López Pueyo, C. (1996), 'La inversión directa extranjera en la industria manufacturera española, 1986–1993', *Papeles de Economía Española*, 66, pp. 176–90.

Bajo, O. and Sosvilla, S. (1992), 'Un análisis empírico de los determinantes de la inversión extranjera directa en España, 1961–1989', *Moneda y Crédito*, 194, pp. 107–37.

Beise, M. and Belitz, H. (1997), *Internationalisierung von Forschung und Entwicklung in multinationalen Unternehmen. Materialen zur Berichterstattung zur technologischen Leistungsfähigkeit Deutschlands 1996*, Berlin: Mannheim.

Blomström, M. and Kokko, A. (1998), 'Multinational corporations and spillovers', *Journal of Economic Surveys*, 12(2).

Buesa, M. and Molero, J. (1998), *Economía Industrial de España*, Madrid: Cívitas.

Campa, J.M. and Guillén, M.F. (1996), 'Spain, a boom from economic integration', in J.H. Dunning and R. Narula (eds), *Foreign Direct Investment and Governments: Catalysts for Economic Restructuring*, London: Routledge, pp. 207–39.

Cantwell, J. (1989), *Technological Innovation and Multinational Corporations*, Oxford: Basil Blackwell.

Cantwell, J. (1995), 'The globalisation of technology: what remains of the product cycle model?', *Cambridge Journal of Economics*, 19, pp. 155–74.

Cantwell, J. and Mudambi, R. (2001), 'MNE competence-creating subsidiary mandates: an empirical investigation' Instituto Complutense de Estudios Internacionales (Complutense Institute for International Studies), ICEI Working Paper, DT 06/2001.

Cantwell, J. and Piscitello, L. (2001), 'The location of technological activities of MNCs in European regions', Fifth Seminar of the MESIAS Network, Reading.

Chesnais, F., Ietto-Gillies, G. and Simonetti, R. (eds) (2000), *European Integration and Global Innovation Strategies*, London: Routledge.

Círculo de Empresarios (1995), *Actitud y comportamientos de las grandes empresas españolas ante la innovación*, Madrid.

Cohen, W.M. and Levinthal, D.A. (1990), 'Absorptive capacity: a new perspective on learning and innovation', *Administrative Science Quarterly*, 35, pp. 128–52.

Criscuolo, P. and Narula, R. (2001), 'A novel approach to national technological accumulation and absorptive capacity: aggregating Cohen and Levinthal', Third Seminar of the MESIAS Network, Budapest.

Dunning, J.H. (1958), *American Investment in British Manufacturing Industry*, London: Routledge.

Dunning, J.H. (1973), 'The determinants of international production', *Oxford Economic Papers*, January 1973.

Dunning, J.H. (1980), 'Toward an eclectic theory of international production: some empirical tests', *Journal of International Business Studies*, 11(1), pp. 9–31.

Dunning, J.H. and Narula, R. (1994), 'The R&D activities of foreign firms in the US', Discussion Papers in International Investment & Business Studies, 189, University of Reading.

Dunning, J.H. and Narula, R. (eds) (1996), *Foreign Direct Investment and Governments: Catalysts for Economic Restructuring*, London: Routledge.

Fernandez-Otheo, C.M. (2002), *Inversión Directa extranjera y desinversión de España, 1993–2001. Una nueva perspectiva*, working paper of the Instituto Universitario Ortega y Gasset (Ortega y Gasset University Institute), Madrid.

Gerschenkron, A. (1962), *Economic Backwardness in Historical Perspective*, Cambridge, Mass: Belknap Press.

Hagerdoorn, J. and Narula, R. (1996), 'Choosing organisational modes of strategic technological partnering: international and sectoral differences', *Journal of International Business Studies*, 2nd quarter 27(2), pp. 256–84.

Ietto-Gillies, G. (2002), 'How internationalised are EU transnationals?', *The Journal of Interdisciplinary Economics*, 13, pp. 13–49.

Inzelt, A. (2000), 'Foreign direct investment in R&D: skin-deep and soul-deep cooperation', *Science and Public Policy*, 27(4), pp. 241–51.

Kuemmerle, W. (1999), 'Foreign direct investment in industrial research in the pharmaceutical and electronics industries: results from a survey of multinational firms', *Research Policy*, 28.

Lall, S. (1996), 'The investment development path, some conclusions', in J.H. Dunning and R. Narula (eds), *Foreign Direct Investment and Governments: Catalysts for Economic Restructuring*. London: Routledge.

Martín, C. and Velázquez, F.J. (1996), 'Factores determinantes de la inversión directa en los países de la OCDE: una especial referencia a España', *Papeles de Economía Española*, 66, pp. 209–19.

Merino, F. and Salas, V. (1995), 'Empresa extranjera y manufactura española: efectos directos e indirectos', *Revista de Economía Aplicada*, 9(3), pp. 105–31.

Merino, F. and Salas, V. (2001), 'La innovación como respuesta a la competencia del exterior', Fundación Empresa Pública, WP 0103, Madrid.

Meyer-Krahmer, F. and Reger, G. (1999), 'New perspectives on the innovation strategies of multinational enterprises: lessons for technology policy in Europe', *Research Policy*, 28, pp. 751–76.

Molero, J. (1996), 'Cambio tecnológico y empresas multinacionales: análisis del caso español', in J.L. García Delgado (eds), *Economía española, cultura y sociedad. Homenaje a Juan Velarde Fuertes*, Madrid: EUDEMA, pp. 871–97.

Molero, J. (2000), 'Las empresas multinacionales y el sistema español de innovación', in J. Molero (ed.), *Competencia global y cambio tecnológico*, Madrid: Pirámide.

Molero, J. (2001), *Innovación tecnológica y competitividad en Europa*, Madrid: Síntesis.

Molero, J. (2002), 'The innovative behaviour of MNC subsidiaries in uneven systems of integration: a comparative analysis of the German and Irish cases', *The Journal of Interdisciplinary Economics*, 13, pp. 305–41.

Molero, J., Buesa, M. and Casado, M. (1995), 'Factores de localización y comportamiento comercial de las multinacionales en España', *Economía Industrial*, 306, pp. 129–42.

Molero, J. and Heijs, J. (2002), 'Differences of innovative behaviour between national and foreign firms: measuring the impact of foreign firms on national innovation systems', *International Journal of Entrepreneurship and Innovation Management*, 2 (2/3), pp. 122–45.

Narula, R. (1999), 'Explaining the growth of strategic R&D alliances by European firms', *Journal of Common Market Studies*, 37(4), pp. 711–23.

Patel, P. (1995), 'The localised production of global technology', *Cambridge Journal of Economics*, 19, pp. 141–53.

Patel, P. and Pavitt, K. (2000), 'National system of innovation under strain: the internationalisation of corporate R&D', in R. Barrell, G. Mason and M. O'Mahony (eds), *Productivity, Innovation and Economic Performance*, Cambridge: Cambridge University Press.

Patel, P. and Vega, M. (1998), 'Technology strategies of large European firms', paper to the International Complutense Seminar, 'Empresas Multinacionales y Sistemas Nacionales de Innovación', November.

Patel, P. and Vega, M. (1999), 'Patterns of internalisation corporate technology: location vs. home countries advantages', *Research Policy*, 28, pp. 145–55.

Pavitt, K. (2001), 'Public policies to support basic research: what can the rest of the world learn from US theory and practice? (and what they should not learn)', *Industrial & Corporate Change*, 10, pp. 761–79.

Pavitt, K. and Patel, P. (2000), 'Empresas globales y sistemas nacionales de innovación: ¿quién domina a quién?', in J. Molero (ed.) *Competencia global y cambio tecnológico*, Madrid: Pirámide.

Pearce, R. (1999), 'Decentralised R&D and strategic competitiveness: globalised approaches to generation and use of technology in multinational enterprises (MNEs)', *Research Policy*, 28, pp. 157–78.

Petit, M. and Sanna-Randaccio, F. (2000), 'Endogenous R&D and foreign direct investment in international oligopolies', *International Journal of Industrial Organisation*, 18, pp. 339–67.

Reger, G. (2001), 'Differences in the internationalisation of research and technology between Japanese, North American and Western European companies', Fourth Seminar of the MESIAS Network, Brandenburg.

Sanna-Randaccio, F. (2002), 'The impact of foreign direct investment on home and host countries with endogenous R&D', *Review of International Economics*, 10.

Sanna-Randaccio, F. and Veuglers, R. (2002), 'Multinational knowledge spillovers with centralised versus decentralised R&D: a game theory approach', CEPR Discussion Paper 3151.

Sembenelli, A. and Siotis, G. (2002), 'Foreign direct investment, competitive pressure, and spillovers. An empirical analysis on Spanish firm level data', paper presented at the Technology and Foreign Ownership Workshop, Oslo (mimeo).

Siotis, G. (1999), 'Foreign direct investment strategies and firms' capabilities', *Journal of Economics & Management Strategy*, 8(2), pp. 251–70.

Solvell, Ö. and Zander, I. (1995), 'Organization of the dynamic multinational enterprise', *International Studies of Management and Organization*, 25(1–2), pp. 17–38.

UNCTAD (2001), *World Investment Report 2001 Promoting Linkages*, New York and Geneva: United Nations.

UNCTAD (2002), *World Investment Report 2002 Transnational Corporations and Export Competitiveness*, New York and Geneva: United Nations.

8. Networks and learning processes: a case study on the automotive industry in Portugal

Vitor Corado Simões*

INTRODUCTION

Learning became in the last decade a fashionable topic. There is a widespread agreement that learning is a critical instrument for firms to cope with, and to anticipate, change. Learning capabilities are envisaged as a key factor in company competitiveness, as indicated by the perspectives of 'the learning firm' (Senge, 1990), 'the knowledge creating company' (Nonaka and Takeuchi, 1995) or the 'individualised corporation' (Ghoshal and Bartlett, 1997).

However, the literature has mainly focused on intra-organisational learning, including the sharing of knowledge within the multinational firm (Szulanski, 1996; Bartlett and Ghoshal, 1989; Doz et al., 2001; Kulkki, 1996). When an inter-organisational perspective was adopted, it was mostly concerned with dyadic relationships between two firms, particularly in joint-ventures (Inkpen, 1997; Tiemessen et al., 1997). Learning processes in the context of inter-firm networks has been a neglected issue in most international business literature, with a few exceptions, namely Kogut (2000), Lam (1997) and the authors associated with the industrial networks approach (Araújo, 1996; Axelsson and Easton, 1992; Haakansson and Johanson, 1993; Blankenburg-Holm and Johanson, 1997).

This chapter is aimed at providing an additional contribution towards the understanding of learning processes in a network context. It will focus on how local partners learn and develop competences within networks whose central actor is a foreign-owned firm. This means that our endeavour has two main facets: one regarding learning in networks; another on the effects of key foreign investment projects which gave rise to the formation of networks. We have chosen two large automotive projects in Portugal, that are landmarks in the development of the industry in that country: the setting up of the Renault complex, in the early 1980s; and the investment by Ford and Volkswagen to create the Auto-Europa joint-venture, in the early 1990s. The characteristics of the automotive industry, particularly the conjunction of 'collaborative manu-facturing' (Kogut, 2000) and continuous improvement, make it particularly interesting for the study of learning within networks.

The theoretical framework for the research combines the concept of the 'flagship firm', introduced by Rugman and D'Cruz (1996 and 2000), with the perspective of business networks suggested by Haakansson (1987). The first highlights the central position held by the automakers. The second enables us to grasp the dynamics of the relationships involving different actors, resources and activities. While taking the network as the frame for analysis, this chapter is mostly concerned with component suppliers' learning processes.

The text is developed along six sections, excluding this introductory note. First, a brief perspective of the main trends in the automotive industry will be provided. Then follows a historical retrospective of that industry in Portugal, underlying the key features of the projects behind our focal networks – Renault and Auto-Europa. A conceptual framework, incorporating the contributions indicated above, is presented in the third section. The fourth deals with the method adopted in empirical research, and particularly how the case studies were developed. The presentation and comparison of the two case studies are undertaken in the next section. The main thrust is to understand the key features of component suppliers' involvement as well as the characteristics and the scope of the learning processes. The chapter concludes with a broader assessment of the relationships between foreign investment, inter-firm networks and learning in the automotive industry.

THE AUTOMOTIVE INDUSTRY: MAIN FEATURES

To understand how networks can foster intra- and inter-firm learning in the automotive sector there is a need to provide a broad characterisation of the industry. Four main features deserve a reference: complexity, with changing patterns of relationships among the main players; market concentration; glo-balisation of activities; and strategic alliances. Let us briefly describe them.

Complexity and Changing Relationship Patterns

The complexity of the automotive system stems from the existence of multiple players linked by different flows of a tangible and intangible nature as well as from the very dynamics of the linkages. Traditionally, three main groups of players, linked through hierarchical relationships and located in distinct layers or tiers, were identified (Chanaron, 1998; Dyer, Cho and Chu, 1997; Stephan and Pfaffmann, 1998; Clark and Veloso, 2000). The leading place was occupied by automotive manufacturers, responsible for designing the vehicle, for assembling mechanical parts (namely engines and gearboxes), for manufacturing the body (pressing, welding and painting), for final assembly, and for marketing (including the image/logo, and the provision of credit, and post-sales service). Then came the first-tier component suppliers responsible for manufacturing sensitive parts of the vehicle under contracts entered into with the automotive manufacturers. Lower down the supply chain was a large number of second-, third- and fourth-tier suppliers, often specialised in a single technological area or in a manufacturing process (stamping, plastic injection and metal protection, for instance).

With the development of lean production systems, automotive manufacturers externalised component sourcing, relying on external suppliers to an increasing extent. Consequently, supply-chain management became a very sensitive topic for automotive manufacturers (Dyer, 1996; Dyer and Chu, 2000; Boyer et al., 1998; Womack, Jones and Roos, 1990). During the second half of the 1990s, the clear-cut pattern of tiered, hierarchical organisation became more blurred, and inter-firm linkages gained more complexity, due to the confluence of three inter-related trends. The first is the decline in the number of first-tiers, direct suppliers, together with the downgrading of weaker firms. The second is a widening of the scope and complexity of the products delivered by direct suppliers: there are no longer single parts, but rather modules and/or systems (Stephan and Pfaffmann, 1998; Veloso et al., 2000). The third trend is the expansion of worldwide supply chains, with suppliers, especially 'systems manufacturers' and 'systems integrators' (Pilorusso, 1997; Veloso et al., 2000),[1] following automotive manufacturers in their international expansion, particularly towards the new platforms set up in the main emerging markets. These trends lead to an increasing complexity of the automotive industry system. Simultaneously, they place increasing demands on suppliers: these should have capabilities to organise supply chains themselves as well as to cooperate with the automotive manufacturers in the development of new, more complex modules and/or systems, even suggesting new solutions, while having an international reach. This raises significant challenges for suppliers based in less advanced countries, whose relationships with automakers were originally based, at least in part, on local value added content clauses. To put it another way, the traditional role of the automotive sector as an 'industrialising industry' may be in jeopardy.

Concentration

The automotive industry exhibits a strong market concentration. According to Vickery (1997), the 20 biggest automakers were responsible, in 1996, for more than 90% of the world output, while the four biggest accounted for a share above 40%. Since then, concentration ratios have increased again, namely as a consequence of the alliances between Daimler and Chrysler, Renault and Nissan, and General Motors (GM) and Fiat as well as the acquisitions of Volvo and Saab by Ford and GM, respectively. The four biggest automakers concentrate now more than one half of the world industry output.

While some observers argue that automotive manufacturers have, in recent years, lost power against direct suppliers (Veloso et al., 2000), we concur with Chanaron (1998) in considering that automakers are still in the driving seat – they control the structure and development of the automotive industry. It is undeniable, however, that concentration was a pervasive phenomenon that has also affected component manufacturers (Clark and Veloso, 2000; Veloso et al., 2000): in 1997, the four biggest component manufacturers (Delphi, Viston, Robert Bosch and Denso) accounted for 29% of the sales of the 50 biggest firms (Stephan and Pfaffmann, 1998).

Globalisation

Although automotive manufacturers' strategies may differ,[2] globalisation is a major shaper of competitive strategies in the industry. The biggest manufacturers have worldwide strategies, while there is an increasing integration of Triadic markets (Ruigrok, Van Tulder and Baven, 1991). The need to make creative syntheses between global and local forces remains, however. The development of the platform approach may be envisaged as a device to match scale and scope economies with the maintaining of local flavours, since markets still have different demands and grant higher value to different features. The international expansion or replication of supply chains, namely in emerging markets, is another expression of the local/global match. These moves to some extent add a new perspective to the strategy taxonomy suggested by Ruigrok, Van Tulder and Baven (1991): 'glocalisation' – that is international, intra-firm division of work – and 'globalisation', characterised by the division of work among geographically concentrated groups of firms. The new perspective might be called global localisation, characterised by the international replication of different locations of variations of a value chain made of global players.

Strategic Alliances

The main automotive manufacturers are adapting to the lean production 'commandments' by externalising their former component divisions: the two key examples were provided by the spin-off of Delphi and Visteon by GM and Ford, respectively.[3] Simultaneously, there has been a surge in strategic alliance formation. Such alliances have involved three main fields of competences: technology, through the development of new, common technical solutions or the sharing of specific technologies; production, encompassing co-production agreements and the common use of manufacturing platforms, to benefit from economies of scale; and marketing, through reciprocal marketing agreements, to counter situations of excessive market segmentation.

In some instances, alliances were pursued still further, involving equity swaps and links as well as the creation of joint-ventures. A number of these happened during the 1990s; examples include the Ford–Volkswagen joint-ventures Auto-Latina and Auto-Europa (which was discontinued a couple of years ago), and Nedcar, launched by Volvo and Mitsubishi in cooperation with the Dutch public authorities. More recently, large acquisitions (such as the purchase of Volvo and Saab by Ford and GM, respectively) and transcontinental tie-ups (Daimler–Chrysler, Renault–Nissan and GM–Fiat) took place. The strategic goals behind these moves are concerned with size and the creation of synergies to enable the leveraging of the capabilities needed to compete globally.

FOREIGN INVESTMENT IN THE PORTUGUESE AUTOMOTIVE INDUSTRY: A HISTORICAL RETROSPECT

The history of the automotive industry in Portugal during the last half century has been shaped by the interaction between two main players: the State, defining (or intending to define) industrial policies specifically addressed to the sector; and international investors, led by the main automotive manufacturers. In the background, but somewhat defining the boundaries for players' behaviours, economic integration processes, from the creation of the European Free Trade Association (EFTA) to the launching of the Economic and Monetary Union.

The 1960s were dominated by the so-called 'assembly law'. This defined the conditions for the import of automotive vehicles, and was aimed at both curtailing imports and stimulating the development of domestic component manufacturing firms (Guerra, 1990). The underlying logic was to substitute imports by local production. The passing of the law generated an immediate reaction by automakers: the launching of assembly plants, in the context of direct foreign investment operations or licensing agreements, with the objective of protecting or even increasing market shares. *Ex-post* evaluation of this policy was clearly negative (Schmidt and Almeida, 1987; Féria, 1999). The multiplication of small assemblying units, addressed to a protected market, did not enable the emergence of a true component manufacturing industry. The negative effect of market size was compounded by the commercial, instead of manufacturing, origin of the Portuguese companies involved in the process.

From 1976 onwards, a policy reorientation, stemming from both a recognition of the meagre results achieved so far and the commitments stemming from the 1972 agreement with the then European Economic Community (EEC), started to take shape. It led to the definition of a new framework law for the automotive sector (Decree-Law 352/79), setting up a mechanism of compensating exports: imports could only be increased to the extent they were offset by exports of manufactured products. Some automakers, of which GM is probably the best example, responded to the new policy by investing in component manufacturing. The main result of the policy is, however, the launching of the so-called Renault project.

Renault was attracted by the exceptional conditions offered by Portugal, not only in terms of direct investment incentives but especially because of the privileged access to the Portuguese market. The project enabled the creation of a relatively coherent automotive manufacturing system, involving a casting unit (Funfrap), an engine and gearbox producing plant, and an assembly unit with a capacity of 80 thousand vehicles per year. The size of the project, the local purchasing policy associated with local value added commitments and the support provided to several Portuguese component manufacturers transformed the Renault project in a landmark for the modernisation of the Portuguese automotive industry. Several authors criticise the Renault project on three grounds: excessive incentives (Santos, 1996); an insufficient level of national value added (Schimdt and Almeida, 1987); and project design mistakes, particularly the low investment in dedicated assets (Féria, 1999). However, even these critics concede that the Renault project was a very important step in enabling the creation of a modern industry of component manufacturing in the country (Schimdt and Almeida, 1987). It may even be argued that Renault provided the ground for the Auto-Europa[4] project to emerge.

With Portugal's accession to the EEC in 1986, the privileged conditions granted to Renault were not sustainable for a long time. This fact, together with the opening of Central and East European markets (Renault undertook significant investments in Slovenia) and the attraction of the Auto-Europa project, led to a fading-out process by Renault. Today, the Renault system no longer exists: the assembly unit was closed; the engine and gearbox plant was granted juridical autonomy to pursue its own independent way; and the metal casting unit is now part of Teksid, a new firm resulting from the merger of Renault and Fiat assets in the metal casting field.

If the investment by Renault was only possible in a context of domestic market protection, the Auto-Europa project was, on the contrary, a consequence of a regional integration process, following Portugal's EEC accession. Auto-Europa, originally a joint-venture between Ford and Volkswagen, was the largest foreign investment ever undertaken in Portugal. Launched in 1991, it involved the setting-up of a vehicle manufacturing plant with a capacity of 180 thousand vehicles per year, the output being addressed to foreign markets. As a greenfield investment, Auto-Europa espoused some of the most recent developments in the automotive industry, regarding the manufacturing process and supply-chain management (just-in-time, close cooperation with suppliers, some of which were located at Auto-Europa premises), organisation (continuous improvement – *Kaizen*), human-resource management (task rotation, team-working, performance stimuli) and environmental protection.

Auto-Europa was envisaged as a key instrument for the development of a 'true automotive cluster' in Portugal, to quote Mr Mira Amaral, who was then the Minister of Industry (Amaral, 1995). Auto-Europa was expected to play a pivotal role on two grounds. First, the dynamisation of the supply chain, namely through the attraction of new foreign investments, including joint-ventures with Portuguese firms, and the upgrading of local suppliers, capable of responding to the challenges raised by Auto-Europa (order size, quality, reliability, logistics, just-in-time delivery, product engineering etc.). Second, 'putting Portugal on the map' of major location alternatives for setting up new automotive manu-facturing plants.

This brief retrospect of the history of the automotive industry in Portugal shows how cumulative processes and change interact, leading to a permanent reconfiguration of industry patterns. To some extent there was a process of punctuated change, where the main foreign investment projects (Renault and Auto-Europa) played a key role. However, these are not stand-alone projects. They gave rise to the formation of supply networks as well as to learning processes inside those networks. Network management and inter- and intra-firm learning become key instruments for integrating cumulativeness and change. Although the automakers are in the driving seat and act as 'flagship firms' (Rugman and D'Cruz, 1996 and 2000), a lot of learning takes place within the network and is internalised by component suppliers. Consequently, instead of focusing on automakers, our target will be the study of component firms' behaviour. More specifically, there is a need to understand how these firms behave and learn in the context of supply networks which are, to a large extent, managed and shaped by the 'flagship' – the final customer.

CONCEPTUAL FRAMEWORK

Bearing in mind the reasoning developed above, it is possible to develop a framework to study how inter-firm learning processes take place in the context of the automotive industry. This general framework will be then applied to the specific networks stemming from the establishment of Renault and Auto-Europa in Portugal.

The automotive industry may be envisaged as a 'value system' in the sense suggested by Porter (1985). The espousing of the lean production concept led to new forms of coordinating the supply chain (Freyssenet et al., 1998; Sako and

Warburton, 2000; Womack, Jones and Roos, 1990). Such a 'value system' corresponds to a network, where firms are linked by resource and information flows and develop mutual expectations which may strengthen the trust required for the network to operate efficiently (Ebers, 1997). Therefore, an appropriate way to study the organisational and learning dynamics in the automotive industry, particularly from the component suppliers' perspective, is to develop a framework combining two different approaches – inter-organisational or business networks, and the 'flagship firm' framework suggested by Rugman and D'Cruz (1996 and 2000).

Business networks are defined as sets of two or more inter-linked business relationships, where each exchange relationship takes place between firms, envisaged as collective actors (Andersson, Haakansson and Johanson, 1994). Haakansson (1987) proposed a framework where the network includes three main elements – actors, resources and activities. Actors control resources and have a certain level of knowledge about them. Through exchange relationships, actors exchange resources. Activities, which may be of transformation or transactional, process the resources or exchange resources through the use of other resources. Networks present multiple features, and may be conceptualised following different perspectives: as relationships, as structures (where stability and change co-exist), as positions or as processes. Relationship dynamics within networks may play an important role as stimulators of learning processes (Haakansson, Havila and Pedersen, 1999; Araújo, 1996). In fact, within a network there are common but also conflicting interests, and 'actors use their knowledge of the network as well as their relationships with other actors in order to increase their control' (Haakansson and Johanson, 1993: 30).

Though some suppliers have recently improved their positions within existing networks (Veloso et al., 2000), automotive industry networks remain, as pointed out above, organised by reference to a central player which has a pivotal role – the automotive manufacturer. This provides coherence to a specific network, although some actors may belong to different networks. The idea of centrality, where an actor develops, around itself, an 'industrial model' (Jurgens, 1998),[5] is particularly relevant for us, since our purpose is to analyse two specific networks led by Renault and Auto-Europa.

This leads directly to the 'flagship firm' framework (Rugman and D'Cruz, 1996 and 2000). The flagship firm is the hub that defines the structure and provides the cohesive force that keeps the network together. To quote Rugman and D'Cruz (1996: 670), it 'provides strategic leadership and direction for a vertically integrated chain of businesses that operate as a coordinated system or network, frequently in competition with similar networks that address the same end markets'. According to the authors, that 'chain of business' involves five types of actors: the 'flagship firm' itself (including different units located in several countries), the main suppliers, the main customers, the competitors and the support infrastructure.

Certainly not by chance, the first example of application of the 'flagship firm' indicated by Rugman and D'Cruz (1996) is an automaker – Chrysler. In fact, this firm, as Belzowski (1998) pointed out, was able to 'reinvent' itself through the development and deepening of the relationships with its suppliers. On the other hand, the network concept was used by Kogut (2000) in his challenging analysis of the Toyota production system. He has shown that the network may be envisaged as a structure that enables the combination of supplier variety with the central position of the automotive manufacturer.

Focusing on two players only – the automaker and the component suppliers – the network may be presented as indicated in Figure 8.1. It provides the structure of the focal network (Automaker A), and places this in a context where the existence of other automakers is acknowledged. Three other features of the figure deserve a reference: several suppliers are linked to more than one automaker (and, for a single automaker, they may supply more than one platform); suppliers' hierarchisation is somewhat blurred, since the same firm may act as a direct supplier for some components and as an indirect one for others; and some suppliers, positioned at higher levels in the network, combine the contributions from different suppliers, playing a role of 'systems integrators'.

METHOD

Since the objective was to understand the learning processes taking place in the Renault and Auto-Europa networks, it was thought that the case study method was the most appropriate. According to Yin (1994) case studies should be undertaken in situations when the researcher is interested in studying how processes unfold. Case studies focus 'on the understanding of the dynamics present within single settings' (Eisenhardt, 1989: 534). The Renault and Auto-Europa networks may be envisaged as 'single settings', although involving multiple players.

Empirical research was developed in four main stages: (1) working out of the structure of the supply networks; (2) selection of suppliers to be studied in each network; (3) undertaking of case studies; and (4) comparative inter-case analysis.

The first stage consisted of applying the framework presented above to depict the Renault and Auto-Europa networks, as shown in Figures 8.2 and 8.3. In this phase interviews were held with sector experts, three of which had played a relevant role in the attraction and setting-up of Auto-Europa in Portugal. The purpose of these interviews was to better understand the organisation of the automotive industry and the challenges faced by component suppliers, as well

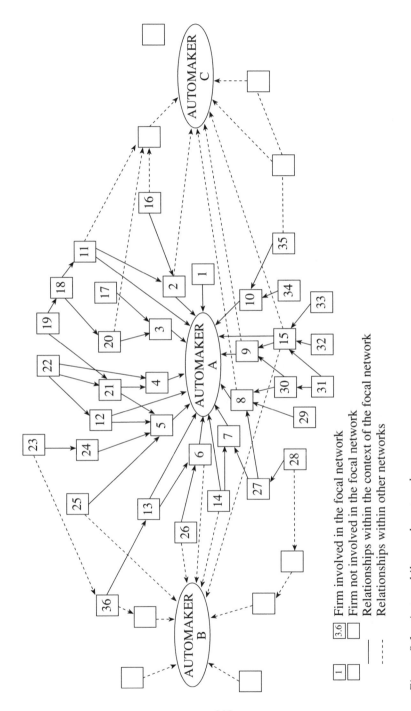

Figure 8.1   Automobile supply network

1   3,6   Firm involved in the focal network

         Firm not involved in the focal network

———   Relationships within the context of the focal network

-----   Relationships within other networks

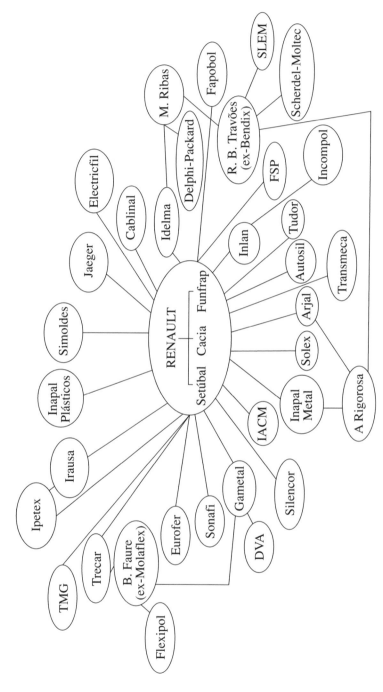

Figure 8.2 Renault network

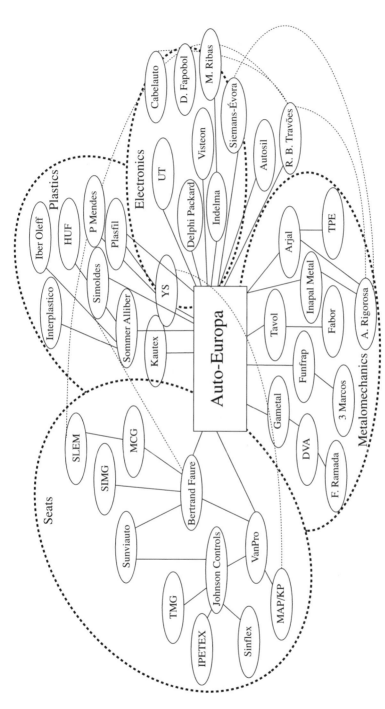

Figure 8.3   Auto-Europa network

217

as to validate our draft of the graphic representations of the networks and to introduce the research team to relevant companies.

The second stage started from the structure of the networks. Since it was not feasible to interview all the suppliers, a selection was needed. This was based on two main criteria. First, to include three different groups of suppliers: members of the Renault network, members of the Auto-Europa network and members of both. This group was very important for our purposes, since it was expected to provide information on inter-network learning. Second, to cover the four main product groups identified: metalomechanics, plastics, electronics and seats. Eighteen firms were selected, besides the two 'flagship firms', but only 12 agreed to participate.

Each case study involved interviews with the 'flagship firm' and the suppliers. Those interviews were open, although based on some common guidelines, and were undertaken in the second half of 2000. Our counterparts were envisaged more as informants than as respondents (Yin, 1994). Whenever possible, multiple informants were used to collect a richer set of contributions, as well as to triangulate information. For both Renault and Auto-Europa several interviews were held, including a very long one (five hours in two rounds) with the former Chairman of the Board of Renault Portugal. Four main topics were considered: decision autonomy and supply-chain management processes by the Portuguese subsidiary of the 'flagship firm'; initial support provided for the accreditation of Portuguese suppliers; relationships between the Portuguese plant (or plants) and the multinational group; and the development of relationships, particularly learning relationships, with the suppliers located in Portugal. Interviews with suppliers followed a set of guidelines structured along seven axes, going from management systems and strategic orientations to the competence basis and assessment of the value of linkages and learning processes in the context of networks. Interviews lasted from 1.5 to 3 hours, with an average of 2.5 hours.

A comparative analysis of the patterns, relationship structures and learning outcomes in the Renault and Auto-Europa networks was undertaken. Although direct comparisons should be made with care, due to the different time frames and environmental conditions in two cases, inter-case contrasts enabled a better understanding of the dynamics underlying the formation and development of automotive supply networks.

INVOLVEMENT OF COMPONENT SUPPLIERS IN THE NETWORKS

Analysis of inter-firm relationships within the networks, from the perspective of component suppliers, may be undertaken according to four dimensions: upstream, concerning the linkages with customers, and namely with the automakers; down-stream, that is, the relationship with other suppliers further down in the chain; other relational spaces, namely horizontal relationships with other players, including the so-called 'suppliers clubs'; and replication of the network in other environments, when a significant number of suppliers follow the automaker in international moves. In this chapter, the focus is on the first dimension: up-stream relationships.

Each network will be studied separately, starting with the oldest – Renault. A closing point will summarise the main findings stemming from the two cases.

The Renault Network

Six of the component suppliers studied have been involved, with different time lengths and positions, in the Renault network. Since for two of them the Renault experience was relatively marginal, our attention will be addressed to the other four firms. Two of them, both foreign-owned, were created in conjunction with the Renault project. For the others, involvement in the Renault network was the key determinant of their specialisation in automotive components.

One of the firms has a very interesting history of belonging to the network. It was set up in the context of the project, and had an equity participation by RNUR.[6] Its main mandate was to supply cast metal products (engine blocks, engine wheels, differential boxes, piston rods and escape collectors) to the Renault plant of mechanical components. It is not surprising therefore that RNUR played a key role in the process of creating a technological and manufacturing base. The launching of this casting plant followed RNUR's routines of inter-unit information transmission and knowledge sharing to enable a smooth start-up. RNUR's contribution mainly consisted in nominating staff for the key posts, professional training (most engineers stayed in other RNUR plants) and providing technological information. Inter-personal relationships played a very relevant role in the foundry's learning process and know-how acquisition. Today, the firm is part of an independent multinational group, that combines the former foundry activities of both RNU and Fiat. In spite of keeping linkages with RNUR (which still accounts for one-third of turnover), the Portuguese firm had to forge its own way with the end of the Renault project.

The two Portuguese-owned firms[7] were, since the inception of the project, involved in the Renault network and still are, more than 20 years later, suppliers to RNUR. They recognise that the Renault project enabled them to upgrade their capabilities as well as to make a stronger commitment to the automotive components industry. As the Chairman of one of them, focused on the casting business, acknowledged, '*the advantage of the [Renault] project was to support the domestic industry*', being a '*dynamisation and modernisation factor*' (Macedo, 1995). The other company, working in the plastic injection field, is an interesting case of capability upgrading, especially in design, and is now an international partner of RNUR. Belonging to the Renault network has enabled the generation of a closer relationship and the forging of trust, leveraging the links from Renault in Portugal to the RNUR group. This accounts for around one-third of turnover. The Portuguese firm now has an engineering unit close to the RNUR Technological Centre in France to streamline and dynamise the relationships in the development of new components and has followed Renault in some international moves, namely to Slovenia and Brazil.[8]

One of the key objectives of the Renault project was to support the creation of an automotive components industry in Portugal. Local value added commitments led Renault to stimulate the upgrading of some Portuguese suppliers, as well as to attract their traditional suppliers to Portugal. According to the former Chairman of Renault Portugal, support was provided to those companies that had the minimum capabilities to become Renault suppliers, and that showed belief in the project; this '*means investing and bearing the inherent risks*'. One of the firms surveyed considered that Renault played a very positive role:

[Renault] provided us with support and training and had the patience for us to upgrade and develop. There was no need for support in process technology. But they helped us in many ways: involvement in training; visits to Renault plants to better understand their operations; visits to other Renault suppliers; investment advice; and quality training. They supported us in learning and enhancing our credibility.

These words confirm our desk research indicating a concern by Renault in developing local suppliers, particularly in the initial phase. Renault support seems to have mostly consisted in the provision of technical assistance and training, to upgrade suppliers' technological capabilities and performance. The automaker has shown forbearance with regard to suppliers, in the first phases, both in terms of prices and quality. Timetables for gradual improvement of prices and quality were defined on a case-by-case basis – the 'patience' mentioned in the quotation above. However, this behaviour needs to be contextualised. In fact, Renault benefited from privileged access to the Portuguese market; the downside was the achievement of local value added objectives. So, Renault was interested in supporting local suppliers. Furthermore, in the early 1980s the Portuguese market was protected and global or regional sourcing policies by automakers were still to be developed. The combined effect of Portugal's EEC accession and the development of new, centralised sourcing policies (Martinez and Jarillo, 1988) led to a significant change in Renault's behaviour from 1987 onwards. Gradually Renault's interest in Portugal declined and, by 1995, it informed the Portuguese government about its decision to close the assembly plant of Setubal and to annul the investment contract entered into in the early 1980s.

In spite of the problems raised by Renault's decision, a long-term perspective of the Renault experience shows that it enabled the modernisation and development of a few Portuguese component suppliers, some of which were able to establish relationships with the RNUR network. In its initial phases, Renault stimulated learning processes by Portuguese potential suppliers and granted credibility to component manufacturers which enabled them to enter other networks. It may be argued that without the Renault project Portugal would not have the domestic manufacturing basis which was instrumental in attracting the Auto-Europa project.

The Auto-Europa Network

The opinions of component suppliers about the impact of the Auto-Europa project on company development and technological, commercial and organisational learning are mixed. Some firms, namely the metal casters, regret engines not being manufactured in Portugal, thereby hindering the opportunities for enhancing and expanding supply relationships. Other firms, however, argue that the main advantages from the Auto-Europa experience are associated with the scale of operations and the extension of linkages with the involved automakers[9] at a wider, European level. Sometimes learning was not achieved through the relationship with the automakers themselves, but rather with first-tier suppliers. For instance, a Portuguese manufacturer of components for seats mentioned the strengthening of the relationship with Bertrand Faure as a consequence of belonging to the Auto-Europa network: '*we already had relationships with them and, since there was an intention to develop [local] suppliers due to national value added obligations, [our company] emerged as a potential supplier*'.

However, the level of autonomy enjoyed by Auto-Europa is limited – and this is perceived as a hindrance by some suppliers. Many decisions are taken by the headquarters, and not by the Auto-Europa plant. For instance, the granting of the 'engineering source approval' is decided by the 'corporate sourcing', and the negotiations regarding most technical aspects of supply agreements are held with Wolfsburg, not with Palmela.[10] In this process, Portuguese affiliates of multinational groups – particularly those that already had a track record of close relationships with Volkswagen – enjoy a clear advantage. In this case, as indicated in Figure 8.4 (Mode 1), there is not a dyadic relationship, but rather a quadrialogue. The leading actors are the headquarters (or regional divisions, namely in the case of US multinationals), while Portuguese subsidiaries play a secondary role, due to their weaknesses in the commercial and technological fields. It may be even argued that the relationships between the Portuguese

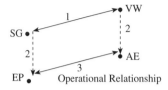

Mode 1:   Multinationals' subsidiaries

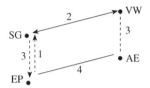

Mode 3:   Portuguese firms with a
          development unit in Germany

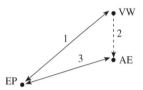

Mode 2:   Direct dialogue from Portugal

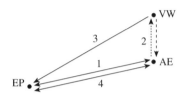

Mode 4:   Intermediation by Auto-Europa

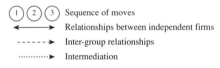

① ② ③	Sequence of moves
──────────►	Relationships between independent firms
------►	Inter-group relationships
············►	Intermediation

VW – Volkswagen (Wolfsburg)
AE – Auto-Europa
FP – Potuguese subsidiary
SG – Headquarters
EP – Portuguese firm
UED – Engineering and Development Unit

Source: Empirical research.

Figure 8.4   Actors and relationship modes in Auto-Europa network

subsidiaries are mostly limited to operational issues (manufacturing and logistics), thereby curtailing the scope of possible learning processes stemming from the interaction.

Portuguese component manufacturers with more ambitions need to set up a direct dialogue with Volkswagen in Wolfsburg. In the absence of such dialogue, and having in mind Auto-Europa's limited influence in sourcing decisions and in product development, those manufacturers face a high risk of downgrading in the supply network. Two possibilities may be considered. The first is to conduct the relationship from Portugal (Mode 2), but this appears to be a transitional stage, since proximity is need for interaction, especially in the product development process. This leads to the second option: the setting up of a product engineering and development unit close to Volkswagen headquarters able to establish direct relationships 'in the German language' with Volkswagen's product development centre (Mode 3). An illustration of this mode is provided by a plastic components firms recognised by our Auto-Europa interlocutors as a success case. '*We learned the way how Volkswagen works*', they told us, and betted on two areas: strengthening the engineering and development division (now staffed by around 40 people) to be able to design '*new things*' for the car; and setting up an office, with engineering capabilities, in Germany, to relate directly with Volkswagen counterparts. The efforts undertaken were highly regarded by Volkswagen, and may be understood as dedicated investments in the relationship. They allowed a feeling of closeness to be generated: '*sometimes it is not so much development [capabilities], but rather being close; there is someone with whom they [the automakers engineers] may talk in German language*'.

Having said this, it should also be acknowledged that Auto-Europa may play a facilitating role in mediating the relationships between Portuguese suppliers and the central sourcing department as well as in confirming the technological and manufacturing capabilities of those suppliers, as indicated in Mode 4. Our interlocutors at Auto-Europa mentioned that this was done with a view to stimulating well-performing Portuguese suppliers. The main instrument used in this endeavour was the so-called '*concept of relevant part*' to indicate a specific part considered by the Auto-Europa plant as very important for streamlining the assembly procedure and for enhancing plant performance. Another relevant initiative of Auto-Europa was the 'tearing down' of the vehicle manufactured in Portugal, decomposing it in all its components, in order to elicit proposals from suppliers for reducing components costs and/or for suggesting better solutions in terms of value for money. It seems, however, that the main benefits of this exercise were appropriated by Auto-Europa itself – in terms of significant cost reductions – and not so much by the component suppliers; in fact, none of the Portuguese-owned suppliers interviewed mentioned *motu proprio* the 'tearing down' initiative.

Auto Europa's autonomy is limited and, as Veloso et al., (2000) pointed out, at headquarters level there seems to be a distrust regarding the product engineering and development capabilities of Portuguese firms in general. Talks with Auto-Europa executives and industry experts enabled the identification of three conditions relevant for component suppliers to enhance their positions in the context of the Auto-Europa network. First, 'they need to be there', that is, to have an office at Wolfsburg to establish a close relationship with Volkswagen's engineering department. The second is the development of linkages with those engineering consultancy companies, such as EDAG, which provide engineering services to Volkswagen. Finally, the setting up of strategic alliances, namely with companies ranked highly by Volkswagen, provides additional visibility and credibility.

In their fields of competence, however, Auto-Europa has provided an important support to local suppliers, and the relationships between these and

Auto-Europa seem to be characterised by a cooperative spirit (Vale, 1999). Such support had two main dimensions: one, of a general nature, associated with the immersion in a lean production context; another, more specific, regarding the establishment of a continuous dialogue with suppliers, including technological or logistic help in problem-solving. Especially in critical instances, Auto-Europa may allocate engineers to stay at suppliers' premises to work together on the solution of specific problems; suppliers' engineers may also be seconded to Auto-Europa to fully understand Auto-Europa's requirements to be incorporated in product improvement. Although the information systems of Auto-Europa and their main suppliers are connected and computer communication is easy, it seems that personal interaction and joint inspection of plant site conditions and product requirements are the main instruments for developing joint solutions and for inter-firm learning.

As indicated above, there is a cooperative spirit within the network, and particularly in the relationships between Auto-Europa and its suppliers. 'Auto-Europa wants to introduce voice mechanisms – in contrast to the exit option – to solve the problems that may emerge in the supply chain' (Vale, 1999: 407). Although, contrary to Renault, Auto-Europa does not appear to have a genuine concern with the development of local suppliers, there is no doubt that mutually profitable vehicles for dialogue and supplier support were set up, particularly personnel exchange (mostly with larger suppliers), diffusion of information and technical assistance. Auto-Europa was, in fact, able to create a new working environment, encouraging the endogeneisation by suppliers of the lean production philosophy. Such an endogeneisation enabled some suppliers to use the experience gained to enter other networks. This was to some extent facilitated by the very fact that Auto-Europa was born as a joint-venture: two of the firms surveyed were able to keep the relationship with Ford after its divestment from Auto-Europa. Looking at supplier behaviour from the Auto-Europa perspective, the assessment is generally positive. It appears, however, that Portuguese component suppliers did not fully profit from the opportunities for learning. Our analysis suggests that this may be due to the convergence of three factors: the frequent absence of a strategic intent of learning and improving position in the network; insufficient resources, namely technological and financial; and low propensity to cooperate, in order to overcome resource constraints and to explore joint learning possibilities.

To sum up, the Auto-Europa experience shows that networks spead over national frontiers and that automakers' plants may not enjoy the autonomy needed to behave as hubs for supply networks. To understand how learning takes place the analysis of the relationships held with headquarters is also needed. Auto-Europa is *prima facie* a plant. It is concentrated on operational activities – manufacturing and logistics. Therefore, it may be labelled a 'specialized manufacturer' and not so much a 'product specialist' (Simões, 1992).

The scope for learning is thereby curtailed. This does not mean, however, that learning – particularly at the operational level – does not take place. On the basis of the collected evidence, one should recognise that Auto-Europa has an important role in consolidating and encouraging the development of component supplier firms in Portugal.

Synthesis: Comparing the Renault and Auto-Europa Networks

A comparative analysis of the two networks reported above enables the identification of differences and similarities. In our opinion, the main differences between the two cases stem from time and context. The Renault project took shape roughly one decade before the Auto-Europa one, at a time when the Portuguese market was insulated (and deliberately insulated for the project to be feasible) and when the concepts of lean production and centralised sourcing had still not been espoused by European automakers. Consequently, for better and worse, the Renault network had stronger local roots and concerns, and Renault Portugal enjoyed more autonomy than Auto-Europa does. Renault was chiefly a domestic market network, while Auto-Europa has a more open and international nature. The former was the last chance to start a local automotive industrial complex before EC accession negotiations, while the latter is itself a consequence of European integration.

These differences do not conceal the underlying similarities, however. Although the existence of several hierarchical levels is more evident in Auto-Europa, both cases gave rise to networks led by a hub subsidiary – and, in real terms, by a decision centre located abroad. In both cases, an attempt was made to involve Portuguese firms in the supply chain, together with the attraction of foreign investments. Most of these were of the implementer type (Bartlett and Ghoshal, 1989), focused on operations, while product and process development, marketing and sometimes sourcing activities were very limited. Of course, there were some exceptions to this general pattern, and a few subsidiaries were able to gradually upgrade their value added activities in Portugal. But the overall pattern reduced the opportunities for learning and for leveraging domestic firms capabilities.

In spite of this, Renault and Auto-Europa experiences were instrumental in enabling the involvement of Portuguese component suppliers in networks where they understood the underlying principles of automotive supply chains and were able to upgrade competences and develop relationships that were later replicated in different contexts. In other words, the interactions held within the networks enabled Portuguese firms to access additional resources (technological know-how, market relationships, logistic tools) as well as to internalise the rules behind automotive supply-chain operations. The process is not complete: Portuguese firms are still typically 'second tiers' (Féria, 1997), and have limited resources and capabilities. But, at the end of the day, it seems that Renault and Auto-Europa were, their shortcomings notwithstanding, relevant factors for most Portuguese component manufacturers to enter automotive networks[11] and to learn about the technological and organisational requirements of the industry.

FOREIGN INVESTMENTS, NETWORKS AND LEARNING: INTERPRETING THE EXPERIENCES

When Portuguese component supplier firms were asked to synthesise the key features of their learning processes in the context of supply networks, the response often focused on aspects such as '*understanding the industry*' or '*understanding the market*'. This may seem, at first sight, very limited. However, in our opinion, this is a critical element. In fact, to operate and succeed in the automotive industry, hierarchically organised but pervaded by a continuous improvement dynamic, there is a strong need to internalise the tacit 'rules of the game' – the philosophy and the standards, implicit and not written, of operation and behaviour. So, learning in this industry is not restricted to transformation activities (Haakansson, 1987), of processing inputs and achieving the required quality of outputs. Learning is not just technologically oriented. A very important area of learning deals with transactional activities, to follow the Haakansson (1987) typology. There is a need to understand the logic of transactional activities to the extent that the balanced working of the network – expressed in the interactions between firms at different levels or tiers, but also increasingly at the same level (supplying systems or modules) – is critical for the lean production. Transactional activities generate new resources, while contributing to strengthening trust and creating relational grounds (Simões, 1999; Nonaka and Konno, 1998), where knowledge sharing may take place. Consequently, learning involves simultaneously explicit elements (well-defined, formalised procedures concerning quality or manufacturing processes) and tacit features, namely on what concerns rules of behaviour within the network and expectations of others' behaviour.

This reasoning leads to the suggestion that the success of newcomers to the network very much depends on their capabilities to understand the implicit structure behind the interaction of the five dimensions of network operations mentioned by Ebers (1997). These include the following: resource flows, information flows, allocation of property rights on the resources, coordination mechanisms and mutual expectations. In automotive supply networks all these five dimensions interact. Some of these are relatively obvious, as is the case of resource and information flows, which are widespread features of the interactions in any network. The allocation of property rights on resources is not straightforward since automakers (and even systems integrators) often compel component suppliers to undertake dedicated investments (in moulds, tools and machinery, for instance) whose recovery very much depends on factors controlled by the automaker. The automaker is still the main orchestrator of the network, and holds the central position. But the coordination works downstream, with every manufacturer reflecting on its suppliers its customer requirements, while being responsible for granting the latter a product meeting the quality and the delivery conditions agreed. The continuous improvement philosophy is also pushed downwards, each company defining specific demands regarding improvements and price cutting on its suppliers.

Our research confirms the critical importance of mutual expectations. The expression, used by one of our interviewees, '*we learned the way how Volkswagen operates*' translates a process of gradual deepening of knowledge about partners' expectations. Such a learning process is key for the weaker partner, which experiences a feeling of dependency towards the other. Sometimes, those suppliers bet on anticipating customers' needs, making credible commitments. Positive surprises are envisaged as an instrument for the weaker partner to strengthen the relationship and improve its position in the network. The promotional literature of one of the firms surveyed explicitly pointed out the purpose of '*creating an environment favourable to the motivation for exceeding our customers' expectations*'. In the same vein, another firm set up an engineering office in Germany, close to Volkswagen headquarters, '*without having business enough to justify*' this investment decision. The purpose was to stimulate a relationship that might be further consolidated through operational performance.

But even for the more powerful partner, including the 'flagship firm', the management of expectations, often based on an analysis of past performance, is important. The shadow of the past is projected towards the future (Parkhe, 1991), and may give rise to small adjustments by the powerful partner, translated into technical assistance to solve specific problems, personnel exchange, the availability to discuss solutions for unforeseen difficulties or even the opening of new opportunities. The idea of 'forbearance', introduced by Buckley and Casson (1988), seems to apply here. There is a risk reduction logic: if the supplier has met the expectations so far (which means that both partners have '*made money together*'), there are no reasons to change. In contrast, if suppliers '*systematically raise problems*' they will sooner or later be discarded, as Auto-Europa has done in the recent facelift of the models. Forbearance may be envisaged as a result of the convergence of expectations, and simultaneously as an input for further convergence. A good track record of performance is the best catalyser for furthering cooperation. The development of mutual expectations may lead to a co-evolution of actors' competences and to a deepening of the dyadic relationship.[12]

The network perspective followed in the automotive industry suggests, however, that it is neither strategically sound to reason in a pure dyadic logic nor in a conflictual perspective of competitive forces *à la* Porter (1980). The 'rules of the game' are clear, although not unchangeable. Although there are centralisation, hierarchisation and power imbalances, cooperation prevails over conflict. Cooperation, responsibility, commitment and learning are stimulated. As Kogut (2000) suggested, contract assemblying and sub-systems manufacturing changed the nature of the industry relationships between automakers and suppliers in favour of 'collaborative manufacturing'. The purpose of the component suppliers surveyed is to play the cooperation game by improving operational and design performance, enhancing internal competencies and better understanding customers' 'mental frameworks'. Although conflict may be latent, one is far away from Porter's perspective, and even Hamel's (1991) competitive collaboration does not translate the industry reality.

Internal competences are necessary for enhancing positioning. Learning processes help a lot. But learning may be improved by the capability to mobilise and orchestrate resources from different actors. Our research confirms the findings by Haakansson, Havila and Pedersen (1999) that learning possibilities are increased when an actor is linked to a larger number of other actors. The new sourcing trends, privileging the supply of systems and modules, still demand an upper level cooperation. This requires further cooperation to achieve larger responsibilities for a wider market. Consequently, suppliers should not look at dyadic relationships with 'flagship firms' or systems integrators only; they need to explore the opportunities for horizontal cooperation.

Operational learning is strongly stimulated by the logic of continuous improvement that pervades the industry. Change capabilities, knowledge accumulation and performance enhancement are badly required: those that are not able to improve, to reduce costs and to increase value are bound to lose position in the network, and to be downgraded. It is interesting to note that the new industry trends enable the avoidance of an excessive concentration on exploiting, that is, an efficiency improvement in a pre-defined framework (March, 1991), expressed in price reduction objectives or the incremental introduction of new features. There is also room for exploring, namely in the area of what concerns suppliers' scope of activities. As the marketing manager of a firm told us, '*the time when [the customer] said you have a part here to reproduce is over*'. To improve a supplier's position static production efficiency is no longer enough: engineering competence, especially in new product development and design, is needed. This point has two main implications for learning. First, it demands a new vision of what a component supplier organisation is. It is no longer just a manufacturer: product design and development capabilities are needed. Second, absorptive capacity becomes a key feature insofar as it shapes a company's ability to identify, access and internalise new knowledge. Sometimes this may be achieved by connecting two different networks.

This research has shown that automotive networks may foster the upgrading and business development by recipient country component suppliers. The network provides a context where learning becomes easier and vertical cooperation is a reality. Learning is not restricted to transformation activities. Much learning occurs in transactional activities and leads to the development of increasing mutual expectations. The dynamics of the industry, however, put increasing demands on component suppliers to gain and maintain position in the networks. Both Renault and Auto-Europa enabled the development of Portuguese component suppliers. But these still have a long process of competitive sustainability ahead. The way is not easy: probably only the fittest, the most capable, the most outward looking or the happiest will succeed.

NOTES

* Work carried out in the context of the MESIAS Network, 'The Relationships between Technological Strategies of Multinational Companies and National Systems of Innovation', supported under the 5th Framework Programme.

1. These authors provide a classification of suppliers in ascending order of their responsibilities and relevance in the supply chain: component manufacturers, process specialists (metal stampers, die casters, injection moulders); sub-assembly manufacturers that correspond to process specialists with additional capabilities (machining or assembly, for instance); systems manufacturers, responsible for the design, development and manufacturing of complex systems; and systems integrators, responsible for the integration of 'components subassemblies and systems into modules that are shipped or placed directly by the supplier in the automakers' assembly plants' (Veloso et al., 2000: 43).

2. See the taxonomy suggested by Freyssenet et al. (1998).

3. However, there are indications that Japanese automakers, such as Toyota, may be moving towards more hierarchical structures (Ahmadjian and Lincoln, 2001).

4. See the description of the Auto-Europa project below.

5. This author refers specifically to the 'model' of Volkswagen. With regard to other automakers, see Freyssenet et al. (1998).

6. The acronym RNUR (Régie Nationale des Usines Renault) is used to indicate the Renault group, and particularly the headquarters.

7. One of them has meanwhile been acquired by a Dutch group.

8. Recent news indicates that this firm is about to set up a plastics plant in Rumania through a joint-venture with a French automotive components group, a traditional supplier of Renault.

9. It should be remembered that Auto-Europa was originally set up as a joint-venture between Ford and Volkswagen.

10. Wolfsburg and Palmela are the locations of the Volkswagen headquarters and Auto-Europa plant, respectively.

11. It should be acknowledged, however, that Renault and Auto-Europa were not the only experiences in this regard. There were others, namely the process of upgrading and development of domestic suppliers by General Motors, Ford and Mitsubishi.

12. It should be acknowledged however that there is a risk of lock-in that is much higher for the supplier than for the automaker, which has a wider set of relationships. More on this below.

REFERENCES

Ahmadjian, Christina L. and James R. Lincoln (2001), 'Keiretsu, Governance and Learning: Case Studies in Change from the Japanese Automotive Industry', *Organization Science*, vol. 12, no. 6, 683–701.

Amaral, Luis Mira (1995), 'Construindo o nosso "Cluster" Automóvel', *Competir*, Vol. VI, nos 3–4, 8–15.

Andersson, J., H. Haakansson and Jan Johanson (1994), 'Dyadic Business Relationships within Business Network Context', *Journal of Marketing*, Vol. 58, 1–15.

Araújo, Luis (1996), 'Knowing and Learning as Collective Work', paper prepared for the symposium Organizational Learning and the Learning Organization, Lancaster, UK, September.

Axelsson, B. and G. Easton (eds) (1992), *Industrial Networks, A New View of Reality*, London: Routledge.

Bartlett, C.A. and S. Ghoshal (1989), *Managing Across Borders – The Transnational Solution*, Boston, Mass.: Harvard Business School Press.

Belzowski, Bruce (1998), 'Reinventing Chrysler', in Michael Freyssenet, Andrew Mair, Koichi Shimizu and Giuseppe Volpato (eds), *One Best Way? Trajectories and Industrial Models of the World's Automobile Producers*, Oxford: Oxford University Press, pp. 242–69.

Blankenburg-Holm, D. and J. Johanson (1997), 'Business Network Connections and the Atmosphere of International Business Relationships', in I. Björkman and M. Forsgren (eds), *The Nature of the International Firm*, pp. 411–32.

Boyer, Robert, Elsie Charron, Ulrich Jurgens and Steven Tolliday (1998), 'Conclusion: Transplants, Hybridization and Globalization: What Lessons for the Future?', in Robert Boyer, Elsie Charron, Ulrich Jurgens and Steven Tolliday (eds), *Between Imitation and Innovation: The Transfer and Hybridization of Productive Models in the International Automobile Industry*, New York: Oxford University Press, pp. 374–9.

Buckly, P.J. and M. Casson (1998), 'A theory of cooperation in international business', in F.J. Contractor and P. Lorange (eds), *Cooperative Strategies in International Business*, Lexington, MA: Lexington Books.

Chanaron, Jean Jacques (1998), 'Automobiles: A "Wait-and-See" Industry?', *International Journal of Technology Management*, Vol. 16, no. 7, 595–630.

Clark, Joel P. and Francisco Veloso (2000), 'The Vertical Integration of the Component Supplier Chains and its Impact on Multi-tier Supplier Relations', paper prepared for the seminar The Automotive Industry: Component Suppliers; Current and Prospective Regulatory Approaches, Lisbon.

Doz, Y.L., K. Asakawa, J.F.P. Santos and P.J. Williamson (1997), The Metanational Corporation, INSEAD Working Paper 97/60/SM.

Dyer, Jeffrey H. (1996), 'Specialized Suppliers Networks as a Source of Competitive Advantage: Evidence from the Auto Industry', *Strategic Management Journal*, Vol. 17, no. 4, 271–92.

Dyer, Jeffrey H.D.S. Cho and Wujin Chu (1997), 'Strategic Supplier Segmentation: A Model for Managing Suppliers in the 21st Century', International Motor Vehicle Programme, Research Note no. 3, October.

Dyer, Jeffrey H. and Wujen Chu (2000), 'The Determinants of Trust in Supplier-Automaker Relationships in the U.S., Japan and Korea', *Journal of International Business Studies*, Vol. 31, no. 2, 259–85.

Ebers, Mark (1997), *The Formation of Inter-Organizational Networks*, Oxford: Oxford University Press.

Eisenhardt, K. (1989), 'Building Theories from Case Study Research', *Academy of Management Review*, Vol. 4, no. 4, 532–50.

Féria, Luis Palma (1997), 'Da competitividade dos Produtos à competitividade dos Sistemas: o Caso dos Componentes para a Indústria automóvel', *Economia & Prospectiva*, Vol. 1, no. 3, 101–14.

Féria, Luis Palma (1999), 'A História do Sector Automóvel em Portugal' (1895–1995), GEPE, Working Paper DT 19-99, Lisboa.

Freyssenet, Michael, Andrew Mair, Koichi Shimizu and Giuseppe Volpato (1998), 'Conclusion: The Choices to be Made in the Coming Decade' in Michael Freyssenet, Andrew Mair, Koichi Shimizu and Giuseppe Volpato (eds), *One Best Way? Trajectories and Industrial Models of the World's Automobile Producers*, Oxford: Oxford University Press, pp. 311–37.

Ghoshal, S. and C.A. Bartlett (1997), *The Individualised Corporation*, New York: Harper Business.

Guerra, António Castro (1990), Formas e Determinantes do Envolvimento Externo das Empresas: Internationalização da Indústria Automóvel e Integração da Indústria Portuguesa na Indústria Automóvel Mundial, Doctoral thesis in Economics, ISEG, UTL, Lisboa.

Haakansson, Haakan (1987), *Industrial Technological Development: A Network Approach*, London: Croom Helm.

Haakansson, Hakan, Virpi Havila and Ann-Charlott Pedersen (1999), 'Learning in Networks', *Industrial Marketing Management*, Vol. 28, 443–52.

Haakansson, H. and J. Johanson (1993), 'The Network as a Governance Structure: Interfirm Cooperation Beyond Markets and Hierarchies', in G. Grabher (ed.), *The Embedded Firm On the Socioeconomics of Industrial Networks*, London: Routledge, pp. 35–51.

Hamel, G. (1991), 'Competition for Competence and Inter-Partner Learning Within International Strategic Alliances', *Strategic Management Journal*, Vol. 12, 83–103.

Inkpen, A.C. (1997), 'An Examination of Knowledge Management in International Joint-Ventures', in Paul Beamish and J.P. Killing (eds), *Cooperative Strategies–North American Perspectives*, (337–369) San Francisco: New Lexington.

Jurgens, Ulrich (1998), 'The Development of Volkwagen's Industrial Model, 1967–1985', in Michael Freyssenet, Andrew Mair, Koichi Shimizu and Giuseppe Volpato (eds), *One Best Way? Trajectories and Industrial Models of the World's Automobile Producers*, Oxford: Oxford University Press, pp. 273–310.

Kogut, Bruce (2000), 'The Network as Knowledge: Generative Rules and the Emergence of Structure', *Strategic Management Journal*, Vol. 21, 405–25.

Kulkki, S. (1996), *Knowledge Creation by Multinational Corporations*, Helsinki: Helsinki School of Economics Press.

Lam, A. (1997), 'Embedded Firms, Embedded Knowledge: Problems of Collaboration and Knowledge Transfer in Global Cooperative Ventures', *Organization Studies*, Vol. 18, no. 6, 973–96.

March, James G. (1991), 'Exploration and Exploitation in Organizational Learning', *Organization Science*, Vol. 2, 71–87.

Martinez, J.I. and J.C. Jarillo (1988), 'La Respuesta de las Multinacionales ante el reto de 1992?', *Información Comercial Española*, October, 71–82.

Nonaka, I. and N. Konno (1998), 'The Concept of "Ba": Building a Foundation for Knowledge Creation', *California Management Review*, Vol. 40, no. 3, 40–54.

Nonaka, I. and H. Takeuchi (1995), *The Knowledge-Creating Company*, Oxford: Oxford University Press.

Parkhe, A. (1991), 'Interfirm Diversity, Organisational Learning, and Longevity in Global Strategic Alliances', *Journal of International Business Studies*, 22, 579–601.

Pilorusso, Felix (1997), 'Finding a Place in the Automotive Supplier Hierarchy in the Year 2000 and Beyond', International Motor Vehicle Programme, Research Note no. 4, April.

Porter, M. (1980), *Competitive Strategy: Techniques for Analyzing Industries and Competitors*, New York: The Free Press.

Porter, Michael E. (1985), *Competitive Advantage*, New York: The Free Press.

Rugman, Alan and Joseph D'Cruz (1996), 'The Theory of the Flagship Firm', in Institute of International Business (ed.), *Innovation and International Business*, Vol. 2, Estocolmo: Institute of International Business, pp. 665–88.

Rugman, Alan and Joseph D'Cruz (2000), *Multinationals as Flagship Firms*, Oxford: Oxford University Press.

Ruigrok, W., R. Van Tulder and G. Baven (1991), *Globalisation versus Global Localisation Strategies in the World Car Industry*, Vol. 13, programme FAST/Monitor, FOP 285, Bruxelas.

Sako, Mari and Max Warburton (2000), 'Modularization and Outsourcing Project: Interim of European Research Team', paper prepared for the seminar The Automotive Industry: Component Suppliers; Current Prospects and Regulatory Approaches, Lisbon.

Santos, Rogério G. (1996), 'Os Efeitos na Economia portuguesa do Investimento directo estrangeiro no Sector automóvel, Master's thesis, ISEG, Lisbon.

Schmidt, Ana and J. Carreira Almeida (1987), *Fabricação Automóvel e Produção de Componentes*, Lisbon: Banco de Fomento Nacional.

Senge, P.M. (1990), *The Fifth Discipline*, London: Century Business.

Simões, Vitor Corado (1992), 'European Integration and the Pattern of FDI Inflow in Portugal', in J. Cantwell (ed.), *Multinational Investment in Europe*, Aldershot and Brookfield: Edward Elgar, pp. 256–97.

Simões, Vitor Corado (1999), 'Organizational Learning and Inter-firm Collaboration: The Case of Licencing', paper presented at the 25th Annual Conference of EIBA, Paris.

Stephan, Michael and Eric Pfaffmann (1998), 'Direct Investment Strategies of Multinational Automotive Suppliers in the German Market: Responses to Outsourcing, Globalization and Supply Chain-Redesign in the 90's', paper prepared for the 24th Annual Conference of EIBA, Jerusalem.

Szulanski, G. (1996), 'Exploring Internal Stickiness: Impediments to the Transfer of Best Practices within the Firm', *Strategic Management Journal*, Vol. 17, Winter Special Issue, 27–43.

Tiemessen, I., H.W. Lane, M.M. Crossan and A.C. Inkpen (1997), 'Knowledge Management in International Joint-Ventures', in P.W. Beamish and J.P. Killing, (eds), *Cooperative Strategies – North American Perspectives*, San Francisco: New Lexington Press, pp. 370–99.

Vale, Mário (1999), 'Geografia da Indústria Automóvel num Contexto de Globalização – Imbricação Espacial do Sistema AutoEuropa', Doctoral thesis in Geography, Universidade de Lisboa, Lisboa.

Veloso, Francisco, Chris Henry, Richard Roth and Joel P. Clark (2000), *Global Strategies for the Development of the Portuguese Auto Parts Industry*, Lisbon: IAPMEI.

Vickery, Graham (1997), 'Crescimiento y Globalización de la Indústria del Automóvil', *Economia Industrial*, no. 314, 27–61.

Womack, James P., Daniel Jones and Daniel Roos (1990), *The Machine that Changed the World*, New York: Harper Collins.

Yin, R. (1994), *Case Study Research: Design and Methods*, London: SAGE Publications.

9. Foreign involvement in acquiring and producing new knowledge: the case of Hungary

Annamária Inzelt

INTRODUCTION

From the very beginning of the transition period the common aim of Central and Eastern European economies was to rouse themselves from their rosy dreamworld and to develop their economies as rapidly as possible. The transition itself had occurred due to the world-wide crisis in the command economies. The post-socialist economies must now manage in parallel the basic transition together with stabilisation and development for the general wellbeing of their societies. Bearing in mind that these transition economies had a starting point lower than that in the majority of West European countries, their tasks are tremendous. The capacity for innovation and competitiveness is lower, and the inherited institutions and traditional modes of behaviour are less supportive than in the advanced economies.

The transformation of these command economic systems into market economies coincided with globalisation and the birth of the knowledge economies. A knowledge economy simply cannot exist without internationalisation, and internationalisation was a clearly defined policy aimed directly at launching the transition economies into the mainstream of knowledge economies.

In these circumstances inter-governmental intermediary institutions are becoming key players in establishing networks and in setting their agendas. For the transition economies the critical question is how may they join existing networks so as to be involved in an internationalised system of innovation?

Internationalisation is a multidimensional process (Archibugi and Michie 1997, Cantwell 1995). Various actors have their own individual roles in the integration of national economic activities and are either the rule-makers or facilitators of internationalisation. National governments, international organisations, inter-governmental agreements and economic actors are the protagonists of this process, and this international arena of multi-part actors became fully-fledged when the transition economies arrived on the scene.

The transformation of Central and Eastern European countries has included the global (re)integration of economic activity. It has assumed new international relationships, a more serious involvement in international trade, participation in cross-national networks and the inflow of foreign capital, all of which may speed up the transition process. During the last decade the CEE national governments have been facilitating the involvement of national actors in internationalisation, and they have arranged national participation in inter-governmental co-operations. Two main instruments have been used to achieve internationalisation in CEECs in reaching their target of becoming a knowledge economy: (1) joining international organisations and building up new (revised) bilateral relationships and (2) attracting foreign business involvement.

This chapter investigates this process of internationalisation in Hungary. It discusses first how the country is emerging from the isolation brought about by its adherence to the socialist system. It touches upon Hungarian participation in international organisations and then describes how government promotes participation in international programmes, finally summarising the first results of reintegration. It goes into detail regarding foreign direct investment in the transformation and investigates the impacts of FDI on technology upgrading, employing statistical data. Inward FDI is influencing knowledge capabilities and capacities, the exploitation of knowledge and the perspective of knowledge production. Interactions between companies (especially foreign-owned ones) and the host country's environment have changed significantly since the beginning of transition and lead to differing types of involvement in research and development and in innovation linkages between investors and Hungary as the recipient country. The chapter employs policy documents, statistical data and administrative data sources. The information base is sporadic; there are no time series. The available data usually do not form a time series since they are *ad hoc* reflections on daily policy questions.

The chapter poses more questions than it answers, although, as Heisenberg opined, a good question is half-way to the solution.

OUT OF ISOLATION

Hungary has placed considerable emphasis on building up an international network of R&D in order to upgrade technology. The legacy of the earlier, bipolar world was that CEECs were outside scientific networks, sophisticated markets, the flow of capital and the mobility of people. Science and technology are *per se* international activities, with an inevitable need for knowledge flow and competition. However, the isolation was also marked by the COCOM

(Coordinating Committee for Multilateral Export Controls) list, which excluded this region from large areas of technology which would have led towards reproductive and parallel R&D activities.

However, after the global political turnaround from 1989–1991, the Iron Curtain disappeared. As a result, most international institutions started to open themselves up to the transition economies and supported the entire process.[1]

The openness of the international community and the partnership of foreign and international public bodies with the transition economies in offering aid, soft loans and intellectual capabilities have been very important factors in the process of transformation and internationalisation.

Framing Internationalisation and Joining International Organisations

The reshaping of the innovation system with a new dimension of internationalisation started in 1982 when Hungary joined the World Bank and the IMF. The framing of new international relationships accelerated when the bi-polar world system disappeared and when the involvement of foreign public organisations became more active. Bilateral and international agreements, together with membership of inter-governmental programmes, provide a legal framework for international R&D and for co-operation in innovation. National policy programmes for internationalisation include:

- Membership of international organisations and participation in bilateral and multilateral agreements,
- Mechanisms to facilitate and encourage various national entities to become involved in international programmes.
- Incentives to foreign investors to invest in knowledge creation and technology upgrading.

Hungary has placed great emphasis on building international networks.[2] The country became a member of S&T-related international organisations and organisation-based R&D co-operations such as EUREKA, COST, CERN, EMBO and the EU RTD Framework Programmes. Several bilateral inter-governmental R&D agreements were born after 1990, reinforcing the contacts with dozens of other countries including CEECs (Table 9.1).

Hungary's revision of intellectual property rights was an entrance fee to several organisations (those relating to US–Hungarian trade, the WTO-TRIPs agreement and the approach to the EPO) and has been broadening existing co-operations.

The OECD, as a think-tank organisation, played an important role in the revision of science and technology policy and in the re-evaluation of the S&T institutional and legal system. NATO membership allows the country to

Table 9.1 Hungarian membership of international organisations

Organisation	Year of membership	Notes
ESF (European Science Foundation)	1990	
ESA (European Space Agreement)	•	Agreement since 1991
COST (Co-operation in the field of Scientific and Technical Research)	1991	
CERN (Centre Europeén Recherche Nucléaire)	1992	Project by project
EUREKA (European Research Co-ordinating Agency)	1992	Associated member since 1993
EU (European Union)	Expected 2004	EU RTD FP membership since 1994
TRIPs (Trade Related Intellectual Property Rights) Agreement	1994	
OECD (Organisation for Economic Co-operation and Development)	1996	PIT Program since 1991
NATO (North Atlantic Treaty Organisation)	1999	Participation in NATO Science Program since 1986
EPO (European Patent Office)	Expected 2003	

Source: Own compilation.

participate at the cutting edge of defence R&D co-operation, and COST and EUREKA offer especially good opportunities to participate in international R&D activities and to belong to professional networks. Hungarian participation in the EU RTD Framework Programmes is, perhaps, the most important tool of international R&D co-operation. At the beginning of the transition period several special schemes were set up for Central and Eastern European countries such as PHARE INCO-Copernicus, essentially to serve as a staircase to (re)-internationalisation.

Promoting project participation

Participation in international programmes has great political importance and, therefore, enjoys full support in CEE countries. In Hungary, as in other CEE countries, new institutions were set up to facilitate this participation. The Hungarian government also launched direct measures to help and encourage participation in international research activity and innovation networks.

Supporting institutions

The experiences of EU member states proved that the so-called bridging organisations can support the search for partners and the partnership building process, whilst shortening the period needed to enter or to form networks. The difficulties for the newly associated countries, including Hungary, also highlighted the problem of their limited partnership connections (and of the scarcely manageable financial rules of the programmes). Policy-makers also supposed that the internationalisation of research organisations would automatically generate organisations devoted to information dissemination and to advise on legal and financial matters relating to co-operation.

CEE governments did, however, build up a special support network in relation to membership of the 5th FP – and, in order to ensure successful participation in both the 5th and 6th FPs, the Hungarian government took measures in the field of support networks to generate the best possible results. One of those is the network of National Contact Points. They are the main links in their professional fields with the EU. The role of NCPs under EU programmes is to give advice on research programmes and on specific key actions, on the administrative rules and requirements of the EU related to the writing of proposals, on reporting and negotiating and on the evaluation criteria. There is a network of liaison offices to promote participation in EU programmes. Liaison offices are located in the various regions. By the middle of 2002 14 thematic and regional liaison offices were operational in eight Hungarian cities, fully covering the country. Their main tasks are as described above.

Many years ago Innovation Relay Centres were formed in each member state of the EU and the adoption of these important knowledge dissemination organisations as 'stairway organisations' in CEECs supports partnership building. The newly associated countries established consortia which formed FEMIRCs (Fellow Member to Innovation Relay Centres). Fellow Members were appointed after an evaluation process to give advice to organisations – especially to SMEs and to RTD institutions – on technology and innovation and to disseminate information throughout their home country on the European research options. They help institutes and companies to identify their technology needs and suitable technologies to match these needs, to give assistance on exploitation and advice on research and technology programmes. The consortia also support partnership building or re-building among CEECs.

Besides these the information dissemination days and training seminars relating to project writing, financial matters and legal conditions are also an important part of facilitating Hungarian participation in international programmes and co-operations.

Financial measures
Several funding schemes were introduced to encourage participation in bilateral and international projects. These funds not only help to overcome the lack of financial capacity of institutions, they also diminish the risks to start-up international co-operations and cover the extra costs which newcomers have to pay to enter an old arena.

The following (still valid) foundation schemes were introduced:

- KMÜFA patronage grants to assist the internationalisation of researchers and institutions, and to cover membership fees (individual or institutional) in international organisations,
- KMÜFA travel grants to support participation in international conferences (if paper or poster presentations have been accepted),
- KMÜFA grants as additional technical resources to organise international workshops or conferences in Hungary,
- KMÜFA travel grants relating to bilateral S&T governmental agreement-based co-operations and covering all travel costs for participating in discussions of interim research findings, of short-term joint research and so on,
- KMÜFA grants for entering or building networks within the EU RTD 5th and 6th FPs to cover, at least partially, the cost of participation or the organisation of network preparatory meetings and of legal and financial advice.

These special direct measures have their own positive roles to play in the facilitating of entry into international networks. However, this direct grant is only a very small fraction of total government expenditure on R&D. The total size of the R&D budget plays a very significant role in long-term internationalisation. Finnish experience proved very well that significantly increased investment in national R&D capabilities, including absorption and co-operation capabilities, can speed up the internationalisation of national R&D organisations. The business involvement is also crucial in financing and performing research and in improving the innovativeness of the economy. I shall return to this issue at a later point.

Performance of Internationalisation

The results and impact of joining international organisations are not easily measurable, and indirect measurements may be needed or employed to observe the strengths and weaknesses of this process. According to statistical data foreign-financed R&D has grown steadily in Hungary (Table 9.2).

Table 9.2   Percentage of GERD financed from abroad in 1991 and 1996–2000

Hungary	1991	1996	1997	1998	1999	2000
% of GERD financed from abroad[a]	[b]1.8	4.6	4.3	4.9	5.6	10.6

Notes:
[a]   Defence excluded (all or mostly).
[b]   Do not correspond exactly to the OECD recommendations.

Source: OECD (2002, p. 25).

Comparing the Hungarian share of GERD financed from abroad to that of five other OECD small economies shows clearly that Hungary was able to obtain a significantly lower share than such EU members as Greece, Ireland and Finland. The rapid growth of the Finnish share is remarkable for newly associated countries and this share soared when Finland joined the EU. As many experts observed (Siune 2002) Finland prepared herself very well to be able to attract and absorb such foreign R&D resources. Nevertheless, Figure 9.1 shows that the Hungarian share is noticeably higher than that which two other transition economies have reached. The Hungarian ranking in this list of countries may be evaluated as indicating good receptive or absorption capability in relation to R&D grants – which may offer good prospects of attaining the average of the smaller EU member states.

International grants and support have a special role to play in the transition process. Foreign funding aid is a small fraction of funding as a whole, but, as 'seed money', it can provide many opportunities and can encourage the restructuring of working modes within science and technology organisations in

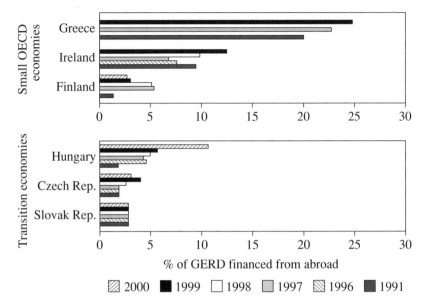

Source: OECD (2002, p. 25).

Figure 9.1   Percentage of GERD financed from abroad in selected small OECD economies

order to adapt themselves to the global environment. This seed money can also help to preserve the resources already accumulated in Hungary (science schools and knowledgeable personnel) and help to promote internationalisation.

Successful 'plug-ins'
Monitoring the output of internationalisation might seem, at first glance, to be successful. This stage of the process may only require a few quantitative measurements which can produce information as to the success rate of applications, and in this sense the output measure of internationalisation is the rate of network-joinings measured by the number of applications approved and the proportion of applications approved in total. Figure 9.2 illustrates activity in the COST programme.

Fast-growing participation in COST and other activities illustrates the effect of opening up networks in the initial years. The growth rate may have normalised in the mid-1990s but the rate continues to increase.

A further scarcely measurable result of participation in joint research activities is that many research groups have learned the rules of the programme and could consequently compensate for their limited partner connections. The 4th EU

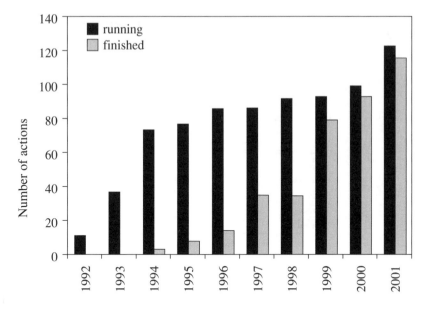

Source: Hungarian Ministry of Education website (om.hu).

Figure 9.2   Hungarian COST activity

RTD FP allowed only restricted participation, but CEECs became fully-fledged partners in the 5th and in following FPs.[3] Hungarian participation in the 4th FP was a mutual learning process for the EU and Hungary. Hungarian participation in EU FPs from 1995–1998 was known to exist in 163 projects, partially financed by the EU. (OMFB 1998, Table 34). It may be assumed that Hungarian research groups were and are good enough and that they were able to enter international networks. Figure 9.3 shows the success rate in respect of the EU RTD 5th FPs.

The proportion of applications granted involving Hungarian participation is quite good, taking into consideration the number of successful projects, the number of participants and the planned amount of Community funding. Successful participation in the STK Framework Programme is not only a matter of finance but also an indicator of the international acceptance of the researchers and of the whole national innovation system.

The success rate of approved projects is no more than a fast indicator. It does not tell us anything about the quality of the network and of the role of the Hungarian research community in the project and so on. The evaluation of the reasons for success and failure in applications for entry, in performance and in

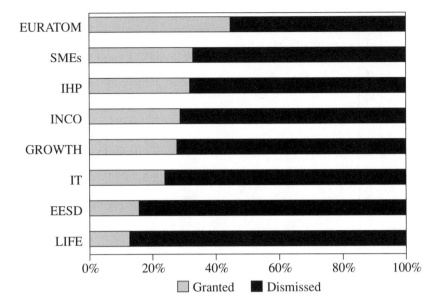

Source: Hungarian Ministry of Education, R&D Directorate.

Figure 9.3 *Percentage of successful applications with Hungarian*
participation by programmes in the 5th Framework
Programme (whole period)

the acceptance of newcomers to these networks is very important for both
national and international policy-making. The information needs to be related
to labour division among the old and new members and to equality/inequality
in partnerships. However, joining the European mainstream in strategic R&D
fields is a long-term learning process.

As figures show, Hungarian participation has grown gradually in COST
activity and in EUREKA and EU R&D framework programmes. Table 9.3
summarises the major Hungarian activities in several international co-operations.

The major activities are in agriculture and biotechnology, chemistry and
telecommunications. It might be assumed that these fields are the strengths of
the Hungarian research community. Another assumption might be that these
fields of science and engineering are those which are facing a shortage of highly
skilled workers. Another factor might be that the networks are more open to
newcomers in relatively new fields; entrance is easier. It should also not be
overlooked that earlier international relationships (in the FAO, UNCTAD or
even in CMEA) can make network-joining easier for research groups who are

Table 9.3 Hungarian activities in international R&D co-operations by field of science (%)

Field of science	COST	Field of science	EUREKA	Program fields	5th EU R&D FP
Environment	8	Environment	27	Environment and Energy	16
		Energy	3		
Medicine	6			Life	16
Agriculture and Biotechnology	14	Biology	14		
Telecommunications	11	IT	17	IST	20
Chemistry	15				
Forests and Forestry products	8				
Social Sciences	7			IHP	23
				Growth	16
				INCO	3
Materials	6	Materials	3	EURATOM	6
Transport	8	Transport	14		
Meteorology	5	Robotics	19		
Physics	4	Lasers	3		
Food Sciences	3				
Urban Civil Engineering	2				
Others	4				
Total	100	Total	100	Total	100

Source: Own compilation.

at least known to some extent. Detailed information should be available for evaluating the results to satisfy policy-making.

Participation in these programmes is important in that it serves to put Hungarian research organisations on the map, to support them in surviving transition crises and to connect with international research communities. However such participation has a limited impact in relation to building up networking capabilities outside the research community.

ATTRACTING FOREIGN BUSINESS INFLOW – CROSSING THE THRESHOLD

Important factors in internationalisation are business entities – mainly multi- and transnational companies and, obviously, business organisations have been the initiators of many inter-governmental agreements and international programmes. Companies are keeping open the different channels of internationalisation, such as trade in goods and services, capital flow, transfer of production facilities and/or technology, research and development (Dunning 1993, Mytelka 2000). In Europe the engines of internationalisation of research and development and of innovation activities are both multi- and cross-national business organisations.

According to a recent OECD study the most dynamic components of international transactions in the last two decades were investments. International trade was three times greater in 1999 than in 1985, whilst foreign direct investment was 18 times and portfolio investment ten times higher during the same period (OECD 2001, p. 183).

Foreign investors vary from the small foreign company located in one or two countries to the giant multinational, and distinguished players in the process of the internationalisation of labour markets are the transnationals.[4] These multinational companies are, world-wide, the greatest investors, the main technology traders and the most important employers. Their investment has an important influence on national labour markets and on the cross-national mobility of their employees and on migration itself.

The regional structure of investment flow has changed greatly during the last three decades. Until the beginning of the 1990s the majority of investment flow took place among the most advanced countries, inside 'the Triad'.

The national system of innovation is an important influencing factor for foreign investment, and the system itself is a strong influence if a country features on the map of foreign investors. The volume of FDI, together with its sector and technology orientation, reflects the potential of the host country in areas such as available skills, capabilities, the legal environment and the presence of other foreign entities.

FDI is a relatively new phenomenon in CEECs. The collapse of the communist regimes and transition towards a market economy have made CEECs important target countries for foreign investors in the new uni-polar world system.

As is well known from the literature, the CEECs were out of the main flow of internationalisation for roughly four decades and there were many political impediments in the way of setting up joint ventures with entities from the market economies.[5]

The first year when the size of CEE inward stock reached the measured international threshold was 1995. Total FDI inward stock amounted to 1.2% of the world total and increased to 2.0% by 2000. The Hungarian share is 0.3% of the world share – that is, the same as the Czech share. This world share is remarkable among CEECs, but it is still below the level of small European economies such as Finland, Greece and Portugal (0.4%).

Figure 9.4 compares the inflow into the OECD member transition economies to small European and non-European OECD member states. In the first decade of transition the level of attractiveness of these countries has been reasonable but the critical question is how the end of privatization and EU membership will change the trend of inflows into this region.

FDI has played a fundamental role in the transformation of the Hungarian economy. Inward FDI flows (as a share of GDP and averaged over the period 1990–1998) put Hungary at the very top of the list among OECD countries. At the same time outflow was very limited and very much at the lower end of the ranking table (OECD 2001, p. 99).

The process of FDI may be analysed on the basis of solid statistical data. The next section investigates this.

FDI in the Transformation

International literature employs three different categories to analyse foreign investment activity: (1) foreign direct investment (2) portfolio investment and (3) foreign affiliates.[6] The borderlines between them relate to the foreign ownership (ordinary shares or voting rights) in the firm. The investor has, or has not, an intention to influence the management of a firm.

The specificity of the transition period means that a general rule, such as that less than 10% investment corresponds to 'short-term' investment transactions, did not work. Investors intended to influence the management of a firm even if their share was very low in the initial period. Many foreign investors started to buy a small stake in a firm during the privatisation process and enjoyed the privilege of influencing management, of behaving as strategic investors. However, the typical short-termism of portfolio investment ('sparrow hawk

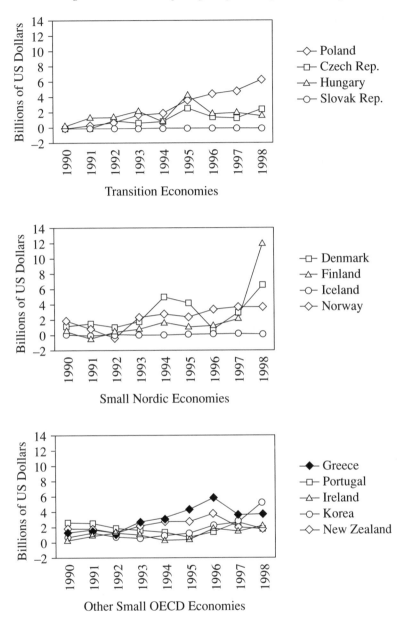

Source: OECD (2001, p. 190).

Figure 9.4   Inward direct investment flows in selected OECD economies

capital') is present in Hungary but it does not correspond to the proportion of
shares held by foreign interests, and many start-up investors (privatisers) have
gradually increased their shareholdings over a few years (Figure 9.5).

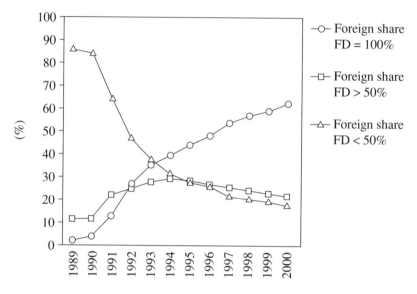

Source: HCSO (2002a, p. 31).

*Figure 9.5   Changes in distribution of firms with foreign shareholdings in
Hungary by the number of firms, 1989–2000*

As Figure 9.5 shows, companies which were 100% foreign-owned
represented only 1.8% of FDI firms in 1989. The proportion of this group has
gradually increased and reached 61.8% in 2000. There was a majority of
domestically owned companies (where foreign shareholding is below 50%) in
1989 (86.7%) and this decreased to 17.2% in 2000, although their number was
four times higher.

All the figures demonstrate that FDI has penetrated rapidly and has affected
every corner of the Hungarian economy (Inzelt 1994a and 2000, Antalóczy and
Sass 2000 and 2002). Foreign investors are now important players in the
Hungarian labour market. As an OECD study (2001, p. 102) highlighted, foreign
affiliates account for about 50% of Hungarian manufacturing employment –
as high as in Ireland and Luxembourg. In several sectors more than two-thirds
of value added is produced by foreign companies. The penetration by FDI and
its role in technology-upgrading research and development activities have
displayed rather different characteristics in two phases of the transition period.

FDI is influenced by a complex set of economic, sociological and legal factors. Naturally, foreign investors behave differently in a country which is moving out from its transition crisis due to an economic recovery and to its growing role of strategic thinking.

The penetration and role of FDI is roughly sketched in Table 9.4.

Several phenomena are typical syndromes of transition. An increasing number of foreign investors illustrate well how foreigners recognise at the beginning of the opening-up process their unique chance, albeit for a limited period, to acquire skilled European labour at a discount price. This situation is temporary, since wages tend to approach the wage levels of EU countries.

The greater part of inward FDI during the first phase of transition corresponds to the privatisation process that meant the acquisition of existing firms.[7] Changing ownership was crucial for the restructuring of existing firms. The creation of new enterprises has also occurred, but brown-field investment was much more common than the green-field variety. One of the most common forms of FDI, that is to say acquisition, was an important part of privatisation. This was the period of the acquisition rush.

MNCs offer international career possibilities to their own employees, although until now this process has worked on a one-way basis: they brought managers and engineers into affiliates and created international career possibilities for people from headquarters. Very scattered examples may be observed from affiliates who posted migrants to headquarters. The other type of internal migration, short-term migration (for example, in training seminars, on-the-job training and study tours within the 'empire') is very frequent. These activities play an important role in knowledge dissemination, diffusion, and in sharing tacit and codified knowledge of the organisations

In the years of the transition crisis Hungary spent a decreasing share of her GDP on R&D. Corporate R&D activities generally show continuous erosion, which is amplified by the privatisation process. The closure of the company's R&D unit was a typical first cost-reduction step of management. Business R&D expenditure declined faster than governmental expenditure. In terms of industry-financed R&D, Hungary, similar to other CEE countries, is considered lowest funded among OECD countries. Businesses maintain only modest funding in terms of both financing and performing R&D.

New foreign owners had typically more strategic thinking than new domestic owners but foreigners also had their own technologies and researchers from their home country. This is perhaps the main reason why corporate R&D units show the greatest decline in Phase I of the transition.

The recovery of the economy affects (after a time lag of 2–4 years) the revitalisation of R&D. By the late 1990s Hungary seems to have reached Phase II and revises its view of falling R&D investment: the strong brain drain stops, R&D investment starts to increase, R&D staff numbers stabilise and the brain

Table 9.4 FDI in two phases of transition

FDI	Phase I	Phase II
• Penetration	Fast growing	Ongoing growth
• Mode of investment	Acquisition through privatisation	Raise the shares, paid-in-capital
• Management	Heavily redeploy	Stabilise
• General behaviour	Wait and see, learning the partners, redeployment	Active involvement, some divestiture
• Role in technology upgrading	Sleeper-keeper position, passive innovations, active incremental innovations, locally new products, processes	Keeper-climber position, more active innovations, incremental new products on sector, regional level
• Involvement in R&D	Limited, scattered skin-deep collaborations, minuscule soul-deep	Increasing, more skin-deep collaborations and investing into soul-deep
• Business R&D		
– Expenditure	Fast decrease	Increase
– Personnel	Fast decrease	Increase
	Strong brain drain	Diminished brain drain, circulation begins
– Laboratories	Close down/redeploy	Open new, invest in
	Reorganisations	Stabilising
• Partnerships		
– With domestic entities	Wait and see	Growing/not growing
– With foreign entities	Same	Involve locals

Notes: For a description of skin-deep and soul-deep co-operation see the section on FDI in R&D activities.

Source: Own compilation.

drain turns into brain circulation. Corporate R&D expenditure starts to develop in this second phase of transition, mainly powered by FDI, creating local R&D facilities as part of global business networks. FDI is important in overcoming several burdening problems associated with the introduction of innovation and in this period technological change speeds up.

In both phases of transition the adjustment to the market environment has changed the mode of management and brought in minor technological improvements with the redeployment of the product structure, supplementary equipment, with more advanced used equipment, and with the introduction of the ISO system.[8] Several companies invested in knowledge, short courses, training seminars and, in a few cases, on-the-job training at another firm under the same ownership, which served to complement existing knowledge and to train personnel in the corporate culture and so on.

The development of innovation-friendly business environments, which is an inevitable precondition of a well-functioning, knowledge-driven market economy, needs several more years or even decades. However Phase II of the transition did bring in changes in business R&D activity, and foreign investors have been important actors in these changes. Quality factors, training, education, rapid response and overall cultural levels have become key issues in sustaining competitiveness.

FDI in Technological Upgrading and R&D

Overall policy aim has consistently been to make Hungary a successful rising economy. Several national policy targets, such as modernisation, which brings the Hungarian economy closer to those of the advanced markets, assume interaction with leading companies to prevent Hungary remaining outside the inner circle of innovation and R&D networking.

S&T and innovation policy measures were introduced that reinforce the policy of improving the relationship between national science and business through internationalisation and of upgrading the innovation capabilities of business entities. New measures of public policy were implemented to encourage any and all FDI into the country to overcome the historical shortfall of the old economy – the heavily burdening factor of the sheer lack of capital.

Several policy measures have been important in affecting those factors which make Hungary attractive to foreigners as a country with a technology-oriented location[9]

- Privatisation contracts in which the discount price has to be compensated by investment in technology,
- Direct measures to encourage technological upgrading and R&D investment for companies active in the Hungarian market.

Available statistical data allow us to investigate a few aspects of technological upgrading with FDI, such as the redeployment of the economy through sectoral distribution of FDI, the reduction of regional underdevelopment by the regional distribution of FDI and the improvement in competitiveness via changes in physical capabilities. Other factors which are also affected by FDI are not included in official statistics, such as FDI-related innovation and R&D activities.[10]

The sectoral distribution of FDI

Almost 50% of FDI went into the manufacturing sector. The size of investment was HUF 5393.9 billion into the whole economy, which is EUR 22.1 billion. The next largest recipient was real estate, both in the rental and business activities sectors. More detailed data are only available regarding larger groupings of manufacturing industries, although two of the most important manufacturing sectors received a slightly lower proportion than did real estate. The share of 'transport equipment' (that is, the car industry) and of the fuel and chemical industry was 10–11% of the total FDI. Car assembly plays an important role in industrial restructuring and technology upgrading, although at the end of the 20th century the automobile industry did not play as important a role in economic modernisation, and innovation as it used to play in the first part of the century. (See more on the redevelopment of the Hungarian car industry and the relationship of foreign-managed assemblers and domestic suppliers in Havas (1997).)

Modern industries such as electrical and optical equipment were also important targeted industries for foreign investors and these received 8.8% of the total investment in Hungary. Table 9.5 shows the sectoral distribution in 2000.

Capital inflow into technology-oriented sectors illustrates well that the available capabilities were good enough in dynamic sectors to attract foreign investment. Foreigners are unquestionably present in many cases of technology upgrading (bringing in equipment and machinery, investing in buildings and training of skilled workers). However different investors followed different policies and so the levels and intensity of technology upgrading are divergent. The problem for the host country is that it is easy to withdraw investment, to close down a factory and to move to countries with a cheaper labour force. Some foreign investors introduced lower-level, 'high-tech' products (as has been done by IBM which will close one of its factories in 2002/2003). Others have introduced high-level, high-tech products and a few of these have involved the Hungarian company in the R&D activities. Such involvement usually means a promise of a more permanent partnership and of recurrent upgrading – or at least of frequent, incremental innovation. Of course many other factors may hamper these positive effects but technology upgrading for lower-level, high-tech products promises much less in the way of long-term advantages. The R&D issue will be discussed later.

Table 9.5   Sectoral structure of FDI in 2000

Industries, branches	Number	%	FDI (billion HUF)	%	Share of FDI from owner's equity (2000) (%)
Manufacturing	4 098	15.4	2 611.3	48.4	82.2
of food products, beverages and tobacco	455	1.7	384.1	7.1	85.6
of textiles and leather products	605	2.3	69.5	1.3	87.0
of wood, pulp, paper, publishing and printing	677	2.5	117.7	2.2	87.8
of coke, refined petroleum products, nuclear products and nuclear fuel, chemicals and chemical products, and man-made fibres	158	0.6	553.9	10.3	63.0
of rubber and plastic products	264	1.0	94.7	1.8	89.9
of other non-metallic mineral products	186	0.7	120.9	2.2	83.0
of basic metals and fabricated metal products	545	2.0	101.6	1.9	87.9
of machinery and equipment	382	1.4	102.4	1.9	87.3
of electrical and optical equipment	480	1.8	476.5	8.8	94.8
of transport equipment	115	0.4	575.3	10.7	91.0
other manufacturing	231	0.9	14.7	0.3	89.1
Mining and quarrying	68	0.3	14.0	0.3	84.3
Wholesale and retail trade, repair of motor-vehicles and household goods	11 348	42.6	489.6	9.1	90.8
Hotels and restaurants	1 283	4.8	82.4	1.5	80.4
Transport, storage, post and telecommunications	846	3.2	491.0	9.1	80.7
Real estate, renting and business activities	5 870	22.0	622.8	11.5	84.4
Electricity, gas, steam and water supply	47	0.2	331.9	6.2	71.2
Other sectors	3 085	11.6	750.9	13.9	86.2
Total	26 645	100.0	5 393.9	100.0	82.7

Source: HCSO (2002a, pp. 32–3).

The Regional Distribution of FDI (Reducing Regional Underdevelopment)

The most advanced Hungarian region is Central Hungary, an area which includes the capital. The regional pattern illustrates very clearly that FDI first of all approached the capital and its immediate, surrounding area. The location of public administration, a good infrastructure and a large educated labour force made this region very attractive.[11] The distribution of FDI by region may be seen in Figure 9.6.

The regional investment pattern shows the largest investor countries. Table 9.6 presents the regions ranked according to GDP per capita and shows the

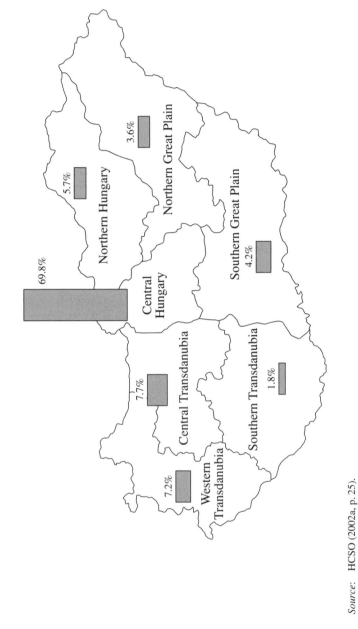

Western Transdanubia — 7.2%

Central Transdanubia — 7.7%

Southern Transdanubia — 1.8%

Central Hungary — 69.8%

Northern Hungary — 5.7%

Northern Great Plain — 3.6%

Southern Great Plain — 4.2%

Source: HCSO (2002a, p. 25).

Figure 9.6   Proportion of FDI by region (%)

Table 9.6 Regional distribution of largest investor countries in 2000

Regions	GDP per capita (thousand HUF)	Total (%)	Austria 3(%)	Germany 1(%)	Netherlands 2(%)	USA 4(%)	France 5(%)	Italy 6(%)
Central Hungary	1 999	69.8	72.8	71.5	81.5	54.8	51.8	58.8
Western Transdanubia	1 492	7.2	16.1	7.0	1.7	4.9	18.3	6.9
Central Transdanubia	1 318	7.7	3.8	3.7	7.2	19.7	4.6	7.4
Southern Transdanubia	979	1.8	3.3	2.8	0.8	0.0	0.4	1.4
Northern Hungary	846	5.7	1.9	10.0	5.4	6.0	3.6	3.1
Northern Great Plain	831	3.6	0.9	2.9	2.2	6.4	1.2	18.7
Southern Great Plain	940	4.2	1.2	2.1	1.2	8.2	20.1	3.7
Total	1 309	100.0	100.0	100.0	100.0	100.0	100.0	100.0

Source: HCSO (2002a, p. 25) and HCSO (2002b, pp. 4 and 16).

regional distribution of FDI by the largest investor countries. In first place is Germany followed by the Netherlands and Austria who have together invested more than 70% in Central Hungary, whilst the next three, the USA, France and Italy, have invested just above 50% in the same area. The regional distribution of their investment outside Central Hungary strongly relates to the industrial structure of their investment and to the size distribution of their companies.

Neighbours of Hungary are very diverse in terms of GDP per capita. Only one of the neighbouring countries, namely the EU member, Austria, is among the largest investors (3rd in rank). Austria has a common border with two regions: Western Transdanubia and Southern Transdanubia, and half of the Austrian investment went into these border regions.

The distance from the advanced market economies does not seem an important influential factor on the large regional level such as NUTS-2[12] and cross-border investment has taken place on a limited scale in other regions. According to anecdotal evidence, the outward investment from eastern regions is more important than inward investment. Without data we may simply assume that mutual technology upgrading may have at least some local value for these border regions. Much more empirical evidence and more detailed regional data are needed to investigate this process.

FDI in physical capacities
Capacity building is an important part of technology upgrading. Physical capacity includes equipment, building and other facilities, and the foreign investment by physical content is also interesting.

At the beginning of the transition period it was supposed that industrial buildings represented important assets, and it was also thought that investment into up-to-date (or better quality) equipment was enough to modernise industry.

During the privatisation process it became clear that modernisation of the manufacturing industry required new buildings and a built-in infrastructure.[13]

The shift from 'dirty' towards 'clean' industry required modern industrial buildings and many brown-field investments were accompanied or followed in a few years time by new construction. Its mark is very visible on the Hungarian-built environment, and there are examples in all economic sectors. In 1999–2000 roughly 30% of new investment was spent on construction. This symbolises that investors are thinking in terms of long-term investment (Table 9.7). For the physical capabilities the proportion of construction was one-third in total economy between 1995 and 2000 and one-quarter in manufacturing industry. During the investigated period the proportion of construction to total investment slightly decreased.

Investment into new equipment brings in new technology, three-quarters of the expenditure on machinery was covered by imports. Imported technology helps to build regional infrastructures and to develop networks and clusters.

Table 9.7 FDI in physical capabilities, 1995–2000 (%)

Industries, branches	Investment	1995	1996	1997	1998	1999	2000
Manufacturing		100.0	100.0	100.0	100.0	100.0	100.0
	Construction	27.4	22.9	24.2	24.0	25.9	23.7
	Domestic machines	23.0	24.1	24.5	25.1	23.1	26.2
	Import machines	41.3	45.6	42.2	42.3	50.9	49.7
Of coke, refined petroleum products, nuclear products and nuclear fuel, chemicals and chemical products, and man-made fibres		100.0	100.0	100.0	100.0	100.0	100.0
	Construction	34.8	26.2	20.6	26.7	32.6	28.2
	Domestic machines	31.4	36.2	34.2	34.4	29.8	40.4
	Import machines	22.0	31.6	32.8	26.2	37.6	31.3
Of machinery and equipment		100.0	100.0	100.0	100.0	100.0	100.0
	Construction	21.8	21.5	28.1	25.2	29.5	20.1
	Domestic machines	15.0	12.3	16.4	30.3	37.1	34.3
	Import machines	56.3	57.3	46.4	32.3	33.3	45.5
Electricity, gas, steam and water supply		100.0	100.0	100.0	100.0	100.0	100.0
	Construction	44.3	57.1	60.0	57.8	60.8	55.1
	Domestic machines	23.7	22.3	18.3	23.2	28.5	32.5
	Import machines	25.8	15.0	13.4	9.0	10.6	12.3
Transport, storage, post and telecommunications		100.0	100.0	100.0	100.0	100.0	100.0
	Construction	39.6	28.7	41.6	30.1	24.2	23.5
	Domestic machines	30.4	23.2	21.2	31.0	39.5	21.3
	Import machines	21.1	40.7	29.1	29.7	36.1	55.1
Total		100.0	100.0	100.0	100.0	100.0	100.0
	Construction	36.0	35.7	35.2	35.7	32.2	29.3
	Domestic machines	23.0	20.0	22.6	23.7	26.7	26.5
	Import machines	32.3	35.9	33.1	32.1	41.0	43.6

Note: The missing sum within years and industries belongs to other investments.

Source: HCSO (2002a, pp. 52–53) and series of HCSO publications over the period.

The proportion of imported technology varied by sector, from very low in many traditional industries to very high in modern industries (the machinery and equipment, electrical and optical equipment, transport equipment and telecommunications sectors).

The proportion of imported machines was much higher every year in the total economy and the manufacturing industry as a whole than investment in domestically made machines. That means changes in the level of technology were influenced significantly by FDI imported machines. The discrepancy between traditional and modern industries for obtaining Hungarian-made or imported machinery illustrates both the strengths and weaknesses of Hungarian engineering in various fields. In modern (high-tech and low-level, high-tech) industries there was a huge demand for up-to-date technology. Besides physical capacity foreign investors brought in complementary knowledge such as new management and new routines to upgrade innovative capability.

FDI in R&D activities
The key question is how the post-socialist economies can fit into the world picture of globalisation in R&D and in innovation. As Florida's overview (1997) on the literature summarised the position, two principal types of foreign direct R&D investment may be distinguished: market- and technology-oriented. Each type creates a different relationship between host and home country. Foreign direct R&D investment is a heterogeneous process with considerable variations across industrial sectors and changes over time (Cantwell 1995). Foreign R&D activities take different forms of collaboration. FDI may bring with it anything from simple contract work to shared strategic research tasks. FDI-related techno-scientific co-operation takes place not only between or among companies but also between and among universities and other R&D organisations. The scale of tasks is varied and depends on many factors. All types of collaboration have very important roles to play in transforming the less-advanced countries into more-advanced ones, and all categories have both positive and negative effects on the host country.

In my previous paper (Inzelt 2000) I introduced categories of what I termed 'skin-deep' and 'soul-deep' collaboration in R&D, in order to classify them by their main characteristics into four categories: (1) Skin-deep-1, (2) Skin-deep-2 (Bangalore type), (3) Soul-deep-1 and (4) Soul-deep-2.

Skin-deep collaboration is demand-side-motivated. FDI in R&D is motivated principally to adapt and tailor products for foreign markets and to provide technical support for offshore manufacturing operations. The organisations within the host countries usually cannot go beyond traditional linkages between home and host countries. FDI may restrict the affiliate acting as passive innovator although the weight of active innovators is not negligible in co-operations of this type. The level of novelty is usually no more than one of being new to the firm, to the country or to the surrounding region.

The aim of *soul-deep collaboration* is to gain and secure access to science and technology and to scientific human capital, and to develop links with the scientific and technical community. In this technology-oriented, supply-side-motivated type of collaboration the actors enter into a deep relationship, with well-balanced interests in co-operation.

The innovation system of the host country and capabilities in particular sectors can encourage or discourage foreign investors to launch soul-deep collaborations. In my previous paper I emphasised that the mode of soul-deep co-operation-2 is less advantageous than soul-deep co-operation-1. In the former the R&D organisations of the host countries are the main partners of foreign investors and their R&D results are used only outside the host country, whilst in the latter case the host country organisations are involved in radical innovation based on the host country R&D efforts.

The internationalisation of innovation has been challenging this evaluation. More and more multinational companies are re-allocating different segments of innovation outside headquarters, and a new regime of international labour division in R&D and innovation may result in new avenues for knowledge flow. New emerging patterns of labour division may produce massively active innovators in host countries on the basis of two-way or multi-directional flows of knowledge.

An important policy issue is how economic organisations are involved in FDI-related R&D activity and innovation.

Governmental programme: setting up and increase of cutting-edge laboratories
The policy aim was to encourage business organisations to set up and run high-quality R&D laboratories which approached the critical mass of research and were involved in business–university co-operative research.[14] It was assumed that such business-led creation of new laboratories could help smooth the restructuring of research organisations, minimising the cost of transition. (The decreasing brain drain and increasing domestic mobility from old R&D organisations caused tremendous problems for new R&D laboratories with up-to-date equipment and efficient R&D management.)

A new programme was launched in 1998 concerning, as the relevant Government document pointed out:

> the establishment of centres of innovation and information which foster the competitiveness of the business sector and its co-operation with research institutes. The technology policy of the Government should facilitate and

stimulate capital investment to be directed into knowledge-intensive high-tech sectors which turn out high-value-added and environment-friendly products. ... Hungary should be made attractive as a research and development location for multinational companies.

The conditions of the Government programme for setting up R&D (high-tech) cutting-edge laboratories were as follows:

* To invest at least HUF 500 million (USD 1.6 million),
* To employ at least 30 higher educated researchers full time,
* To run the R&D laboratory for at least five years according to its original aim.

The Government programme offered a grant of 25% of the total budget of those meeting these criteria. The original scheme was renamed and extended following a change of government and additional grants would become available after a few years of operation of the establishment, if the owners were to increase the number of higher educated R&D employees by at least ten persons and invest at least an additional HUF 150 million (USD 0.5 million).

This programme is open to any business organisation but the Hungarian reality is that only foreign-owned companies have been able to meet these criteria. However, the programme could facilitate the policy aim which declared that Hungary should be made an attractive research and development location for multinational companies. The assumption was that these laboratories would create more valuable jobs and could help the further internationalisation of Hungarian R&D and innovation activities: they may link other entities in the national system with sophisticated partners. Table 9.8 shows the list of approved laboratories which were set up or restructured significantly within the framework of this support scheme.

The last column of Table 9.8 shows that the percentage of government support in the total budget was 4–25% and that the majority of companies used much less in the way of grants than the supporting scheme offered them. All approved laboratories are more or less involved in the European or global R&D operations of investors.

From the dozen or so approved R&D laboratories seven were related to the car and car component industries. That illustrates that FDI in this sector has an effect on its own knowledge base in the host country in that foreigners are investing in knowledge creation locally. The ICT sector ranks second among approved laboratories, and three companies invested in large-scale R&D laboratories in this sector. These laboratories are involved in the global R&D labour division of their funding companies. Two other laboratories enjoyed

Table 9.8 Results of the programme to set up high-tech laboratories (million HUF)

Year of application	Granted firms	Relating sector	Total support from KMÜFA	Firm		Total budget	Percentage of KMÜFA support
				Source	Other		
1998	KNORR-BREMSE Brake Systems Ltd.	Vehicle and vehicle parts	75.0	764.4	125.0	964.4	7.8
	NOKIA Hungary Communication Ltd.	ICT	53.7	1 144.7	89.4	1 287.8	4.2
1999	AUDI Hungaria Motor Ltd.[1]	Vehicle and vehicle parts	171.4	3 181.9	285.6	3 638.9	4.7
	Continental Teves Hungary Ltd.	Vehicle and vehicle parts	125.0	465.0	–	590.0	21.2
	TEMIC TELEFUNKEN Microelectronic Hungary Ltd.	Vehicle and vehicle parts	125.0	628.6	–	753.6	16.6
	FLEXTRONICS INTERNATIONAL Product and Service Off-shore Ltd.	ICT	125.0	389.6	–	514.6	24.3
2000	GE HUNGARY Industrial and Trade Co.[2]	Lighting technology	125.0	583.8	–	708.8	17.6
2001	Denso Production Hungary Ltd.	Vehicle and vehicle parts	125.0	583.8	–	708.8	17.6
	VISTEON HUNGARY Product and Trade Ltd.	Vehicle and vehicle parts	200.0	693.7	–	893.7	22.4
	ZENON Systems Product and Service Ltd.	Environmental production equipment	200.0	673.3	–	873.3	22.9
	SAMSUNG SDI Hungary Product and Trade Co.	ICT	200.0	600.0	–	800.0	25.0
	W.E.T. Automove Systems Hungary Ltd.	Vehicle and vehicle parts	200.0	963.3	–	1 163.3	17.2
			200.0	681.5	–	881.5	22.7

Notes:
1 has to pay back 40% of the support.
2 no contract has been signed.

Source: Compiled from the records of the R&D Division of the Hungarian Ministry of Education.

grants – one in lighting technology and another in the field of environmental protection equipment.

There are several other important R&D laboratories in Hungary which were either set up or significantly upgraded without Government R&D grants. The multinational and large foreign companies could usually afford such investment and, for many reasons, they may prefer to avoid any interference in their business.[15]

As regards the number of applications and grant approvals for laboratories it can be seen that the number of applications is decreasing while the number of organisations approved for grants remains stable (Table 9.9).

The reasons vary from those citing the global recession to the emergence of new, competing host countries. The small-country effect – a relatively smaller base of excellence in research – is interesting for firms searching for partners and locations.[16]

The direct impact of this incentive was positive in that many new laboratories were born and knowledge-intensive jobs created. The type of activity of these laboratories differs: some of them run basic/applied research whilst others are involved in experimental research as testing laboratories.

The Government incentive has been an important factor in putting Hungary on the map of multinationals as a location for R&D laboratories. The launch of such a Government incentive was the most significant message: Hungary had reached the second phase of transition and could afford new R&D support schemes and wished to build long-term partnerships with foreign investors. The message was more important than the sum offered.

The policy expectations from these laboratories are high. Following the period of the grant there must be an evaluation of the output and results of these laboratories with a view to continuing, modifying or cancelling the programme. The available statistical data is needed for this evaluation since overall figures concerning total business R&D activity suggest that there is a shift from basic research towards experimental development. The percentages for basic research performed by business enterprises were 7.0% in 1994 and 4.0% in 2000, whilst those for experimental research were 74.6% and 78.9% in the same years. Expenditure on experimental development was 14 times higher than on basic research in 1991 and 24 times higher in 2000. There is no data as to how the grant-aided laboratories have influenced this shift.

As an OECD study (2001, p. 102) highlighted, foreign affiliates account for about 70% of industrial R&D in Hungary. This high figure reflects the foreign affiliates' economic activity, since they carry out relatively more R&D than do national firms.

Table 9.9 *Changes in the number of applications and grants for setting up high-tech laboratories*

Year of application	Number of		Contracts signed	Granted application %	Total public support (million HUF)	(%) of public support to total budget
	Applications	Granted organisations				
1998	10	3	3	33	800	13.6
1999	7	3	3	43	375	20.2
2000*	6	2	1	17	250	30.0
2001	5	4	4	80	1 000	21.7
1998–2001	28	12	11	39	2 425	18.4

Note: * One application was withdrawn before contracting.

Source: Compiled from the records of the R&D Division of the Hungarian Ministry of Education.

CONCLUSIONS

Hungary, like the other transition economies, has arrived at a new crossroads. The framework of the related internationalisation is now becoming established. Hungary is a full member of OECD and of NATO and membership of the EU is now open for her. As a full member of the Union she may enjoy many new options for internationalisation, but she will lose some of those transition-related tools which were part of her success.

Hungary successfully crossed several thresholds of internationalisation in her system of innovation. The economy tends to reach a development level where knowledge-oriented networking with R&D institutions and other companies is a factor of survival. The complex thinking of the new network economy can gain a central role as an opportunity for latecomers, and Hungary can be a part of a knowledge-driven Europe on an equal basis, overcoming the handicaps inherited from an unfortunate political and economic system.

The success rate of grant-aided international projects is no more than a fast indicator. It tells us nothing about the quality of the network, the role of Hungarian research community in the project and so on. The evaluation of the reasons for successful and failed entries, performance and acceptance of newcomers in these networks is very important for both national and international policy-making. Information is needed on labour division among the old and new members and on equality–inequality in partnerships.

It is still an open question as to how Hungary, or any other transition economy, can influence the agenda of the networks in order to contribute to their own development-relevant questions. Partnership building is a long-term learning process.

Integration into the global networks is the basic ingredient of the rising economy, and FDI is an important part of this process. Within the transition economies the case of Hungary as an attractive country for investors is quite interesting. In the first decade of the transition period Hungary was very successful in attracting FDI in knowledge-based and/or export-oriented sectors. Hungary also was able to become host economy to many different types of R&D activity. The overall effect of the transformation system and of direct and indirect measures for FDI has been technological upgrading, fresh investment in R&D and some improvements in business-to-business and business-to-academia interaction.

Hungary might become the Ireland of Central and Eastern Europe, Ireland being the most successful among the small, less-advanced EU member states in attracting foreign investment and technology upgrading through these investments. Although the basic domestic roots – and several forms of capacity – are very different in Hungary and Ireland, a repetition of the Irish success may occur.

FDI is only one of the protagonists on the stage of technology upgrading, and changes in potential depend on the successful transformation of the environment, and the receptive/absorption capabilities of the country. The inflow of FDI can mobilise and upgrade these capabilities, and so policy has an important role in shaping the environment, in improving receptive/absorption capabilities and in encouraging the inflow of FDI and its involvement in additional capability building.

Improving the innovativeness of a country via FDI is clearly a complicated issue. The great policy challenge for any laggard economy is to create an environment which protects the country from a one-way (outward) flow of knowledge, from remaining on the periphery or from further marginalisation.

NOTES

1. Mushrooming literature on this topic prevents us going into detail. A few examples from this literature are: Inzelt and Auriol (2002), Radosevic (1999 and 2001), Veress (2000), Jasinski (2002), Widmaier and Potratz (1999), the EBRD series of Transition Reports, the OECD series on selected transition economies, the European Commission reports on transition economies, and the OECD reviews on transition economies.
2. Inter-governmental state responsibilities started with mega-science programmes after World War II in a bipolar world system (e.g. CERN, ESA). Since the late 1960s, international R&D co-operation has gone beyond mega-science to reinforce the scientific and technological basis of industry and support its international competitiveness (e.g. EU Framework Programmes, EUREKA, COST.)
3. The CEE countries associated with the FP comprise Bulgaria, the Czech Republic, Estonia, Hungary, Latvia, Lithuania, Poland, Romania, Slovakia and Slovenia. Other Central and Eastern European countries can also participate, as can any country which has concluded a bilateral S&T agreement with the EU.
4. According to the recent World Bank 2000 report, roughly 40 000 multinational companies run 300 000 firms in 130 countries of the world, although MNCs actually originate in very few countries. (Of the 100 top MNCs 88 originated from 'the Triad'.) These companies produce one-third of the world's gross product, and one-third of world trade is the internal business of MNCs.
5. In the bi-polar world system the planned economies decided to set up joint enterprises inside the framework of the CMEA and a few transnational socialist enterprises were created. However, it was the system itself which was the blocking factor to internationalisation at the micro-level, even within the CMEA framework. The first laws on foreign direct investment were enacted in this region in the late 1960s, but with many constraints. The first country to enact a law on FDI was Yugoslavia in 1965, although the country was not a member of the CMEA. The first CMEA country was Romania in 1970, followed by Hungary in 1972, and then by Bulgaria in 1980, Czechoslovakia in 1985 and Poland in 1986 (Hunya (2002) – and EBRD (1999). Between 1972 and 1988 only six joint ventures were set up in Hungary – by way of illustration of the constraints of the law and of the whole system in the field of globalisation. One hundred per cent foreign ownership was first allowed only in 1988 (Hungary and Poland).
6. Foreign investment is classified as a foreign direct investment if the foreign investor holds at least 10% of the ordinary shares or voting rights in an enterprise and exerts some management influence. Portfolio investments are those cases where the foreign investor holds less than 10% of the capital of a firm (OECD 2001, p. 92). The term foreign affiliate is restricted to foreign affiliates which are majority-owned.

7. The transition from command economy to market economy is a long-term process and it has different stages. Parallel tasks, transition, stabilisation and development are present at all stages although the management of 'development' was ranked lower in the years of so-called transition crises than in later years. Two phases of the transition period are distinguished (Dyker and Radosevic (1999), Inzelt (2000), Inzelt and Balogh (forthcoming), Radosevic et al. (2001). According to the experts' opinion a country is in the second stage of transition if a new legal and institutional system has been set up and new structures have begun to work, if the macro-economy has stabilised somewhat and declining trends are being reversed and if the transformation and privatisation of the majority of socialist-type enterprises into market economy-type companies has been concluded.

8. See empirical studies on the initial years of transformation, such as Havas (1994), Inzelt (1994a), Tóth (1994).

9. As the National Development Programme (the Széchenyi Plan) declared: 'in the allocation of state research and development resources special attention needs to be paid to the funds for technology investment, and to encouraging knowledge and technology transfer, the more efficient use of existing research and development capacities. A review of the economic incentive schemes aimed to simplify them and thereby to create an economic environment which favours innovation. The current 120 per cent writing off of R&D expenditure as cost should be increased to 200 per cent. (It has done.) Moreover, a higher rate of amortization for equipment used in the innovation process should be made possible. The development and dissemination of these technologies have to be stimulated indirectly through so-called horizontal means and activities in a sector-neutral manner, avoiding distortion of market and competition.'

10. The minuscule statistical information is available on knowledge upgrading and the R&D activities of foreigners. Sporadic case studies have collected some information on these topics although their main focus was different (e.g. the economic impact of German investors, studying the economic role of FDI and regional development) (Szalavetz (2000), Antalóczy and Sass (2000 and 2002),, Hamar (1997), Biegelbauer et al. (2001)).

11. In the process of upgrading regional capabilities to make them more attractive to foreign investors it is worth mentioning the role of foreign and international organisations. Both European Union and US supporting policy paid attention to less advanced regions to help cohesion among different parts of Hungary. The revitalised regional authorities themselves have done a lot to put their region on the agenda of investors. They are implementing a very attractive infrastructure (setting up industrial parks and off-shore fields), investing in human resources and developing regional marketing policy. Regional authorities need many more tools to become protagonists of regional development.

12. NUTS regions have not yet been introduced in Hungary. In preparation for EU membership Hungarian regional classification tries to follow the NUT classification. Hungary was divided into seven regions but the regions have not yet became legal entities.

13. Several old industrial buildings have historical value as national heritage and may be transformed into museums, theatres or malls but are too costly to reconstruct for industrial purposes.

14. In this context, policy aims such as the 'elaboration of a support scheme for establishing and strengthening knowledge- and technology-intensive enterprises that start up at research institutes' and the 'stimulation of co-operation in innovation between domestic companies, especially the small and medium-sized ones' are important. To this end, horizontal target-oriented projects should be launched. The Government has to play a greater role in these programmes as an awarder of contracts.

15. A full list of foreign-based companies carrying out R&D in Hungary does not exist. From Government documents, newspapers and case studies we may add to the previous list several non-grant-aided laboratories: pharmaceuticals (Sanofi-Chinoin, Astra, Teva-Biogal), household chemistry (Unilever), ICT (IBM, Ericsson, Philips, Siemens, Mannesmann/Rexroth, Motorola), vehicles and vehicle components (Volkswagen, Michelin), agriculture (Novartis/Sandoz Seeds) and material science (Zoltek, Furukawa).

16. The size effects of the research base are discussed in Patel and Pavit (1998), Niosi (1996), Chesnais (1995) and Florida (1997).

REFERENCES

Antalóczy, K. and M. Sass (2000) 'Zöldmezős működőtőke-befektetések magyarországon: statisztikai becslés, vállalati motivációk, gazdasági hatások' (Green-field foreign direct investments in Hungary: statistical estimation, company motivations, economic effects), *Külgazdaság*, XLIV (2000/10), pp. 4–19.

Antalóczy, K. and M. Sass (2002), 'Vállalaton belüli kereskedelem a világgazdaságban és Magyarországon: elméleti keretek, nemzetközi tendenciák, magyarországi jellegzetességek' (Intra-firm trade in the world economy and in Hungary: theoretical framework, international developments, Hungarian relevance), Part 1, *Külgazdaság*, XLV (2001/12), pp. 4–21, Part 2, *Külgazdaság*, XLVI (2002/1), pp. 52–70.

Archibugi, D. and J. Michie (1997), 'The globalisation of technology: a new taxonomy' in Archibugi, D. and J. Michie (eds), *Technology, Globalisation and Economic Performance*, Cambridge: Cambridge University Press.

Biegelbauer, P., E. Griessler and M. Leuthold (2001), *The Impact of Foreign Direct Investment on the Knowledge Base of Central and Eastern European Countries*, Political Science Series, Vienna: Institut für Höhere Studien.

Cantwell, J. (1995), 'The globalisation of technology: what remains of the product cycle model?' reprinted in Cantwell, J. (ed.), *Foreign Direct Investment and Technological Change*, Cheltenham, UK and Brookfield, US: Edward Elgar.

Chesnais, F. (1995), 'Some relationships between foreign direct investment, technology, trade and competitiveness' in Hagedorn, J. (ed.), *Technical Change and the World Economy. Convergence and Divergence in Technology Strategies*, Aldershot, UK and Lyme, US: Edward Elgar.

Dunning, J.H. (1993), *Multinational Enterprises and the Global Economy*, Wokingham: Addison-Wesley.

Dyker, D.A. and S. Radosevic (eds) (1999), *Innovation and Structural Change in Post-Socialist Countries: A Quantitative Approach*, Dordrecht: Kluwer Academic Publishers.

EBRD (1999), 'Transition report 1999, ten years of transition: economic transition in Central and Eastern Europe, the Baltic States and the CIS', European Bank for Reconstruction and Development. [This report gives an overview on all transition economies.]

Florida, R. (1997), 'The globalization of R&D: results of a survey of foreign-affiliated R&D laboratories in the USA', *Research Policy* 26, pp. 85–103.

Hamar, J. (1997), 'A multinacionális vállalatok szerepe a magyar gazdaság világpiaci integrálódásában' (How and why to integrate into the world economy. The role of the MNCs in Hungary), working paper, Budapest: Kopint Datorg.

Havas, A. (1994), 'Incentives to Innovate in Transition: The case of Laser Technology in Hungary', *Economic Systems*, 18(2), pp. 197–214.

Havas, A. (1997), 'Foreign direct investment and intra-industry trade: the case of the automotive industry in Central Europe', in Dyker, D. (ed.), *Technology of Transition. Science and Technology Policies for Transition Countries*, Budapest: Central European University Press.

HCSO (2002a), *Foreign Direct Investment, 1999–2000*, Budapest: Hungarian Central Statistical Office.

HSCO (2002b), *Pocket-Book of Hungarian Regions 2001*, Budapest: Hungarian Central Statistical Office.

Hunya, Gabor (2002), 'Recent inputs of foreign direct investment on growth and restructuring in Central European transition countries', *Online Research Reports No. 284, WIIW*, Vienna: The Vienna Institute for International Economic Studies.

Inzelt, A. (1994a), 'Privatization and innovation in Hungary: first experiences', *Economic Systems*, 18(2), pp. 141–58.

Inzelt, A. (1994b), 'Restructuring and privatisation of the Hungarian manufacturing industry', *Technology in Society*, 16(1), pp. 35–63.

Inzelt, A. (2000), 'The FDI in R&D: from skin-deep collaboration toward soul-deep co-operation', *Science and Public Policy*, 27(4), pp. 241–51.

Inzelt, A. and L. Auriol (2002), *Innovation in Promising Economies*, Budapest: Aula.

Inzelt, A. and T. Balogh (forthcoming), 'Changing innovation system of economies in transition (CEE)', in Rigas Arvanitas (ed.), *Encyclopedia of Life Support Systems*, Oxford: UNESCO Publishing – EOLSS Publishers.

Jasinski, H.A. (ed.) (2002), *Innovation in Transition: The Case of Poland*, Warsaw, Poland: Wydawnictwo Naukowe Wydzialu Zarzadzania Universytetu Warszawkiego.

Mytelka, Lynn K. (2000), 'Mergers, acquisitions, and inter-firm technology arrangements in the global learning economy' in Archibugi, D. and B. Lundvall (eds), *The Globalising Learning Economy*, Oxford: Oxford University Press, pp. 127–44.

Niosi, J. (1996), 'The globalization of small industrial countries' R&D. A contribution to the evolutionary theory of the MNC', Stanford: Centre for Economic Policy Research, Stanford University, manuscript.

OECD (2001), *Science, Technology and Industry Scoreboard – Towards a Knowledge-Based Economy*, Paris: OECD.

OECD (2002), *Main Science and Technology Indicators*, Vol. 2002/1, Paris: OECD.

OMFB (1998), *Research and Development (R&D) Hungary, 1998*, Budapest: Stádium Kft.

Patel, P. and K. Pavitt (1997), 'Uneven (and divergent) technological accumulation among advanced countries: evidence and a framework of explanation' in Archibugi, D. and J. Michie (eds), *Technology, Globalisation and Economic Performance*, Cambridge: Cambridge University Press.

Radosevic, S. (1999), *International Technology Transfer and Catch-Up in Economic Development*, Cheltenham, UK: Edward Elgar.

Radosevic, S., A. Reid, C. Nauwelaers, B. Musyck, S. Georgiu, K. Mueller, E. Terk, S. Kurik, A. Navas, J. Koslowski, M. Bucar and M. Stare (2001), 'Innovation Policy Issues in Six Candidate Countries: The Challenges', Luxembourg: Office for Official Publications of the European Communities.

Siune, K. (2002), 'Building European research capacity', Discussion paper for the third MUSCIPOLI Workshop, University of Athens, October 2002, mimeo.

Szalavetz, A. (2000), 'Hanyatló iparágak?' (Declining industries?), *Külgazdaság*, XLIV (2000/9), pp. 17–34.

Tóth G.L. (1994), 'Technological change, multinational entry and re-structuring: the Hungarian telecommunications equipment industry', *Economic Systems*, 18(2), pp. 179–95.

Veress J. (2000), 'A globalizáció hatása a vállalati magatartásra' (The influence of the globalization to the behaviour of the firms), *Külgazdaság*, XLIV (2000/9), pp. 50–56.

Widmaier, B. and W. Potratz (eds) (1999), *Frameworks for Industrial Policy in Central and Eastern Europe*, Aldershot, UK and Brookfield, US: Ashgate Publishing Company.

World Bank (2000), *Entering the 21st-Century: World Development Report 1999/2000*, New York: World Bank and Oxford University Press.

10. National innovation systems: absorptive capacity and firm competitiveness

Theodosios Palaskas and Maria Tsampra

INTRODUCTION

The contemporary debate on the technological adjustment capacity and growth of national production systems evolves around the fact that competitiveness in today's globalising world is related with dynamic 'knowledge-based economies'. Empirical cross-country and cross-industry surveys suggest that variation in economic performance is related to different technological patterns. Moreover, diversion in technological and innovation capabilities, hence growth, results from different combinations of structure, institutions, and culture of national production systems.

National systems of innovation provide economic agents with *territorialised* capabilities and context conditions not available to competitors located abroad. Consequently, the knowledge-absorbing and diffusing capacities of firms vary across different innovation systems, as they are strongly marked by territory-specific socio-economic factors. Technology transfer and development is prescribed in the interaction between user- and producer-sectors, hence in the structure of national production systems. Economic structures, additionally, have strong institutional dimensions that define the organisation of firms and markets in different countries.

Nevertheless, not all combinations of structures, institutions, and culture are equally prone to enhance national economic growth. Moreover, even in the same environment some firms are more innovative and competitive than others. The capacity to absorb and capitalise knowledge may differ, not only between labour-intensive and technology-intensive industries, but among firms of the same industry as well. The factors defining the investment strategy and technology capabilities of firms constitute a broad set: firm size, production mode, management, competition strategy, market efficiency in labour skills, maturity and quality of demand, are considered important among others.

On the basis of the 'national innovation systems' approach, the present chapter explores the *direct* and *indirect* impact of technological and socio-economic inputs on firm absorptive capacity, hence innovativeness and competitiveness. The following section discusses the theoretical concepts relating knowledge to competitiveness in the new economy context. The absorptive and innovative capacity of national production systems is analysed in the third section. The impact of technological and non-technological factors on learning and competitiveness is specifically explored (Tsampra 2000). The results of the analysis of cross-country and cross-industry research findings (Palaskas and Arapoglou 1999) are discussed and summarised into conclusions in the fourth section. Implications for policy intervention are considered in the final section.

COMPETITIVENESS IN THE NEW ECONOMY OF KNOWLEDGE

The major contemporary globalisation phenomena are increasingly connected with the shift of production to science-based industries in the advanced countries. This process was partly initiated by the massive public investments in research and development (R&D) during World War II and the following cold war period. R&D expenditures and the creation of new economic knowledge shape a temporary comparative advantage driving the flow of foreign direct investment (FDI). This comparative advantage is based on the products and production techniques not yet adapted by foreign competitors (Gruber 1963).

During the oil crisis of the 1970s, it became apparent that advanced industrial systems could add value to their products and production process only by upgrading their knowledge base (Leydesdorff et al. 2002). Competitiveness shifts from the 'low-wage' advantages of less-advanced countries to the 'knowledge-based' advantages of high-wage countries. This shift is increasingly connected to knowledge-driven innovative activity (Audretsch 2000), which is reflected in the rise of patent applications (Kortum and Eaton 1995) and the dramatic decrease in low skills at the same time as increasing demand for highly skilled workers (Berman and Philips 1995).

The emerging technological and institutional changes, primarily in the US economy, marked the beginning of the 'knowledge-based economy'. The correlation between a nation's pattern of specialisation in production and trade on the one hand, and the national knowledge base on the other is broadly established in research (Freeman 1987; Archibugi and Pianta 1992). Knowledge and technology are acknowledged as major factors in shaping production, employment and economic growth, driving qualitative changes in the specialisation and role of countries in the world economy.

The assumption of most international economics is that trade is an effective mechanism of growth rate and income convergence (through price and quantity adjustments in local economies) (Grossman and Helpman 1991). However, empirical evidence on growth and income convergence indicates that trade is driven by differences in the rate and direction of technical progress between economies (due to localised, strongly endogenous forms of technical change). Thus, the traditional models of international trade – originally focused on the factor input of capital and labour – are expanded to include skilled labour, and technology (Storper 2000).

Technology and growth differences between nations are attributed by many scholars primarily to the *production structure* of national economies (the 'national system of production' approach) (Dosi and Malerba 1995). But empirical surveys have established that national structural characteristics and interactions between agents involve non-market relationships of co-ordination and co-operation, prescribed in the elements of power, trust and the way markets are organised (Lundvall 1985).

Thus, emphasis was put on the *institutional* set-up of national economies (the 'national business systems' approach) defined by the *historical pattern* of production and trade specialisation (Whitley 1992; Guerreri and Tylecote 1997). Different national contexts offer disparate organisation possibilities, depending on the established inter-firm relationships, financial markets, industry–university interaction and training system. Still, however, institutional differences do not sufficiently explain the differences in the organisation of firms and national markets (Tylecote 1997).

The analytical concepts of the 'national innovation systems' approach integrate both structural and institutional characteristics. According to this approach, a nation's economic structure is considered as the reflection of accumulated national learning. The differences between national systems of knowledge creation and learning point to the fundamental role of intellectual and social human capital. Mismatches and tensions between structure and institutions can either hamper economic growth (Freeman 1995) or trigger socio-economic change in innovation systems (Lundvall and Maskell 2000).

An *innovation system* consists of the relationships between elements 'which interact in the production, diffusion and use of new and economically useful knowledge' (Lundvall 1992). The term 'innovation system' includes all institutions and actors that contribute to the development and the diffusion of inventions or new technologies (Freeman 1987; Lundvall 1992; Nelson 1993; Metcalfe 1996). The innovation system is not just the sum of actors such as private R&D departments, universities and public research facilities; it is substantiated by the interaction of all these different elements (Audretsch 2000).

It is a paradox that analytical concepts such as 'national systems of innovation' are broadly used in a period of accelerated globalisation and integration. The reason is that competitiveness is built on *heterogeneity* – that is, competitive firms are capable of achievements that others are not, or producing at lower cost than others. Moreover, knowledge and ideas are embodied in localised human capital – that is, skilled individuals. Thus, patent citations are highly localised, indicating the geographical limits of knowledge spillovers (Kogut 1993). The globalisation process induces firms and governments to focus on localised, hence *immobile*, capabilities that 'preserve heterogeneity' across space (Maskell et al. 1998; Lundvall and Maskell 2000).

In other words, innovation systems are by definition localised and immobile, thus providing economic agents (firms) with territory-based capabilities and context conditions *not available* to competitors elsewhere (Lundvall and Maskell 2000). As dynamic learning-based social systems, they are identified at the regional and national, as well as European, level (Lundvall 1992). Local and regional factors are also important as national factors to the formation of innovation conditions (Tödtling and Kaufmann 2002; Storper 1997; Braczyk et al. 1998; Leydesdorff et al. 2002).

Nevertheless, national systems of innovation are still essential domains of economic and political analysis – despite shifts to upper ('globalisation') and nether ('new regionalisation') geographical entities (Freeman 1995). Trajectories of research institutions, educational and financial systems, and regulations are more distinct on the national level; thus knowledge creation and transmission is more easily captured within national boundaries (Freeman 1987; Lundvall 1992; OECD 1996). Policy intervention may rectify identified weaknesses in the nation-specific interaction between structure and institutions, further contributing to the variation of national business environments. On this ground, the analysis of technology absorptiveness, innovativeness, and competitiveness in contemporary globalised industries and national innovation systems is facilitated by cross-country comparisons. Moreover, the distinction between low- and high-technology industries further rectifies the evaluation of the endogenously developed technological capabilities of national innovation systems. Within this context, the following analysis gives eminence to the socio-economic tangible and intangible transactions rooted in structural and institutional characteristics that define knowledge dissemination and exogenously affect the innovation capacity of national production systems.

ANALYSING ABSORPTIVE CAPACITY AND INNOVATIVENESS

Continuous learning and exploring processes, which result in new products, techniques, organisation forms and markets, are found in all parts and times of the economy (Lundvall 1992). But today, technological adaptability and innovativeness have become the principles of competitiveness. Innovation is rather a process than a single event in the economic system, reflecting already existing knowledge, combined in new ways (Schumpeter 1934). In the models of standard economics, innovations appear as rare *exogenous* events temporarily disturbing the general equilibrium, until a new state of equilibrium is established via the price mechanism. This approach however is inadequate in modern capitalism where innovation is a *fundamental and inherent* phenomenon (Lundvall 1992).

The innovative capacity of a firm is directly related to the learning ability of the national production system. The rate and direction of innovation – the end product of learning is the combined effect of the *prevailing economic structure* and *institutional set-up* of the national production system (Lundvall 1992). Institutions define *how learning takes place*, and economic structures define *what is learnt* (Lundvall and Maskell 2000). Thus, innovation, R&D efforts and the science and technology institutional set-up are much analysed in terms of technological traditions, with regard to national specialisation, performance, and differences in growth rates (Nelson and Winter 1977). Economic performance is closely related to the national knowledge base (Nelson 1989).

The knowledge base consists of important tacit parts emanating from learning-by-doing, learning-by-using, and learning-by-interacting – and not only from science and R&D activities (Lundvall and Maskell 2000). Entrepreneurial R&D efforts constitute important inputs to the process of learning and innovation; but learning-by-doing in routine production, learning-by-interacting and learning-by-using in distribution and consumption are also involved (Petrakos and Tsiapa 2001). These are not costless processes; they rather involve production process improvements that require a flow of investment. Furthermore, firms learn not only from their own efforts, but also from their rivals (knowledge spillovers, networking).

Summarising these notions, the related literature distinguishes among several forms of entrepreneurial learning (Petrakos and Tsiapa 2001): intra-firm learning is based on internal R&D efforts (Harris and Trainor 1997; Konstandakopoulos 1997); learning from the environment is a function of clustering and agglomeration economies, spillover effects, and the institutional science and research base (Audretsch and Feldman 1996; Asheim 1996; Morgan 1997; Antonelli 2000a); and inter-firm learning is based on industrial networks capable of managing collective know-how (Amin and Robins 1990; Saxenian 1994; Zuscovitch and Justman 1995; Dodgson and Bessant 1996; Garnsey 1998).

The learning capacity of firms, hence their knowledge- and technology-absorptiveness, is indicated by their innovative output. Innovation and innovativeness have been measured in research (Feldman 2000) as outcomes or dependent variables of R&D inputs (laboratories, expenditures), patents or innovation citations (indicating knowledge flows), new entries or new investment (indicating innovative activity), wage or employment growth, and total factor productivity at the firm level (indicating process innovation).

In brief, innovativeness is illustrated on product innovations, their roots in the interaction between producers and users, and the cultural and distance dimension of such relationships (Lundvall 1992). The process of enterprise learning has significant geographical dimensions: clustering or density, proximity and distance have decisive implications for knowledge absorption and diffusion (Krugman 1995a; Audretsch and Feldman 1996; Storper 1997; Sun 2000). Patent citations of product innovations are broadly used in recent surveys as the main indicators assessing innovation (OECD 1996). Nevertheless, the analytical framework adopted here takes into account all previously elaborated concepts.

The Impact of Technological Factors on the Absorptive Capacity

Our analysis is primarily oriented towards the identification and definition of the technological factors that determine the knowledge-absorption and innovation capacity of firms.[1] In the related literature, such factors are distinguished in endogenous- and exogenous-to-the-firm technological transactions (OECD 1993; Clark et al. 2002). The *endogenous* factors directly affecting firm absorptiveness and innovativeness are prescribed in the internal technological effort of the firm, based on continuous knowledge accumulation activity (Brouwer and Kleinknecht 1996).

Intra-firm technological effort is primarily illustrated in R&D expenditures – more commonly carried out by larger firms. The capacity of firms to invest in technology is restrained by small size and limited assets, traditional organisation (family ownership and management) and production mode (family personnel, low-value-added customisation), as well as poor modernisation structures (production equipment, marketing). In other words, small traditional firms have limited resources to access information and funding, assess market conditions, and adopt dynamic technology adjustment strategies (Tsampra and Palaskas 2002).

Moreover, empirical evidence indicates that the R&D in-house activity of small firms involves development (D) rather than research (R). Nevertheless, the most important factor in the innovative capacity of firms is the quality of their human capital (skilled key-employees) (Palaskas and Arapoglou 1999). Highly skilled employees facilitate the adoption of new technology and innovations, and further stimulate the generation of know-how and innovation (Storper 2000). This factor is captured in the ratio of skilled key-employees (scientists and engineers) to total firm employment.

However, high technological skills merely stocked within the firm are not enough to enhance its learning and innovation capacity. Firms need to substantially invest in the continuous upgrading of their labour skills through training, and the involvement of their personnel in R&D activities. This investment process is reflected in firm R&D expenditures per employee, which is considered a measure of technology input less dependent on exogenous conditions (such as demand and sales) and more dependent on endogenous characteristics (such as firm size, organisational structure, and investment strategy) (Symeonidis 1996; Malecki 1980).

The *exogenous* factors directly determining the absorptive and innovative capacity of firms are prescribed in their technological inputs through purchase of patents and licenses, and inter-firm technological transactions (such as partnerships with innovators) (Caves 1982; Symeonidis 1996). There is no strong research evidence suggesting that firm engagement in licensing, or technology-transfer networks, enhances innovation output (Brouwer and Kleinknecht 1996). Nonetheless, the more technological transactions and R&D activity a firm undertakes, the greater is the opportunity for technological advancement and product innovation (Acs and Gifford 1996).

Multinational enterprises (MNEs) and FDI play a decisive role in technology transfer to indigenous firms. The supply chain may be an important channel for this type of technology input, particularly when highly developed local and regional institutional and producer service infrastructures are absent (Phelps 1997). However, evidence suggests that weak local supply chains result in a lower than the socially optimal level of knowledge transfer to indigenous firms (Crone and Roper 2001). Consistently with the 'path dependence' theory, little influence of foreign firms on the initial technological advantages of indigenous firms is indicated in research (Cantwell 1992).

The level of knowledge transfer depends on the nature of supplier relationships: collaborative forms are more conducive to interactive learning, than the 'arm's length' practices of MNEs (Lall 1996). Moreover, learning processes from MNEs are rather transmissions of process- and systems-related knowledge, than of product-related knowledge (Crone and Roper 2001). In any case, technology transfer depends on the local learning capacities: the recipient has to invest in the absorption of new knowledge; technology embodiment in skills requires further investment in knowledge accumulation (Tsampra and Palaskas 2002).

Two main strands of argument have been further stressed in the innovation literature, concerning the relationship between the endogenous technological effort and exogenous technological input, and their impact on firm innovativeness (Acs and Audretsch 1988). The first suggests that intense technology inputs discourage in-house technological effort: in the context of dense spillovers, a firm can take advantage of innovations produced by leading neighbouring firms, without investing much in technology. The second sustains that in-house technological effort is more influential to firm innovativeness than external technological input: it motivates intra-firm assets in a more dynamic way than the latter.

The Impact of Non-technological Factors on Innovativeness and Competitiveness

The innovation capacity of a firm is not defined by merely technological factors. Technological capabilities are not fully prescribed in purchased mechanical equipment, blueprints or patents, formal skills, and R&D expenditures. These are only some possible sources of technological learning, while the absorption and dissemination of production-based technology also depends strongly on territorialised socio-economic, non-purely technological tangible and intangible transactions (Storper 1997; Audretsch 1998; Maskell and Malmberg 1999; Larsson and Malmberg 1999). Nevertheless, the adoption of advanced knowledge and the adaptation to complex technologies require a formal technological and R&D base (Lall 1996).

Territorialised socio-economic transactions are ascribed to the concept of firm *embeddedness*, suggested by Grannoveter (1985, 1992) to denote the impact of social relations on different possible outcomes (Grabher 1993a and 1993b). Economic actors are influenced by socio-cultural elements of common business values and ethics, networks of interpersonal relationships, social consensus, class forces shaped by institutions, and so on. (Hirst and Zeitlin 1992; Salais and Storper 1992; Amin and Thrift 1994). Such elements are strongly *territorialised* as they result from local traditions and historical development patterns not reproducible elsewhere. In this sense, modes of information exchange and expertise diffusion – both traded and untraded – constitute important territorial assets (Scott 1996; Storper 1997).

In other words, technological advancement is embedded in national cultures. Cultural and geographical distance are important dimensions of learning. The common environment, shared norms and cultural systems, enhance interactive learning and innovation – especially when the exchanged knowledge is tacit and difficult to codify (Freeman 1995). At the same time, geographical and cultural proximity to advanced users, and institutionalised (even if often informal) user–producer relationships, is an important source of diversity and comparative advantage, as is the local supply of managerial and technical skills, and accumulated tacit knowledge (Storper 1997).

On the other hand, important elements of the innovation process are becoming transnational and global rather than national – especially in science-based areas where communication is easier to formalise and codify (Lundvall 1992). The international transfer and sharing of economically useful and complex types (partially codifiable, partially tacit, and relationally dependent) of knowledge are made feasible by structures and practices that specialise in global–local relationships (Eaton and Kortum 1995; Coe and Helpman 1995). Multinationals play an important role (Chesnais 1992), but such efforts require the institutional support of indigenous technological capability within the recipient countries (Freeman 1995).

In summary, the 'embeddedness approach' attributes a strong social nature to labour skills and knowledge, as these are not merely technological input but related to the 'generic' and 'learning' capabilities of human resources. Moreover, it points out that important parts of knowledge are tacit, and emanate from learning-by-doing, learning-by-using, or learning-by-interacting, and not only from formal R&D activities (Storper 1997; Lundvall and Maskell 2000). It further substantiates networking effects on economic performance, by suggesting that frequent firm interaction implies trust, openness, and better economic output (Grannoveter 1992). Knowledge is developed within networks as a function of collective learning, based on clustering and agglomeration economies, spillover effects, and joint R&D (Audretsch and Feldman 1996; Morgan 1997).

On this analytical basis, the 'linear' indicators of standard technology input and output are not adequate for the prescription of innovation capacity. An additional set of indicators is required, in order to measure 'soft' processes like socio-cultural linkages and networking. The direct impact of socio-economic transactions and non-technological factors on the firm's economic output is captured in the firm's local/national and international embeddedness. Firm embeddedness can be measured in terms of: (i) *volume* – that is, the frequency of firm interactions with local/national and international actors (competitors, suppliers, customers, financial institutions) which establishes 'strong' or 'weak' ties; and (ii) *reach ability* – that is, the extent of inter-firm networks, which constitutes 'long-' or 'short-reaching' ties (Bridge 1997; Murdoch 1995).

Inserting the dimension of competitiveness into the elaborated analytical framework, we argue that the absorptive and innovative capacity of firms – reflected in their technological output – directly affects their economic performance, as illustrated in their sales growth. The latter is broadly considered as a dynamic measure of firm competitiveness on the local, national and international markets (Ettlinger and Tufford 1996; Clark et al. 2002). In this sense, the (endogenous and exogenous) technological factors that directly affect firm innovation output have an indirect impact on firm competitiveness.

ANALYSIS RESULTS AND CONCLUSIONS

In the preceding sections, we sought to identify how technological and socio-economic factors affect the technology-absorptive and innovative capacity of firms, and to demonstrate, using econometric analysis results, their impact on firm economic performance and the competitiveness of national innovation systems. We will now assess the role of the national structural and institutional setting in firm learning. The structural factors are related to more fundamental economic or spatial conditions, beyond the control of the individual firms, than the behavioural. In any case, learning is not only an intra-firm affair but also a social affair requiring public policies of specific focus.

We tested this assumption across various national innovation systems and industries of different technological intensity – specifically, for labour-intensive, low-technology industries, as well as capital-intensive medium- or high-technology industries.[2] To this purpose, we econometrically explored the relationship between competitiveness – defined as growth of sales – and innovativeness – defined as product innovation output of the firm (Palaskas and Arapoglou 1999). Our statistical analysis indicates that both economic performance and innovation capacity are positively associated with technological intensity.[3]

In other words, firms in labour-intensive industries (garments manufacturing) are less innovative than firms in capital- and knowledge-intensive industries (electronics and software). This observation is indicative of the different quality of labour skills, level of production technology, and product sophistication of firms across industries (Tsampra and Palaskas 2002). However, empirical data further indicate wide and persistent variations in the technological and competitive efficiency of firms within the same industry, across different countries (see note 3, Tables 10.1 and 10.2).

Such diversity, as already argued, emanates from the territorialised characteristics and conditions of national innovation systems (Tsampra and Palaskas 2002). National economies differ regarding their production system structure and institutional set-up – as reflected in the pattern of intra-firm organisation and inter-firm relationships, the role of public and financial sectors, and the intensity of the R&D base. Nevertheless, our survey identified firm-level variations in innovation capacity and competitive efficiency, not only within the same industry but within the same business context too.

The interpretation of firm technological and economic performance requires the examination of firm strategy and investment practices. These depend on the development stage and specialisation of the firm, its size and management pattern (Clark et al. 2002; Cohen and Levinthal 1989). Firm investments in technology and R&D activities play the critical role for innovativeness and competitiveness. As already argued, skilled employees are effective to firm absorptive and innovative capacity only when they are engaged in training and R&D. Our empirical evidence also suggests that internal effort is more effective to firm technological upgrading than external-to-the-firm technology inputs (adopted process technologies, etc.) (see Table 10.3, equation 1).[4]

Despite the previously noted significant impact of territorial intangible transactions (embodied in labour skills and niche-production mechanisms) on knowledge absorption and diffusion (through learning-by-doing, learning-by-using, and learning-by-interacting) within national innovation systems, firm technological and economic performance is determined by codified, rather than tacit, knowledge. Low tacitness allows for higher standardisation and transmission of knowledge via tangible mediums (patents, licensing). In conclusion, technology absorptive capacity and innovativeness are related to proprietary, rather than tacit, learning processes and knowledge spillovers (Von Hipple 1994).

We previously distinguished also between international and local/national technology transfer channels, in terms of their impact on firm performance. According to Grannoveter (1985, 1992) long-reaching networks are more effective than big-volume networks; this effect he calls 'the strength of weak ties'. That argument is coherent to our research findings (Palaskas and Arapoglou 1999) which point out the bigger importance of international linkages (international embeddedness) for firm economic performance, in comparison to local linkages (local embeddedness).

The analysis of our fieldwork information further reveals that competitiveness and technological capabilities improve when firms are engaged in 'internationally traded knowledge' networks of even not-frequent ('weak') transactions. In other words, even the weak ties of firms to international technological leaders offer them the advantage of higher 'exposure', and allow them to play a brokerage role in the connection of local/national to international actors (Grannoveter 1992; Palaskas and Arapoglou 1999). In conclusion, the knowledge-absorbing and innovating capabilities of firms depend on their interaction with international technology leaders rather than with local innovators.

According to empirical evidence, local ties do not contribute much to innovation, but rather to knowledge assimilation through learning-by-doing processes. Nevertheless, our analysis does not suggest a positive impact of geographic proximity and local embeddedness on the costs of transmitting tacit knowledge. On the other hand, international embeddedness has a strong positive impact on absorption and innovation capacity – either on the supply (imported technology and innovations), or the demand side (international promotion of indigenous technology) (see note 4, Table 10.3, equation 2). Although local embeddedness is not significant in this sense, it is nevertheless helpful for the creation of favourable conditions for international transactions.

The degree of international embeddedness varies between high- and low-technology industries. The technology-intensive firms of our sample present higher levels of international embeddedness than traditional labour-intensive firms. The latter, although highly territory-based, are hardly embedded (either locally, nationally or internationally) in outsourcing, niche-production, and exporting networks. In other words, territorialisation does not always imply embeddedness; it may signify weak inter-firm transactions due to fragmented local/national specialisation, and diverse niche-market orientation. Under such conditions, embeddedness may just involve the links with local/national institutions (business associations, education, banks, and so on).

POLICY LESSONS FOR NATIONAL INNOVATION SYSTEMS

The complex relationships established by the results of our econometric analysis are depicted in Figure 10.1. The main conclusions are summarised and a basis for policy suggestions is provided. More specifically, Figure 10.1 illustrates the substantial relationships among the previously analysed factors and conditions that define a national innovation system. It is however a challenge for policy-making not just to build upon established links, but also to reinforce weak ties and bridge the gaps that inhibit technological adjustment and development.

The identified relationships denote that successful learning and innovativeness – reflected in product innovation – are principal elements of thriving

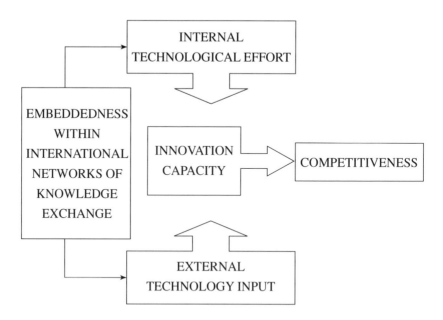

Figure 10.1   Absorptive capacity and firm competitiveness in national innovation systems

economic performance and competitiveness. The absorptive and innovation capacity of firms is mainly determined by their internal effort for technological development – employing key labour skills, investing in training and R&D engagement of personnel. Firm innovativeness is largely defined by external technology inputs, too – transfer of process technology, purchased patents and licensing – but the essential preconditions are absorptiveness and strong learning capacities.

The generic and learning capacities of national innovation systems are not the outcome of merely technological factors. It is the path-dependent, socio-economic dimensions of national innovation systems that determine the effectiveness of the endogenous and exogenous technological inputs – hence, knowledge absorption and diffusion. These are rooted in the structural and institutional business settings of nation-specific production mode and specialisation, supply chain and consumption pattern, and networking.

Innovative capacity and the associated learning ability are directly related to the density and quality of networking among actors within the national production system. Innovation, as the end-product of learning, depends on the quality and density of the above relationships (Oughton et al. 2002). In particular, embeddedness within international networks of knowledge exchange gives a strong impetus to both innovativeness and competitiveness.

Policy intervention should therefore aim at extending and strengthening knowledge transfers within the local supply chain, and promoting knowledge transfers from multinational plants to indigenous firms. Consequent suggestions point towards the development of infrastructures that boost the collaboration between indigenous firms and international technology suppliers, and also sustain the effort of local innovators to internationalise their technological output, and become 'innovative mediators' through exports to niche markets.

To this purpose, the formation of a reliable institutional framework is essential: primarily, to enhance intra-firm technological efforts – supporting firm R&D expenditures, participation in technology development programs, and venture capital; and secondarily, to sustain inter-firm technological transactions at the local/national level, in order to establish stronger exchanging and absorptive structures, which are also necessary for potential internationalisation.

The major drawbacks for competitiveness are identified in the inadequate human resources and poor knowledge base of national innovation systems. Big differences between countries in their formal and informal education and training systems affect their innovative capabilities. These refer to quantitative investment in education, the enrolment in science and engineering, the investment in training of skilled workers, and so on. Also, qualitative differences related to the social norms and values are reproduced by the system.

Thus, policy agencies need to upgrade local labour skills – even in traditional craftsmanship activities – through training processes. Successful policy lessons should also be drawn from the collaboration of firms with local technological and educational institutions. The realisation of knowledge- and technology-related competitive advantages leads to the structural adjustment of the post-war knowledge infrastructure (Freeman et al. 1982). This involves, among others, the institutional divides between public and private, academic and industrial, and related science-based innovation policies (Leydesdorff et al. 2002).

Through such policies, the handicaps of technologically lagging nations – such as dependence on foreign investment, and difficult access to foreign markets (Katzenstein 1985) – can be overcome. Lagging national innovation systems – characterised by specialisation in low-technology production, and slow growth of technological opportunities and market volume (Freeman and Lundvall 1988) – can be upgraded today by developing dynamic technology-based competitive advantages.

NOTES

1. The *direct* and *indirect* implications of the technological factors and socio-economic transactions among firms for innovativeness and competitiveness are econometrically estimated in the following simultaneous equation system:

$$SALGR_i = a_1 + b_1\ EMBI_i^{**} + c_1\ INP\hat{R}OD_i + d_1\ NINDE_i^{**} + f_1\ SEMPL_i^* + e_{1i},\ \hat{R}^2 = 0{,}27 \tag{1.1}$$

$$INPROD_i = a_2 + b_2\ RDEXEMP_i^* + c_2\ LICEN_i^* + d_2\ SC\&EN_i^{**} + f_2 TPROC_i^{**} + e_{2i},\ \hat{R}^2 = 0{,}77 \tag{1.2}$$

where i = firm, and e_{1i} and e_{2i} the unexplained part of the regression. [**] denotes significant at 1%, and [*] significant at 5%.

BOX 10.1   DEFINITION OF VARIABLES INVOLVED IN THE ESTIMATED MODEL (1.1) (1.2)

SALGR: growth of sales, competitiveness
INPROD: product innovation, innovativeness
EMBI: international embeddedness
NINDE: non independent firms
SEMPL: employment size
RDEXEMP: R&D expenditures per employee
LICEN: licensing
SC&EN: ratio of scientists and engineers to total employment
TPROC: process technology

---

2. Interesting evidence is provided by an empirical survey carried out in five European and two East Asian countries: England, Scotland, Italy, Greece, Israel, Korea, and Taiwan; and two industrial sectors: traditional labour-intensive garments manufacturing, and the technology-intensive microelectronics and software industry. The analysis was based on quantitative primary

data, complemented with qualitative information obtained via interviews with firms and questionnaires. The results point to the effective alteration of the relation between inputs and achievements, and suggest strategies supporting competitive knowledge-based economies. The survey was made possible through an EU FP4 grant for Targeted Socio-Economic Research (TSER) on 'SMEs in Europe and East Asia: Competition, Collaboration and Lessons for Policy Support – Greek Report', and the participation of our partners from Italy, England, Scotland, and Israel.

3. The aim of the following analysis is to examine whether the growth of sales (*SALGR*) and innovativeness (*INPROD*) differ statistically significantly between high-technology (HT) and low-technology (LT) industries: The ANOVA results presented in Table 10.1, show that the ratio of the means of *SALGR* of the HT to the LT industries (see the 4th column) is bigger than 1. This primarily suggests that the HT firms across all seven countries perform better than the LT firms, in terms of sales growth. The mean differences in *SALGR* for all countries together (see the last row) between HT and LT firms were statistically confirmed at a level of 99% (F'statistic = 13.149).

Table 10.1   ANOVA results for SALGR *across industries and countries*

Sales Growth: ratio 97/95	High-tech industry Mean	Low-tech industry Mean	HT/LT Ratio
Taiwan	1.16	1.03	1.13
Korea	1.75	1.54	1.14
England	3.00	2.60	1.15
Scotland	2.36	1.12	2.11
Italy	1.85	1.01	1.83
Greece	1.44	0.94	1.53
Israel	4.55	0.97	4.69
Total	2.08**	1.16**	1.79

Note: **Significantly different at 99%.

The same approach was adopted to examine whether innovativeness (*INPROD*) differs statistically between HT and LT industries, in the seven countries under examination. The obtained results in Table 10.2, suggest that the innovation ratio of HT firms to LT firms is higher than 1 (excluding Korea). The ANOVA results confirmed that, on average (see the last row) and at a 95% level of significance (F'statistic = 37.778), HT firms are more innovative than LT firms.

Table 10.2   ANOVA results for INPROD *across industries and countries*

Innovativeness	High-tech industry Mean	Low-tech industry Mean	HT/LT Ratio
Taiwan	0.84	0.73	1.15
Korea	0.48	0.53	0.91
England	0.79	0.15	5.27
Scotland	0.71	0.46	1.54
Italy	0.56	0.31	1.81
Greece	0.48	0.17	2.82
Israel	0.76	–	–
Total	0.67*	0.36*	1.86

Notes:
INPROD variable lies between 0 = no product innovation, and 1 = yes product innovation.
*Significantly different at 95%.

4. The Regression Analysis results on the impact of in-house R&D activity (*IHRD*) and external technology input (*LICEN*), i.e. purchased licenses, on firm innovativeness suggest that at a 99% level of significance both factors have a positive impact (see the first row of Table 10.3).

The estimation of the impact of local and international embeddedness on firm innovativeness indicates that local embeddedness (*EMBLO*) is statistically insignificant, whereas international embeddedness (*EMBIN*) has a positive effect and is statistically significantly different from zero at 95% (see the second row of Table 10.3).

More specifically, the results suggest that firm embeddedness in a local context of dense technology spillovers does not initiate (or even hamper) internal technological effort, hence firm innovativeness, whereas the ability of firms to be internationally embedded (*EMBIN*) enhances their innovative capacity.

Table 10.3   Regression estimations

eq. 1. INNOVATIVENESS	0.200** LICEN	0.254** IHRD
eq. 2. INNOVATIVENESS	0.121* EMBIN	–0.096+ EMBLO

Notes:
*   at 95% level of significance.
**   at 99% level of significance.
+   not significantly different from zero.

REFERENCES

Acs, Z.J. and Audretsch, D.B. (1988), 'Innovation in large and small firms: an empirical analysis', *American Economic Review*, 78 (4): 678–90.
Acs, Z.J. and Gifford, S. (1996), 'Innovation of entrepreneurial firms', *Small Business Economics*, 8: 20–218.
Amin, A. and Robins, K. (1990), 'The re-emergence of regional economies? The mythical geography of flexible accumulation', *Environmental Planning D*, 8: 7–34.
Amin, A. and Thrift, N. (eds) (1994), *Globalization, Institutions, and Regional Development in Europe*, Oxford: Oxford University Press.
Antonelli, C. (2000a), 'Collective knowledge communication and innovation: the evidence of technological districts', *Regional Studies*, 34 (6): 537–47.
Antonelli, C. (2000b), 'Restructuring and innovation in long-term regional change', in G.L. Clark, M.P. Feldman and M.S. Gertler (eds), *The Oxford Handbook of Economic Geography*, Oxford: Oxford University Press.
Arapoglou, V., Palaskas, T. and Tsampra, M. (2000), 'Local and international ties of regional innovation systems: the Greek IT SMEs', paper presented at the Thematic Network MESIAS (STRATA) Workshop, Oslo.
Archibugi, D. and Michie, J. (1995), 'The globalisation of technology: a new taxonomy', *Cambridge Journal of Economics*, 19: 121–40.
Archibugi, D. and Pianta, M. (1992), *The Technological Specialization of Advanced Countries: A Report to the EEC on International Science and Technology Activities*, Boston: Kluwer Academic.
Asheim, B. (1996), 'Industrial districts as learning regions: a condition for prosperity', *European Planning Studies*, 4 (4): 379–400.
Asheim, B. and Dunford, M. (1997), 'Regional futures', *Regional Studies*, 31: 445–56.
Audretsch, D. (1995), *Innovation and Industry Evolution*, Cambridge, MA: MIT Press.

Audretsch, D. (1998), 'Agglomeration and the location of innovative activity', *Oxford Review of Economic Policy*, 14: 18–29.

Audretsch, D. (2000), 'Corporate For and Spatial Form', in G.L. Clark, M.P. Feldman and M.S. Gertler (eds), *The Oxford Handbook of Economic Geography*, Oxford: Oxford University Press.

Audretsch, D. and Feldman, M. (1996), 'R&D spillovers and the geography of innovation and production', *American Economic Review*, 86 (3): 630–40.

Berman, Y. and Philips, D.R. (1995), *Human Services in the Age of New Technology: Harmonising Social Work and Computerisation*, Aldershot: Avebury.

Braczyk, H., Cooke, P. and Heidenreich, M. (eds) (1998), *Regional Innovation Systems*, London: UCL Press.

Bridge, G. (1997), 'Mapping the terrain of time–space compression: power networks in everyday life', *Environment and Planning D: Society and Space*, 15.

Brouwer, E. and Kleinknecht, A. (1996), 'Firm size, small business presence and sales of innovative products: a micro-econometric analysis', *Small Business Economics*, 8: 189–201.

Brouwer, E. and Kleinknecht, A. (1999), 'Keynes-plus? Effective demand and changes in firm-level R&D: an empirical note', *Cambridge Journal of Economics*, 23: 385–91.

Camagni, R. (ed.) (1991), *Innovation Networks: Spatial Perspectives*, London: Belhaven.

Cantwell, J. (1992), *Multinational Investment in Modern Europe: Strategic Interaction in the Integrated Community*, Aldershot and Brookfield: Edward Elgar.

Cantwell, J. and Iammarino, S. (1998), 'MNCs, technological innovation and regional systems in the EU: some evidence in the Italian case', *International Journal of the Economics of Business*, 5 (3): 383–408.

Cantwell, J. and Santagelo, G.D. (1999), 'The frontier of international technology networks: sourcing abroad the most highly tacit capabilities', *Information Economics and Policy*, 11 (1): 101–23

Caves, R.E. (1982), *Multinational Enterprise and Economic Analysis*, Cambridge: Cambridge University Press.

Chesnais, F. (1992), *L'armement en France: genèse, ampleur et coût d'une industrie*, Paris: Nathan.

Clark, G., Palaskas, T., Tracey, P. and Tsampra, M. (2002), 'Globalization and SME competitive strategies in Europe's vulnerable regions: firm, industry and country effects on employment in four labour-intensive industries over the late 1990s', paper presented at the Dialogue Workshop on The Internationalisation of European SMEs: Culture, Entrepreneurship and Competitiveness, EU, Socio-Economic Research Key Action, Brussels.

Coe, D.T. and Helpman, E. (1995), 'International R&D spillovers', *European Economic Review*, 39.

Cohen, W. and Levinthal, D. (1989), 'Innovation and learning: the two faces of R&D', *The Economic Journal*, 99.

Cooke, P. and Morgan, K. (1991), 'The network paradigm: new departures in corporate and regional development', paper presented at the International Conference: Europe after Maastricht, Lemnos, Greece, 2–5 September.

Crone, M. and Roper, S. (2001), 'Local learning from multinational plants: knowledge transfers in the supply chain', *Regional Studies*, 35 (6): 535–48.

Daly, A., Hitchens, D.M. and Wagner, K. (1985), 'Productivity machinery and skills in a sample of British and German manufacturing plants – results from a pilot study', *National Institute Economic Review*, February: 48–61.

De Vet, J. (1992), 'Globalization, local and regional competitiveness', *STI Review*, 13.

Dodgson, M. and Bessant, J. (1996), *Effective Innovation Policy: A New Approach*, London: International Thomson Business Press.

Dosi, G. and Malerba, F. (1995), *Organization and Strategy in the Evolution of the Enterprise*, Basingstoke: Macmillan.

Dunning, J.H. (1994), 'Multinational enterprises and the globalization of innovation capacity', *Research Policy*, 23.

Eaton, J. and Kortum, S. (1995), *Trade in Ideas: Patenting and Productivity in the OECD*, Cambridge, MA: National Bureau of Economic Research.

Edquist, C. and McKelvey, M. (eds) (2000), *Systems of Innovation: Growth, Competitiveness and Employment*, vol. I, Cheltenham and Northampton, MA: Edward Elgar.

Ettlinger, N. and Tufford, M. (1996), 'Evaluating small firm performance in local context: A case study of manufacturers in Columbus, Ohio', *Small Business Economics*, 8: 139–57.

Feldman, M. (1994), *The Geography of Innovation*, Dordrecht: Kluwer Academic Publishers.

Feldman, M. (2000), 'Location and innovation: the new economic geography of innovation, spillovers, and agglomeration', in G.L. Clark, M.P Feldman and M.S Gertler (eds), *The Oxford Handbook of Economic Geography*, Oxford: Oxford University Press.

Foray, D. and Lundvall, B.-Å. (1996), 'The knowledge-based economy: from the economics of knowledge to the learning economy', in OECD (eds), *Employment and Growth in the Knowledge-Based Economy*, Paris: OECD, 11–32.

Freeman, C. (1987), *Technology Policy and Economic Performance: Lessons from Japan*, London: Pinter.

Freeman, C. (1995), 'The "national system of innovation" in historical perspective', *Cambridge Journal of Economics*, 19 (1): 5–24.

Freeman, C., Clark, J. and Soete, L. (1982), *Unemployment and Technical Innovation: A Study of Long Waves in Economic Development*, London: Pinter.

Freeman, C. and Lundvall, B.-Å. (eds) (1988), *Small Countries Facing the Technological Revolution,* London: Pinter.

Garnsey, E. (1998), 'The genesis of the high technology milieu: a study in complexity', *International Journal of Urban and Regional Research*, 22 (3): 361–77.

Geroski, P., Machin, S. and Van Reenen, J. (1993), 'The profitability of innovating firms and RAND', *Journal of Economics*, 24: 198–211.

Grabher, G. (1993a), 'Rediscovering the social in the economics of interfirm relationships', in G. Grabher (ed.), *The Embedded Firm: On the Socio-Economics of Industrial Networks*, London: Routledge.

Grabher, G. (1993b), 'The weakness of strong ties: the lock-in of regional development in the Rurh area', in G. Grabher (ed.), *The Embedded Firm: On the Socio-Economics of Industrial Networks,* London: Routledge.

Grannoveter, M. (1985), 'Economic action and social structure: the problem of embeddedness', *American Journal of Sociology*, 91 (3): 481–510.

Grannoveter, M. (1992), 'Economic institutions as social constructions: framework of analysis', *Acta Sociologica*, 35: 3–11.

Grossman, G. and Helpman, E. (1991), *Innovation and Growth in the Global Economy*, Cambridge, MA: MIT Press.

Grossman, G.M. and Helpman, E. (1994), 'Endogenous innovation in the theory of growth', *Journal of Economic Perspectives*, 8: 23–44.

Gruber, H. (1963), *Science and the New Nations: The Proceedings of the International Conference on Science in the Advancement of New States*, Israel: Rehovoth.

Guerreri, P. and Tylecote, A. (1997), 'Interindustry differences in technical change and national patterns of technological accumulation', in C. Edquist (ed.), *Systems of Innovation: Technologies, Institutions and Organizations*, London: Pinter Publishers.

Gustavsson, P., Hansson, P. Lundberg, L. (1999), 'Technology, resource endowments and international competitiveness', *European Economic Review*, 43: 1501–30.

Harris, R. and Trainor, M. (1997), 'Innovation and R&D in Northern Ireland manufacturing: a Schumpeterian approach', *Regional Studies*, 29 (7): 593–604.

Hipple, E. von (1988), *The Sources of Innovation*, Oxford: Oxford University Press.

Hipple, E. von (1994), 'Sticky information and the locus of problem solving: implications for innovation', *Management Science*, 40: 429–39.

Hirst, P. and Zeitlin, J. (1992), 'Flexible specialisation versus post-fordism: theory, evidence and policy implications', in A.J. Scott and M. Storper (eds), *Pathways to Industrialization and Regional Development*, London: Routledge.

Hudson, R. (1999), 'The learning economy, the learning firm and the learning region: a sympathetic critique of the limits of learning', *European Urban and Regional Studies*, 6 (1): 59–72.

Hughes, K. (1986), *Exports and Technology*, Cambridge: Cambridge University Press.

Katzenstein, P.J. (1985), *Small States in World Markets: Industrial Policy in Europe*, New York: Cornell University Press.

Keating, M. (1998), *The New Regionalism in Western Europe*, Cheltenham and Lyme: Edward Elgar.

Kleinnknecht, A. and Reijnen, J.O.N. (1992), 'Why do firms cooperate on R&D? An empirical study', *Research Policy*, 21: 347–60.

Kogut, B. (1993), *Country Competitiveness: Technology and the Organizing of Work*, New York: Oxford University Press.

Konstandakopoulos, D. (1997), 'Regional and local network systems for innovation', paper presented at the Regional Frontiers International Conference, Frankfurt.

Kortum, S. and Eaton, J. (1995), *Trade in Ideas: Patenting and Productivity in the OECD*, Cambridge, MA: National Bureau of Economic Research.

Krugman, P. (1995a), *Development, Geography and Economic Theory*, Cambridge, MA: MIT Press.

Krugman, P. (1995b), 'Technological change in international trade', in P. Stoneman (ed.), *Handbook of the Economics of Innovation and Technological Change*, Oxford: Blackwell.

Lall, S. (1996), *Learning from the Asian Tigers: Technology and Industrial Policy*, London: Macmillan.

Larsson, S. and Malmberg, A. (1999), 'Innovations, competitiveness, and local embeddedness. A study of machinery producers in Sweden', *Geographisca Annaler*, 81B (1): 1–18.

Leydesdorff, L., Cooke, P. and Olazaran, M. (2002) 'Technology transfer in European regions: introduction to the special issue', *Journal of Technology Transfer*, 27.

Lundvall, B-Å. (1985), *Product Innovation and User–Producer Interaction*, Industrial Development Research Series no. 31, Aalborg: AUC.

Lundvall, B-Å. (ed.) (1992), *National Systems of Innovation: Towards a Theory of Innovation and Interactive Learning*, London: Frances Pinter.

Lundvall, B-Å. and Maskell, P. (2000), 'Nation states and economic development: from national systems of production to national systems of knowledge creation and learning', in G.L. Clark, M.P. Feldman and M.S. Gertler (eds), *The Oxford Handbook of Economic Geography*, Oxford: Oxford University Press.

Malecki, E.J. (1980), 'Firm size, location and industrial R&D: a disaggregated analysis', *Review of Business and Economic Research*, 16: 29–42.

Maskell, P. and Malmberg, A. (1999), 'Localised learning and industrial competitiveness', *Cambridge Journal of Economics*, 23: 167–85.

Maskell, P., Malmberg, A., et al. (eds) (1998) *Competitiveness, Localised Learning and Regional Development: Specialisation and Prosperity in Small Open Economies*, London: Routledge.

Metcalfe, S.J. (1996), *Wealth from Diversity: Innovation, Structural Change, and Finance for Regional Development in Europe*, Boston: Kluwer.

Morgan, K. (1997), 'The learning region: institutions, innovation and regional renewal', *Regional Studies*, 31 (5): 491–503.

Murdoch, J. (1995), 'Actor-networks and the evolution of economic forms: combining description and explanation in theories of regulation, flexible specialisation and networks', *Environment and Planning A*, 27.

Nelson, R. (ed.) (1993), *National Innovation Systems: A Comparative Analysis*, New York: Oxford University Press.

Nelson, R.R. (1989), *End-User Computing: Concepts, Issues, and Applications*, New York: Wiley.

Nelson, R.R. and Winter, S. (1977), 'In search of a useful theory of innovation', *Research Policy*, 6 (1): 36–76.

OECD (1996), *Innovation, Patents and Technological Strategies*, Paris: Organisation for Economic Co-operation and Development.

OECD (1993), *Territorial Development and Structural Change: A New Perspective on Adjustment and Reform*, Paris: Organisation for Economic Co-operation and Development.

Oerlemans, L. et al. (1998), 'Do networks matter for innovation? The usefulness of the economic network approach in analysing innovation', *Tijdschrift voor Economische en Sociale Geografie*, 89 (3): 298–309.

Oughton C., Landabaso, M. and Morgan, K. (2002), 'The regional innovation paradox: innovation policy and industrial policy', *Journal of Technology Transfer*, 27.

Palaskas, T. and Arapoglou, V. (1999), 'SMEs in Europe and East Asia: competition, collaboration and lessons for policy support', Greek report for the Targeted Socio-Economic Research (TSER) project financed by the EC-FP4. (FP4-EU), Department of Economic and Regional Development, Panteion University of Athens.

Park, S. (1996), 'Networks and embeddedness in the dynamic types of new industrial districts', *Progress in Human Geography*, 20 (4): 476–93.

Pavitt, K, Robson, M. and Townsend, J. (1987), 'The size distribution of innovating firms in the UK: 1945–1983', *Journal of Industrial Economics*, 35: 297–316.

Petrakos, G. and Tsiapa, M. (2001), 'The spatial aspects of enterprise learning in transition countries', *Regional Studies*, 35 (6): 549–62.

Phelps, N.A. (1997), *Multinationals and European Integration: Trade, Investment and Regional Development*, London: Jessica Kingsley.

Phelps, N.A. and Alden, J. (eds) (1999), *Foreign Direct Investment and the Global Economy: Corporate and Institutional Dynamics of Global Localisation*, London: Stationery Office.

Rauch, J.E. (2001), 'Business and social networks in international trade', *Journal of Economic Literature*, 39: 1177–203.

Salais, R. and Storper, M. (1992), 'The four worlds of contemporary industry', *Cambridge Journal of Economics*, 16: 169–93.

Saxenian, A. (1994), *Regional Advantage. Culture and Competition in Silicon Valley and Route 128*, Cambridge, MA: Harvard University Press.

Scott, A.J. (1996), 'Regional motors of the global economy', *Futures*, 28 (5).

Scott, A.J. and Storper, M. (eds) (1986), *Production, Work, Territory*, London: Allen & Unwin.

Schmitz, H. (1995), 'Collective efficiency: growth path for small-scale industry', *Regional Studies*, 31 (4): 529–66.

Schumpeter, J. (1934), *The Theory of Economic Development*, Cambridge, MA: Harvard University Press.

Sölvell, O. and Zander, I. (1998), 'International diffusion of knowledge: isolating mechanisms and the role of the MNE', in A.D. Chandler, P. Hagström and O. Sölvell (eds), *The Dynamic Firm*, Oxford: Oxford University Press.

Sternberg, R. (2000), 'Innovation networks and regional development – evidence from the European Regional Innovation Survey (ERIS): theoretical concepts, methodological approach, empirical basis and introduction to the theme issue', *European Planning Studies*, 8: 389–407.

Stoneman, P. (ed.) (1995), *Handbook of the Economics of Innovation and Technological Change*, Oxford: Blackwell.

Storper, M. (1997), *The Regional World: Territorial Development in a Global Economy*, New York: Guildford Press.

Storper, M. (2000), 'Globalization, localization, and trade', in G.L. Clark, M.P. Feldman and M.S. Gertler (eds), *The Oxford Handbook of Economic Geography*, Oxford: Oxford University Press.

Sun, Y. (2000), 'Spatial distribution of patents in China', *Regional Studies*, 34 (5): 441–54.

Symeonidis, G. (1996), *Innovation, Firm Size and Market Structure: Schumpeterian Hypotheses and Some New Themes*, Paris: Organisaton for Economic Co-operation and Development.

Tödtling, F. (1992), 'The uneven landscape of innovation poles: local embeddedness and global networks', *University of Vienna IIR*, 46.

Tödtling, F. and Kaufmann, A. (2002), 'SMEs in regional innovation systems and the role of innovation support – the case of upper Austria', *Journal of Technology Transfer*, 27.

Tsampra, M. (2000), 'A study of regional diversity in a global sector: the case of the Greek information technology industry', PhD thesis, Department of Geography, King's College, University of London.

Tsampra, M. and Palaskas, T. (2002), 'Technology adjustment strategies of labour intensive industries in vulnerable European regions', paper in the Conference on 'New Economy Statistical Information Systems: the New Information Economy and Human Investment', Olympia, Greece, 9–14 June.

Tylecote, A. (1997), *Environment, Technology and Economic Growth: the Challenge to Sustainable Development*, Cheltenham, and Lyme: Edward Elgar.

Whitley, R. (1992), *European Business Systems: Firms and Markets in their National Contexts*, London: Sage.

Zuscovitch, E. and Justman, M. (1995), 'Networks, sustainable differentiation and economic development', in D. Batten et al. (eds), *Networks in Action*, New York: Springer.

Epilogue – after the stock market turnabout: questions and hypotheses

François Chesnais

In this 'epilogue' I argue that the collapse of Nasdaq and the initial public offering (IPO) market, followed by the deep downturn on Wall Street and other Bourses, are not minor events. They reveal significant weaknesses in the current accumulation regime, thus clouding the future for the hundreds of thousands of people employed by multinational enterprises (MNEs) throughout the world. They also have quite strong implications for the financing of innovation, hence calling for a reconsideration of current policy if the capacity of national systems of innovation to meet social needs is to be maintained.

THE THEORY OF ACCUMULATION REGIMES AND THE ADVENT OF A FINANCE-DOMINATED ONE

The capitalist economy is not a structural invariant. Since its birth, it has gone through many successive phases marked by different production technologies and modes of work organisation, different transport and communication technologies and so different degrees and modes of internationalisation, different international monetary systems and international institutional arrangements. To these must be added changes in the modes of ownership and in the concentration of capital. Interrelation between all these and other parameters has given successive phases marked systemic features. Until fairly recently, the fact that the capitalist economy undergoes periodically structural and indeed systemic change was recognised at least partially and worked into analytical frameworks.[1] With the conquest of academia by a brand of economics which uses exclusively totally a-historical concepts, as well as with the advent of very strong compartmentalisation among sub-disciplines, awareness of this need has receded quite seriously. In economics, as distinct from economic geography or urban studies, the main exceptions to this trend are the French 'Ecole de la régulation' (Boyer, 1987) and scholars belonging to the neo-Marxian current now close to them (Dumenil and Levy, 1999).

The theory of 'accumulation regimes' seeks to capture structural changes in the capitalist economy and their systemic impacts on institutions and corporations.[2] In the use that I make of the notion, an accumulation regime refers to a specific pattern or structure of relationships which emerge out of the interaction between: (1) the institutions and economic mechanisms which command the prevailing dominant forms of capital ownership and of corporate management, and so the relationship between capital taken as a whole and labour; (2) those that shape dominant forms of competition and hence *inter alia* the nature of the linkages and value-sharing relationships between small and large firms; (3) the institutions and 'institutional' arrangements which shape the way domestic economies manage their insertion into the international economic system or are integrated into it without much choice or say; and (4) the key traits of prevailing technological paradigms. In this approach 'institutions' and the relationships they give birth to, and the changes they all undergo from one historical phase and one accumulation regime to another, are viewed as 'crystallising' and consolidating shifts in economic as well as in political *'power relationships'* between social classes and also between countries, along with their concomitant effects on the distribution of wealth and well-being. During the historical phase a given accumulation regime prevails, this structure of relationships will strongly impinge on the issues defined by Lazonick and O'Sullivan (1998) as representing 'the essence of economic development', namely *'who makes investment decisions* in the economy, *what types of investment* they make and *how returns from investments are distributed'* [emphasis in the original].

Systemic change, leading to a new accumulation regime, started in the late 1970s as the outcome of two parallel processes. One was the trade, investment and financial liberalisation and deregulation initiated at that time and pushed forward ever since. The other was the re-emergence of concentrated interest-bearing money or financial capital.[3] The alliance between specific sections of capital and labour, born in the US during the New Deal and in other countries during or just after the Second World War, has been superseded by a less clearly formulated, uneasy and yet real alliance between industrial, traditional financial capital and the managers of Pension and Mutual funds, the latter being bent on imposing a purely financial paradigm for industrial activity, namely the maximisation of 'shareholder value'. A central notion of Keynesian theory, namely the power wielded by rentier capital, has reappeared in a new configuration, along with many of the ills of the 1930s, notably high income inequality, strong job precariousness and strong financial market bred instability.

Financial accumulation by Pension funds and Mutual funds in the form of retirement benefits and wage-saving schemes lie at the heart of the contemporary dominant economic and social power structure.[4] One indicator is the structure of capital ownership. In the US capital market, Pension and Mutual funds held less than 2% of corporate equity in 1945, 11% in 1965, 20% in 1975, jumping to 31% in 1985 and 42% by the end of 1999. This change in the pattern of ownership has gone hand-in-hand with a huge increase in the market value of holdings and an empowerment of stock markets as a result of the function attributed to them by several major countries in the payment of pensions. The attractiveness of financial investment gave a strong boost to the centralisation of individual savings in large non-bank financial institutions, notably Mutual funds. Financial globalisation and the competition it generates between financial institutions has generalised these trends throughout the Organisation for Economic Co-operation and Development (OECD) and subsequently in 'emerging market' economies. In countries where funds are not germane, large banks and insurance companies have undertaken the centralisation of unspent income. Once centralised, these savings become financial capital seeking returns in the form of dividends, interest and windfall stock market profits. The criteria for this particular type of investment involve different mixes of security, profitability and liquidity (the possibility of transforming assets back into cash at very short notice). In this regard, the economy we live in is that analysed in Chapters 12 to 16 of Keynes's General Theory. It combines the ills of rentier appropriations from investment and wages with the instability of the casino-like financial markets and, excepting the very special case of the US, it pushes economies down to varying levels of unemployment equilibrium.

SOME IMPORTANCE FEATURES OF THE FINANCE-DOMINATED ACCUMULATION REGIME

Here we must select only the most salient features.[5] The first relates to the position now occupied by financial markets in the pattern of *income distribution*. Financial institutions, primarily institutional investors, stand at the heart of the entire structure of income distribution in contemporary capitalism. This occurs in several inter-connected ways. Interest payment on public debt ensures the transfer of large flows of income (several percentage points of Gross Domestic Product (GDP)) from tax payers, primarily salary-owners (*largo sensu*) to bond-holders, first and foremost to large financial investors (non-bank but also banks). The other major, and now dominant, mechanism builds on the distribution of profit between retained profits and dividends and on the priority given to corporate decisions enhancing 'shareholder value' on stock markets. This notion refers to criteria devised by financial analysts which combine yields from dividends and the level of share prices. They include criteria regarding 'normal' (e.g. acceptable to financial investors) profit, its distribution in favour of dividends and so the level of tangible and intangible investment. In the new configuration dividends have priority over retained profits while wages are to a greater extent than previously a variable cost on which the brunt of cyclical and financial instability is brought to bear. In countries where US and UK institutional investors have gained control over a large fraction of the stock market, their financial power is used to line 'normal' rates of profit up with the ones in the US.

With the downgrading of retained profits to the status of a residual[6] (e.g. the sums remaining at the disposal of firms for investment outlays after the payment of dividends), managers are placed in a position where the reduction of real wages and the increase in labour productivity are the only means of ensuring the capacity to invest without having to borrow too heavily. Increasing the flexibility of labour is a major objective. Firms are powerfully aided in this by the mechanisms of competition and de-location of plant and jobs triggered off by the liberalisation and deregulation of foreign direct investment (FDI) and trade, as well as by the changes made in labour legislation under the effects of the overall shift of political and social 'power relationships'. As will be seen, maximising 'shareholder value' forces corporations to build up large debt nonetheless.

A second key feature of the new regime is that in most countries Governments and public authorities (the 'State') have accepted, or been forced to make, very extensive retreats from their previous position of institutions capable of either making important investment decisions with large structural effects or of strongly influencing these when made by the private sector. The investment decision is, as before the New Deal and the post Second World War reforms, increasingly or in some cases totally back under the direct control of private capital. The shift in the locus of the investment decision is also largely true for research and development (R&D), but here there are exceptions. Among these are countries where government R&D has been central to the innovation system and where the privatisation of the public sector is meeting some resistance. The other exception is that of countries that have had no qualms – or suffered no contrary pressures – in recognising the public good attributes of science and technology and in deciding that their national interests as States (e.g. as true Sovereigns), which include ensuring key externalities for their firms, call for the support of R&D. Today the US fits this definition closest.

Third, not only is the investment decision almost completely back into private hands, but it is also in those of a *new type of manager*, acting under the sway of a new type of relationship with shareholders and more broadly with financial markets. This is one of the most decisive features of the present regime. If we take the US as the 'benchmark example', outside the information technology (IT) industry, decisions about investment and R&D are no longer in the hands of Chandler type independent corporate managers (Chandler, 1977), but in those of corporate officers trained according to the management criteria devised to meet – or to appear to meet – the portfolio objectives of large institutional shareholders. These managers enjoy stock markets based forms of remuneration which reward their capacity to keep share prices high. In principle their strategies are subjected to a number of related forms of discipline, notably the threat that the company be sold in the 'market for corporate control' or that by selling the shares they hold (the 'Wall Street walk'), investors can make a firm's shares collapse. Recent experience (Enron, WorldCom, Vivendi, etc) has shown that this discipline can, for a time at least, quite easily be skirted. Skilful managers can deceive shareholders with serious consequences for corporations and employees. However fraud is not the sole or even the major problem. It is the stock market mechanism *per se* that requires close critical scrutiny in the way that it permits the use of shares as 'cash' for innovation-related ventures aimed at skirting the need for a genuine financing of R&D.

MNEs are one of the pillars of the finance-dominated regime. For institutional financial investors 'new-style MNEs' (Dunning, 1988) play a vital role as key points of interface with the real economy. The 'ideal type' of firm in the finance-dominated accumulation regime is the highly concentrated but productively decentralised 'network' firm. The appropriation of rentier type income channelled through non-government routes in the 'private economy' (e.g. dividends and interest payments by firms) is easier to monitor once manufacturing and service sectors have experienced both concentration and internationalisation. The network firm and the large firm small firm relationship acquire a new perspective once shareholder value is introduced into the analysis. One of its functions is that of encroaching on the value chains of firms not quoted on stock markets. The issue of the market power – both individual and collective – of the large firms emerging from the merger process must also be considered in this context.

The fourth and last feature of the finance-dominated regime which must be stressed here is the accentuation it has brought about in the degree of differentiation between countries in the world economy. Globalisation has increased homogeneity in production and consumption patterns and brought about convergence among some countries and upper social groups, but the complementary trends towards divergence have been even stronger. Hierarchy and differentiation are the hallmark contemporary international relationships even between OECD countries. The Triad powers dominate the rest of the world, but the United States is in a class of its own. The roadblock to world growth this increased hegemony may have created can be approached by interpreting the US recession and the downturn in the stock markets.

IMPLICATIONS AND CAUSES OF THE STOCK MARKET DOWNTURN

For a finance-dominated accumulation regime in which Bourses shape the direction and rate of investment and the distribution of income, notably regarding pensions, a deep downturn in the stock markets is not a minor event. This is particularly true when it is marked by a genuine crash in one of the major and seemingly most promising compartments (Nasdaq) and accompanied by spectacular corporate fraud (Enron, WorldCom, etc.) injuring the trust of professional investors and households and representing the tip of the iceberg of much broader problems. Such events touch the foundations on which the accumulation regime is built.

Pension funds belong to two categories. The first are schemes with defined benefits in which employees enjoy a number of guarantees regarding the safety of their retirement benefits. Here a booming stock market allows temporarily firms to defer their contributions or to pay them at a lower level than they forecasted. The second are schemes with defined contributions in which employees lack such guarantees. On the contrary the schemes have strings attached (the holding of the firm's own stock, time constraints on access to savings, etc.) while benefits depend totally on stock market performance. During the 1990s new firms offered their personnel only the second category of scheme while many older ones forced, or attempted to force (bringing about many industrial disputes), their personnel to accept a shift from the more stable system. Even in cases where no fraud occurred, as with Enron, for employees approaching retirement, the 'disappearance' during 2000 and 2001 of some US$8 trillion's worth of asset value has meant the loss of part or of all the revenue on which they counted and thus the obligation to stay at work or to find new employment.[7] The fall of the stock market gravely injures the social contract contained in private (just as much as in public) pension schemes. Full realisation of this injury has not taken place among workers and employees, but further falls could change this. Some of those who persist in advocating corporate pensions now suggest that these be paid only at the age of 70.

There is considerable debate about the factors behind the deep downturn in the stock market and the related US recession. Some factors are cyclical and quite classical. This is the case for the US domestic investment boom, which was in fact highly concentrated in IT, and indeed outside of communications infrastructure investment, in software. Inevitably this boom had to come to an end and be followed necessarily by over-capacity. This has shown to be quite severe. Since the recovery of US productivity growth was largely concentrated in the IT producing sector, it is affected by the slump in IT. This will end as all cyclical troths have done even if a future upturn will be hampered and delayed by very high corporate and household debt. The second set of factors lying behind both the downturn in the stock market, and the difficulty for other parts of the world economy to grow and to help the US move out of the recession, are infinitely more serious since they stem from one of the accumulation regime's founding traits. They have to do with implications and contradictions arising from the high concentration of growth in the second half of the 1990s in one single economy, namely the US itself.

The US represents some 20–21% of world GDP, but it accounted for over 40% of GDP growth since 1995. As a small number of analysts[8] and scholars have started to argue, this gap is not without relation to the US's share of world stock market capitalisation, over 35% of the total unto the mid-1990s, but nearly 50% at the height of the bubble in 2000. The US's unique growth performance has also to be related to the country's unique external deficits, both in the trade and capital accounts, as well as to its unique situation with respect to saving, e.g. the negative rating of private saving. Alongside the strong inflow of inward FDI, the main factor accounting for the deficit in the US external capital account is the unique attractiveness of the US capital markets for financial investors coming from all over the world. Simultaneously the external capital account deficit reflects the strong need for these markets, if they are to uphold the high levels of market capitalisation required to pay pensions, have of being fuelled by a continual inflow of financial capital from abroad. This is all the more so given the negative rating of US domestic saving, now coupled with the new Federal deficit triggered off by tax cutting at a time of renewed high military outlays. The situation imposes a high exchange rate of the dollar, since this is the currency in which financial assets are denominated, and liquidity recovered by foreign financial investors. In turn the high dollar is one of the causes of the huge US commercial deficit.

An easy quip has often been made regarding the status of the US economy as 'consumer in last resort' for the world. Given the American households' status of negative savers, they can hardly be anything else. The US stock markets have stood at the heart of a very special type of global cumulative process, temporarily 'virtuous', but potentially quite 'vicious'. Their buoyancy attracted financial investment from all over the world, which in turn had income and investment spill-over in the economy. Through the transfer of significant fractions of their capital to the US (both in the form of 'true investment' in plant and R&D and of portfolio funds), other parts of the world, notably EC member countries, contributed, consciously or unconsciously, to make the US economy the world's *only* 'growth zone' outside China. After a lag, this is now the source of backlash mechanisms which are also affecting the US Stock Exchange. With only a few exceptions (the US aerospace firms), the corporations which form the backbone of the New York Stock Exchange (NYSE) are Transnational corporations (TNC's) with productive units and markets spread all over the world whose profits depend ultimately not only on the buoyancy of US demand, but also on the health of other economies. The bad results TNCs have been announcing to shareholders during 2002 are rooted in overall world growth performance. No amount of credit creation and 'market wizardry' by the Fed in the US will resolve the problems born from the particular forms of international polarisation induced by the combined interplay of trade, investment and financial liberalisation and deregulation and so by the particular form of globalisation associated with the finance-dominated accumulation regime.

A third set of factors lying behind the stock market downturn and aggravating its severity concern the trap into which a number of firms, including important ones, have fallen as a combined result of the need to comply with the requirements of 'shareholder value' and of the facilities offered transitorily by the buoyant stock market, notably but not exclusively during the 1999–2000 asset bubble. Several inter-connected cumulative mechanisms have been at play. First, once the initial floating of stock in IPO markets is over, the Stock Exchange has become quite the opposite of a source of finance for firms. Firms *supply* cash to the share market rather than the reverse.[9] The commitment imposed on firms by the theory of 'shareholder value' to keep the price of shares up, coupled with the threat of take-over through hostile public offerings, has pushed more and more firms (including very large and well-established corporations) to buy back their shares. IBM, for instance, managed to do this in favourable conditions in November 1997, when Wall Street fell brutally in the wake of Hong Kong at the height of the Asian crisis. Other firms have been less lucky or wise in their timing and have had to retrieve their shares at very high prices. Another factor leading to 'reverse financing' has been the introduction of stock options remuneration plans by firms to retain qualified or key personnel. In order to fund stock option plans without causing undue dilution of shareholding, firms have been forced to repurchase stock.[10]

Deprived of accumulated retained earnings and even forced to pay cash to the market, firms have had to resort to other sources of finance for acquisitions, investment and innovation-related outlays. Whenever they needed finance in the form of cash, they have had to resort to large-scale borrowing, through the floating of corporate bonds or through bank credit. Even here the stock market has not been out of the picture. Both form of debt terms were negotiated on the basis of share prices, explaining why the difficulties of many large firms (notably in telecomms and media) increased so brutally when the stock market began to fall, leading to bankruptcies or quasi-bankruptcies. The very heavy load of corporate debt is now one of the factors jeopardising a movement out of recession. As long as the boom lasted, the other major technique for offsetting the dearth in finance created (in an apparent paradox) by the finance-dominated accumulation regime, was the use of shares by firms as *purchasing power*, as 'currency' in mergers and acquisitions. This quite salient feature of the 'new economy' has been subjected to close scrutiny from the standpoint of 'shareholder value'. A detailed survey by *Business Week* of the 302 largest mergers and acquisitions having taken place between mid-1995 and mid-2001, found that 61% resulted in loss of value for the shareholders of the acquiring firms, both because the price paid through the transfer of shares to sellers (e.g. the shareholders of targeted firms) was too high, and also because in many cases the merger following the acquisition created no real synergy.[11]

Unfortunately there are very few studies on the consequences of mergers and acquisitions on R&D.[12] Likewise very few scholars seem to view the impact on innovation capacity of the mergers made through the use of shares as currency during the Nasdaq high-technology asset bubble as a worthy research area.[13] Let me suggest why the issue is important. Acquiring a small firm, or indeed a start-up only just floated on the IPO market, can be a short cut to investing in R&D oneself. For large oligopolies, this represents a way of accessing quickly complementary technologies and new markets as well as a defensive weapon against entry by innovative firms into their own ones. Competition is then corseted by the forms of rivalry characteristic of oligopoly. The use of stock at inflated prices to pay for acquisitions may encourage firms to be much less regarding and cautious in acquiring control of another company than is the case if they have to use cash for the transaction. Strategies devised in artificial financial conditions can disrupt the R&D and in-house technological accumulation in acquiring firms[14] and if integration fails, perhaps simply because it takes place too early, it may have a destructive effect on R&D investment by innovator firms.

THE VULNERABILITY OF THE VENTURE CAPITAL MODE OF R&D FUNDING

The 1990s saw the expansion, notably in the US, of forms of innovation-related funding characteristic of and indeed specific to a finance-dominated regime. This was the case notably for the venture capital industry. In Europe it has been presented as a novel and genuine boost to innovation and a model which could be imported quite easily from the US. This requires closer examination, notably after the crash on Nasdaq.

Venture capitalists are specialised financial firms which use funds entrusted to them by large institutional investors, on the basis of a limited partnership agreement,[15] to provide dedicated investment finance to start-ups or early-stage innovative companies. At the height of the industry's growth, it was estimated that venture capital had risen to some 0.16% of GDP, thus representing some 7% of US non-defence R&D outlays.[16] Alongside specialised foundations, investors became pension funds, investment banks and insurance companies, all of which put a small percentage of their total funds into high-risk investments. Since 1978, regulatory changes allow private pension funds to invest a part of their assets into the private equity market.[17] Pension funds became the largest investor groups, holding roughly 40% of capital outstanding and supplying close to 50% of all new funds raised by partnerships.[18] Pension funds generally expect a return of between 25% and 35% per year over the lifetime of the investment, which is much higher than the historical return experienced in the stock market.

Most capital goes to development, only a small part actually supporting R&D. The National Science Foundation (NSF) has calculated the breakdown in funding made available to entrepreneurs at different stages of the innovation life cycle. The data shows that only a very small proportion is available in earlier phases (*seed, start-up and first stage*).[19] This proportion actually fell with the onset of the new economy and the Nasdaq market boom. Since 1995 the bulk of venture capital has gone to firms that had already financed their initial development and reached their expansion phase, suggesting that venture capitalists and institutional investors are willing to takes risks, but not too strong ones. Start-ups are referred to as '*portfolio firms*', stressing that they are part of the specialised financial firms' array of portfolio assets. Like other financial investment venture capital is governed by investor 'conventions' and marked by herd behaviour. This explains the high concentration of funding in the high technology industry segments viewed with most favour by the stock market at any given time. In the first part of the 1990s ventures were mostly in biotechnology and genetic engineering. During the Nasdaq boom that started in 1998, the favoured firms were initially in telecommunications and software. In the second phase the rush was on Internet firms, until the speculative bubble collapsed.

Venture capitalists support their portfolio firms until they reach a sufficient size and credibility to be sold either through an IPO on a specialised public-equity market (Nasdaq being the main example), or to a 'real' corporation ready to buy the start-up with cash or with shares. Since venture capitalists are financial investors and act in an institutional environment in which secondary markets ensuring the liquidity of assets are available for practically all financial assets, they are looking for a similar characteristic in this industry. Hence rapid exit routes are key to the working of the industry. The ones provided by the US financial and corporate system were hard to duplicate before the stock market downturn. Now the venture capital mechanisms have broken down, at least temporarily, even in the US. The spectacular fall in the number of IPOs from an average of 50 a month between May 1999 and October 2000 to 15 a month in 2001 and 2002, is one expression of the high degree of dependence of this form of funding on a buoyant stock market.[20]

CONCLUDING REMARKS

The funding of innovation-related investment has always depended on a mix of private and public sources. In the 1990s financial market forms of financing became increasingly important. This shift from public to private funding and from managerial control to market control entailed changes in the level, the objectives and priorities and in the time horizon of innovation-related investment. It represented a transition from situations where *'finance was in support of industry'* to ones where *'industry is required to support finance'*,[21] or to be more precise to satisfy the stringent requirements of institutional share-holders. For a time, the finance-dominated accumulation regime seemed to offer novel sources of funding: international private bond markets for firms with strong reputations and venture capital.

At the height of the enthusiasm about the 'new economy' and the US-centred IT investment boom, arguments questioning the long or even the medium term viability of these new forms seemed to be belied by the US's performance. Now that this phase is over, they have to be taken seriously. In the case of the US, held up as a model of best corporate governance practice, there is evidence that before the mirage of the 'new economy', major 'old economy' corporations were following 'downsize-and-distribute' restructuring policies that shifted massive amounts of income from labour to capital, alongside adaptive strategies for technology based on the exploitation of the capabilities accumulated in the past, hence without putting in place the foundations for renewed innovation.[22] US Federal government agencies are conscious of this. They are well aware that the stock market feeds on innovation, but will only support it quite marginally. Science needs absolutely direct funding. The neo-liberal discourse of the Washington Consensus is for outside consumption. After having funded Star-Wars as a 'dual purpose' project, aimed at Japan as much as at the Soviet Union and China, and re-established a part of its lost lead in advanced technology, the US first offset the relative fall in military R&D of the 1990s through a very important increase in public outlays supporting life-science and biotechnology-related research. This is aimed at giving US pharmaceutical and agro-technology corporations the full and also lasting pre-eminence now permitted by the inclusion of industrial property rights within the jurisdiction of the World Trade Organization (WTO). Since 2000, military outlays, including those for R&D, have grown again rapidly. This began well before September 11th, Afghanistan and Iraq and will continue to allow the US government to support R&D while continuing to preach to others that this is not to be done.

Elsewhere[23] I have put the case for halting the process of liberalisation, deregulation and downgrading of the functions of Government in Europe and making European Union institutions, as well as Member states, the locus for a much stronger, more focused and integrated policy for industry and technology. This can be seen as a way of starting to reduce the imbalance between MNEs and other social forces in the European Commission (EC) and of moving towards stronger, but also much more democratic, forms of economic and social integration. Here successful technology policy instruments are less those of research funding *per se* than of government or public science-based product development and procurement in health, telecommunications, the environment and public transport. This is not the road the EC has taken. The failure of financial investor funding can only prompt me to repeat that it is time for a new social alliance to take the reins in the European Union and to fund the technological priorities a truly democratic Europe needs.

NOTES

1. In saying this, I realise of course the privilege I enjoy of belonging to a generation grounded in the work of Keynes and Schumpeter – and in my case of Marx – subjected as a student to numerous courses on economic history and the history of economic thought and lucky enough to have been prompted by Joan Robinson, Paul Sweezy and others to view 'the present as history'. This helped even those that were not Marxian to recognise the capitalist economy as marked by phases possessing distinct features. This is partially captured by the best work on the internationalisation process and on MNEs by scholars of this generation who make calls on history. Michalet (1976), Dunning's essay on 'new-style multinationals' (Dunning, 1988) and Chapter 5 of his *magnum opus* (Dunning, 1993) are examples in point.
2. For a full-length presentation of my approach to the theory of accumulation regimes, see Chesnais and Sauviat (2003).
3. Regarding these notions, see also Guttmann (1994), pp. 40–41 and 294–5.
4. See R.J. Schiller (2001) and A.A. Kennedy (2000).
5. These and other dimensions of the current accumulation regime are developed at greater length in Chesnais and Sauviat (2003).
6. In the 1990s corporate governance theorists built their case for 'maximising shareholder value' on the purported 'residual claimant' status of shareholders. At least until the fall in the price of shares gained momentum, the success of stock markets in enforcing this view shifted relations quite radically in their favour and made retained profits the 'residual'.
7. The expression 'disappearance' stresses that this asset value, and so the sense employees and retirees had of possessing a capital, was a *mirage*. Their capital was purely *fictitious* in the sense Marx gave the term in *Capital*, Volume III (1959). For a clear explanation see Guttmann (1994).
8. These include notably staff at *The Economist*, whose warnings go well back (see *The Economist* (1999 and 2000) and in France at the Département des études économiques et bancaires of Credit Agricole. In international organisations, only the work at United Nations Conference on Trade and Development (UNCTAD) by the staff producing the annual UNCTAD Trade and Development Report is noteworthy.
9. See Lazonick and O'Sullivan (2002a).
10. For instance during the 1997–2001 period, even a very successful firm like Microsoft had to repurchase US$19.6 billion worth of its stock, of which $4.9 billion in 2000 and $6.1 billion in 2001. Over the same five-year period Microsoft spent $15.6 billion on R&D. See W. Lazonick and M. O'Sullivan (2001), p. 62.
11. Among a 150-strong group of losing buyers whose acquisition was not overshadowed by another subsequent deal, about four-fifths still showed negative returns after 24 months. About two-thirds of those showed no improvement at all over the survey period. Companies that

paid for their acquisitions with stock (65% of the cases) showed the worst results. See *Business Week* (2002), p. 74.
12. Work by Browyn Hall (1990) on this issue examines the effects on R&D of restructuring after the 1980 wave of mergers. No similar work is available on the impact of the finance-dominated merger mania of the 1990s.
13. In particular Mary O'Sullivan and William Lazonick at INSEAD in Fontainebleau.
14. For instance, case study work by the INSEAD team on the acquisitions made by large telephone equipment firms such as Lucent, Nortel and Alcatel in data communications technology concludes that 'besides encouraging the use of dubious accounting practices and overexposure to financing risks, the use of stock as an acquisition currency appears to have distorted or disrupted the normal strategy process at the companies concerned, thus helping to account for a number of poor acquisitions that they made'.
15. In this kind of agreement, which runs usually between seven and ten years, venture capitalists act as general partners and institutional investors as limited partners.
16. See OECD (2000).
17. The Department of Labor modified the Employment Retirement Income Security Act (US Congress) (ERISA) diversification rule four years after its adoption. The 'prudent man rule' is now based on the entire position of the private pension fund's portfolio and not to each investment committed by the fund, see Moye and Barber (2000).
18. CalPERS has 117 venture capital partnerships valued at US$7.5 billion in commitments, of which $4.1 billion has been invested, cf. *Pension & Investment*, 14 June 1999, p. 20.
19. National Science Foundation (2000), appendix tables 7–15.
20. In 2002 venture capital outlays had fallen to their 1998 levels. See *Washington Post*, 28 January 2003.
21. This is the title and theme of a little-known but very suggestive article by Gonenç (1993). Regrettably the author never took the subject up again or pushed any further analysis.
22. This is documented in Lazonick and O'Sullivan (1998) and more recently in Lazonick and O'Sullivan (2002b).
23. See the final chapter in Chesnais, Ietto-Gillies and Simonnetti (2000).

REFERENCES

Boyer, R. (1987), *La théorie de la régulation: une analyse critique*, Paris: Editions La Découverte.
Business Week (2002), 'Mergers: why most big deals don't pay off', 14 October.
Chandler, A.D. Jr (1977), *The Visible Hand: The Managerial Revolution in American Business*, Cambridge, MA: Harvard University Press.
Chesnais, F. and Sauviat, C. (2003), 'The financing of innovation-related investment in the contemporary global finance-dominated accumulation regime', in J. Cassiolato, H. Lastres and M.L. Maciel (eds), *Systems of Innovation and Development*, Cheltenham, UK and Northampton, MA: Edward Elgar.
Chesnais, F., Ietto-Gillies, G. and Simonnetti, R. (2000), *European Integration and Corporate Global Strategies,* London: Routledge.
Duménil, G. and Lévy, D. (eds) (1999), *Le triangle infernal: crise, mondialisation, financiarisation*, Paris: Actuel Marx Confrontations, PUF.
Dunning, J.H. (1988), *Explaining International Production*, London: Unwin Hyman.
Dunning, J.H. (1993), *Multinational Enterprises and the Global Economy*, Wokingham, UK: Addison Wesley.
Economist, The (1999), 'Shares without the other bit', 20 November.
Economist, The (2000), 'America's economy: slowing down, to what?', 9 December.

Gonenç, R. (1993), 'De la finance pour l'industrie à l'industrie pour la finance', *Revue d'économie financière*, 27: 29–41.

Guttman, R. (1994), *How Credit Money Shapes the Economy: The United States in a Global System*, New York: M.E. Sharpe.

Hall, B.H. (1990), 'The impact of corporate restructuring on industrial research and development', *Brookings Papers on Economic Activity*, 1990 (1): 85–136.

Kennedy, A.A. (2000), *The End of Shareholder Value? Corporations at the Crossroads*, Cambridge, MA: Perseus Publishing.

Lazonick, W. and O'Sullivan, M. (1998), 'Governance of innovation for economic development', Report for the TSER Programme of the European Commission, Brussels, March.

Lazonick, W. and O'Sullivan, M. (2001), 'Corporate governance, innovation, and economic performance in the EU: project policy report', Targeted Socio-Economic Research (TSER) Programme of the European Commission (DGXII) under the Fourth Framework Programme, European Commission (Contract SOE1-CT98-1114; Project 053).

Lazonick, W. and O'Sullivan, M. (2002a), 'The changing role of the stock market in the US economy', paper presented to the Annual Business History Conference, April.

Lazonick, W. and O'Sullivan, M. (eds) (2002b), *Corporate Governance and Sustainable Prosperity*, London: Palgrave.

Marx, K. (1959), *Capital*, vol. III, Moscow: Foreign Language Publishing House.

Michalet, C.-A. (1976), *Le capitalisme mondial*, Paris: Presses Universitaires de France.

Moye, M. and Barber, R. (2000), 'Institutional power in corporate transactions', paper presented at the 52nd annual meeting of the Industrial Relations Research Association, Boston, January.

National Science Foundation (2000), *Science and Engineering Indicators 2000*.

OECD (2000), *A New Economy? Innovation and New Technologies' New Role in Growth*, Paris: OECD.

Schiller, R.J. (2001), *Irrational Exuberance*, Princeton, NJ: Princeton University Press.

Index